PI

LEADING
COMPETITIVE ADVANTAGE

"I have known and worked with Peter Linkow for more than thirty years. We have each been in an advisor role to the other. He is an intuitive, penetrating thinker. Four messages: (1) tactics and strategy are critical to the people wars of workplace, marketplace, and community; (2) the issue of 'difference' is the greatest challenge of our generation, and there aren't common sense or off-the-shelf solutions, only situations requiring looking, listening, and talking between people who are different; (3) consistency of leadership is required. Every generation having a 'I can do this better, faster, or smarter' is a recipe for failure. 'Progress is over time, not overnight' and is only possible through consistency; (4) this book is an opportunity for a look in the mirror. For line executives to understand when it is anchored in marketplace and talent, you can't duck; for practitioners—this is not social work 101 and is not for everyone. This book is not to tell you what or how to do. It is to prod you to look at yourself, leader or practitioner, assess your culture and situations, and determine how to work together to ensure the culture, those situations, and business performance will be better years after your departure."

—Ted Childs, Thought Leader, Strategist, and Catalyst
for Change at Ted Childs LLC; former Vice President
for Global Workforce Diversity at IBM

"*Leading Diversity for Competitive Advantage* is a timely book by someone who knows what he is talking about. No recent convert to diversity, equity, and inclusion initiatives, Peter Linkow has devoted his entire career to DEI leadership. Distilled from Linkow's considerable practical experience are enduring insights about effective change management in our time. The future belongs to those who can master the principles of DEI leadership set forth here. This book offers clear thinking masterfully written. It should be read by all who care for their organizations and want to make a lasting impact."

—W. Carl Kester, George Fisher Baker Jr. Professor of Business Administration, Emeritus at Harvard Business School

"There are many publications purporting to help organizations with their diversity, equity, and inclusion (DEI) efforts, but most fall short. *Leading Diversity for Competitive Advantage* and the twelve competencies as laid out by Peter Linkow offer a comprehensive and practical approach to leading DEI and is written in plain language with helpful infographics and charts. As a DEI practitioner for more than thirty years, I can attest that Peter's recommendations are spot on in every regard. He speaks to the reader assuming they are an adult with positive intent. I will be recommending this book early and often to my clients and mentees as the primary book they need to grasp and implement what constitutes a sound systems methodology for developing a high impact strategy that is aligned to the culture they are operating in. I also want to commend Peter for including the community I identify with, people with disabilities, thoughtfully throughout the book."

—Deb Dagit, President of Deb Dagit Diversity LLC, and Former Chief Diversity Officer at Merck

"In this critical moment, *Leading Diversity for Competitive Advantage* is a must-read about seizing opportunities that advance diversity and competitive edge together. Drawing on deep expertise, Peter Linkow offers the potent guidance leaders and influencers need to take on their most significant DE&I challenges. Clear, highly engaging, and distinctive, this book will prepare and energize you to launch strategies that take DE&I and your business to the next level."

—Rebekah Steele, Consultant and Coauthor of *INdivisible: Radically Rethinking Inclusion for Sustainable Business Results*

"Peter Linkow has written a down-to-earth, easy-to-read, and practical handbook not only on how to think about diversity but how to take steps, both within oneself and one's organization, to make significant progress towards an equitable society. Linkow has leveraged his years of experience as a leader, consultant, and professor to generate a multitude of straightforward ideas that are easily understood and require only that one make the internal decision to act and implement."

—Mike Markovits, Leadership Consultant, Former HR Executive at GE and IBM

"Peter Linkow's book, *Leading Diversity for Competitive Advantage*, provides a practical approach to addressing the systems and practices that affect the bottom line along with the twelve competencies required to embed diversity, equity, and inclusion in the workplace. He introduces the values and deep work in which organizational leaders must engage to achieve diverse, equitable, and inclusive workplaces. His lifelong work in becoming an ally is something all business leaders should emulate if they want to be effective leaders in a global and multicultural economy."

—Amanda Fernandez, CEO of Latinos for Education

"Peter Linkow not only exposes the deeply innate problems with diversity, equity, and inclusion, he shows us how to fix them. The depth, breadth, and detail of this book is rooted in the Einstein principle that if we don't thoroughly understand a problem, we can never find a solution. This book is an imperative for changing what Linkow says is 'progress proceeding at a glacial pace.'"

—**David H. Hughes, Author,** *Thoughtware: Change the Thinking and the Organization Will Change Itself* **(with Philip Kirby) and others, Retired Business Executive and Venture Capitalist**

Leading Diversity for Competitive Advantage:
The Twelve Strategic Competencies

by Peter Linkow

© Copyright 2022 Peter Linkow

ISBN 978-1-64663-835-2

All rights reserved. No part of this publication may be reproduced, stored in a retrieval system, or transmitted in any form or by any means—electronic, mechanical, photocopy, recording, or any other—except for brief quotations in printed reviews, without the prior written permission of the author.

Published by

◤ köehlerbooks™

3705 Shore Drive
Virginia Beach, VA 23455
800-435-4811
www.koehlerbooks.com

LEADING
DIVERSITY
FOR COMPETITIVE
ADVANTAGE

THE TWELVE
STRATEGIC COMPETENCIES

PETER LINKOW

VIRGINIA BEACH
CAPE CHARLES

*The journey to Leading Diversity for Competitive Advantage
began in childhood. This book is dedicated to those two great
childhood influences who inspired my journey:
my father, Bill Linkow, who bequeathed to me his obsession
with fairness and justice,
and my mother, Shirley Lowy Linkow, who taught me the joy
of bridging differences
and the power of an open mind.*

Table of Contents

Introduction

*"The arc of the moral universe is long,
but it bends toward justice."*
Martin Luther King, Jr.

KING'S HOPEFUL APHORISM WAS ADAPTED from an 1853 sermon by the abolitionist Reverend Theodore Parker titled "Of Justice and Conscience." In that sermon Parker notably affirmed that he did not pretend to understand the moral universe, nor could he perceive or calculate its long arc, but his conscience instructed him that it bends toward justice. Leading diversity is an act of conscience built on a foundation of competence. Each strategic leader must examine her own conscience to divine the righteous path to diversity for herself and the institution she leads. The competence to successfully traverse that path—to bend the arc toward institutional justice—is the topic of this book.

The Audience

Leading Diversity for Competitive Advantage is written for leaders who play a strategic role in diversity, equity, and inclusion—boards of directors; the C-suite; strategic business unit and function leaders; top diversity, human resources, human capital, and talent leaders; and those emerging leaders who wish to leave a diversity legacy engraved in the stories of their lives.

The *sine qua non* of a successful diversity initiative, as it is for any strategic initiative, is top leadership commitment. While those leaders in the middle are the linchpin of successful diversity initiatives, it is leaders at the top who empower, motivate, and steer them. These responsibilities cannot be purely delegated. Top leaders who push these responsibilities down the organization or, worse, ignore them, do not show up, do not commit the relatively modest time required, and do not personally commit and engage are destined to preside over a moribund diversity initiative.

Leading Diversity for Competitive Advantage provides the competencies strategic leaders require to fulfill their commitments and turn those commitments into results. It offers a foundation on which to establish new diversity initiatives, resuscitate waning initiatives, or simply move diversity onto a strategic, evidence-based footing.

Every organization and every leader is unique. *Leading Diversity for Competitive Advantage* does not provide a "how-to" script but offers the strategic models, methods, templates, and tools to enable leaders to craft diversity initiatives that fit their organizations' unique situations and characteristics while being true to their own personal style.

The Author

After forty years of examining thousands of diversity data points, I can count on one hand the number of times women, Black, Latino, and other underrepresented people have achieved equity and inclusion. In this era of increasing multiculturalism (maybe because of it), institutional bias remains insidious—hiding in backrooms and subconscious thoughts, woven into the fabric of national and organizational culture, aided and abetted by impervious and imperious hierarchies of power. Leaders of goodwill speak earnestly about creating inclusive institutions in which all people thrive and achieve their highest levels of productivity and effectiveness. Yet exclusion all too frequently predominates. For employment, the promises of civil rights and a post-racial society have too often been frustrated.

This reality tears at my soul. And then there is my own complicity, coming face-to-face with my own racism, sexism, and privilege. What can I do to repair myself and the world in which I reside?

Over a long career journey, much of which has been devoted to diversity, equity, and inclusion, I have undertaken the following:

◇ Worked with a wide array of top leadership teams on strategic issues in the for-profit, nonprofit, and government sectors

◇ Guided numerous organizations in the formulation and implementation of diversity strategies

◇ Reviewed thousands of scholarly studies on the science of diversity, equity, and inclusion and related topics

◇ Conducted global research on diversity and strategy, including a three-year study of gifted strategic thinkers as a Kellogg Foundation Fellow

◇ Pored over diversity assessments of business, government, and nonprofit organizations

◇ Advocated for people with disabilities

◇ Led four organizations serving underrepresented people

◇ Interviewed top organizational leaders and chief diversity officers

◇ Guided strategic diversity conversations with senior leadership teams, diversity councils, employee resource groups, and diversity leaders

◇   Taught strategy to top and emerging leaders as a management professor and consultant

◇   Designed and facilitated an abundance of diversity learning experiences

◇   And questioned and questioned and questioned

The knowledge I have gained about strategy in general and diversity, equity, and inclusion strategy in particular and the skills I have developed for improving organizations are my most significant strengths and thus the foundation of my potential to make a contribution to repairing the world. I have committed the remainder of my life to advancing diversity, equity, and inclusion in the world's institutions. This book is one step, hopefully a consequential step, toward honoring that commitment.

The Content

Many, many books and articles have been written, research studies conducted, and consultants retained to point organizations and their leaders in the direction of diversity, equity, and inclusion. Though the knowledge and insights gained from these sources have been widely applied over many years, progress is proceeding at a glacial pace.

This interminably slow progress is rooted in a wide range of causes, including lack of top management commitment, genuinely committed leaders taking low-impact actions, a goal of inclusion without the knowledge and skill set to achieve it, the absence of a common language and guidelines for civil conversations about diversity, not treating diversity as a change process, failures of implementation, middle-management resistance, ineffective measurement, and inadequate accountability. While *Leading Diversity for Competitive Advantage* addresses all of these and other root causes, three core causes frame the twelve competencies advanced in this book: an overreliance on best practices, a spotty foundation of empirical evidence, and gaps in the knowledge leaders need to successfully guide a strategic diversity initiative.

OVERRELIANCE ON BEST PRACTICES

Diversity strategy in many organizations is more an agglomeration of bright, shiny best practices than a cogent, integrated strategy. Best practices—gleaned from conferences, webinars, articles, consultants, and similar sources—engender distinct problems. Whether wrapped in a cloak of strategy or adopted wholesale, best practices tend to drive organizations toward the tactical. Under pressure to advance rapidly, best-practice programs, often artfully designed, are a shortcut to strategy but are often nothing more than an assemblage of tactics. As Sun Tzu, one of history's greatest military strategists, famously declared, "Strategy without tactics is the slowest route to victory. Tactics without strategy is the noise before defeat."

A prime business value of diversity is that it differentiates an organization in its talent and product/service markets, those markets in which it competes for diverse talent and customers. Differentiation is a primary source of competitive advantage. By their nature, best practices are copies of the practices of other organizations. The adoption of best practices is often a rush to sameness, forgoing the talent and product/service market differentiation that diversity should provide. Critical to sustaining competitive advantage is to establish barriers to competition. Adopting the best practices of others does not establish barriers to competition. If you can copy a best practice, others can too.

A best practice for one organization may not be a very good practice for another organization. Best practices must fit the context, culture, and mission of the organization in which they will be implemented. Great strategists do not respond to the consequential challenges their organizations face with an assemblage of the best practices of other organizations. They craft the answers in light of the unique people, characteristics, industry, opportunities, and circumstances of their own organizations.

Finally, best practices often lack an evidence base. Exactly who is the arbiter of whether a diversity practice is a best practice? Evidence based on rigorous, systematic, objective evaluation and science is often weak or nonexistent.

SPOTTY EMPIRICAL EVIDENCE

Although the empirical foundation of diversity practice is growing, management decisions about diversity initiatives are often based on inadequate or spurious scientific grounds. In addition, diversity practice has made insufficient use of the vast spectrum of exciting interdisciplinary scientific evidence.

The empirical foundation of *Leading Diversity for Competitive Advantage* is based on several thousand rigorous, peer-reviewed scientific studies that apply to strategic diversity leadership. They come from the fields of sociology, social psychology, cognitive psychology, neuroscience, behavioral economics, decision science, leadership, prejudice studies, gender and race studies, education, business strategy, and others. Yet this vast body of research leaves gaps in an empirical foundation for strategic diversity leadership practice.

To close these gaps and to provide a complete picture of strategic diversity leadership, I have drawn upon interviews with chief diversity officers and top leaders of major institutions, surveys by professional and academic organizations, and a long career of poring through internal organizational data on diversity and guiding top leadership teams through the diversity strategy process. These steps have been applied in a framework of rigorous critical thinking. By critical thinking, I mean observation and data gathering, rational and objective analysis, interpretation and conclusions, and ongoing evaluation of the process and results. These steps have been carried out under the conditions of discipline (staying consistent with a critical thinking framework) and open-mindedness (consciously challenging my own tendencies, attitudes, and prejudices).

At some point the question must be asked, "Does the empirical and practice evidence assembled in this book provide an adequate foundation of competence on which to lead a successful diversity initiative?" My colleague and friend Andrew Hahn, the former assistant dean of the Heller School at Brandeis University, professor, and long-time policy researcher, grappled repeatedly with this question of when research establishes an adequate foundation on which to initiate policy. He has often admonished, "Enough is known for action." After a nearly fifteen-year odyssey of exploring the empirical basis for strategic diversity leadership, preceded by thirty years of practice, I believe enough is known for action. The challenge, then, becomes how to prepare top leaders to take the helm.

GAPS IN LEADERSHIP COMPETENCE

This book is for strategic leaders who are committed to bending the arc of the institutions they serve toward justice. But many leaders have gaps in their competence for leading diversity. In numerous presentations on strategy to senior executive teams, I have found that strategic leaders express these gaps by asking four questions:

◇   What exactly are diversity, equity, and inclusion?

◇   Why should we make diversity a priority?

◇   What does our organization need to do to make diversity successful?

◇   What do I personally need to do to make diversity successful in my organization?

Many strategic leaders do not have the full, evidence-based competencies to enable them to answer these questions. *Leading Diversity for Competitive Advantage* provides those competencies. It is organized around the four questions and guides organizational leaders to find answers for the unique people, characteristics, and circumstances of the organizations they lead, no matter the size, sector, or location. The table below elaborates the organization and content of *Leading Diversity for Competitive Advantage.*

The Four Diversity Leadership Questions			
What exactly are diversity, equity, and inclusion?	Why should we make diversity a priority?	What does our organization need to do to make diversity successful?	What do I personally need to do to lead the organization to success?
Competency 1: Voicing a Language of Diversity	Competency 2: Constructing a Business Case for Diversity	Competency 4: Mastering Diversity Strategy	Competency 10: Talking the Walk: Leadership Communications
	Competency 3: Envisioning a Diversity Philosophy	Competency 5: Advancing Toward Equity	Competency 11: Walking the Talk: Top Leadership Commitment
		Competency 6: Instituting Inclusion	Competency 12: Leading Change
		Competency 7: Engineering Sustainable Diversity Competitive Advantage	Epilogue: Forging a Legacy
		Competency 8: Designing a Diversity Management Structure	
		Competency 9: Measuring for Accountability	

How to Use This Book

Leading Diversity for Competitive Advantage is designed to be used just in time—when a strategy is being formulated or implemented or a challenge arises, review the corresponding competency for background and guidance. The twelve competencies of strategic leadership are arranged in the logical order in which strategy formulation and implementation typically progress. Before proceeding, read "Competency 1: Voicing a Language of Diversity."

The act of writing *Leading Diversity for Competitive Advantage* has been a deeply personal awakening, an opportunity to explore in great depth how I, as a strategic leader, have advanced diversity, equity, and inclusion in the leadership opportunities I have had and, more importantly, to come to terms with my many missteps and failings as a leader.

My fervent hope is that in addition to a pathway to strategic diversity leadership, this book will provide a pathway for strategic leaders to explore their attitudes, values, and beliefs about difference, define the role they wish to play in fostering diversity, equity, and inclusion in the organizations they lead and the societies in which they dwell, and forge the diversity legacy they wish to leave.

COMPETENCY 1:
Voicing a Language of Diversity

"People fail to get along because they fear each other; they fear each other because they don't know each other; they don't know each other because they have not communicated with each other."
Martin Luther King, Jr.

DIVERSITY REQUIRES DIALOGUE. DIALOGUE IN real life, as in theater, reveals character—how a person thinks, feels, and behaves, her motivation, her moral backbone and temperament, her personality, the essence of her being. It is that character that Martin Luther King, Jr., spoke about when he proclaimed, "I have a dream that my four little children will one day live in a nation where they will not be judged by the color of their skin but by the content of their character." Considerable social science research demonstrates that connecting with the essence of another human being—her character—deepens mutual understanding and empathy, bridging differences and overcoming the stereotypes and prejudices that separate us. Without dialogue, those connections are impossible.

Dialogue is rooted in language. Nuances of language may elevate dialogue or diminish it, conveying enlightenment or confusion, conflict or collaboration, respect or disdain, empathy or indifference, integrity or deceit, equality or inequity. Language choices can create barriers to dialogue. Two of these barriers are highly consequential for diversity and need to be addressed if dialogue is to flourish and diversity is to be productive: disagreement about the meaning of diversity, and the words we choose to refer to someone who is different.

Whether explicit or implicit, most people have a definition of diversity in their minds. When those definitions are different, which is all too often the case, people talk past each other. When those definitions are in conflict, communication serves only to magnify differences.

How people refer to each other across the divide of differences, the labels they use for each other, can unwittingly—or sometimes wittingly—undermine, humiliate, and alienate. Is the proper term Black or African American or African ancestry? Should the reference be to LGBT people or LGBTQ or LGBTQQIA? Which term is least offensive—Latino, Hispanic, or Latinx? Use the wrong label and the conversation can easily turn from goodwill to acrimony. Or worse, don't engage in dialogue at all or retreat into political correctness for fear of being censured for using the wrong term. Where can we find the right words?

Top leaders must ensure that diversity is defined clearly and in resonance with the unique characteristics and context of the organizations they serve. They must also ensure that the organization has guidelines that promote civil conversations about differences. Then, they must relentlessly communicate these definitions and guidelines throughout the organization.

Defining Diversity

In a largely open-ended survey of 10,000 leaders in an organization of about 200,000 that I conducted with colleagues, the vast majority of the leaders defined diversity as quotas, often substituting the term *affirmative action*. In numerous surveys and focus groups, I have found this point of view to be widespread. The implication of diversity as quotas articulated as affirmative action is that affirmative action will force organizations to hire and advance people from particular underrepresented groups rather than the best candidate for the position, eroding the quality of the organization's talent.

A review of over a hundred definitions of diversity in books and articles and on websites found two distinct underlying views of diversity: primary demographic differences, such as race, sexual orientation, and physical and mental ability; and primary plus secondary differences, such as thinking styles, education, and functional expertise. Expanded definitions of diversity, although they encompass everyone and add important cognitive differences, can weaken the purpose and focus of diversity initiatives.

WHAT DIVERSITY ISN'T

Before proceeding with a definition of diversity, the reality of quotas and whether diversity should be only primary demographic differences or both primary and secondary differences needs to be sorted out.

Quotas

In employment, quotas are requirements to hire, advance, or retain individuals on the basis of their social characteristics, usually race, ethnicity, and gender. In effect, quotas are discrimination, often labeled reverse discrimination, in behalf of people who have historically been underrepresented in organizations and in their leadership.

In numerous interviews, focus groups, and open-ended survey questions, I have observed that employees conflate quotas with reverse discrimination and affirmative action. The widespread perception of the existence of reverse discrimination isn't surprising. For example, a 2011 study of Blacks' and Whites' perceptions of bias from the 1950s to the 2000s found that in the early 2000s, Whites began to "see anti-White bias as more prevalent than anti-Black bias," even though by virtually any measure, including education, employment, and wages, "statistics continue to indicate drastically poorer outcomes for Black than White Americans."[1] Reverse discrimination is prohibited by federal laws and regulations. In reality, reverse discrimination is rare. Among the three thousand discrimination opinions issued by the federal courts from 1990 to 1994, only a hundred were reverse discrimination cases, and in only six of those was reverse discrimination established.[2]

Quotas do exist in some countries—for example, for the appointment of women to corporate boards in many European Union countries, racial employment quotas in Brazil, and employment quotas for people with disabilities in Eastern and Central Europe and China. In some countries failure to meet a quota is enforced by penalties such as fines or tariffs.

Quotas are often confused with affirmative action. Federal contractors are required to file affirmative action plans. Occasionally, the courts will require affirmative action in cases where there has been a proven history of discrimination. Organizations also may voluntarily enter into an affirmative action plan. Affirmative actions are steps taken to remedy past or present discrimination or prevent it from occurring in the future. A plan is developed for removing obstacles to equal opportunity, and numerical goals and timetables may be established. Goals are not quotas. The measure of compliance is not whether or when the goal is met but that a good-faith effort is made to reach the goal. No penalties or sanctions may be imposed for not reaching a goal or meeting a timetable. Affirmative action does not include quotas for protected classes. Sometimes organizations establish quotas under the label of affirmative action, but that is a misuse of affirmative action.

Quotas may undermine the achievements of underrepresented people; for example, the query "Did she get the promotion because of her achievements or because she was a woman?" might be raised. For that reason, opposition to quotas is often strongest among underrepresented people themselves.

Affirmative action programs, which affect about 25 percent of organizations, do not erode the quality of the workforce through reverse discrimination; they have precisely the opposite effect. Affirmative action by statute and regulation seeks to redress a history of discrimination and level the playing field, not to tilt it in the reverse direction. Affirmative action programs are aimed at removing barriers to fairness and putting initiatives in place that promote merit in employment decision-making. When job-relevant merit, such as training and education, skills and knowledge, experience, and past performance, is the sole qualification for a position—not who you know, the color of your skin, or who you are in a relationship with—then the quality of the workforce will improve.

Secondary Differences

Most definitions of diversity relate to legally protected differences, called primary, demographic, or social group differences, including race, ethnicity, gender orientation, sexual preference, immigration status, caste or class, religion, veteran status, physical and cognitive ability, and age. In recent years, organizations have added secondary differences, including communication, learning, and cognitive styles; function, department, or unit; education; life and work experiences; union affiliation; etc. The addition of secondary differences has advantages and a disadvantage.

The inclusion of secondary differences affords two advantages. Politically, secondary differences encompass everyone, helping to ensure widespread support for diversity. In addition, many secondary differences relate to the cognitive differences that create advantages in problem-solving, decision-making, and innovation by bringing diverse perspectives and thinking processes to the challenge at hand.[3] Cognitive differences in groups and organizations create competitive advantage. The disadvantage is that a focus on secondary differences diminishes the emphasis on diversity in ending discriminatory practices, policies, and behavior.

This quandary can be resolved by placing emphasis on primary differences. For the most part, primary differences have been shown to yield the same benefits as secondary differences. A wide range of research demonstrates that people from different social groups have different cognitive styles and strengths. Women, for example, generally have superior perceptual skills and language fluency, while men tend to have better spatial abilities and mathematical reasoning.[4] People who are bilingual or multilingual not only have a significant aptitude for cross-cultural communication, but they also have better attention capacities and task-switching capacities.[5] Those of European heritage are more likely to base decisions on expertise and analytics, while African Americans are more likely to base decisions on relationships and individual perspectives and take a more holistic approach to information.[6] The prevalent European approach will help ensure organizations make effective decisions, while the prevalent African American approach will help ensure that those decisions will actually be implemented.

Consider people with severe, longstanding physical disabilities. They have a lifetime of experience adapting to their environment by developing new and unique ways to accomplish work. Wouldn't they be likely to enhance innovation in their work teams? To maintain the focus on those who have been historically underrepresented in the membership and leadership of institutions, secondary differences, although important, will not be a part of the conversation here.

WHAT DIVERSITY IS

Diversity rarely stands alone. In current parlance, diversity is often accompanied by equity and inclusion—diversity, equity, and inclusion, or DEI. In many institutions, especially higher education, the word *belonging* is added. Here, belonging is one of the core components of inclusion.

Diversity is typically defined as the range of differences and similarities in race, ethnicity, religion, gender identity, sexual orientation, physical and mental abilities, and age and the resulting differences in perspective that those differences produce. Some organizations include secondary differences in their definition. Missing from such descriptive definitions is the sense of purpose that animates diversity. Without purpose, diversity is moribund. Diversity is defined as *the equitable representation of historically underrepresented groups at all organizational levels in a manner that creates sustainable diversity competitive advantage.*

Diversity is the goal, not the method of achieving the goal. Diversity strategy focuses on methods. Achieving diversity is primarily a function of equity and inclusion, represented by this equation: diversity = $f(E,I)$.

Equity occurs *when human capital or talent decisions are based exclusively on fairness and merit.* Inclusion is *amplifying the unique voice and talents and maximizing the performance of every employee, creating a workplace where everyone thrives.* Both equity and inclusion are aspirational. No state of perfect equity nor optimal inclusion exists. Some organizations, however, do much better than others.

Three elements in the definition of diversity require refinement: (1) equitable representation of historically (and currently) underrepresented groups, (2) at all organizational levels, and (3) sustainable diversity competitive advantage.

Equitable Representation

Equitable representation begs the question "Equal to what?" The "what" is the availability of underrepresented people in a relevant labor pool or job group. The CEO of one manufacturing company, a leader in diversity, established the US census as the relevant labor pool so that Black people, Latinos, Asians, and women in his company would be represented as they are in the US population. This is a very aggressive, lofty goal, especially for a company that employs a significant number of mechanical engineers, a labor pool in which women and Black and Latino people are significantly underrepresented.

A good way to determine the relevant job group is to follow the US Department of Labor's procedure for developing affirmative action plans. Those procedures define job groups as having "1) similar wages; 2) similar job duties and responsibilities; and 3) similar opportunities for training, promotion, transfer, and other employment benefits."[7] A simpler but less precise method is to use the Equal Employment Opportunity Commission's (EEOC) ten job categories (table 1-1), also taking into account whether the labor pool is internal or external to the organization and the geography from which the candidate will be drawn:[8]

EEOC's Ten Job Categories

- Executive/Senior-Level Officials and Managers
- First/Mid-Level Officials and Managers
- Professionals
- Technicians
- Sales Workers
- Office and Clerical Workers
- Craft Workers
- Operatives
- Laborers
- Service Workers

Table 1-1

In establishing a job group, care must be taken to ensure that the job group is not a biased population. For example, Black and Hispanic people have a lower proportion of bachelor's degrees than would be predicted by their proportion in the overall population census. In cases like this where bias is outside the direct control of the organization, organizations may wish to normalize the labor pool by targeting a higher proportion of a particular underrepresented group than is actually represented in that labor pool. For example, if Latinos are only 3 percent of the available labor pool but are approximately 17 percent of the civilian, noninstitutional labor force, organizations might wish to set their targets between 3 and 17 percent.

All Levels

"At all organizational levels" refers to the proportion of each group at each step of the organizational hierarchy. Proportion at all organizational levels is calculated by dividing the number of members in a particular group by total employees at each hierarchical level. Suppose that the proportion of Asians at the entry professional level in an organization is 11.5 percent, but the proportion is 5.9 percent at the supervisory and managerial levels, and 4.6 percent at the executive and senior manager levels. Do these numbers signify that bias exists? The numbers do not definitively indicate that bias is occurring; other causes might explain the disparities. However, they certainly raise a suspicion of bias and point to areas where organizations should dig deep to explain the root causes of the results.

Sustainable Diversity Competitive Advantage

Few organizations will continue to invest in diversity if it does not substantially contribute to the achievement of business results, notably improved organizational performance, and sustainable diversity competitive advantage. For diversity, improved organizational performance results from cost reduction, revenue increases, and improved decision-making, problem-solving, and innovation, the mechanisms of which are covered throughout the book.

Sustainable diversity competitive advantage occurs *when organizations distinguish themselves in talent markets and product/service markets in ways that are advantageous and difficult to overcome* (see "Competency 7: Engineering Sustainable Diversity Competitive Advantage"). If a workplace welcomes those who identify as LGBTQ+, then it is more likely to be attractive to prospective LGBTQ+ employees and enjoy a competitive advantage over the firms that compete for the best talent. If an organization is widely identified among its clients and consumers as being welcoming to people who identify as LGBTQ+, then they and their families and friends will be more likely to purchase the organization's products and services. In addition, each diverse identity group is a consumer market with considerable purchasing power. The University of Georgia's Selig Center for Economic Growth, for example, estimates that African

American purchasing power was $1.2 trillion in 2016, just short of the GDP of Spain, the fourteenth largest economy in the world.

Businesses often require their vendors to be diverse or show evidence of diversity progress. A frequently told story tells of an all-White IBM team descending upon an all-Black Atlanta company only to be told to come back when they mirrored their client.

Equity

Organizational leaders make judgments about employees all day, every day. These might be formal decisions about who gets hired, who receives a development opportunity, what rating an employee receives, or who gets promoted; or they can be informal, often below-the-radar judgments, such as offhand comments heard or made and perceptions gained in meetings and conversations. When those decisions are not made exclusively on the basis of fairness and merit, when bias enters the judgment process, inequity follows.

An organization that makes human judgments exclusively on the basis of fairness and merit, a meritocracy, will always be an aspiration. To imagine that leaders are able to develop objective criteria and then apply them objectively is a mirage. Bias will always enter—for example, in the form of prejudice or objective-appearing criteria that are actually biased. An example of the latter is the Scholastic Aptitude Test. Although debated by the Educational Testing Service, the group that oversees the SAT, scholars have found that equally talented Black students score lower than their White counterparts on many questions.[9] The challenge is not to lock the door on bias—that won't happen—but to press hard enough against the door to mitigate bias.

Mitigating bias requires knowing whether and where bias is operating, understanding its sources, and designing solutions to address those sources. None of these steps is straightforward. The existence of bias is typically measured by looking at the outcomes of talent decisions across demographic groups or by asking the possible subjects of bias whether they have been discriminated against. An inequitable outcome might have many causes—some biased, some legitimate. Perceptions of bias can be incorrect, perhaps influenced by overgeneralized data and observations. Bias does not have one or even two sources but numerous sources, each with a different set of solutions. Some solutions are targeted to specific sources, while others are universal. Determining the right mix of solutions to mitigate bias is a complex undertaking. "Competency 5: Advancing Toward Equity" describes how to establish awareness of bias, systematically deconstructs bias into its many sources, and offers solutions targeted to each source, as well as two solutions that are universal across all sources.

Inclusion

The goal of inclusion is to establish the programs, practices, management knowledge and skills, leadership, and climate that virtually ensure all employees are engaged and able to deliver exceptional results. A key variable in creating inclusion is the behavior of leaders. Unfortunately, inclusion just isn't in the bones of most leaders. They often have neither the mindset nor the skills and knowledge to manage the dilemmas of inclusion— when to speak and when to listen; how to inquire without taking a position; and when to delegate, when to look for consensus, and when to take control. They know little about how to establish the programs and practices and create a climate in which employees of all stripes flourish. It is no surprise, then, that all too often leaders give lip service to inclusion, falling back into exclusivity, power, and control. "Competency 6: Instituting Inclusion" elaborates the conditions and offers the tools for creating an inclusive workplace that is more highly engaging and delivers superior performance.

The Power of Language

CHOOSE YOUR WORDS WISELY

Dialogue that deepens contact and relationships is at the heart of bridging our differences. However, the language that powers dialogue is caught in a double bind: use improper language and dialogue is often cut off, yet the fear of using improper language also shuts off dialogue.

I have been challenged for using the word *Black*, and I have been challenged for using the term *African American*. I have hesitated to engage in diversity discussions with colleagues for fear of committing a faux pas. I go frequently to the Human Rights Campaign website to keep up with the evolving language about sexual orientation and gender identity. The Census Bureau uses the term *minority*, which offends many people. How can I refer to their research without offending? If we are going to engage in dialogue that transcends and builds bridges across differences, then we need an arbiter of what language is appropriate and what is inappropriate. Political correctness is one such arbiter, but it has a host of imperfections.

Moving Beyond Political Correctness

With every word I write in this book, I am concerned that I will violate someone's interpretation of what is politically correct and offend them. While political correctness may beneficially set the normative boundaries between what is decent and indecent language, it can be the bane of diversity dialogue. It too often creates an environment of fear where people avoid dialogue about diversity for fear of using the wrong word and being assailed. Even more, in this virtual and sometimes vicious world, many will hesitate to speak their thoughts and ideas for fear of being the next internet non-sensation.

Political correctness exists for a reason. In theory, it should work like a dictionary, identifying the correct words to use in any conversation. Correctness requires an arbiter. For example, the arbiters of the *American Heritage Dictionary*, which sits on my desk, are a staff of experts in such areas as definitions, pronunciations, etymology, usage, biographical and geographic entries, etc. In addition, the dictionary has a usage panel made up of writers, academics, and other distinguished experts, such as Maya Angelou, Jacques Barzun, Julian Bond, Isaac Asimov, Langston Hughes, and Katherine Anne Porter, and a group of consultants with expertise in such arenas as arts and humanities, physical sciences and mathematics, and religion.

The problem with political correctness is in identifying the arbiters who set the rules of correctness. Is it you? Is it me? Is it a panel of experts? Are they a fixed set of rules, or do they vary with whomever happens to be making them at the moment? If they aren't fixed, how do I navigate? Are they rules by which people can have the depth of dialogue that is required to bridge our differences?

Until a *Dictionary of Diversity Language* exists, if that is even possible or desirable, how can people of goodwill navigate to the right words? The answer lies in the context in which a word is used, the history of the word, and in the intent of the speaker. Consider the use of the N-word in hip-hop. The history and context of its usage in hip-hop are "'gangsta' rap, music that celebrated West Coast gang violence, during the early 1990s."[10] By ripping the word out of the mouths of White supremacists,

Black people have taken control of the word, diminishing its power to enforce hierarchy and inflict humiliation. The word has evolved into a term of friendship between young Black men and morphed into the language of young White men. A Tribe Called Quest give the best explanation of the history and current context of the N-word in their rap "Sucka Nigga," in which they rhyme about how the N-word was first used by White people in the Deep South as a tool of oppression, but today young Black people have embraced the term as a way of taking control of the word and reducing its acrimony, even though some senior members of the Black community oppose its use. The rap deserves a look.[11]

Contextually, the use of the N-word in hip-hop or among young Black men and women might be fine. However, a young Black man might not use the word with his pastor or grandmother. This is where history is helpful. Neal Lester, dean of humanities at Arizona State University who designed and taught a course on the N-word, points out that "as early as the seventeenth century 'negro' evolved to 'nigger' as intentionally derogatory." He goes on to say, "The word is inextricably linked with violence and brutality on black psyches and derogatory aspersions cast on black bodies."[12] While the context might be right for young White men to use the N-word, its history makes its use inappropriate among White people.

Although context and history are important guideposts, they are often not definitive in guiding language. This is where intent comes in. Is the speaker talking out of hatred and anger, the desire to subjugate, or the expression of power, or is the speaker a person of goodwill, however inept, seeking to understand and advance the dialogue? While the responsibility to discern context and understand history falls mainly to the speaker, the responsibility to ascertain intent falls mainly to the person hearing the language.

West African author Chimamanda Ngozi Adichie told the following story about context and intent to graduating students at Harvard about a woman who had taken great pains to pronounce her name correctly for an introduction at a London event:[13]

> My name is Chimamanda. In Igbo, it means "My personal spirit will never be broken." I'm not sure why, but some people find it difficult to pronounce.
>
> [About the woman who was to introduce her, she said] I could tell she was very eager to get it right. And then she went out to the stage, and gave a lovely introduction, and ended with the words, "Ladies and gentlemen, please welcome Chimichanga!" I told the story at a dinner party and one of the guests seemed very annoyed that I was laughing about it. "That was so *insulting*," he said. "That English woman could have tried harder."
>
> But the truth is, she did try very hard. In fact, she ended up calling me a fried burrito *because* she had tried very hard and ended up with an utterly human mistake that was the result of anxiety. The point of this story is that intent matters. That context matters. . . . We now live in a culture of "calling out," a culture of outrage. And you *should* call people out; you *should* be outraged. But always remember context, and never disregard intent.

Distinguishing between positive and negative intent is largely based upon trust. If the speaker is trusted, the listener will be more likely to assume positive intent. Trust is forged in the give-and-take of relationships. Facilitators of trust in relationships include the following:

◇   Entering relationships with the assumption that the other
     person deserves respect
◇   The courage to act consistently with one's moral principles
◇   Honesty
◇   Empathy and consideration of the other person's needs and
     interests
◇   Following through on commitments
◇   Sharing aspects of oneself, particularly membership in a
     protected class, family background, critical life experiences,
     values and beliefs, and education
◇   Listening more than talking
◇   Openly addressing conflicts

In any relationship, the development of trust takes time
to percolate. First and foremost, leaders must give diverse
employee teams and individuals clarity about what builds trust
and opportunities to build trusting relationships before they dive
into dialogue about diversity.

The choice of language can be black and white or gray.
Words that are black and white, such as the use of certain racial,
ethnic, and religious epithets, are relatively easy to discern.
When language is black and white, the majority of people in
organizations are clear about what is and isn't proper. The
challenge is that much of diversity dialogue, if it is to be honest
and open, falls into the world of gray.

In addition to being trustworthy, effective dialogue in a
largely gray world requires that the participants allow themselves
to be vulnerable. Vulnerability is about leaning into challenging
dialogue, risking exposure and criticism, tightrope walking across
the divide of difference, and, ultimately, making connection. As
Theodore Roosevelt said in his "Man in the Arena" speech at the
Sorbonne in 1910,

> It is not the critic who counts; not the man who points out how the strong man stumbles, or where the doer of deeds could have done them better. The credit belongs to the man who is actually in the arena, whose face is marred by dust and sweat and blood; who strives valiantly; who errs . . . who at the best knows in the end the triumph of high achievement, and who at the worst, if he fails, at least fails while daring greatly, so that his place shall never be with those cold and timid souls who neither know victory nor defeat.[14]

The net effect of being invulnerable, leaning away from the fray, and controlling expressions is to be cut off from the depth of connection that is required to transcend differences. Political correctness will not stop the ignorant and hateful; it will only block those who are uncertain about what is politically correct in an interaction with people who are different from themselves (i.e., most of us). Besides engendering trust and approaching uncertainty with vulnerability, how do we find the language to initiate dialogue?

LANGUAGE GUIDELINES

How can people weave through the minefield of language to find words that don't offend? The answer: they probably can't. To minimize the risk of offending, the first guideline is that speakers should consider history and context for the language they use, and listeners should consider intent.

Some reference organizations, such as the Human Rights Campaign (HRC), a leading advocate for LGBTQ+ equality, recommend language for an evolving world. The HRC moved from LGBT to LGBTQ. Other advocates of gender preference and gender identity equality use acronyms such as GLBTTQ or LGBTTTQQIAA (lesbian, gay, bisexual, trans or transgender, transsexual, two-spirited, queer, questioning, intersex, asexual, ally). By the publication date of this book or thereafter, the correct reference language may well have changed again, so organizations must keep up with reference organizations. An organization's own employee resource groups are often the best arbiters of language.

Even reference organizations disagree on the correct terms. Chris Bartlett, executive director of the William Way LGBT Community Center in Philadelphia, sheds light on finding the right term: "The diversity of acronyms reflects the vibrant diversity of thought about what our communities should look like. Inclusion is our byword, and if that requires more or different letters, I'm all for it. But I would never box us in by saying that any particular acronym could express this diversity."[15]

When in doubt about the use of a word, whether addressing an individual or a group, ask preference and obtain agreement on the reference word. For example, until widely accepted gender-neutral pronouns exist, ask what pronoun employees prefer when referring to themselves. Or if you need to use the word *minority* to refer to people of color, obtain agreement before using it. Better yet, use *underrepresented people.*

A key consideration in finding the right word is "people first." For example, don't say "the disabled"; use "people with disabilities." Reference words like *Black, White, Caucasian,* and *Latino,* whether used as an adjective or noun, should be treated as proper nouns and adjectives and be capitalized.

When referring to a group, be as specific as possible. For example, the term *Asian* lumps many culturally distinct groups together. Ideally, use the most specific national, tribal, or local regional reference. If referring collectively to people of Chinese, South Korean, Taiwanese, and Japanese ancestry, for example, use the term *East Asian.*

In many circles, *African American* is preferred to *Black*. However, the term *African American* refers to people of African ancestry who live in the United States. In some cases, it is further modified to only include people who trace their ancestry to slavery, and it can be an exclusive term in global organizations since it refers only to the US. For most organizations, context will determine the proper word. Where context doesn't work, an internal reference group, such as an employee affinity or resource group, or external reference group may offer the right language.

In most cases, following the six guidelines in table 1-2 will guide leaders to the most effective language.

The Six Language Guidelines

1. Consider context, history, and intent.
2. Check with reference organizations.
3. Ask preference and obtain agreement on the right reference words up front.
4. Follow the "people first" rule.
5. Treat references to demographic groups as proper adjectives and nouns and capitalize them.
6. Be as specific as possible.

Table 1-2

THE LANGUAGE OF THIS BOOK

Since I can't obtain preferences and agreement up front, I commit myself to following the other five guidelines in table 1-2. When a sentence calls for a singular pronoun (he, she, him, her, his, her, hers), I randomly use just one gender identity to avoid clunky terms such as him/her, s(he), or she or he. I sometimes use they, them, their, or theirs as singular pronouns out of respect for those people whose gender identity is nonbinary.

Substantial controversy exists over the terms to use for referring to members of different social groups. The book uses the following terms:

◇ *Historically underrepresented people*—or the shorthand *underrepresented people*—is used to refer to those who have historically been discriminated against and marginalized in employment and advancement opportunities.

◇ *People of color* is used when referring collectively to African Americans/Black people, Latinos/Hispanics/Latinx, Asians, Native American or Indigenous people, and people of multiple races.

◇ The term *minority* is not used, except when referencing a source that uses the term, such as the Census Bureau.

◇ *Latino* is employed because at the time of this writing, it is relatively inclusive (though the *o* ending is masculine, it has come to be regarded as inclusive of all genders) and the least likely to offend. Though *Hispanic* is preferred over *Latino* by more people, according to Pew Research Center, it excludes the large number of people from Brazil who trace their heritage to Portugal and speak Portuguese. Some feel *Hispanic* is a colonialist word. Recently, the gender-neutral term *Latinx* (pronounced La-teen-ex, although other pronunciations are used) has come into use. *Latinx* is gender neutral, but its use is still controversial. The best way to resolve this conundrum is to ask preference of the person or people to whom you are speaking or to be country specific (e.g., Mexican or Guatemalan).

◇ *Black* is utilized instead of *African American*, and *Asian*, if further specificity is not possible, instead of *Asian American* because the scope of this book is global. When citing a reference that uses *African American, Asian American,* or another word, the reference language is used.

◇   The proper language with which to refer to Indigenous people is complicated. No consensus on language exists. In the US, some prefer Native American, which is widely used by many tribes, while others prefer American Indian, First Nations Peoples, or other language. Generally, the specific tribe or nation is preferred (using the original name, not the name assigned by outsiders), such as Diné or Numa in the US or Maasai in Kenya or Himba in Namibia. When citing a reference, as long as the term the reference uses is respectful, it will be used. Otherwise, if the specific tribal name is inappropriate or unknown, either *Indigenous people,* if the reference is global, or *Native American,* if the reference is to the US, will be used.

◇   *LGBTQ+* is used to refer to sexual orientation and gender identity to be consistent with the HRC recommendation. The plus sign has been added to maintain full inclusion as the reference term evolves.

◇   *People with disabilities* is used in general when referring to people with physical and cognitive disabilities. The terms *people with a physical disability, people with a developmental disability,* and *people with a cognitive disability* are used when references are more specific. The general term *ableism* is used to refer to systemic discrimination against people with disabilities.

◇   *Older people or person* is used instead of *elderly, aged,* or other terms because it is generally preferred. *Eldercare* is used to refer to time spent caring for older people.

◇   In most cases, the term *woman* is preferred to *female.* *Woman* is a noun, whereas *female* can function as a noun or an adjective. However, *woman* is "an apposite noun— explaining, even identifying, the noun it 'stands next to'—

but [is] syntactically stronger than an adjective. Both words can be used as modifiers of nouns, but the noun woman has more weight." Deborah Tannen, a linguistics professor at Georgetown University, notes, "We're hearing woman as an adjective more often now. Female connotes a biological category. I think many feminists avoid it for the same reason they prefer gender to sex. . . . I avoid female in my own writing because it feels disrespectful, as if I'm treating the people I'm referring to as mammals but not humans."[16] For these reasons, *women* is used, although when *woman* sounds inappropriate or a reference uses the term, *female* is used.

◇   Still a relatively uncontroversial choice, the term *veteran* is used to refer to people who have served in the armed services.

Even these choices are not without complexity. For example, some resist the use of the term *people of color*. They are concerned that it harks back to the term *colored*. Historically, *people of color* comes from the French *gens de couleur*, which is a shortened version of *gens de couleur libres*, "free people of color," which referred to people with both European and African ancestry who were not enslaved and were concentrated in cities controlled by the Spanish, largely New Orleans in the US. Lumping all groups together under *people of color* might negate the individual histories and unique experiences the groups have had with discrimination. Some Whites object to the term because, as they argue, "We have color, too."

No pure language of diversity will ever exist. Language exists in the real world where conversations about diversity can be charged and opinionated. If society is going to gain greater acceptance and respect across differences, and employees greater capacity to work together for the benefit of the organization and its customers and communities, dialogue will always be more important than words. Critical to getting past words to the vital dialogue is the presumption, until clear disproval, of positive intent.

Thus, I hope the reader will consider my intent, however inadequate my choice of words. This book is intended to ensure that employees and their leaders are able to reach across differences to achieve equity in talent decisions and workplaces in which everyone can do their highest-quality, most productive, most engaging work.

Constructing a Business Case for Diversity

"How do you bring people into the change process? Start with reality. Get all the facts out. Give people the rationale for change, laying it out in the clearest, most dramatic terms. When everybody gets the same facts, they'll generally come to the same conclusion."

Jack Welch
Former Chairman and CEO, General Electric

IN ORGANIZATIONS, REALITY EXISTS IN three dimensions: the business, the organizational, and the personal. For change to occur, organizational stakeholders must understand and accept how diversity will help the organization fulfill its mission (the business case), how diversity will influence day-to-day life within the organization (the organizational diversity philosophy), and the personal meaning of diversity for each employee (the personal case). The creation of a business case and the organizational diversity philosophy is the responsibility of strategic leadership. The personal case is the responsibility of each employee, with senior leaders serving as the role model. Together, the three dimensions establish the organization's rationale for diversity. Constructing the business case—the second competency of strategic leaders—is covered below. The third competency, envisioning organizational and personal diversity philosophies, is the subject of the next chapter.

The business case for diversity is a clear, dramatic, compelling statement of the reality faced by the organization and how engagement in a diversity initiative improves that reality, bringing economic and organizational benefits to the organization. The personal case, which is addressed by the next competency, is composed of the personal philosophy that animates a leader's own commitment to diversity and the values and beliefs that provide a signpost for how the organization will address differences among its employees and customers. It is a leader's articulation of his singular reality and commitment that animates his personal engagement in advancing diversity. Together, the business and personal cases form the rationale for diversity. A diversity rationale should be composed of very public statements, living as much in the commentary, dialogue, and presentations of an organization's leaders as in its analog and digital documents.

The Business Case for Diversity

A business case for diversity is confirmed when a positive relationship is demonstrated between diversity and individual, group, and organizational performance. Generally, the research literature views the relationship between diversity and performance through three lenses: positive, negative, and paradoxical views. The positive view holds that demographically diverse groups and organizations produce superior results. The arguments for the positive point of view are that a wider range of viewpoints, life experiences, and cultural backgrounds leads to better and more creative problem solutions and decisions and greater connection with a diversity of customers and clients.

The negative view is typically based on the argument that increased diversity leads to increased conflict among group members, leading to poorer performance. The paradoxical view incorporates elements of both the positive and the negative views, demonstrating that demographic diversity produces positive effects but also increases conflict. The argument for the efficacy of the paradoxical view is that if conflict is effectively managed, it will produce a wider range of ideas, approaches, and strategies, leading to better solutions and decisions and greater creativity. Though research presents a complex weave of perspectives and conclusions, the paradoxical view currently holds sway.

A business case is composed of the interweaving of up to eight different business or organizational cases: the talent case, the legal case, the return-on-investment case, the product market case, the operating effectiveness case, the multiplier effect case, the moral case, and the political case. This review focuses on the strategic considerations required to build a business case.

THE TALENT CASE

Diversity is a talent strategy. And, increasingly, that talent is coming from underrepresented groups. Yet bias against people from underrepresented groups, whether in North America, South America, Europe, Asia, Africa, or Oceania, is undermining the ability of organizations to maximize their talent.

A Demographic Evolution

The argument most frequently heard against embracing diversity is that it will cause the quality of the organization's talent to decline. This would be true if diversity were a system of forced quotas. But except in a miniscule number of cases and in some countries outside the US that enforce quotas, diversity is a process of equity (fairness in attraction, retention, and advancement of all employees) and inclusion (ensuring that those employees are welcome and perform to the best of their ability). Both equity and inclusion, key components of diversity, increase the quality and contributions of the workforce. Diversity is fundamentally a strategy to maximize talent.

When the changing demographics of the workforce are considered, the focus on equity and inclusion for underrepresented populations should not be a surprise. The civilian labor force tells the story of changing demographics in the US (table 2-1).[17] The number of White people in the labor force is actually declining for both men and women, while the number of underrepresented people is growing in every category. The numbers are stark. In the ten years between 2009 and 2019, the number of White men in the labor force declined by over one million and the number of White women declined by over six hundred thousand. At the same time, the numbers of people who are Black, Asian, and Hispanic grew by over ten million, a difference of over twelve million workers. Some employers might argue that this doesn't apply to them since this is the broad civilian employee population and they are primarily hiring more educated professionals.

Changes in the US Civilian Labor Force, 2009–2019
(in thousands, twenty and over)

	2009	2019	Change 2009-2019	Percent Change
White Men	65,372	64,070	(1,302)	(2.0%)
White Women	54,976	54,304	(672)	(1.2%)
Black Men	7,914	8,883	969	12.2%
Black Women	8,988	9,910	922	10.3%
Asian Men	3,777	5,257	1,480	39.2%
Asian Women	3,248	4,729	1,481	45.6%
Hispanic Men	12,730	15,204	2,474	19.4%
Hispanic Women	8,560	11,516	2,956	34.5%

Table 2-1

The statistics on those who have a bachelor's degree or higher, though not as stark, show a trend away from non-Hispanic White men (table 2-2).[18] While the number of non-Hispanic White men attaining an advanced degree has grown by nearly six million, the number of underrepresented people—including White, Non-Hispanic women and Black, Asian, and Hispanic people—receiving advanced degrees has grown nineteen million, a difference of over 300 percent. And the growth rates are much higher for people of color.

Changes in the Attainment of a Bachelor's Degree or Higher, 2010–2020, in the US

(in thousands, eighteen and over)

	2010	2020	Change 20010-2020	Percent Change
White Non-Hispanic Men	23,751	29,568	5,817	24.5%
White Non-Hispanic Women	24,261	32,041	7,780	32.1%
Black Men	1,885	3,244	1,359	72.1%
Black Women	2,887	4,894	2,007	69.5%
Asian Men	2,554	4,409	1,855	72.6%
Asian Women	2,625	4,762	2,137	81.4%
Hispanic Men	1,843	3,561	1,718	93.3%
Hispanic Women	2,050	4,262	2,212	107.9%

Table 2-2

The Ubiquity of Bias in the United States

While changing demographics and markets are driving increased demand for employees from underrepresented groups, bias is creating a barrier to the effective employment of members of these groups. Bias is difficult to prove since it is challenging to draw a direct line between acts of bias and individuals not being hired, retained, and advanced, especially when so much of bias is unconscious.

Data from over a quarter million medium and large business units in the US demonstrates that something is limiting the progress of White women and people of color (figure 2-1).[19] In considering advancement of a group, the relevant comparison is to the labor pool from which they are drawn. Those prospective employees with a bachelor's degree or higher are the labor pool for professional employees. From there, professionals become the labor pool for first-line and mid-level managers, who in turn are the labor pool for executive positions. The labor pools are approximations since, for example, it is likely that the ranks of first-line and mid-level managers include nonprofessionals. However, most executive positions in mid- and large-sized firms come from the professional ranks. The figure shows that US companies are doing a good job of recruiting and hiring professional men and women of color, but men and women of color are not progressing into top leadership in proportion to their presence in the labor supply. Most shocking is that while White men are 35.7 percent of professionals, they represent 59.9 percent of executives.

Proportion of Positions Held at Three Organizational Levels Compared with Educational Attainment, 2018

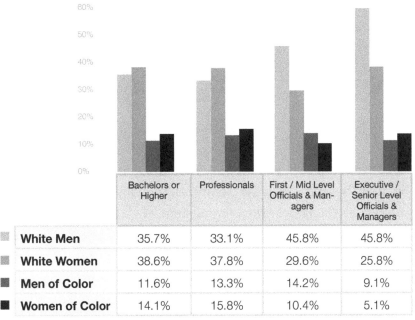

	Bachelors or Higher	Professionals	First / Mid Level Officials & Managers	Executive / Senior Level Officials & Managers
White Men	35.7%	33.1%	45.8%	45.8%
White Women	38.6%	37.8%	29.6%	25.8%
Men of Color	11.6%	13.3%	14.2%	9.1%
Women of Color	14.1%	15.8%	10.4%	5.1%

Figure 2-1

Progress is being made, but it is at best interminably slow and at worst declining. Between 2008 and 2018, the proportion of White men in first-line, mid-level, and executive positions declined, while the proportion of White women has increased slightly (figure 2-2).[20] The proportion of men and women of color in management roles is progressing at around 2.2 percent year over year.

Ten Years of Change in Manager Demographics

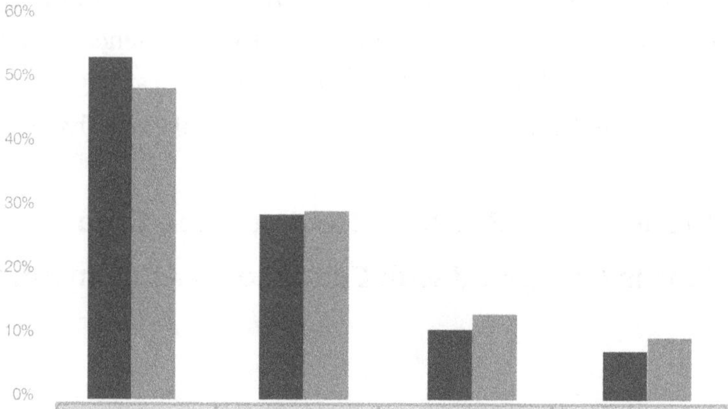

	White Men	White Women	Men of Color	Women of Color
2008	52.8%	28.6%	11.0%	7.6%
2018	47.9%	29.1%	13.4%	9.6%

Figure 2-2

At 2.2 percent it will take decades for equity to be achieved, but it can be argued that the picture is improving. However, when we look at changes in the employment of professionals (table 2-3)[21] another picture emerges: the rapid entry of people of color into the professional ranks appears to be driving progress but not so much a reduction in bias. Given the dramatic changes in demographics, we would expect there to be faster growth in the proportion of women and men of color in management positions.

Percent Increase in Professional Employment
2008–2018

White Men	18.9%
White Women	22.1%
Minority Men	55.5%
Minority Women	49.0%

Table 2-3

Wage gaps between Black and White and White male and female workers have been widening. For example, "Black men earned 18 percent less than White men in 2010. By 2019, that gap had grown to 24 percent"; while wage gaps for White and Black women were declining before 2010, since then they have increased substantially.[22]

Below are a number of additional data points and studies which underscore the ubiquity of bias in the US and across the globe:

◊   Even where great pains have been taken to eliminate bias, it can be significant. Among NBA referees, which former NBA Commissioner David Stern called "the most ranked, rated, reviewed, statistically analyzed and mentored group of employees of any company in any place in the world," bias is ubiquitous. In a study of NBA referees, Joseph Price and Justin Wolfers found "systematic evidence of an own-race bias. Notably, players receive up to 4% fewer fouls or score up to 2½% more points when they are the recipients of a positive own-race bias by referees, rather than a negative opposite-race effect."[23] Over the course of a season, this level of bias is significant enough to affect a close championship race.

◇   In a classic study, fictitious resumes that systematically varied the experience of imaginary job applicants were sent in response to help-wanted ads in Boston and Chicago. Employers were significantly more likely to call back applicants with White-sounding names (Emily and Greg) than African American–sounding names (Lakisha and Jamal). The researchers also found that a White name yielded as many callbacks as an additional eight years of experience for a member of an underrepresented group.[24] Similar results were found in studies of job applicants who were disabled and from the LGBTQ+ community.[25]

◇   Young White men with felony convictions were more likely to receive callbacks than young Black men with comparable qualifications and a clean record.[26]

◇   Simply introducing a screen to obscure the gender of musicians auditioning for symphony orchestra positions "increases—by 50 percent—the probability that a woman will be advanced from certain preliminary rounds and increases by severalfold the likelihood that a woman will be selected in the final round."[27]

◇   Religious discrimination in employment is on the increase. EEOC complaints about religious discrimination were up nearly 50 percent in the ten years between 2005 and 2015.[28]

◇   In a survey of 1,197 LGBTQ+ people, 21 percent believed they had "been treated unfairly by an employer."[29] People who are transgender experience considerable employment bias. Thirty percent of employees responding to the National Center for Transgender Equality's 2015 US Transgender Survey reported that in the previous year they had "be[en] fired, denied a promotion, or experienc[ed] some other form of mistreatment in the workplace due to their gender identity or expression, such as being verbally harassed or physically or sexually assaulted at work."[30]

◇ Twenty states and the District of Columbia have employment nondiscrimination laws that cover sexual orientation and gender identity. Two additional states have nondiscrimination laws that cover only sexual orientation.[31]

◇ Forty-three percent of people with disabilities believe they have experienced employment discrimination.[32]

◇ "Disabled workers are commonly perceived as possessing high warmth, but low competence, triggering emotions of pity and sympathy."[33]

◇ In 2016, for people with a disability, the unemployment rate— unemployed and actively seeking a job—for those twenty-five and over with a bachelor's degree or higher was 6.6 percent, 275 percent higher than the 2.4 percent rate for those with a bachelor's or higher who do not have a disability.[34]

The Ubiquity of Bias Across the Globe

The forms bias takes, the laws and regulations that govern bias, and how those laws are enforced vary substantially across the globe. For example, law in the People's Republic of China (PRC) institutes a quota requiring that 1.5 percent of employees be people with disabilities and prescribes levies or fines for those organizations that do not comply. While US laws and regulations strongly prohibit discrimination against people with disabilities, legally enforced quotas and fines are also prohibited. Enforcement mechanisms in the PRC are weak compared to the US, often left to local or regional authorities.[35]

The racial and ethnic identities of those who are the objects of discrimination vary considerably across regional and national boundaries. Across Europe, for example, immigrants and Roma people are subject to discrimination. In the UK, people of African and Caribbean origin experience discrimination; in the Russian Federation, it's migrants and especially people from

Caucasian and Central Asian countries; in South Asia, caste-based discrimination, especially against Dalits, is significant; in the PRC, workers from rural areas suffer extensive discrimination in employment in the coastal industrial cities,[36] as do Uyghurs, a largely Muslim ethnic group;[37] in Africa, bias against people with HIV/AIDS and caste members such as the Ilkunono in Kenya and the Osu in Nigeria is significant; and in Latin America, discrimination against the poor, Indigenous peoples and Afro-descendants is consistent across all countries.[38] The following are examples of discrimination across the globe:

◇   The International Labour Organization (ILO), the United Nations' labor office, assessed the percentage of female CEOs of companies traded on fourteen international stock exchanges. Percentages ranged from 5.6 percent (of 2,100 listed companies) in China to 0 for the CAC 40 (France) and the DAX 30 (Germany).[39]

◇   The percentage of board seats held by women ranged from greater than 20 percent in Finland, Norway, Sweden, and the UK to less than 5 percent in Japan, Russia, India, the Republic of Korea, Chile, and such Middle Eastern states as Bahrain, Kuwait, Oman, Qatar, Saudi Arabia, and the UAE.[40]

◇   The global gender pay gap is estimated to be 22.9 percent, comparable to the pay gap in the US. It ranges from 2 percent in Panama to over 50 percent in Azerbaijan. "At the current rate," the ILO estimates, "it would take over seventy years to bridge the gender pay gap."[41] The gender pay gap is widening in several countries, such as Peru, Dominican Republic, Belarus, and Bulgaria.[42]

◇   Around 6 percent of the people in Sweden to about 55 percent of the people in Lithuania believe "it is unfair to give work to handicapped people when able-bodied people can't find work."[43]

◊   In a global survey, in answer to the question "Is the city or area where you live a good place or not a good place to live for gay and lesbian people?" the Netherlands (87 percent) and other European countries, Canada (84 percent), and Uruguay (79 percent) were most likely to say "good place," while Senegal (1 percent) and other sub-Saharan countries, Azerbaijan (2 percent), Pakistan (2 percent), and Indonesia (3 percent) were least likely. Gallup was not allowed to ask the question in such countries as "China, Saudi Arabia, Iran, Egypt, Malaysia and a host of other nations in the Middle East and Central Asia."[44]

◊   When asked who they would like having as neighbors, 78 percent of Africans responded that they would somewhat or strongly dislike having homosexuals as neighbors.[45]

◊   At this writing, Mauritania, Sudan, Iran, Saudi Arabia, and Yemen all have active legislation leading to the death penalty for people who are LGBTQ+.[46]

◊   Since the early 1990s, with encouragement from the United Nations, some forty-five countries have decriminalized homosexuality and more than thirty have introduced full legal recognition of same-sex relationships.[47] Sixty-two countries prohibit employment discrimination on the basis of sexual orientation. Although some courts have ruled that Title VII of the Civil Rights Act prohibits employment discrimination against the LGBTQ+ community, the United States does not have an explicit employment antidiscrimination law for LGBTQ+ people.[48]

The Denial of Bias

Many leaders deny that bias is significant in their organizations. When asked to explain why their underrepresented employees are not advancing, the most frequent answers these leaders give are that underrepresented people simply don't have the leadership skills to advance and that talented women are leaving organizations to care for family. Neither conjecture has a sound footing. Indeed, for women, a number of studies conclude that they have better leadership skills than men or different leadership skills that are equally in demand. For example, in a comprehensive study of 7,280 leaders, using 360-degree assessments, women were found to outrank men on twelve of the sixteen competencies that exemplify outstanding leadership, while men outranked women on only one competency. Men are perceived to be superior strategic thinkers, although when only top executives of both genders are compared, they are perceived to be equal on strategic thinking. For the other three competencies, women are slightly superior, although the differences are not statistically significant.[49]

An array of other reasons, generally supported by research, suggest why women and people of color do not ascend into leadership:[50]

◇   The performance of employees of color is scrutinized more rigorously and they receive lower ratings, even though their performance is equivalent or better.
◇   Women and employees of color lack access to the networks that factor strongly into promotions.
◇   Cultural perceptions that White men make better leaders than people of color and women

Another reason for the low proportion of promotions among women and employees of color is that significant numbers leave organizations before they can be considered for promotion. Though the data on voluntary turnover is generally weak, one robust study of companies, which included 475,458 professionals and managers, showed that women, African Americans, and Hispanics were considerably more likely to leave in their first three years.[51] Reasons considered for why underrepresented employees leave sooner are job ghettoes, an unwelcoming climate for diverse employees, lack of peers in higher status positions, and slower career progress. *Job ghettoes* are roles that tend to be occupied by members of underrepresented groups, such as women in human resources. Bias plays a role in each of these.

The drain of top female talent for family reasons has been overstated, although the pandemic may have altered the equation. A study of well-educated, top-talent women revealed that 37 percent take an off-ramp for an average of only 2.2 years (1.2 years in business organizations). While family responsibilities are cited by 45 percent of women, 29 percent (52 percent for business) cite unsatisfying careers, and 23 percent (26 percent for business) cite career stagnation. Fully 93 percent of top-talent women step off the career track with the intention of returning to their careers. To stem the tide of top employees, namely women, leaving to care for family, many organizations offer an array of work–life benefits, including flexible work arrangements and dependent-care supports. However, most leaders send a mixed message about taking advantage of work–life supports, saying on the one hand that work–life is vital to the business, while implying on the other hand that those who utilize work–life must sacrifice their careers. In effect they are sending the mixed message "Take advantage of the wonderful work–life benefits we are offering you, just as long as you are sitting outside my door when I need you."[52]

Another reason—perhaps the fundamental reason—why many organizations are in a state of denial about bias is that beginning in the late nineties, White people have increasingly come to believe that they are more the targets of discrimination than Black people (figure 2-3).[53]

White and Black Perceptions of Anti-White and Anti-Black Bias over Six Decades

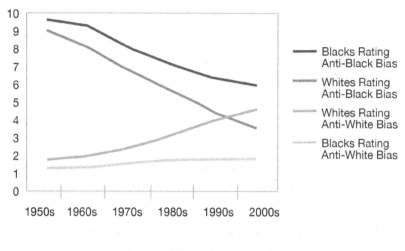

Figure 2-3

No credible data supports the belief that bias against White people is greater than bias against Black people.

THE LEGAL CASE

In 2016, of the 97,443 charges brought against employers and resolved by the Equal Employment Opportunity Commission, 15,832 (16.2 percent) were resolved in favor of the charging party, amounting to $348 million in monetary awards. These do not include charges filed with state and local fair employment practices agencies.

Insofar as they address the causes of employment discrimination, diversity initiatives can prevent these charges. Many charges emanate from biased employment decisions, including hiring, compensation, evaluation, development, advancement, and separation decisions, and from hostile work environments. By addressing the employment decision-making processes that contain bias and creating inclusive work environments (see competencies 5 and 6), organizations can reduce their exposure to discrimination charges.

THE RETURN ON INVESTMENT (ROI) CASE

The ROI case monetizes diversity investments and returns. The ROI is usually expressed as a percentage, using the formula ROI=Return/Investment x 100. It is typically calculated on an annual basis or over the lifetime of the initiative. Because they express investments and returns in dollars, ROIs allow comparison among projects to determine which was more successful or to determine which would be the better investment. Investments typically include dollars spent directly on diversity initiatives, such as diversity staff, trainers, consultants, and employee time spent in diversity activities, and may include an allocation of indirect costs or organization overhead. Returns include monetized versions of improved overall economic performance, as well as its key drivers; reduced absenteeism and turnover; increased innovation and employee engagement; and improved problem-solving and decision-making. Although in most cases, returns far exceed investments, the ROI business case is a difficult one to make because of the difficulty of monetizing investments and returns.

Monetizing Investments

On the investment side, accounting and budgeting systems do not usually record employee time spent on diversity activities, especially training, which is often the largest investment component. These activities typically need to be recorded by a separate accounting system. Then, they must be monetized by multiplying the time spent in diversity activities by the actual salary and benefits costs of each employee. Because of the resource requirements of recording time and making these calculations, average salaries and benefits are sometimes used.

The purchase of external resources, such as training content, workshop facilitation, consulting, and recruiting, are recorded in accounting systems. They are already monetized. The challenge is in making sure to fairly identify and monetize all external costs.

Monetizing Returns

The return side is far more challenging. Whether the demographic diversity of the workforce or a subset of the workforce, such as a board of directors or executive team, leads to improved economic performance—profit and loss, market performance, market share, sales, or shareholder returns—cannot be definitively confirmed. While several studies have demonstrated the relationship between demographic diversity and economic performance, others have minimized the effect or found the relationship to be negative.[54] Critics point out that the direction of causality is difficult to determine; does diversity of the workforce lead to higher economic performance, or does higher economic performance make it more likely that an organization will invest in workforce diversity? Another criticism is that some studies do not effectively control for other variables that could be affecting economic performance—for example, firm size (i.e., large firms are more likely to have diversity initiatives).

Reduced absenteeism and unwanted turnover, two factors often included in return calculations, are usually measured by assessments of employees' perceptions, including employee surveys and exit interviews. Monetizing absenteeism is usually a process of looking at costs saved because an employee wasn't absent. Unwanted turnover is usually measured by a question on the employee survey about an employee's intention to leave. Of course, people don't always follow through on their intentions. Monetizing turnover is usually based on lost productivity from an employee's absence, time consuming and difficult to assess accurately, and the costs of recruiting, hiring, and training a new employee. In cases where measures of actual turnover are used, the causes are usually based on self-reports from exit interviews. Exit interviews are notoriously inaccurate because employees do not wish to burn bridges.

The returns on absenteeism and unwanted turnover are not real. A diversity initiative prevents absenteeism and unwanted turnover. Returns are determined by what costs would have been incurred had the diversity initiative not prevented absenteeism and unwanted turnover. These are called avoided costs. They are not real because no one actually left and no dollars were actually spent to replace them. Executives tend to be far more concerned with real costs and so frequently discount avoided costs.

Although there is strong evidence that diversity is positively correlated with superior decision-making, problem-solving, innovation, and employee engagement, determining what proportion is caused by diversity initiatives and monetizing that proportion is extremely difficult. Improved problem-solving, for example, would have to be monetized by comparing the returns from the decision made to the returns from the decision or decisions not made, a virtually impossible undertaking outside of a highly controlled experimental environment.

Building an Effective ROI Case

An effective ROI business case is difficult to build. However, because diversity investments are typically modest and returns often substantial, a sensitivity-analysis approach may be useful. Sensitivity analysis tests how sensitive the results of an analysis are to the assumptions made about investments and returns by developing two ROI cases: the most conservative case and the best-estimate case. In the most conservative case, the highest cost assumptions are made for investments, the lowest benefit assumptions are made for returns, and discounting is used to bring the dollar amount of returns and investments into the same base year. The best-estimate case is an attempt to be as accurate as possible on each assumption. A standalone best-estimate analysis is often greeted with skepticism. A conservative case that shows a positive ROI when juxtaposed against the best-estimate case is often very convincing to senior management. At minimum, a sensitivity analysis should be reviewed by the CFO. At best, the sensitivity analysis should be prepared by the CFO or a respected member of her team before being presented to the top leadership team.

Interpreting the meaning of an ROI requires a comparison either against some external standard or organization or against one's own ROI measures over time. Because no standard for the calculation of diversity ROI exists, comparison against an external standard does not make sense until such time as a measurement standard, similar to the FASB's Generally Accepted Accounting Principles, exists. Comparison against an organization's own diversity ROI over time requires a minimum of three measures separated by equal amounts of time.

The Magnitude of Returns Problem

ROIs, called benefit/cost ratios in government and nonprofits, are often used to prioritize organizational initiatives. To establish priorities, organizations typically compare projected ROIs ((Total Return on Investment – Total Cost of Investment)/Total Cost of Investment x 100) while also looking at the magnitude of returns (Total Return – Total Cost) for each initiative. Even though a conservative estimate of the diversity ROI may be exceptionally positive, the magnitude of returns from diversity initiatives often pales in comparison to the returns from pure business and organizational initiatives.

For example, a business initiative might have an ROI of 167 percent (($80 million − $30 million)/$30 million x 100), while a diversity initiative has an ROI of 500 percent (($600,000 − $100,000/$100,000) x 100), three times the business initiative. However, the magnitude of return is $500,000 for the diversity investment and $50 million for the business investment. If the risk and other factors are relatively similar for each investment, then from a business or budgetary point of view, the business initiative is likely to receive priority.

THE PRODUCT/SERVICE MARKET CASE

A product or service market is a grouping of customers who have similar needs and requirements for the goods and services they purchase. The diversity product market is the conglomeration of consumers and businesses who make purchase decisions based, at least in part, on their membership in an underrepresented or ally group or the vendor company's demographic characteristics or diversity activities. The diversity product market can be segmented in numerous ways. For making a business case, the most useful perspective from which to view the diversity product market is by type of customer, typically either business-to-business (BtoB) or business-to-consumer (BtoC). The term *business* is used to refer to any institution, whether a commercial business or a nonprofit organization.

The Business-to-Business Market

The BtoB market contains two major categories: companies that are predominantly owned and staffed by members of one or more underrepresented groups, called women-owned business enterprises (WBE) and minority-owned business enterprises (MBE), and companies with strong vendor or supplier diversity initiatives that require suppliers to show a strong commitment to diversity. Diverse organizations have an advantage in competing for business in both of these categories.

Underrepresented Owners

According to the Commerce Department's Minority Business Development Agency, the most recent data available shows that MBEs' growth rates in gross receipts, employees, and number of firms are significantly outpacing NMBEs' rates (figure 2-4).[55]

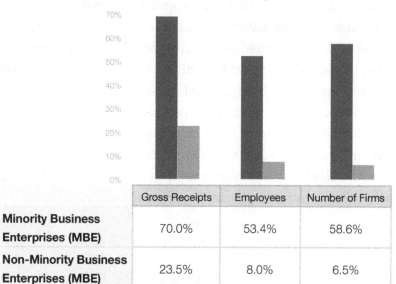

MBE and NMBE Growth Rates, 2007–2017

	Gross Receipts	Employees	Number of Firms
Minority Business Enterprises (MBE)	70.0%	53.4%	58.6%
Non-Minority Business Enterprises (MBE)	23.5%	8.0%	6.5%

Figure 2-4

Women-owned business enterprises are growing in number, employment, and revenues faster than all firms (figure 2-5).[56] The growth rate in the number of WBEs is being driven by growth in minority women–owned business enterprises (MWBEs). While the overall growth rate in the number of WBEs was 114 percent between 1997 and 2017, the number of MWBEs grew 467 percent.[57] NMBEs and NWBEs are the markets of today, but the future will increasingly belong to minority- and women-owned, especially minority women–owned, businesses.

Growth Rates for Women-Owned Businesses vs. All Firms, 2014–2019

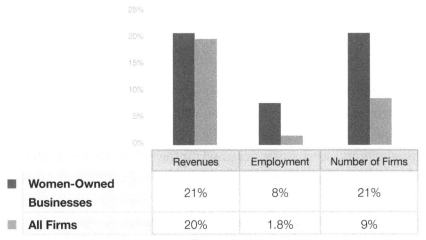

	Revenues	Employment	Number of Firms
Women-Owned Businesses	21%	8%	21%
All Firms	20%	1.8%	9%

Figure 2-5

Vendor Requirements

The asset management division of a leading financial services company made a pitch to a large state pension fund. The presenters were all White men. As a condition for doing business, they were told to return with data about their diversity demographics and evidence that they were taking substantive action on diversity.

Many companies require their suppliers to show evidence of diversity plans, policies, and achievements, with some even requiring their suppliers to demonstrate that they are, in turn, requiring their own suppliers to demonstrate similar evidence. The US Office of Federal Contract Compliance requires that contractors who supply the US government with goods and services and who do $700,000 in revenues ($1.5 million for construction companies) must set and meet goals for subcontracting with underrepresented suppliers (tier one), and in some cases their subcontractors must also set and achieve spending goals with underrepresented suppliers (tier two). These requirements can be seen in two ways: as a burden or as an opportunity to establish competitive advantage through diversity.

The Business-to-Consumer Market

The diversity consumer market also has two major categories: a universal market, in which the same products and services are offered to all customers, and a specialized market, in which products and services are designed for the unique characteristics of individual underrepresented groups.

BtoC Universal Market

The universal market includes the vast range of products and services that appeal across social groups (e.g., toilet paper, automobiles, and hot dogs). When the buying power of an underrepresented segment is substantial, it behooves an organization to appeal directly to that segment through positioning. For nonprofit organizations, positioning might involve designing fundraising or client solicitations aimed at an underrepresented group, or, in government, designing materials that use different languages to address underrepresented segments. Buying power is usually defined as the total personal income after deductions for taxes and federal retirement benefits. Positioning is largely a communications strategy that uses such marketing tools as advertising, promotions, packaging, or a unique sales force to appeal directly to that segment. A simple example is the ubiquity of people of color portrayed in television advertisements for consumer products.

The business case for diversity is that the organization will have a competitive advantage when people from the targeted underrepresented groups are a vital component of the marketing team. They have the language and cultural knowledge to tune marketing so that it appeals to the segment from which they are drawn. This is particularly important when positioning an organization's products and services for a global market. When Chevrolet sought to sell the Nova line in Latin America, it was shocked to find that *no va* means "no going" in Spanish.

Diversity consumer markets in the US are substantial (table 2-4).[58] Growth in buying power (disposable income) in all diversity segments is outpacing growth in the White segment (figure 2-6).[59]

Multicultural Buying Power in the US, 2019 (trillions)

WHITE	$13.2
BLACK	$1.4
LATINX	$1.7
ASIAN	$1.2
AMERICAN INDIAN	$0.13
MULTIRACIAL	$0.25

Table 2-4

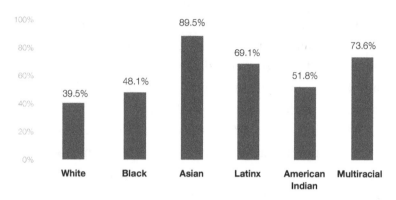

Figure 2-6

Estimates of the buying power of people with disabilities vary substantially, depending on whose estimate of the size of the population with disabilities is used. In 2018, the American Institutes for Research estimated the buying power of people with disabilities to be $490 billion.[60] When family members are incorporated into the calculations, buying power may more than double.[61] Estimates of the buying power of the LGBTQ+ community have been fairly consistent with Witeck Communications' estimate of $917 billion in 2015. Research indicates that women directly control or influence 73 percent of household spending.[62] Applying that percentage to real disposable personal income in the US, women control about $9.3 trillion in buying power, the equivalent of nearly twice the GDP of Japan.[63] Globally, women control between $20 and $30 trillion in annual consumer spending.[64]

For many US companies, the future is global. According to the Small Business and Entrepreneurship Council, "Two-thirds of the world's purchasing power is in foreign countries."[65] The countries where economic growth is most rapid are in Asia, Africa, and Latin America.[66]

Business overseas appears to offer a greater opportunity than domestic business, requiring a diverse workforce in the US and abroad. Notwithstanding future changes in US trade policy, exports are growing considerably faster than the US gross domestic product. From 2005 to 2014, the GDP grew at 2.9 percent annually,[67] while exports grew at an annual rate of 6.23 percent,[68] over 200 percent faster. For many US companies, across most industries, exports are a vital component of their revenue. For example, in 2011, General Electric earned 54 percent, IBM earned 64 percent, Dow Chemical earned 67 percent, and Intel earned 85 percent of their revenues abroad.[69]

In considering universal markets, organizations should be aware of secondary influences in those markets. Companies that are responsive to diversity constituencies may influence the purchasing decisions of families and friends of diverse consumers. For example, 87 percent of consumers who responded to a 2005 survey said they "agreed" or "strongly agreed" that they would prefer to give their business to companies that employ people with disabilities. Ninety-two percent of respondents were "more favorable" or "much more favorable" toward companies that hire people with disabilities.[70]

The BtoC Specialized Market

The specialized market includes those products and services designed specifically to serve the unique needs of a particular diversity group. For example, market research firm Mintel estimates that Black people spent $2.56 billion per year on hair care products designed for them. People with disabilities and their families purchase a host of support services and assistive technologies, including wheelchairs, ramps, and hearing aids. A 2011 study estimated the annual revenue for services, excluding medical services and overnight housing, to be $34 billion,[71] and another study from July 2011 estimated that the US market for assistive technologies, including eyeglasses and contact lenses, was $55 billion in 2016.[72]

The business case for the specialized market is that to establish competitive advantage in the targeted market, not only do organizations need segment representatives in important marketing functions, but also underrepresented people need to be a vital component of research and development and product planning and design. In addition, the human resource function should also include underrepresented people to effectively serve their counterparts in the rest of the organization.

THE OPERATIONS EFFECTIVENESS CASE

Diversity has been shown to have a positive impact on two operational areas: employee engagement and work group performance, including creativity, problem-solving, and decision-making.

As noted above, the case for operations effectiveness—that diversity, equity, and inclusion in operations leads to better business performance—is equivocal. However, a strong relationship exists between diversity, equity, and inclusion and employee engagement,[73] the commitment an employee has to an organization's welfare and outcomes and the willingness to act on that commitment. In turn, employee engagement—as demonstrated by a number of practitioner studies, including those from Gallup and TowersWatson, and limited academic studies—has a positive relationship with organizational outcomes, such as total shareholder return, stock price, employee retention, and customer attitudes.[74]

One study found two diversity factors related to employee engagement. The first factor, labeled *diversity and inclusion*, was defined as "the degree to which employees sense that people 'like themselves' are valued at the company and included in work decision-making processes, agree that company policies and practices foster diversity, and perceive that management believes that diversity is vital to company success." The other factor, *work–life support*, was "the degree to which employees feel supported by top management, their immediate manager or supervisor, co-workers, and company policies as they strive to balance work with family or personal responsibilities."[75] Both diversity and inclusion (0.62) and work–life support (0.61) are highly correlated with employee engagement.[76]

Diverse work groups are more creative and better problem solvers and decision makers than homogeneous work groups. A factor that works against the effectiveness of diverse work groups is that demographic diversity has been shown to increase conflict, reduce cohesion, complicate internal communications, and hamper coordination within the team.[77] These negatives seem to decline over time as group members overcome differences and take advantage of diverse knowledge, values, and experience,[78] and they tend to be absent in groups with high levels of training in career development and diversity management.[79] The positive effects of diverse groups are not automatic and require time and effective management.

Social scientist Scott Page, using mathematical modeling to examine the impact of diversity on performance, found that "diversity trumps ability." Expert problem solvers tend to be similar in approach, so "a collection of the best problem solvers performs little better than any one of them individually." A group of intelligent, randomly selected problem solvers provides a wider range of approaches to problem-solving, generates more solutions, and offers more ways to back out of dead ends.[80] In addition, diverse groups tend to have more information and a richer range of perspectives and ways of representing problems.[81] Because people with disabilities have typically had to make more adaptations and accommodations to be successful in their work lives, they are especially likely to bring a wider range of problem-solving repertoires.

Innovation and creativity are often confused. Creativity focuses on the generation of novel and utilitarian ideas, while innovation focuses on the implementation of those ideas. Innovation is dependent upon creativity. In a large-scale analysis of 108 empirical studies covering 10,632 teams, a significant positive relationship was found between cultural diversity and creativity.[82]

THE MULTIPLIER EFFECT CASE

The multiplier effect case is that "a rising tide lifts all ships"—what is beneficial for underrepresented employees is beneficial for all employees. Though logical, research evidence on the existence of a multiplier effect is scant.

Logically, equity and inclusion should have benefits for all employees. Increased equity works to eliminate bias from talent decisions. But for those who enjoy a privileged status, the promise of equity is unlikely to be perceived as beneficial to them.

However, for the highest performing, or, at least, for those who perceive themselves to be high performing, a level playing field should be perceived as advantageous. Inclusion, amplifying the unique talents and maximizing the performance of every employee, is beneficial to all employees.

THE MORAL CASE

Morals are an individual's principles about what behaviors and beliefs are right and what are wrong. As such, the moral case for diversity is relatively straightforward—diversity is either the right thing to do or not the right thing to do. The moral case can take many forms, from the statesmanlike "Our workforce must match the composition of our customers, clients, and markets" to the religious "There is neither Jew nor Greek, there is neither slave nor free, there is no male and female, for you are all one in Christ Jesus (Galatians 3:28)" to the purely moral "Establishing a just workplace is the right thing to do."

Two arguments go against the moral case. First, for businesses, the argument is that the business of business is business (or for government and nonprofits, the mission of the mission is the mission). This argument, most notably advanced by the economist Milton Friedman, is that a robust economy requires that businesses, competing on a level playing field, focus exclusively on profits. Ultimately, Friedman would argue that a robust economy lifts underrepresented people. This argument, however, fails with regard to diversity. If the business of business is truly to make a profit, then, as demonstrated by the talent and product market business cases, bias and exclusion are getting in the way of profitability.

The second argument, similar to political correctness, is "Whose morals should predominate?" The moral case is typically made by the chief executive. Does she have the right, or even the authority or influence, to impose her will on the entire workforce? Will they accept her will? Do the board of directors, stockholders, and other stakeholders approve? These are the same questions that can be raised about the organization's strategy. Though effective strategies incorporate stakeholder voices, they are typically top down. They are accepted and embraced by the workforce because of the authority of their leaders and because they make sense for the business and ultimately for the welfare of all stakeholders.

Where moral cases seem to be most effective is in organizations where the founder or an early leader established a moral case which has become part of the culture. Where an organization does not have the benefit of a founder or early leader's moral vision, current leaders may be able to establish a strong moral case. In building a moral case, actions speak louder than words. Indeed, words usually only speak when they have been preceded by action. To be effective, actions must be sustained and reinforced over time. It's never too late to take direct action in advocating for the rights of underrepresented people or serving their cause.

At their core, moral cases should transcend business purpose. Nevertheless, a moral case can have a business purpose. Effective moral cases not only guide the beliefs and behaviors of employees; they can, if effectively marketed, send a clear message to customers, consumers, and prospective employees about where the organization stands on diversity and positively affect the purchase decisions of markets and the attraction and retention of employees that are positively moved by the moral case.

The research on the market effects of diversity itself is limited. The best example is a subset of the research on corporate social responsibility (CSR). In the *2017 Cone Communications CSR Study*, the definition of CSR includes job growth, racial equality, women's rights, the cost of higher education, immigration, climate change, gun control, and LGBTQ+ rights. The Cone study found that 70 percent of Americans "believe companies have an obligation to take actions to improve issues that may not be relevant to everyday business operations."[83] Eighty-seven percent of Americans "would purchase a product because that company stood up for or advocated for an issue that they care about."[84] Eighty-eight percent of Americans "say it is acceptable for companies to include a cause or issue in their marketing," and 90 percent of consumers "want companies to tell them the ways they are supporting causes."[85] In a review of 128 studies on corporate social performance, financial performance was positive in 59 percent of the studies, neutral or mixed in 27 percent, and negative in 14 percent.[86]

Organizations high in corporate social performance "have more positive reputations and are more attractive employers."[87]

In a review of 588 journal articles and 102 books, it was found that CSR led to increased identification with the organization; higher employee engagement, retention, task performance, and creativity; and improved employee relations.[88] CSR—and by implication, diversity—influences customer, consumer, and employee decisions. Yet CSR is the best kept secret in many organizations. Communications about CSR to customers, consumers, and employees are often limited or kept under wraps for fear of being seen as unseemly. Organizations with a deep commitment to diversity are wise to communicate that commitment to relevant internal and external target segments.

THE POLITICAL CASE

Within twenty-five years, White people will be the minority in the United States. With the vast wave of immigration being driven by war, famine, and the drug trade, and the more rapid population growth among low-income people, all of which may pale in the face of population migrations wrought by global warming, the racial and ethnic makeup of the developed countries of North America and Europe is changing. As these new populations garner voting rights, albeit slowly but likely with increasing acceleration, their power in democracies will only increase. It is no wonder that so many rightest movements have gained currency in recent years as current majorities perceive that politics will increasingly be dominated by underrepresented racial and ethnic minorities and therefore attempt to erect barriers to immigration and voting rights.

Organizations that embrace the political case will follow a strategy of getting out in front of this wave of demographic change. They will seek to resemble the body politic at all their organizational levels. What organization wants to look like the currently dominant group when political power increasingly resides in the hands of those currently underrepresented?

A more radical movement for racial equity, called critical race theory (CRT), is currently gaining credence. At the foundation of CRT are the following principles:

◇ Racism is so embedded in our society that it is systemic.
◇ Colorblind meritocracy, which is enshrined in our legal system, is not effective at rectifying deeply ingrained structural racism.
◇ Race has no biological basis but is socially constructed.
◇ Racial groups cannot be viewed as homogeneous (the essentialist viewpoint) but must be viewed as heterogeneous (the anti-essentialist viewpoint).
◇ The fundamental methodology for developing knowledge is uncovering the lived experiences of African Americans through counterstory, meant to overcome prevailing views of race and the African American experience formulated by White hegemony.

CRT has been extended to other forms of discrimination through Latina/o critical theory (LatCrit), queer-crit, American Indian CRT (TribalCrit), disability CRT (DisCrit), and Asian American legal scholarship, depending on the group being discussed.

Critical theorists call for "race-conscious decision making as a routine . . . a more or less permanent norm."[89] In other words, where the current laws in the US forbid the use of race or ethnicity in decision-making about employees, critical theorists argue for proactive decision-making that focuses on hiring and advancing those who have been systemically discriminated against.

Critical race theory has its antagonists. However, those who are anti-CRT have tended to inaccurately portray CRT as a sort of bogeyman and then rail against their own definitions of CRT. A legitimate counterargument can be made against the rejection of colorblind meritocracy—that meritocracy has not been effective because it has been so poorly conceived and implemented. Nevertheless, CRT is gaining adherents and momentum. In a nation that will be majority minority in twenty-five years, a strong probability exists that Americans will see laws passed that provide playfield-leveling advantages to members of underrepresented groups in talent decisions. In addition to improved optics and the obvious product/service market and talent benefits, those who advance diversity at an accelerated pace will reduce the conditions that give rise to more radical strategies of redress.

The political case is a longer-term case. Demographic changes, although relatively certain, will take time to occur. Organizations may wish to wait and play catch-up when demographic changes are a reality. After all, as the COO of a large bank said to me when I showed him an analysis demonstrating that his institution would face labor shortages in key occupations within three to five years if it didn't change its diversity policies, "Three years is an eternity in this business."

Organizations must make a strategic decision today about whether they want to be seen as a leader or play catch-up in the fourth quarter of changing demographics.

Crafting a Business Case for Diversity

Most business cases are based on research studies, surveys, and databases, much like the data presented above. Sound logic and quantitative proof are necessary to win the acceptance and understanding of the analytically minded. But it is largely emotion, not logic, that motivates action. Diversity is connected to emotion through story, what Professor Brené Brown called "data with a soul." The story of a Latina women rising from a secretarial position to become a vice president is not only testament to her heart, talent, and effort but also a deep acknowledgement of the diversity initiative that supported and encouraged her. Stories work by conveying images of success, stimulating imagination, and connecting thought to action.

Neither data and logic nor story and emotion work in a generic form. While leaders and employees will certainly be interested in how their numbers compare to others and in stories of success from other organizations, it is numbers and stories from their own organization that are truly compelling. In this respect, the best business cases are local.

This is illustrated by the DLP® Products division at Texas Instruments, which first created a business case based purely on industry quantitative data. The senior management team rejected what to them felt like a generic business case with no heart—unlikely to be seen as credible or meaningful to employees. Management staff built a new business case unique to DLP® Products. The new case started with their three diversity objectives of that time: diversity of thought, speaking the "language" of their customers (much of their business consisted of supplying chips to manufacturers in Asia), and doing the right thing. Each objective was illustrated by examples with which employees could resonate—effectively, stories about how employees utilized diversity for business advantage; how DLP® Products benefited; and how TI could benefit more broadly going forward. John van Scoter, president of DLP® Products, presented that business case as he traveled throughout the world to various business sites, winning strong acceptance and support.

To build a local business case, diversity strategists need to answer a series of strategic questions about each element of a business case. Some of the questions will pertain to their unique situation; others won't. Organizations should create their own questions to reflect their unique context and reality. Table 2-5 offers a series of questions to serve as a starter template for crafting a local business case.

Strategic Questions for Crafting a Local Business Case

The Talent Case
- What are the diversity-related demographic trends in our domestic and foreign labor pools?
- Are underrepresented employees being hired, retained, and advanced relative to their proportions in appropriate labor pools (e.g., see, for example, table 2-1)?
- Is there greater unwanted turnover among high-potential diverse employees?
- Do employee surveys or exit interviews demonstrate perceptions of inequality or exclusion among underrepresented groups?

The Legal Case
- Does our organization have a history of employment discrimination?
- Are we susceptible to employment discrimination and other diversity-related legal actions?

The ROI Case
- What is our diversity ROI trend over the last three or more years?

The Product Market Case
Business to Business
- Does our organization qualify as a woman- or minority-owned business enterprise?
- Do our customers and clients demand or give special advantage to vendors who meet prescribed diversity requirements?

- Are a significant proportion of our clients owned or led by members of underrepresented populations?
- Does a significant proportion of our revenue come from WBEs or MBEs?
- Do we have opportunities to expand our business with diversity-related clients?
- Do our customers and clients have diversity-related requirements—explicit or implicit—for their suppliers?

Business to Consumer

- Are diversity-related markets a significant proportion of our business?
- What are the growth trends in our current and potential diversity-related market segments?
- Are there opportunities in diversity-related markets—universal and specialty, domestic and foreign—that we are not exploiting?
- What are the demographic trends in our diversity-related markets?
- Do our products and services compete effectively in diversity markets (e.g., competitive advantage, market share, share of wallet)?
- Do any entities in the supply chains we serve demand a demonstrated commitment to diversity?

The Operations Effectiveness Case

- Are diversity or its components significantly correlated with employee engagement?
- How dependent is our business on creativity and innovation?
- Are diversity or its components significantly correlated with creativity and innovation?
- Are diversity or its components significantly correlated with the quality of solutions or decisions?

- Do we have high potential return-on-investment opportunities from increased employee engagement, improved decision-making, problem-solving, and innovation?

The Multiplier Effect Case

- Is it reasonable to conclude that improvements in equity and inclusion will benefit all employees, including White males?
- In what ways will equity and inclusion benefit all employees?

The Moral Case

- Do we have a moral responsibility to ensure our organization has a level playing field for all prospective and current employees and a work environment where they can succeed?
- Do we have a moral responsibility to the communities from which we draw our talent, in which we are located, and in which we do business?
- Have senior leaders articulated a diversity philosophy, diversity principles, or other morally based statement?

The Political Case

- How rapidly are diversity voting demographics changing in our stakeholder communities?
- To what degree are stakeholder communities likely to support diversity-related legislation and regulations?

Stories of Success

- Is diversity embedded in our culture? What are the myths about diversity, who are its heroes, and what are the artifacts that reflect a commitment to diversity?
- How have diverse teams come together to achieve extraordinary results?
- What have been our achievements in diversity talent and product/service markets?

* What other successes have we had as a result of the diversity of our workforce or work teams?
* What recognition have we received for our diversity initiatives, and does it square with reality?

Table 2-5

The next competency presents the companions to the business case: the organizational diversity philosophy and the organization's aspirational values and beliefs about diversity; and the personal case: each individual leader's aspirational diversity philosophy. Insofar as story captures the emotion that can motivate commitment and action, a leader's personal case or story of her commitment to diversity values and beliefs, to the degree that it is honest and heartfelt and well communicated, can be a platform for positive change.

COMPETENCY 3:
Envisioning a Diversity Philosophy

"Culture eats strategy for breakfast."
Peter Drucker

DIVERSITY CULTURE COMPRISES THE VALUES and beliefs about diversity, equity, and inclusion that most employees share. Through informal norms or rules of behavior about how employees should behave toward each other and other stakeholders, these values and beliefs are brought into everyday behavior.

Peter Drucker, one of the great management thinkers, illustrates in the above quote not that culture is more vital to achieving diversity, equity, and inclusion than strategy but rather that if an organization's strategy is misaligned with its culture, then no matter how robust and ingenuous the strategy, it is merely a delusion.

For diversity strategy to align with an organization's culture, that culture must be imbued with diversity values and beliefs, including equity and inclusion (e.g., respect, dignity, equal treatment and opportunity, trust, etc.). The primary mechanisms for creating diversity culture are a clear, well-communicated statement of the organization's diversity values and beliefs—the organizational diversity philosophy—and accountability by all employees to that diversity philosophy; great clarity about each leader's own philosophy for engaging in diversity, equity, and inclusion—their personal case; and a deep commitment to authentically living organizational and personal values and beliefs as reflected in the daily work and personal lives of the organization's strategic leaders. Articulating an organizational diversity philosophy is the responsibility of strategic leaders. Every strategic leader and aspiring leader is responsible for their own personal case for diversity.

The remainder of this chapter introduces the elements of organizational diversity philosophies and personal cases and offers examples of each.

Organizational Diversity Philosophy

The diversity philosophy is an aspirational statement, typically composed of a set of values and beliefs designed to serve as a guidepost for employee behaviors toward diversity principles and diverse people. Diversity philosophies can be broad, carefully crafted statements, usually attributed to the CEO, or consist of the diversity mission, vision, and values of the organization. A diversity philosophy often combines elements of the business case with diversity values and beliefs. In a review of nearly 100 diversity philosophies from leading organizations, seven core diversity values and beliefs were identified (table 3-1).[90]

Core Diversity Values and Beliefs

Psychological Safety	Employees should be free from harassment, discrimination, and intolerance, and free to speak up without fear of reprisal.
Value Differences/ Foster Inclusion	All differences should be respected and valued. An organization will achieve superior outcomes when it effectively acknowledges and embraces a wide range of different cultures, perspectives, thought processes, assumptions, and beliefs.
Advancement through Merit	All employment decisions, including hiring, evaluation, development, promotion, and compensation decisions, should be made purely on the basis of objective merit.
Reflect Customers and Communities	The practices and demographics of the organization should mirror the practices and demographics of its customers and communities.
Value Chain Diversity	All suppliers throughout the value chain should demonstrate successful diversity practices.
The Right Thing	Taking action in the interest of diversity is morally correct.
Competitive Advantage	Organizations that achieve a significant level of diversity will enjoy a competitive advantage in the talent and/or product/ service marketplaces.

Table 3-1

Diversity philosophies range from bulleted lists to flowing narratives. Subscribing to the admonition that less is more, they usually incorporate three to five values and beliefs.

Johnson & Johnson has won numerous awards for its diversity initiatives. Their diversity philosophy (see below) is effectively an employer branding statement aimed at current and prospective employees:

Johnson & Johnson Diversity Philosophy

Diversity at Johnson & Johnson is about your unique perspective. It's about you, your colleagues and the world we care for—all backgrounds, beliefs and the entire range of human experience—coming together. You view the world from a unique vantage point; a perspective that gives you problem-solving potential ideas, solutions & strategies that, when mobilized, can bring health to billions.

Inclusion at Johnson & Johnson is about creating a deep sense of belonging. It's about a culture where you are valued, your ideas are heard and you advance this culture for everyone.

Diversity & Inclusion at Johnson & Johnson means - You Belong.

Our Vision

Be yourself, change the world.

Our vision at Johnson & Johnson is for every person to use their unique experiences and backgrounds, together – to spark solutions that create a better, healthier world.

Our Mission

Make diversity and inclusion how we work every day.

Our mission is to make diversity & inclusion our way of doing business. We will advance our culture of belonging where open hearts and minds combine to unleash the potential of the brilliant mix of people, in every corner of Johnson & Johnson.

Cornell has achieved a strong representation of underrepresented people in its undergraduate student body (54 percent are women, 49 percent are US minorities, and 10 percent are international). However, like most universities, representation on its staff (14.4 percent) and in its academic posts (13.2 percent) has not kept pace. Nevertheless, Cornell aspires to a culture in which diversity, equity, and inclusion flourish.

Cornell's Vision for Diversity: Open Doors, Open Hearts, Open Minds

Open Doors

"I would found an institution where any person can find instruction in any study." This statement, made by Ezra Cornell in 1865, proclaims Cornell University's enduring commitment to inclusion and opportunity, which is rooted in the shared democratic values envisioned by its founders. We honor this legacy of diversity and inclusion and welcome all individuals, including those from groups that historically have been marginalized and previously excluded from equal access to opportunity.

Open Hearts

Cornell's mission is to foster personal discovery and growth, nurture scholarship and creativity across a broad range of common knowledge, and affirm the value to individuals and society of the cultivation of the human mind and spirit. Our legacy is reflected in the diverse composition of our community, the breadth of our curriculum, the strength of our public service, and the depth of our commitment to freedom, equity, and reason. Each member of the Cornell community has a responsibility to honor this legacy and to support a more diverse and inclusive campus in which to work, study, teach, research, and serve.

Open Minds

Free expression is essential to this mission, and provocative ideas lawfully presented are an expected result. An enlightened academic community, however, connects freedom with responsibility. Cornell stands for civil discourse, reasoned thought, sustained discussion, and constructive engagement without degrading, abusing, harassing, or silencing others. Cornell is committed to act responsibly and forthrightly to maintain an environment that opens doors, opens hearts, and opens minds.

The creation of an organizational diversity philosophy should not be purely delegated. At Fidelity Investments Institutional Services, the top management team engaged in an extensive exercise to craft organizational values and beliefs themselves. At the DLP® division of Texas Instruments, the top leadership team asked its director-level managers to draft a diversity philosophy. Top leaders then engaged deeply with those values and beliefs, themselves crafting the final statement.

Personal Case for Diversity

A personal case must be not only logical and convincing but also free from hypocrisy and insincerity, both as it is written and as it is spoken, in company gatherings and to the public. As the Reverend Eugene Rivers was told by a street-gang member while working to quell violence in Boston's neighborhoods, "If you're faking the funk, we'll smoke you." Although the consequences are not as profound here, leaders will undermine their relationships with employees if they fake their commitment. And they cannot hide from their employees, no matter how distant and isolated. As a Navy admiral once said, "Every lieutenant [front-line supervisor] can fathom when the boss is being a hypocrite."

No algorithm exists for writing a personal case for diversity. Since of necessity they must be from a leader's head and heart, personal cases range widely. For example, one leader stated that his commitment had come from observing the travails of institutional sexism experienced by his three daughters. Another pointed to her religious commitments, and yet another pointed to the importance of behaving consistently with organizational values. In crafting a personal case, consider what convinces you to personally take action to bend the arc toward justice in your own organization:

◇   The role played by your religion or personal values
◇   Your upbringing, lessons from your parents, and early influences
◇   Your personal and professional life experiences and observations
◇   A rationale that captured your imagination

Below is my own personal case for diversity. I offer it both as
an example and as my personal rationale for writing this book.
I have labored to ensure it is a sincere, heartfelt statement. The
determination of whether I have transcended "faking the funk"
I leave in the hands of the reader.

WHAT'S A WHITE MAN DOING IN DIVERSITY: A PERSONAL CASE FOR DIVERSITY

People are often surprised that an older, affluent, White guy
like me is committed to diversity, equity, and inclusion. I am
occasionally asked—sometimes directly, oftentimes furtively—
about what I am doing in diversity. My commitment did not
materialize in a single, blinding flash of self-discovery, nor
from suffering the indecencies of discrimination, but from my
heritage and a lifetime of experiences observing and resisting
bias, inequality, exclusion, and injustice.

As far back as I can remember, I had a compelling desire to
do good, best characterized by the Hebrew words *tikkun olam*,
"to repair the world." My efforts, beginning as a child, ranged
from gathering pennies for UNICEF on Halloween and selling
peanuts for Kiwanis to raise funds for "underprivileged" children
to, as I grew older, advocating for disenfranchised students and
youth and people with developmental disabilities and working
with numerous organizations to create more equitable, inclusive,
and productive workplaces.

Who I am is also a reflection of my parents. I was bequeathed
my father's indignation at injustice and my mother's open-
mindedness and joy in reaching across differences. I seem to
have been born with a good dose (sometimes an overdose) of
sensitivity, empathy, and well-meaningness.

Numerous personal and professional experiences have shown me, time and time again, that the playing field is desperately, woefully, agonizingly tilted against people of color, people of particular religions and ethnicities, women, people with disabilities, older people, veterans, immigrants, the poor, Dalits (members of the lowest caste), and the LGBTQ+ community.

Once while I was walking down my suburban street as an eight-or-so-year-old, a middle-aged Black man who was cutting a neighbor's lawn stopped me and inquired, "Excuse me, sir, do you have the time?" I answered, but the experience left me reeling. I had been firmly taught that a younger person always addresses an older man as "sir," certainly not the other way around. But that wasn't the only thing. I had a watch and he didn't.

As a high school student, I watched news reports of the Freedom Riders as they made their way through the South to accomplish the unfulfilled intent of the previous year's Supreme Court decision in Boynton v. Virginia, which declared that segregation in interstate travel is unlawful. I am overwhelmed with admiration for such paladins of justice as John Lewis, the morally courageous son of Alabama sharecroppers who became a universally admired US congressman, and Genevieve Hughes Houghton, a daughter of affluence and Cornell University graduate who left a career as a stockbroker to put her life on the line for freedom and dedicated her life to social justice. The determination and extraordinary courage of the Freedom Riders to maintain nonviolence in the face of such hatred and savagery have been an example, and a beacon of hope, in my life.

As a young professional, I went to work in Washington, DC. One night, my date and I were robbed at gunpoint by three Black teenagers just behind the Cannon House Office Building of the House of Representatives. They took my wallet and my black Timex watch. Later, riding with two Washington police detectives, we were driven to where they were holding a suspect, in his thirties, arms raised with a silver-banded watch in his hand, whose only commonality with those who had robbed us was the color of his skin.

Throughout my life, I have witnessed many highly capable and accomplished women of color go unrecognized, unexalted, excluded, and stifled. Etched in my memory is the admonition valiantly delivered in a workshop on bias by a Black financial services senior manager to her predominantly White, male colleagues: "Some of you"—her finger sweeping the room—"have walked right past me on the street without noticing me."

In a long career as a diversity advocate, researcher, consultant, and business leader, I have been immersed in a vast sea of data on employee recruitment, hiring, evaluation, development, and advancement but can recall only a miniscule number of times when the conclusions of data analysis did not favor White men. Having conducted numerous surveys, interviews, and focus groups and reviewed myriad studies to better understand the root causes of these unjust outcomes, the findings have convinced me that bias is ubiquitous in even our most cherished and celebrated institutions.

I understand that my experiences pale in comparison with those of people who have been subjected to injustice and to justice so haltingly and insufficiently perfected. I understand that looking into the fire can never be the same as being consumed by the searing antipathy of its flames. I understand that I have led a life of relative privilege. I understand that those who are underrepresented rarely seek special privilege, only equal privilege. And I understand that I can never truly understand.

I believe that this lack of fairness, justice, and equal opportunity is one of the most catastrophic transgressions of our time, significantly diminishing our global competitiveness. It prevents organizations from assembling and retaining the best talent, achieving the highest productivity from that talent, and surmounting the competition in domestic and global markets. How disheartening for the majority of the workforce to live their work lives running the race uphill while others of us are running downhill. My fundamental commitment, then, is to participate in creating the playbook for leveling the playing field in the globe's institutions. That commitment, which I will carry to the end of my life, is the purpose of this book and a measure of my contribution to bending the arc toward justice.

Mastering Diversity Strategy

"The essence of strategy is choosing what not to do."
Michael Porter
Professor, Harvard Business School

STRATEGY IS NOT A SIMPLE, straightforward concept. Numerous perspectives exist about what strategy is and how it is developed. Added to this hodgepodge of views is the challenge of defining the strategic subgenre of diversity strategy. To sort out these perspectives, this chapter elaborates the purposes and unravels the meanings of diversity strategy, identifies its central functions, and proposes an overarching strategic process for fulfilling the purposes of diversity strategy.

The Purposes of Diversity Strategy

Diversity strategy has three fundamental purposes: to establish equity, inclusion, and sustainable diversity competitive advantage in talent and product/service markets. Equity focuses on creating talent decisions that are purely based on merit. Inclusion is concerned with creating a workplace in which all employees can thrive and rise to the highest levels of productivity and achievement their talents can carry them. Sustainable competitive advantage focuses on winning the competition for the most talented employees in each labor pool and winning the competition in the business-to-business, business-to-consumer, and specialized product/service markets.

The Meaning of Diversity Strategy

Numerous schools of thought exist about the meaning of strategy. Henry Mintzberg, a leading strategic thinker, identified ten different schools of thought.[91] Although a great deal of research indicates that organizations that formulate and implement strategies achieve higher levels of performance, no single school of thought has been proven superior to others. The school of strategic thought an organization adopts depends on its unique context, circumstances, and culture. As these change, so too might the school of thought the organization pursues. It is particularly useful to consider four schools of thought about the meaning of diversity strategy: reflected choice, incrementalism, opportunism, and formal planning.

REFLECTED CHOICE

All organizations have a diversity strategy, whether intended or not. Because strategies are about the fundamental choices organizations make, the pattern of choices that an organization makes (or doesn't make) about diversity reflects its strategy. A reflected choice strategy is likely to have an excess of unintended consequences, or, as that sage Baseball Hall-of-Famer Yogi Berra admonished, "If you don't know where you're going, you'll end up someplace else."

INCREMENTALISM

While formal planning imposes needed structure on the strategic planning process, it often doesn't take account of the qualitative, human factors and complexities that permeate organizational decision-making and action. Some attempt to impose their will on the outcomes of the diversity strategy process, while others resist the very notion of diversity and find diversity strategy a misuse of resources. Carefully calculated analytics prove wrong, and organizational events and the diversity environment change faster than a formal planning process unfolds. Emerging ideas and interests and the diversity strategy process itself galvanize coalitions that support different interpretations of strategy or resist it in various ways. Reality itself, which formal planning attempts to model, is fraught with ambiguities.

The late Brian Quinn of Dartmouth's Tuck School of Business studied strategic processes as they actually were rather than as they should be conducted and observed that they "are typically fragmented, evolutionary, and largely intuitive." He concluded that real strategies follow a path of "logical incrementalism" on which they tend "to *evolve* as internal decisions and external events flow together to create a new, widely shared consensus for action among key members" of the decision-making group.[92]

Though formal planning should be the starting point of diversity strategy, strategies must be developed and implemented with respect for the fact that they rarely follow a logical path. Strategy leaders should be prepared for analytic errors, resistant or dominating coalitions, and especially the fact that strategic processes are processes of human change. "Competency 12: Leading Change" helps address the reality of the incremental world.

OPPORTUNISM

The same flow of events that drives strategic incrementalism also presents opportunities. These are often unpredictable or unseen opportunities to advance the strategic diversity agenda and deliver business results that emerge out of the organizational and environmental mist.

One of the enduring issues in healthcare is adherence—patients actually purchasing, picking up, and taking the drugs they have been prescribed. As Deb Dagit, Merck's former chief diversity officer, described it, "Several sources of data demonstrate that about a third of prescriptions that doctors write are never picked up. And then a whole bunch aren't followed as directed. And even people with PhDs . . . often do not understand the instructions from their doctor and/or pharmacist."

As adherence gained credence as a critical issue facing Merck, Dagit seized the opportunity. Among their many products, Merck produces medications for diabetes and hypertension, which are particularly significant health issues in the Black, Latino, and Native American communities. When patients who have been prescribed Merck's medicines do not pick up and take their medicines, their health suffers and Merck potentially loses millions of dollars in sales, creating a win-win opportunity. Dagit linked diversity directly to helping to address the adherence issue. Working with marketing and sales, the diversity organization asked Merck's employee resource groups (ERGs) to get involved.

The small Native American ERG initially focused on diabetes. Type 2 diabetes is a significant public health problem in Native American communities.[93] At the Native American Basketball Invitational (NABI), in which a large swath of tribes and nations are represented, a third-party provider funded by Merck provided diabetes screening and general education for parents while, at the same time, ERG members introduced the children of these attendees to Merck Institute for Science Education learning opportunities through interactive games and demonstrations. Adherence awareness improved considerably at this gathering of the Native American community, as did Merck's image and the influence of adherence on Merck's profitability. Today, sales and marketing continue to look to the ERGs for innovative ideas, to review advertisements and patient inserts, for their advice on community partnerships, and for other input. Similar initiatives in the Black, LGBTQ+, and disability communities were linked to even greater revenue opportunities.

Taking advantage of emerging opportunities is one of the matchmaker roles of diversity leaders. Diversity leaders should have business acumen and be strongly networked with business leaders at higher organizational levels and in the geographies within their scope of responsibilities. They should constantly scan for emerging internal business issues and external environmental changes for win-win diversity opportunities and be ready to pounce as opportunities emerge.

FORMAL PLANNING

The classic definition of formal planning was provided by Kenneth Andrews, the seminal thinker on corporate strategy. The definition has been adapted for diversity strategy:[94] "Diversity strategy is the pattern of decisions in an organization that determines and reveals its overall objectives and goals or targets, produces the principal policies, programs, and plans for achieving those goals, and defines the range of opportunities the organization will pursue, the kind of organization it intends to be, and the nature of the contributions it intends to make to its clients, customers, communities, shareholders, and other stakeholder groups."

If Andrews's definition stopped at "the pattern of decisions," it would be a reflected choice strategy. Formal planning is a logical process that begins with a situational assessment, proceeds to the formulation of strategic objectives, goals, plans, programs, and policies, and continues with an implementation structure and process. This book is fundamentally about formal planning for diversity. However, it recognizes that plans do not necessarily follow a rational process (incrementalism) and often take advantage of unpredicted, serendipitous events as they arise (opportunism).

The Central Functions of Diversity Strategy

The primary function of strategy is focus: weighing various directions against others and choosing a path. As Robert Frost observed in his poem "The Road Not Taken," "Two roads diverged in a yellow wood, / And sorry I could not travel both / And be one traveler, long I stood." Imagine if Frost chose to follow both paths at the same time. Not a pretty sight, yet many organizations are inundated with strategic pathways. As Michael Porter's quote at the beginning of this chapter urges, an organization doesn't really have a strategy until it has said no to some available paths.

In addition to focus, effective strategies concentrate on the functions of integration, uncertainty reduction, and complexity management.

FOCUS

Focus is a response to the fact that an organization has limited resources to invest in any initiatives it undertakes. The traditional way to talk about focus in business organizations is to concentrate on that part or segment of the product/service market in which the business can be dominant. Peter Drucker, the management thought leader, famously observed, "Concentration is the key to economic results."[95]

Concentration is particularly important when organizations are competing in product/service markets composed of underrepresented people. It is also important in the competition for top diversity talent. In both cases, focus is about concentrating resources to dominate the competition in one or a few aspects of the marketplace. Concentration, however, is most vital when considering the totality of the diversity strategy.

Focus in diversity strategy is largely about containing the number of strategic objectives to be pursued by choosing those that fit the current context and offer the greatest leverage for positive change. As Frost reminds us, however attractive and compelling it may be, an organization cannot (and should not) follow every viable path.

In working with leadership teams to formulate strategies, I ordinarily try to limit the number of strategic objectives for any one time period to three (at most five), believing that attempting to pursue more numerous objectives spreads resources too thin. I almost always get pushback. The process of narrowing choices to focus on a strategy is one of productive conflict. When pressing for agreement on a strategy, it is tempting to settle conflict by providing everyone with strategic objectives that fulfill their interests. The result of such a proliferation of objectives is that resources are spread thin, leading to unachieved outcomes.

The tendency toward proliferation of objectives can be addressed by the following:

◇   Leadership discipline
◇   Viewing diversity strategy as a series of cumulative strategies, evolving over a number of time periods
◇   Aligning with organizational imperatives and the diversity philosophy
◇   Following an inclusive process to focus and agree on strategic objectives

Leadership Discipline

Discipline requires strong leadership from the top and an understanding from the outset of the strategic process that choices will have to be made and objectives limited. This includes top leadership being clear on the maximum number of strategic diversity objectives to be pursued and that it will allow neither a proliferation of objectives nor a basket of everyone's strategic interests to be crammed into a few strategic objectives.

Cumulative Strategies

Strategies must be fit to time periods—a longer period in a more stable environment, a shorter time period in a rapidly changing or chaotic environment. By viewing a strategic initiative as a series of time periods, each with its own strategic objectives integrated with other time periods, those valuable strategic objectives that do not fit the time period under consideration can be reconsidered in future time periods. Some organizations have strategies with two or three phases, with strategic objectives for each phase.

For example, one organization, just beginning a diversity initiative, had three phases over thirty months. Phase one (startup to six months), Build Momentum, had four strategic objectives that focused on developing an infrastructure, including the establishment and education of a diversity council of senior leaders; conceiving and promulgating a diversity philosophy; establishing a measurement system; and debiasing three troubled talent processes. Phase two, Deepen Understanding & Action (seven to eighteen months), had three strategic objectives that focused on implementing a work–life initiative, education of all levels on diversity, equity, and inclusion, and the debiasing of three additional processes. Phase three, Institutionalize Gains (nineteen to thirty months), had three strategic objectives focused on creating a mentoring process, developing diverse leaders, and the continuous debiasing of critical talent processes.

Alignment with Organizational Imperatives and Diversity Philosophy

Two strategic mandates—organizational imperatives and diversity philosophy—constitute the true north and south of a diversity initiative. Organizational imperatives state the overall strategic direction of the business or organization. They include the business or organization strategy; mission, vision, and values; top management pronouncements; and other statements and intentions that have the force of organization-wide strategic mandates. Aligning strategic diversity objectives with these mandates and the diversity philosophy provides focus by demarcating and therefore narrowing the field of strategic choices.

Inclusive Process

An inclusive process opens with broad-based inclusion of the widest variety of viewpoints and data points on diversity, identifies the full range of issues raised by those viewpoints and data points, determines which issues are most salient, develops strategic objectives for the most salient issues, and concludes with top leadership determining the critical few strategic objectives to be pursued over the strategic horizon.

INTEGRATION

A strategy should be designed to integrate employee implementation roles and responsibilities horizontally across organizational units and vertically across organizational levels. In assessment and in the formulation of a strategy, integration is achieved through a cross-functional and representative top management team, diversity council, or other leadership group that represents the views of a wide swath of the organization and reviews the analysis and recommendations and formulates the strategy.

In implementation, integration is achieved through a process of deployment. Deployment links goals horizontally and then vertically. Horizontal linkage is achieved by appointing a cross-functional group to oversee each strategic objective and then by delegating components of each strategic objective to the appropriate function or operating unit and determining how any overlaps will be managed. This delegation can only be done by top management. Then, to create vertical linkage, objectives should be deployed down the organization by requiring each successive level to have objectives in their performance plans that link with the objectives of the level above. All employees should have a few critical objectives that articulate their role in achieving organization-wide diversity objectives.

UNCERTAINTY REDUCTION

A strategy should integrate current plans and actions with the uncertainties of the future. Some changes evolve in long arcs, such as the increasing educational attainment of people of color, while others are relatively unpredictable events that instantaneously change the organizational environment, such as the #BlackLivesMatter and #MeToo movements. Two ways in which strategies can address future uncertainties are in building robustness to change and planning for alternative futures.

Building Robustness to Change

Building a strategy that is robust to change can be difficult since robustness is likely to come from sacrificing focus. Robustness could ostensibly be achieved by being prepared for any eventuality. However, because resources are spread so thin, to be prepared for everything is to be prepared for nothing.

Robustness can also be found in the strategic process as distinct from the strategy itself. A robust strategic process never stops. It is dynamic, constantly monitoring the organization and scanning the environment so that the organization can move quickly in the face of significant change. To accomplish this, the diversity infrastructure must be designed for resilience—able to anticipate, plan for, and rapidly adapt to change. To anticipate and plan for change requires that someone be placed in charge of monitoring and preparing for material changes in the diversity environment. That can be one person from the diversity organization or a member of the cross-functional team accountable for implementing each diversity objective. The responsible person should continuously scan for emerging environmental changes that might impact strategic diversity objectives, including new developments in scientific and practice evidence, and legal, regulatory, cultural, and competitive changes.

Rapid adaptation to change comes from anticipation by top leadership that changes are inevitable, an infrastructure experienced at implementing changes, and slack resources. Building continuous improvement into the implementation process seasons the organization to make change. Continuous improvement comes from frequently monitoring actions and results and making required incremental improvements on an ongoing basis. Slack resources come from having excess budget and capacity. The diversity organization should preserve a percentage of its budget in anticipation of changes. In today's lean organizations, having excess personnel is unlikely and impractical. Preparing key human resources to jump into the fray if needed, somewhat akin to a volunteer fire department, is a more sensible approach. The best-prepared individuals are likely to be found in employee resource groups.

Planning for Alternative Futures

Numerous techniques have been applied to planning for alternative futures, including environmental scanning, the Delphi technique, emerging issues analysis, visioning, and backcasting. The most widely used in recent years is scenario planning, developed by Pierre Wack, an executive at Royal Dutch Shell. Scenario planning is widely recognized as having prepared Shell to weather the oil shocks of the 1970s.

Scenario planning creates a series of stories, usually two or three, that anticipate and consider how to react to changes in the external environment. Many different approaches exist to scenario planning.[96] Most contain the following elements:[97]

◇   Define the timeframe, scope, and change issues that are likely to impact the diversity strategy. The timeframe is how many years out the scenario will look (further in more stable environments, shorter in turbulent environments). Scope is whether the scan is for the whole organization or a subunit and whether the scan is for one country, a region, or the entire globe. Change issues are those categories of change that most need to be monitored (e.g., employment laws and regulations protecting the rights of underrepresented employees, and judicial decisions affecting the employment of underrepresented people).

◇ Identify the key stakeholders who have an interest in the change issues, both those most likely to be affected by them and those with the most influence over them.

◇ Determine the cultural, demographic, governmental, technological, economic, and industry trends that are most likely to affect the change issues and how they might impact those issues, and how key stakeholders will respond and how their actions will impact the change issues.

◇ From this analysis, identify the most significant uncertainties.

◇ Create two extreme scenarios in which one represents all positive outcomes for the critical uncertainties, the other negative outcomes.

◇ Evaluate the scenarios for plausibility and internal consistency and rewrite the scenarios until all internal inconsistencies are eliminated.

◇ Consider the scenarios in the formulation of strategic objectives and in preparing for the inevitable internal and external changes.

COMPLEXITY MANAGEMENT

A diversity initiative is composed of numerous variables, including stakeholder interests, organization structures, resources, priorities, options, analyses, uncertainties, processes, talent and product/service markets, choices, and decisions, interacting in numerous ways. Warning signs of a complexity problem are difficulty making decisions and accomplishing objectives, and the proliferation of unintended consequences.

Focus, insofar as it reduces the number of variables to be addressed by a diversity strategy, is the key to managing complexity in the strategy process. Other methods of managing complexity include reducing the complexity of programs, processes, and infrastructure, and ensuring that diversity leaders have the capabilities to manage complexity.

Program Complexity

Diversity programs have a tendency to gain complexity over time, particularly in global and multidivisional organizations. The number of different programs grows, and programs tend to take on multiple forms to meet regional variations and stakeholder interests. Reducing complexity is a straightforward process of conducting a comprehensive program audit to evaluate the benefits/costs of programs, compare all programs, and eliminate those that do not provide adequate impact for dollars spent. If benefit/cost is too difficult to assess, then a survey of employees who have participated in the programs is second best. The survey should assess employees' perceptions of both the performance and the importance of the various programs.

Process Complexity

Most process complexity resides in either diversity planning and management or talent decision-making processes. Usually, those who hold a stake in planning and management processes will have a good sense of where the complexity lies. This can be discovered by creating a list of all the planning and management processes and then surveying the stakeholders to determine which processes are overly complex and least effective. To reduce complexity in the identified planning and management processes, each process should be flowcharted and unnecessary, redundant, and low-value steps eliminated. Sometimes, a process may be so overly complex or convoluted that it needs to be reengineered altogether. In addition, where possible, the number of decision makers for each decision should be reduced.

Reducing complexity in talent decision-making processes can be piggybacked on the debiasing of those processes as described in "Competency 5: Advancing Toward Equity."

Infrastructure Complexity

An old aphorism states, "Structure follows strategy," meaning that organizational structure should be designed to support strategy. As strategies evolve and new strategies are introduced, the existing infrastructure may prove to be overly complex or obsolete. Each time the strategy is significantly modified or a new diversity strategy is formulated, the infrastructure should undergo a zero-base review. A zero-base review examines infrastructure development from scratch, as if no diversity infrastructure ever existed. Of course, this review will be highly threatening to diversity staff, whose roles and responsibilities may be on the line. The review should be conducted by an unbiased group of leaders, ideally with expertise in organizational structure, with involvement of the diversity staff.

Another approach to reducing complexity in infrastructure is to decentralize decision-making, moving it as close to the action as possible. Beware, decentralization can also contribute to the proliferation of programs, processes, and infrastructure, adding to complexity.

Complexity Management Capability

Leaders who are effective at managing complexity tend to have "ambidextrous capabilities: the ability to keep the business ticking on a daily basis while looking for ways to expand and improve it."[98] In addition, effective complexity managers tend to be highly competent at three strategic thinking capabilities:[99]

◊   *Multivariate Thinking*: the ability to balance many dynamic variables simultaneously and see the relationships among those variables

◊   *Abstracting*: grasping the essential theme or discovering the synergy among often disparate bits of information in a way that informs choice and focuses action

◊   *Valuating*: seeking the underlying values, beliefs, and attitudes held by current and potential stakeholders and sensing a direction that incorporates a balance of interests

In managing complexity, keep in mind that not all complexity is bad. Every time complexity is encountered, the question should be asked, "Is it contributing to diversity progress or detracting from it?"

The Diversity Strategy Process

The diversity strategy process presented here (figure 4-1) is a formal planning process with three phases: assessment, formulation, and implementation with a feedback loop from implementation to assessment.

Diversity Strategy Process

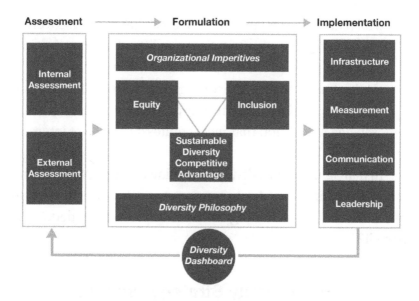

Figure 4-1

An assessment examines the current state of diversity in the organization, including the diversity climate, lingering diversity issues, and diversity business opportunities, and identifies and estimates the impact of external environmental trends on the organization. The assessment results in a series of findings about what is working, what needs improvement, and what the future portends for the organization, and a set of recommendations for action.

Formulation considers the assessment findings and recommendations along with the business and organizational imperatives, the diversity philosophy, and contingencies. Strategic objectives, action plans, accountabilities, and measures are formulated for equity, inclusion, and sustainable diversity competitive advantage and for the design and installation of the four implementation levers—infrastructure, measurement, communication, and leadership.

Implementation is concerned with how diversity leaders actually operate the four levers to achieve the strategic plan. A comprehensive measure of diversity progress, the "diversity dashboard" (see "Competency 9: Measuring for Accountability"), provides feedback to leadership and guides the next round of strategy development as the current diversity strategy expires, continuously improving diversity strategy.

The first step in the strategy process is to determine its horizon, the period of time for which the strategic plan is being formulated and at the end of which it expires. The horizon is primarily dependent on the turbulence in the internal and external environments. Internal turbulence, for example, might be caused by increasing employee activism or acceleration in global business growth. External turbulence might include rapidly changing labor supply demographics or changes in the political environment that raise or lower protections for underrepresented people. The greater the turbulence, the shorter the horizon should be, since the strategy becomes less and less relevant as the conditions in the internal and external environments change.

How organizational imperatives and diversity philosophy affect the strategic process is discussed in the "Focus" section above. Contingencies are considered below. Assessment, formulation, and implementation constitute the remainder of this book.

CONTINGENCIES

Three contingencies that can significantly influence diversity strategy should be considered: priority, life-cycle stage, and scope.

Priority

Priority refers to an organization's level of commitment to diversity, equity, and inclusion on a scale of high to low. The most highly committed organizations are characterized by a deeply engaged leadership team that models inclusion and the diversity philosophy, commits the financial and human resources necessary to achieve success, and aggressively and personally supports the diversity initiative and its leaders and participants. The leadership of the least committed organizations resist diversity or simply allow the diversity initiative to proceed with only nominal involvement.

Low-commitment organizations tend to shut off diversity or force it underground. Without active support from the top, diversity leaders and employees may not be able to engage with integrity in a formal planning process. Often, incremental and particularly opportunistic strategies are the only available choices. One approach that leaders of subunits utilize is to establish a formal strategic plan for their own organization. This works particularly well for leaders who head a division, function, or strategic business unit. If this work is performed by well-respected leaders and is effective, it is likely to galvanize action among leaders of comparable organizational units and eventually among the top management team.

The Diversity Lifecycle

Like most organizational endeavors, diversity initiatives progress through life-cycle stages that mirror an S curve (figure 4-2), in which they take some time to accelerate to full takeoff, then expand rapidly, mature into a slow-growth mode, and ultimately decline unless they are revitalized. From a strategic perspective, revitalization occurs through either innovation or a new strategic process that, while recognizing advances previously made, essentially wipes the slate clean and rebuilds the diversity strategy.

Stages of the Diversity Lifecycle

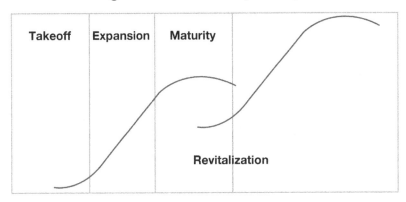

Figure 4-2

Takeoff Phase

Organizations that need or wish to make a quick start will often use a rapid takeoff approach. Typically, rapid takeoff is accomplished by bringing top leaders together for a half day or so to formulate three to five strategic objectives with action plans and measures for each objective. They use pre-existing data, such as from EEO-1 reports, employee surveys, and often interviews with senior leaders, to frame strategy development. Once a rapid takeoff strategy is in place and momentum has been established, a formal strategic diversity plan is developed.

At Global Asset Management–Americas, a division of UBS, the regional executive diversity committee (REDC) was already in place. However, no strategy existed, and inadequate progress on diversity was being made despite pressure from client institutions. Kai Sotorp, president, led a quick-start process. He pulled together the REDC for three hours for a facilitated strategic planning meeting. After committee business and a review of progress to date, followed by a briefing on the elements of diversity strategy, the REDC launched a ninety-minute planning process in which it discussed the diversity challenges facing Global Asset Management–Americas, identified four diversity challenges (they were asked to identify two to three), and set short-term strategic objectives and established measures, identified key activities, and created an action plan with accountabilities to achieve the strategic objectives. Subsequent to the planning meeting, sub-teams for each strategic objective met to refine the language and actions and establish a current baseline and targets for each of the measures they had established.

The takeoff phase may also be a more experimental period in which equity, inclusion, and competitive initiatives are implemented on a limited scope and evaluated and refined or discarded. Most often, the takeoff phase begins with a comprehensive strategy, a two-to-three month process, and is largely engaged with standing up infrastructure, creating baseline measures, developing and implementing basic awareness education, and other start-up activities.

Expansion Phase

In the expansion phase, strategy implementation moves into full bloom. Initiatives are rolled out across the organization, and leadership at all levels is engaged. Four months after their takeoff meeting, the REDC, having progressed significantly on their initial strategic objectives, moved into takeoff phase by launching a full-blown diversity strategy process, including in-depth interviews and focus groups to understand employee perceptions of the current state of diversity, equity, and inclusion at Global Asset Management–Americas and the creation of a formal strategic plan.

Maturity Phase

The maturity phase is often characterized by limited new initiatives or an overabundance of tactical program initiatives, less-engaged leadership, and a declining diversity budget. In many cases, it is predicted by the departure of the CEO or senior leadership sponsor. Maturity has two possible outcomes: decline or revitalization.

The chief diversity officer has two critical responsibilities to prevent the maturity phase from moving into decline. One responsibility is to be an aggressive advocate for making diversity a key qualification for the appointment of any new top leader. The other is to move the organization into the revitalization phase as early in maturity as possible.

Revitalization Phase

The first action in revitalization is to launch a new strategic planning process. This must include an assessment that not only examines employee perceptions but also takes a hard look at diversity leadership, objectives, and infrastructure. About the only aspect of diversity that should remain relatively untouchable is the diversity philosophy, and even that may have to be recreated to revitalize the diversity initiative.

The other action is to focus on innovation. Innovation primarily occurs in equity, inclusion, and sustainable diversity competitive advantage initiatives and programs. While internally generated innovations are best because they exercise and build the capacity for innovation and create the foundation for sustainable diversity competitive advantage, partnerships with academics or consulting firms known for their evidence expertise and creative thinking can be a productive way to generate innovations. Consulting firms that have collaborated on successful innovations are the first to trumpet them in the marketplace, bringing positive attention to the innovating organization.

Innovation not only breathes new energy into a diversity initiative, but it can also begin a cycle that sustains revitalization, builds brand, and creates legacy. If diversity innovations are noteworthy, they garner the attention of the diversity community. When other organizations begin to incorporate those innovations into their own diversity initiatives, the institutions that give awards and recognition begin to take notice. As the organization moves onto center stage, senior executives are asked to receive awards and give speeches, which brightens their focus on diversity. CEOs who anticipate retirement at the time the diversity initiative is approaching or is in maturity should launch a revitalization effort, engaging a new generation of leadership, ideally a year before they leave.

Scope

The scope of the strategy, whether it is being developed for the entire organization or a subunit and whether the organization is geographically consolidated or dispersed, colors the strategy process and especially the implementation infrastructure. How to consider scope depends on the point of view—looking up or looking down—of those who are guiding the strategic process.

Looking Up

If the organization for which strategy is being developed is either a subunit or geographically dispersed, then it may need to look up to headquarters for imperatives and diversity philosophy and often for organization-wide strategic objectives. If the subunit is a strategic business unit, it will have its own imperatives. Where no organization-wide diversity philosophy exists, the subunit should create its own. Where strategic diversity objectives are cascaded from above, then those strategic objectives join the imperatives and diversity philosophy in determining strategy in the subunit.

Looking Down

The major dilemma for diversity leaders who are looking down is balancing centralization versus decentralization of the diversity strategy process. On the one hand, centralization ensures a consistent approach up and down the organization and better control of diversity spending and programs. On the other hand, a decentralized process is usually more inclusive and allows better customization to local culture and needs.

Veronica Villalobos, director of the Office of Diversity and Inclusion in the US Office of Personnel Management (OPM), solved this dilemma during implementation of President Obama's Executive Order 13583, "Establishing A Coordinated Government-Wide Initiative to Promote Diversity and Inclusion in the Federal Workforce." The executive order required OPM to create that initiative within ninety days of its issuance.[100] To fulfill this mandate, Villalobos established a highly inclusive process to create overarching goals that would allow individual agencies to institute strategy initiatives that fit their unique circumstances. Working with agency leaders and diversity experts and adhering to inclusion throughout the process, OPM, with Villalobos's leadership, established three very broad goals relating to workforce diversity, workplace inclusion, and sustainability, and seven top leadership commitments, responsibilities, and requirements that largely offered wide latitude while establishing a consistent foundation for centralized measurement of progress.[101]

DIVERSITY STRATEGY PROCESS LEADERSHIP: THE DIVERSITY COUNCIL

The strategic process should be led by a diversity leadership council, committee, or task force called a "diversity council" or another appropriate name. It should be composed of the top strategic leaders in the organization or a cross-organizational group of top leaders and key stakeholders and meet at least quarterly.

The diversity council should be substantially diverse. Thirty percent diverse membership is a good rule of thumb. Because top leaders are often White males, this can be challenging. One useful approach is to use the diversity council as a leadership development and visibility opportunity by selecting diverse leaders of the future for participation. If the organization has employee resource groups (ERGs), which are affinity groups of underrepresented people, the leaders of those ERGs, insofar as they are members of underrepresented groups, can be appointed to the diversity council.

The council should be chaired by the CEO or the top leader of the organization for which strategy is being formulated. The chief diversity officer (CDO) should serve as lead staff person and be a member of the council.

The first responsibility of a new diversity council is its own education. The purpose of education is to provide the council with a common language of diversity; the meaning and implications of diversity, equity, inclusion, and sustainable diversity competitive advantage; an understanding of the unique issues faced by various underrepresented groups; and the most significant, evidence-based practices for advancing equity and inclusion. Guided by the CDO in collaboration with the CEO, educational purpose can be fulfilled in numerous ways, including formal lectures, workshops, and experiences. Most frequently, leadership diversity education relies on the CDO, ERGs, and outside experts. Interactive, engaging educational programs work best. Even better, where appropriate, is action learning, in which action follows learning. Actions are real. They are either recommendations for action or decisions (e.g., council members learn a tool to identify barriers to implementation and then actually implement strategies to remove those barriers).

DON'T START WHAT YOU CAN'T FINISH

Diversity strategy is a process of formulating and implementing measurable strategic objectives. Once formulated and announced, concerted action to achieve the strategic objectives is critical. Nothing will generate cynicism about diversity (and its leaders) faster than a commitment made that is halfheartedly or not kept. Better to not start a diversity initiative at all than to not keep its promise.

The Diversity Assessment

Diversity assessments have abundant uses. They define the current state and determine barriers to advancement. They offer a baseline against which progress (or lack thereof) can be measured. They uncover the root causes behind a lack of progress. They identify the talent processes that need to be made more equitable. They provide input into the local business case. And most vitally, they can be a force for change by creating the burning platform that motivates decisive action on diversity. In July 1988, Andy Mochan, a superintendent on the Piper Alpha oil-drilling rig in the North Sea, was awakened by a loud explosion. Leaving his bed to go to the platform, he was immediately engulfed in flames. He had two choices: be consumed by the flames or jump into the fiery ocean. He chose the latter, and, although injured, he was one of the few to survive. When asked why he jumped, Mochan responded, "It was either fry or jump." As Lawrence Bossidy, former chairman and CEO of Allied Signal, later Honeywell, noted, "To inaugurate large-scale change, you may have to create the burning platform. You have to give people a reason to do something differently." For leaders, especially strategic leaders, assessments can be transformative.

Assessments are either *formative*, providing information that supports the formulation of strategic diversity objectives, or *evaluative*, determining whether those objectives were achieved and the impacts—intended and unintended—of achieving those objectives. This competency focuses on formative assessment, while "Competency 9: Measuring for Accountability" focuses on evaluative measures.

This competency reviews the two sides of formative assessments: *content*, what should be measured and analyzed, and *process*, how to measure and analyze the content, focusing on surveys, interviews and focus groups, manager appraisals, and post-exit interviews.

FORMATIVE ASSESSMENT CONTENT

Formative assessments measure and analyze both the internal and external work environments. Below are some suggestions for the assessment content that organizations should gather.

Internal Work Environment

◇   Employee perceptions of bias and exclusion in policies and practices, managerial behavior, and interpersonal interactions
◇   Formal complaints of bias

◇ Bias in talent decision-making processes

◇ Root causes of bias, such as unconscious bias, favoritism, and bigotry

◇ Diversity climate, including employee perceptions of the degree to which the diversity philosophy is enacted; equity, bias, and discrimination; equity programs and practices; harassment and hostile work environment; multiculturalism; inclusion policies and practices; inclusive leadership; developmental and career support; respect; physical and psychological safety; cross-difference interactions; microinequities; trust; supervisor behavior; and diversity progress

◇ Measures of self-determination, locus of control, and employee engagement

◇ Clarity of the organization's definition of diversity, business case, diversity strategy, and line of authority for diversity

◇ Progress on diversity, equity, and inclusion

◇ Top management commitment to diversity, equity, and inclusion

◇ Contingencies, including priority, life-cycle stage, and scope, and their implications

◇ Diversity and functioning of the talent and product/service supply chains

◇ Current state of the talent market, including talent pool segments, positioning, differentiation, dependency on diverse talent, and competitive success

◇ Current state of the product/service market, including domestic and global market segments, positioning, and barriers to entry

◇ Functioning of social networks, including those that facilitate talent-market competition, product/service market competition, task accomplishment, mentoring and support, and cross-difference relationships

External Environment

◇ Trends that impact diversity within the organization, including demographic, public policy, industry, technology, economic, and cultural trends of relevance to the diversity strategy

◇ Current state and future developments in talent pool segments, including growth and change, competitors, diversity best practices, and employee brand awareness, reputation, and loyalty

◇ Current state and future developments in diverse domestic and global product/service market segments, including size; market share; brand awareness, reputation, and loyalty; growth; unrealized opportunities; and positioning of competitors

FORMATIVE ASSESSMENT PROCESSES

Assessing the Internal Work Environment

In addition to existing sources of data—such as the Human Resources Information System, EEO-1 reports, employee satisfaction and engagement surveys, external sources of data, and formal complaints—four additional sources should be considered: focus groups and interviews, diversity climate surveys, upward and 360-degree leadership appraisals, and post-exit interviews.

Depending on their unique circumstances, organizations should take one of two approaches to the formulation of an assessment strategy and the development of any new tools to support that strategy. The first approach is to establish a working group of the diversity council to take on these tasks. The other is to assign assessment tasks to diversity staff. In either case, the group should report to the diversity council through the CDO. Unless the expertise is readily available in-house, the assessment working group or diversity staff should partner with a firm or individual with deep expertise in survey, interview, and focus group design, and data collection, analysis, and reporting.

Focus Groups and Interviews

Focus groups are essentially group interviews. Interviews are typically reserved for top managers, while focus groups are targeted toward salient demographic groups, such as women, Black people, Latinos, White people, the LGBTQ+ employee community, people with disabilities, parents, single parents, supervisors, and middle managers. Out of good intentions, some leaders will resist having focus groups composed of people from a single underrepresented social group. The advantage of single-population focus groups is to be able to identify with some precision, insofar as the group is representative, the concerns and opinions of a particular social group. Furthermore, people of one social group might be less likely to speak up if members of another social group are present.

Focus groups and interviews serve two purposes: data gathering and inclusion. They gather leadership and employee judgments and perceptions about individual and organizational attitudes, behavior, and progress and the root causes of those perceptions. They also function as a mechanism of inclusion. At the end of a focus group I conducted with riggers at a New Mexico gas liquids plant, one of the participants thanked me, saying, "I've been with this company thirty-four years, and this is the first time anyone asked my opinion." Interviews and focus groups set a tone of inclusion for the strategy process and ensure that representative voices from across the organization and its social groups are effectively heard.

Although well-trained staff can successfully conduct interviews and focus groups, ideally external consultants who have expertise and deep experience conducting interviews and focus groups should be brought in. The organization should execute a confidentiality agreement with the consultant's firm. External consultants bring authority conferred by their expertise and do not carry any historical baggage with the individuals being interviewed, two factors that tend to elicit more straightforward answers.

The first step is to determine who should be interviewed and what focus groups should be conducted. In general, interviews should be reserved for those senior leaders who will participate in formulating the diversity strategy objectives. Focus groups should ensure adequate representation of the voices of members of salient demographic groups. Because separate functional and organizational units may have different diversity perspectives, focus groups should also have adequate representation from the units about which conclusions are intended to be drawn or separate groups for each relevant unit.

In keeping with studies of good group size, focus groups should include eight to twelve people. Fewer than eight participants precludes the kind of interaction that stimulates good dialogue; when more than twelve people participate, not all voices are able to obtain airtime. Focus groups should never exceed eighteen people. Interviews should be scheduled for one hour (never less than thirty minutes) and focus groups for two hours (never less than ninety minutes).

Prior to the actual interviews and focus groups, questionnaire protocols (the questions and procedures for facilitating the dialogue) should be prepared and reviewed with the diversity council working group. The questionnaire protocol should draw upon the internal and external environmental categories presented above. Different demographic, functional, and business groups will require distinct questionnaires, although many questions will overlap. In designing the protocol, a good rule of thumb is "Begin with the end in mind," which means that those preparing the protocols should have a solid picture of how the results will be used. Protocol designers should keep in mind that everyone has their own story to tell about diversity, equity, and inclusion. While the protocol must obtain answers to the questions, it must also give impetus and space for the individual to tell their own story.

At the outset of the interview or focus group, the facilitator should anticipate and answer four questions that interviewees typically have: "What will happen to my input? Is what I say confidential? Will I receive a copy of the report? Will I receive feedback on what happens as a result of my input?"

Surveys

Surveys are quantitative assessments of employee perceptions. Many organizations experience survey fatigue and resist an additional survey. This barrier can be overcome by administering a diversity survey every two or three years or, if the organization is large enough, by sampling different people every year so that employees are only asked to participate every three or four years. Another barrier is that surveys can be expensive to construct, administer, and analyze. A way to overcome both barriers is simply to eliminate the survey and limit the assessment to focus groups and interviews or add a small number of questions to an existing employee survey.

It is even more important that a survey be designed with the end in mind. In particular, designers need to be clear about distinctions to be made among demographic groups, functions, business units, etc. Those distinctions determine the number of employees of different social groups needed in the respondent pool.

Anybody can construct a survey. However, surveys are highly technical tools, requiring precise question design and sophisticated statistical analysis. Unless the organization is using a prepackaged survey that has been adequately tested for validity and reliability, the survey design, administration, and analysis should be left to expert partners. This can be an outside consultant or an internal technical advisor. At minimum, the consultant or advisor should be skilled in diversity questionnaire construction, question design, determining sample size, selecting the sample, analyzing the data, and reporting the results.

The key survey instrument to assess the state of diversity, equity, and inclusion is the diversity climate survey (see "Competency 7: Engineering Sustainable Diversity Competitive Advantage" for a thorough presentation of diversity climate).

A temptation in designing a survey is to overload it with questions to satisfy everyone's interests. However, after twenty minutes, respondents become fatigued and are increasingly likely to exit the survey. To address survey fatigue, keep the survey under twenty minutes, usually around fifty questions.

Upward and 360-Degree Leadership Appraisals

Upward and 360-degree leadership appraisals assess the degree to which leaders are exhibiting effective diversity leadership behaviors. Upward appraisals include the perspectives of direct reports only, while 360-degree appraisals include the perspectives of direct reports, peers, and supervisors.

Appraisals have two purposes. First, they shape leadership behavior by assessing key diversity behaviors, providing performance feedback, and comparing each leader's performance to the normative performance in the organization being assessed. Second, aggregating all the appraisals allows organization-wide conclusions to be made.

The questions in appraisals are drawn from internal work environment topics. In particular, categories of questions should include the following:

◊ The degree to which the leader's behaviors are aligned with the diversity philosophy
◊ The leader's commitment to diversity
◊ The degree to which the leader creates an inclusive work environment, including modeling and support for belongingness, authenticity, collaboration, autonomy, relatedness, competence, respect, trust, physical and psychological safety, developmental and career support, and support for inclusion policies and practices
◊ The degree to which the leader creates an equitable work environment, including actively recruiting and hiring diverse employees, standing up against biased and discriminatory behavior, and allocating developmental opportunities and conducting performance evaluations on the basis of merit
◊ If possible, an employee engagement index should be included to determine which organizational attributes, such as trust, respect, and inclusion, drive both diversity effectiveness and employee engagement.

Examples of appraisals can be found on the internet, although they should be customized to fit the unique characteristics of the organization, especially its diversity philosophy.

Post-Exit Interviews

Exit interviews can be a great source of insight into "regretted losses" of underrepresented and well-represented people from the organization. The problem with exit interviews is that in the rush of exiting, they can be perfunctory, obtaining little valuable information. Furthermore, those exiting the organization usually do not wish to burn bridges out of concern for maintaining relationships and receiving good recommendations down the road, so many tell white lies about why they are leaving. Six months after exiting the organization, former employees are usually willing to take the time and tell the truth about why they left. They are especially willing to be direct with an interviewer who is not an employee of the organization they left.

Clearly, the interview protocol should include questions about the departed employee's motivation for leaving, especially asking about how their relationship with their direct supervisor played into their decision and whether discrimination or exclusion influenced them to leave. In addition, post-exit interviews should address the former employee's views on whether the employer brand was fulfilled; what, if anything, would have been required to keep the employee; what they liked and disliked about the organization; their last position in the old organization and their new position; a comparison of their old and new organizations, including differences in pay and benefits; and their recommendations for change.

Assessing the External Environment

An environmental assessment examines external trends in demographics, economics, technology, public policy, economics, culture, and the organization's industry that are likely to have an impact on diversity in the organization over the strategic horizon. In addition, market analyses should be conducted to better understand product/service and talent-market trends. These are covered in "Competency 7: Engineering Sustainable Diversity Competitive Advantage."

Trends, Cycles, and Fads

Before examining the remainder of the environmental assessment process, trends need to be distinguished from similar-appearing but distinct phenomena, including cycles and fads.

Trends are long-term effects—such as growth in the employment of women or the educational attainment of Latinos—that have an impact on the formulation of diversity strategy. Trends move in one direction (up or down) over the course of the strategy horizon.

Cycles are activities in the external environment that go up and down over the course of a horizon. An excellent example is the gross domestic product (GDP), a measure of the market value of all the goods and services produced by a country or other state entity over a specified period of time. To build a diversity plan based on a country's expanding GDP is unwise because the country will experience a recession at some point, a point which no one has been able to successfully and continuously determine. Sometimes, if the horizon is short enough, a cycle can behave like a trend and may be useful for strategy purposes. For example, in a two-year horizon, the GDP may be relatively consistent and predictable and can be used for planning purposes. However, cyclicality should give pause and always requires contingency planning should the cycle turn.

A fad is an activity that behaves like a trend but is of limited duration, like a shooting star that fades out. Work–life integration has, to some degree, the characteristics of a fad. The growth of work–life integration initiatives increased rapidly in the 1980s and 1990s, only to decline in the 2000s. This is not to suggest that work–life integration is not substantive; rather, it has likely reached maturity, having been adopted at most mid- and large-sized organizations.

Trend analysis is always a precarious undertaking since the future is always uncertain. Confusing trends with cycles and fads can increase the precariousness of the environmental assessment.

The remaining steps in the environmental assessment are identifying relevant trends, assessing the impact of those trends on the diversity strategy, and determining which trends should receive priority attention in strategy formulation.

Trend Analysis

The analysis of external trends is a five-step process. First, the horizon should be established if it hasn't already been. Second, for each of the six trend analysis categories—demographics, economics, technology, public policy, culture, and industry—trends of interest should be identified (see table 4-1 for examples). Most external trends will relate to the organization's talent and product/service markets. Trend identification can be assigned to expert diversity staff or to the diversity council's assessment working group. Facilitated brainstorming encourages an interplay of minds that generates many useful trend ideas. Do not spend time determining which category a trend fits into. The categories are useful for generating thinking about trends and serve no other purpose once trends are identified.

Trend Categories	
Demographics	♦ Proportion of underrepresented and well-represented groups with postsecondary degrees ♦ Job-to-job mobility rates of underrepresented and well-represented groups
Economics	♦ Share of total spending of underrepresented groups ♦ Pay equity among the various underrepresented groups and well-represented groups

Technology	♦ Proportion of underrepresented people who have access to the internet
	♦ Relative skill levels among underrepresented groups with office productivity software used by the organization
Public Policy	♦ State and local legislation on equal employment opportunity for the LGBTQ+ community
	♦ How tough appellate courts are on affirmative action programs
Culture	♦ Proportion of underrepresented people who use the internet for job finding
	♦ Attitudes of underrepresented and well-represented groups toward occupations relevant to the organization
Industry	♦ Most popular diversity programs
	♦ Proportion of sales force from underrepresented groups

Table 4-1

Third, identify the impact of each trend on diversity, equity, and inclusion in the organization and the intensity of the impact.

Fourth, determine which trends should be priorities for the attention of the organization in formulating a diversity strategy. This should be done by the diversity staff group or the diversity council working group, using a facilitated group process. An excellent tool for establishing priorities is the priority matrix (figure 4-3). For each trend, the group should establish the probability that it will actually occur (high, medium, or low) and the impact on the organization (high, medium, or low) if it does occur. Those trends in the upper left are most important for the organization to consider in constructing the strategy and to monitor over the course of the strategy. The quality of the conversation about impact and probability is almost always more important than which box the trend lands in.

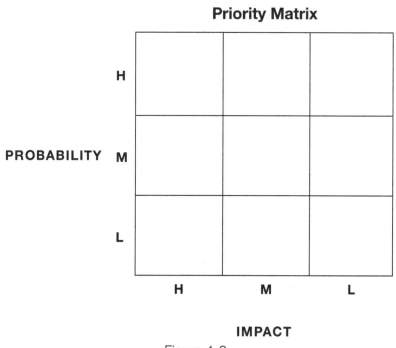

Figure 4-3

THE ASSESSMENT REPORT

The assessment report is a vital component of the assessment process. Besides the insight that it provides for determining where to focus strategy development, the assessment report can be a force for change, creating the burning platform that focuses leadership attention on diversity. The assessment report typically has three sections:

◊   An overview, including who and how many participated in the survey, the actions taken to gather the data, and how data was selected to be included in the assessment report

◊   Findings, including an integrated analysis of external environmental and internal focus groups, interviews, surveys, appraisals, and exit interviews

◊   Recommendations, including strategic objectives with action plans, accountabilities, and metrics

Recommendations are just what they say they are: suggestions, based on data and analysis, about the actions the organization should take to further diversity. The diversity council or other leadership group must make the final determination of the strategic diversity objectives the organization will undertake.

Diversity Strategy Formulation

Strategic diversity objectives are the heart of the diversity strategy. They translate the assessment and diversity philosophy into action, ensure the diversity strategy aligns with the organizational strategy and other imperatives, account for contingencies, guide the development of activities and measures, and frame implementation.

No algorithm exists for formulating strategic objectives. The formulation process is more craft than science. The objectives that result from the formulation process garner much greater commitment when the formulation process and the forces driving it have been highly inclusive.

A strategic diversity objective is *an endpoint toward which action is directed to achieve a particular strategic outcome in diverse representation, equity, inclusion, sustainable diversity competitive advantage, or implementation.* Strategic objectives should start with a verb, be short (one or two sentences), simple (to promote wide understanding), and measurable. Where common organizational vernacular uses *goal* or some other term instead of *objective*, then use the common term. An example of a strategic diversity objective is "Capture 50 percent market share for Product X in African American and Latino markets." The example is short, unambiguous, and measurable, assuming that measures of market share are available.

For each strategic objective, a measure or measures should be established. A baseline for each measure should be calculated to set the current state of the measure as a basis for determining progress at subsequent points in time. Next, a target should be established for each measure. Finally, tactical programs and policies should be developed for moving the measure to the target. Either the diversity council or top management is responsible for strategic objectives. Measures, targets, and programs and policies are ordinarily within the purview of the diversity staff with upward approval, although in some cases the diversity council or top management may wish to retain these responsibilities.

THE THREE DOMAINS OF DIVERSITY STRATEGY

Diversity strategy objectives are formulated in three domains: (1) equity, (2) inclusion, and (3) sustainable diversity competitive advantage. The first two drive the representation and effectiveness of those who have been historically underrepresented in employee populations and leadership roles. The third domain derives in large part from the first two and ensures that the organization has a sustainable competitive advantage in attracting, retaining, and advancing the highest-quality talent and in capturing expanded opportunities in diversity product/service markets. Equity, inclusion, and sustainable diversity competitive advantage are covered in the next extremely consequential competencies (competencies 5 through 7).

The initiating actions of strategy formulation are the assessment, organizational and leadership imperatives, diversity philosophy, and contingencies. The concluding actions are to consider the impact of unintended consequences on the strategic objectives and reframe the objectives as warranted.

UNINTENDED CONSEQUENCES

The act of determining unintended consequences is a highly uncertain enterprise. However, the simple act of systematically asking the unintended consequences question, as inclusively as possible, often does identify potential unintended consequences and raises awareness about them so they can be monitored throughout the implementation process.

In his classic work on unintended consequences, Robert Merton identified four essential sources of unintended consequences: inadequate knowledge, error, self-interest, and meta-action.[102]

◇ *Inadequate Knowledge*: Unintended consequences may emerge from carefully, even rigorously considered actions that nonetheless do not result in the intended outcome. Take, for instance, efforts to change attitudes toward people from underrepresented groups through sensitivity training. The expectations of these structured interactions are that members of all social groups will develop deeper understanding of each other, greater empathy, and positive changes in attitudes. However, racial and ethnic tensions have often been exacerbated by sensitivity training. This is a key reason why it is so important to include the voice of knowledge and expertise in strategic and program considerations.

◇ *Error*: Errors tend to occur because of incomplete or biased analysis in assessing the current state of diversity and in selecting a course of action. They also occur because of poor implementation.

◊ *Self-Interest*: When one or more of the decision makers has a vested interest in a particular course of action or outcome, unintended consequences are more likely to occur. A particularly challenging source of unintended consequences is values-driven self-interest since the values are often noble. Organizations should be cautious about hiring consultants or advisors with a one-size-fits-all approach or an approach that is calculated to obtain further business.

◊ *Meta-Action*: Action encourages action. Most well-meaning leaders, once they observe that the diversity initiative is serious, will try to get out in front by taking actions of their own. While actions by well-meaning actors may reinforce intended actions, they might also create unintended consequences. Consider what actions leaders might take with the positive intent of leading the diversity initiative but which might create unintended consequences. Alter the objective or action or put measures in place to prevent those consequences.

In the deployment of the diversity strategy, all employees will be asked to take action in support of the strategic objectives. Having all employees embrace diversity in their daily actions is a key to strategic success. Yet, at the same time, it can create an insidious form of unintended consequences. Because these consequences are often deep in the organization, they might be out of view of diversity program leaders and end up driving the diversity initiative in unintended directions. For example, I have spoken with many middle managers who have been told by a well-meaning senior leader that they must improve the diversity of the unit they manage. Many middle managers take these instructions for direct orders and, instead of hiring the best person for the job, hire the most available diverse person for the job. Even when middle managers resist and ignore such orders, the directives lead them to see the diversity initiative as a quota system, leaving them to believe that the quality of the workforce is being undermined by diversity and causing them to perceive diversity with a cynical eye.

For each measure and its target, the team should brainstorm the question "What can we, individually and collectively, do to achieve the targets we have established, no matter how inappropriate or ludicrous these actions might be?" Answering this question usually identifies unintended consequences that can be avoided by adjusting or adding measures. Asking this question more widely in the organization can be an excellent signal of inclusion.

Diversity Strategy Implementation

Strategy implementation is the action that propels the diversity strategy to success. Implementation is composed of the following: a management structure that establishes the management roles needed to guide the diversity strategy; measures that operationalize and propel strategy and form the foundation for accountability; top leadership communication that inculcates commitment, meaning, and direction; a high level of leadership commitment that sustains implementation; the resources to support strategy implementation; and a written plan that incorporates all of the above. After the plan has been documented, the first step is to evaluate that plan.

THE WRITTEN STRATEGIC PLAN

Dwight Eisenhower, the late US president and supreme commander of the Allied Expeditionary Force in Europe in World

War II, notably said, "Plans are nothing; planning is everything." While a documented, written plan is necessary as a vehicle of organizational alignment and accountability, Eisenhower reminds leaders that the planning process trumps the written plan itself. The value of the strategic product is directly proportional to the degree of inclusion in the strategic process. Without a deeply inclusive process, and the buy-in and commitment it engenders, even the best plan can be unimplementable. Furthermore, a written plan is a static statement in a dynamic environment. As the environment races forward, opportunities that were once palpable may disappear from the screen. And new threats emerge that were not foreseen. Plans undergo entropy—the process of deterioration—the moment they are concocted. How, then, can the entropic character of diversity strategy be managed?

In the 1980s, strategists moved from talking about strategic planning to discussing strategic management. They reasoned that because of the dynamic environment in which strategy making takes place, it is more valuable to think of strategy as an ongoing, everyday management challenge than as a static, formal document. Organizational executives should see the written strategic plan as a stake in the ground and build strategy into their everyday conversations and decisions rather than wait two or three years for a new or revised strategy.

In addition, in particularly dynamic environments, leaders should shorten the time between plans, called the plan–replan cycle. When the plan is speeding toward irrelevance, it is time to initiate a new process.

The remainder of this section discusses the purposes of a written plan, components of a strategic plan, and how to evaluate the plan. The diversity organization is responsible for drafting the written plan.

The Purposes of a Written Plan

Though the highest value is in the process, documenting the strategic plan has three primary purposes: alignment, accountability, and evaluation. A written plan allows for easy communication to the entire organization. When everyone has a consistent understanding of the strategic plan, the probability that they will largely act in concert rises, giving power to the diversity strategy. A communicated, mutually understood diversity strategy also promotes deployment. In deployment, individual employees and their managers, working through the performance management system, link their individual objectives to the targets defined in the strategic diversity plan. Communication and deployment create the conditions for vertical and horizontal alignment to the diversity strategy from across the organization.

A written plan not only provides clarity about the intent of the organization but also serves as a project plan for accomplishing the strategy. In the action plans and scheduling of specific tasks, the strategy offers clarity about who is responsible for what and when they are expected to achieve results. Being a static document, a strategic plan does not create alignment and accountability; it only provides the vehicle. Execution of the strategy, primarily in the hands of leadership at all levels, determines whether alignment and accountability are attained.

If an organization values diversity as a competitive advantage, then some will be concerned that a published diversity strategy will fall into the hands of competitors, eroding competitive advantage. However, the diversity strategy itself, while critically important, is not the difference maker. How the strategy is executed makes the difference. When a strategy is developed with widespread and meaningful inclusion, diversity programs and policies are highly innovative and evidence based, leaders are disciplined and committed to the diversity strategy, employees are aligned and have clarity about their roles and fulfill them, the climate supports a diverse workplace, systems and processes promote equity and inclusion, and everyone holds each other accountable, then an organization could deliver its strategy into the hands of its competitors and dare those competitors to outcompete them. Assuming a high-quality diversity strategy, the organization that out-executes the other competitors almost always wins the competition.

Components of a Written Strategic Plan

The strategic plan should contain six sections: the diversity philosophy, contingencies, assessment summary, the strategy, an implementation plan, and the budget. The strategic plan is an amalgamation of decisions made during the assessment, formulation, and implementation phases of strategy development. Most of the components have been addressed in previous competencies, especially "Competency 4: Mastering Diversity Strategy," so creating a strategic plan is largely an exercise in integration and documentation.

Diversity Philosophy

The purpose of including this in the strategic plan is to convey the context for the strategy and the broad intent of engaging in the diversity enterprise. Further, the philosophy is one of the four guideposts for strategy formulation.

Contingencies

Priority, life-cycle, and scope considerations should be presented here. Contingencies are also one of the four guideposts.

Assessment Summary

The assessment summary should start with an overview of the external assessment that includes the critical trends and market opportunities identified in competency 4. The internal assessment, also covered in competency 4, should recount the key themes identified in the assessment process and within them present areas of achievement (what is working, where the organization is succeeding in diversity) and areas in need of improvement (what isn't working and needs to be improved).

The Diversity Strategy

The strategy includes strategic objectives, measures, and targets, and the program and policy plans to effectuate the strategic objectives.

Implementation Plan

The implementation section should include any additional program plans for implementing infrastructure, a measurement system, a communications plan, and leadership development and change. The implementation section should also display the phasing of the diversity initiative. The implementation of diversity programs will not occur simultaneously. Some programs logically precede or succeed others, and many organizations do not have the capacity to implement simultaneously on all diversity fronts.

A good tool for displaying the phasing of diversity programs is the Gantt chart (table 4-2). While it's easy to create a Gantt chart in Microsoft Word or Excel, there is excellent, robust Gantt-chart and project-planning software on the commercial market. The simple example below is for an organization just kicking off its diversity initiative and is phased over the two-year horizon of the diversity strategy.

Simple Gantt Chart Example

Programs/Policies	Lead	Q1	Q2	Q3	Q4	Q5	Q6	Q7	Q8
Determine Diversity Infrastructure	PJ	▓							
Form Diversity Council	TM	▓							
Educate the Diversity Council	Consultant		▓						
Craft the Diversity Philosophy	MJ	▓							
Establish the Business Case	BR		▓						
Conduct Organizational Assessment	Consultant		▓						
Formulate Diversity Strategy	MJ			▓					
Create Diversity and Inclusion Scorecard	MJ			▓					
Develop Communications Plan	PMcC					▓			
Establish Employee Resource Groups	XK						▓		
Conduct Dependent-Care Assessment, Planning, and Implementation of Child-care Options	Consultant							▓	
Develop and Implement Disabilities Signature Initiative	TM								▓

Table 4-2

Budget

Budgets are composed of two components: the dollar costs by line item and an estimate of the time away from other duties required for the entire diversity effort by each program and for leadership and administrative duties. Often, dollars for diversity programs and the time commitment required of leaders are more modest than anticipated. However, when such costs as time away from the primary job for training or time to lead the development, implementation, and oversight of a program are thrown in, the costs may appear daunting. Of course, these time commitments can be reduced by hiring diversity staff or external consultants to do the work. For those organizations that are too small to afford such supports, the ambition of the diversity initiative should be scaled back with limited strategic objectives, less infrastructure, a tight communications plan, and a more modest pace.

EVALUATING THE STRATEGIC DIVERSITY PLAN

The strategic plan should be evaluated in two steps. After each evaluation, the strategy will likely need to be revised. First, it should be reviewed by the top leadership team and the diversity council, according to the seven criteria presented in table 4-3.

Strategy Evaluation Criteria	
Alignment	Is the diversity strategy aligned with organizational imperatives, diversity philosophy, the assessment, contingencies, and the organizational culture?

Strategy Evaluation Criteria	
Inclusiveness	Was there broad-based involvement in formulating the strategy, including the rank and file, middle managers, and relevant external communities? Do key internal stakeholders, particularly middle managers, believe their voices were heard well enough for them to actively support diversity strategy implementation?
Internal Consistency	Do the components of the strategy reinforce each other and guide behavior in a consistent direction? Have the unintended consequences of the strategy been considered and addressed?
Feasibility	Is the strategy supported by organizational competencies and capabilities? Is leadership prepared to commit the resources and the managerial bandwidth and employee time to executing the strategy?
Robustness	Is the strategy able to withstand changes in the external environment? If change is necessary, does the organization have the agility to execute rapid, effective change?
Evidence Base	Are the programs based on firm, scientific or practice evidence?
Differentiating Practice	Are programs built on differentiating practices (i.e., they are likely to differentiate the organization in talent and product/service markets) rather than being best practices which do not necessarily differentiate?

Table 4-3

Consideration should be given to whether these criteria are adequate for the unique organizational context and what other criteria are merited.

Second, the strategy should be presented to one or more focus groups, composed of middle managers, to gauge their response to the strategy. This not only provides an opportunity to obtain feedback from the group most pivotal to the strategy's success, but it also contributes to inclusiveness. Though it is usually best that the organization has undergone the consolidation process required to create a written plan, diversity leaders need not wait until the diversity strategy has been committed to paper to conduct any of these evaluations.

Strategy implementation is a study in Newton's third law: "For every action, there is an equal and opposite reaction." The propelling forces are always met by a reaction that can stymie the diversity strategy, including bigotry, middle-management intransigence, concerns that diversity will take resources and attention away from the organization's mission and strategic imperatives, fears that diversity will lower the quality of the workforce, and the common foot-dragging that accompanies any large-scale change effort. "Competency 12: Leading Change" elaborates the strategist's role in preventing and overcoming these reactive forces.

Advancing Toward Equity

". . . a problem well put is half solved."
John Dewey

AT THIS JUNCTURE, EMPLOYMENT BIAS remains ubiquitous, and progress toward solutions has been scant and exceptionally slow. Creating equity and justice in talent judgments requires understanding and solving the problem of bias. However, given the numerous manifestations of bias and its complexity, understanding bias is elusive. As Dewey's quote illustrates, a clear problem statement facilitates problem-solving. After reviewing the somber state of equity, this competency deconstructs bias into its many components and then constructs a representation of the problem that facilitates problem-solving and offers a host of innovative, evidence-based problem-solving strategies.

The talent case for diversity (see "Competency 2: Constructing a Business Case for Diversity," figures 2-1 and 2-2 and table 2-3) established that while companies are doing a decent job of recruiting members of underrepresented groups, those individuals are simply not progressing up the corporate ladder in proportion to the numbers being recruited. Progress toward equity has been slow and is likely decelerating, requiring decades before some semblance of equity will be achieved.

At the root of this sluggish progress lies the quagmire of bias with its numerous interpretations, suspected causes, and competing solutions abetted by retrogressing social and political systems, labyrinthine organizational environments, and lack of real commitment. Finding a route out of this morass to arrive at solutions begins with unraveling the problem of bias and framing the problem with clarity, precision, and rigor. From there, the organizational and human components of the solution can be determined.

Deconstructing Bias

Bias is complex, nuanced, and composed of a jumble of causes, such as prejudice and stereotyping, bigotry, privilege, implicit bias, internalized oppression, microinequities, microaggressions, and favoritism. As a first step, achieving a firm grasp on the problem of bias requires a process of deconstruction that differentiates and then reorganizes that jumble of causes into a coherent model that more effectively states the problem as a framework for solution.

The problem of bias can be viewed through five frames: valence, locus, magnitude, cognizance, and identity (see table 5-1 for definitions).

The Five Frames of Bias	
Valence	The degree to which bias is negative (bigotry) or positive (favoritism)
Locus	The source of the bias, whether it arises from inside an individual or in-group or from an out-group
Magnitude	The scope of the bias, whether it emanates from an individual, from a group or institution, or from social, political, and economic systems
Cognizance	The level of awareness that biased individuals have of their own biases—conscious and unconscious
Identity	The social group membership of the person to whom bias is directed

Table 5-1

Each frame is composed of two or more dimensions that guide strategic thinking about solutions to the problem expressed by that dimension (figure 5-1). In the middle of the model are spaces to develop targeted solution methodologies keyed to the problems expressed by the dimensions and intersections between dimensions. At the very center of the model are two universal solutions—attitude change and debiasing systems that address all of the dimensions of bias.

Solution methodologies are highly inclusive practice- and evidence-based tools designed to generate solutions that are relevant to the organization's unique context. Methodologies draw upon evidence from numerous disciplines and fields, including cognitive and social psychology, neuroscience, sociology, behavioral economics, decision sciences, strategy, prejudice studies, and total quality management, as well as effective organizational practices.

Bias Deconstructed

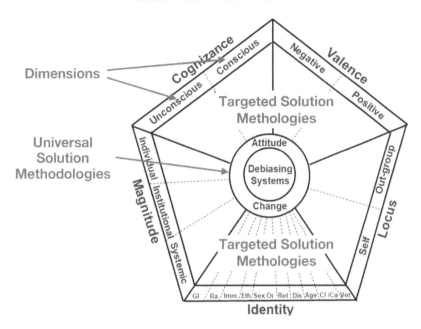

Figure 5-1

Determining which dimensions are the primary root causes of bias and should therefore be a focus of the diversity strategy is part of the assessment process. Survey, interview, and focus group questions that examine each of the dimensions should be added to the assessment. For example, using a scale of strongly agree to strongly disagree, questions such as "Hiring decisions are often based on favoritism" and "Promotions are often based on favoritism" should be added to the survey, and questions such as "Is bigotry a problem at [name of organization]?" and "How is bigotry expressed at [name of organization]?" should be added to interview and focus group questionnaires. Unconscious bias as a root cause should be assumed since, because it is unconscious, employees cannot judge whether it is a significant root cause of bias. Whether unconscious bias or any other dimension of bias should be a focus of the diversity strategy is the responsibility of senior management.

Constructing Equity

Individual, institutional, and out-group biases are best addressed through universal solution methodologies. Targeted solution methodologies are offered for unconscious bias, favoritism, self-based bias, systemic bias, the intersection between conscious and negative bias, and identity-based bias.

UNIVERSAL SOLUTIONS

Changing Attitudes

Attitudes are feelings, beliefs, and actions directed toward other people, groups, and ideas. Attitudes based on stereotypes and prejudice influence biased behavior toward people and groups.[103] Organizations have had limited success in changing attitudes, in part because biased attitudes are so difficult to change and in part because organizations have used inadequate methods to bring about behavior change. Research evidence, however, offers an array of tactics for changing attitudes.

Changing attitudes would be much simpler if there were a prototypical biased attitude that could be fixed; however, biased attitudes exist on a continuum from blatant bigots to inclusive multiculturalists (figure 5-2). Each evolution along the continuum presents different challenges for overcoming bias.

At one extreme are the blatant bigots, estimated to be 10 percent of the population: people outspoken in their intolerance toward other groups. The primary challenge with blatant bigots is deselection—discouraging them from seeking employment and weeding them out of the recruitment process.

In the left middle are employees who have a prejudiced self-identity they are unlikely to consciously act upon. They are aware of their prejudices but aren't motivated to make any changes. The challenge is to motivate them to do the hard work to change their attitudes and then provide them with the tools and methods to make the changes. Motivation must be deftly managed. Press too hard and those with a prejudiced self-identity will go underground with their thoughts and feelings—or worse, their bias will increase.[104] Press too softly and they won't be motivated to change their attitudes.

The Bias Continuum

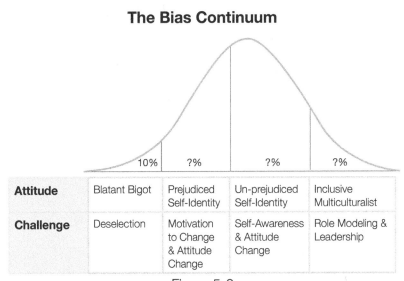

		10%	?%	?%	?%
Attitude		Blatant Bigot	Prejudiced Self-Identity	Un-prejudiced Self-Identity	Inclusive Multiculturalist
Challenge		Deselection	Motivation to Change & Attitude Change	Self-Awareness & Attitude Change	Role Modeling & Leadership

Figure 5-2

In the right middle are those who are unaware of their biases but identify themselves as unbiased. The first step for these unconsciously biased individuals is to help them recognize their biases. The guilt from the contradiction between their unprejudiced self-identity and their revealed unconscious bias creates the motivation for attitude change as long as they are presented with tools and methods to make changes.

While they may hold unconscious biases, inclusive multiculturalists are largely open, respectful, and empathetic individuals who not only reach across differences and endeavor to embrace the full chorus of voices but also find richness and personal fulfillment in people who are different. The organizational challenge with inclusive multiculturalists is to motivate and recruit them as role models to influence their peers and provide leadership and support to the diversity initiative.

The need to vary diversity programs and tactics to meet the challenges of the bias continuum requires a toolbox from which diversity leaders can draw. The attitude-change tools (see table 5-2) are the most proven, research-based tools available. They can be deployed through numerous media, including human resources, human capital, and talent programs and policies; classroom and on-the-job training; workshops; action learning; work design; and leadership development programs. The tools are not so much solutions in and of themselves as they are templates for the design of attitude-change interventions.

Attitude-Change Tools

Awareness

◊ Raising individuals' awareness of their own prejudicial behaviors and biases in an environment that is safe, private, and free from political correctness. Also, increasing understanding of the presence and mechanisms of bias and the personal and organizational benefits of mitigating bias.

Common Group Identity

◊ Placing people in categories that transcend the in-group and out-group (e.g., emphasizing being an IBMer, and the prestige and status that referent confers, rather than being a person with disabilities at IBM). Social activities, sports teams,

work and project teams, and a strong institutional identity
promote common group identity. Also called recategorization.

Counter-Stereotypic Imaging

◊ In this approach, the employee imagines a person with the
same characteristics as the stereotyped person who is a
"positive exemplar."[105] For example, for a stereotype based
on age, the employee might imagine an abstract exemplar,
such as a highly energetic and contemporary older person;
a famous example, such as Albert Einstein; or a friend or
acquaintance with counter-stereotypical characteristics.

Empathy

◊ Empathy is a combination of perspective taking (cognitive
empathy) and emotions (affective empathy). In perspective
taking, an employee examines a situation from the other
person's perspective, taking a walk in their shoes. Empathic
emotions are literally translating the perspective gained into
feelings. What feelings did that situation elicit when you
took the other person's perspective? Role-playing has been
effective in developing empathy, although it can be a hard sell.

Individuation

◊ Emphasizes the individual's unique attributes rather than the
categories to which they belong (e.g., "Amanda is strong
analytically, a strategic thinker, and has excellent supervisory
skills" rather than "Amanda is a Latino woman"). Training
supervisors to assess and manage employees as individuals
rather than making assumptions about them based on
social group membership promotes individuation. Also called
decategorization.

Intergroup Contact

◊ The most proven approach to attitude change, intergroup contact is activated when members of one social group are in contact with members of another social group, increasing "mutual appreciation" and reducing bias. Intergroup contact is most effective when contact is among those with equal status in the organization who share common goals, work together cooperatively and collaboratively in pursuit of those goals, and receive support from institutional policies, norms, and leadership.[106] For example, as a component of leadership development, a real organizational challenge might be assigned by senior management to a diverse group of high-potential employees. Affinity or employee resource groups, usually composed of members of particular identity groups, should encourage non-group-member allies to join the group, providing opportunities for collaboration and cooperation around group tasks.

◊ Intergroup contact that leads to friendship is particularly effective in reducing bias. The chances for friendship are increased when employees reach across differences to include another employee in their inner circle.

◊ In the close of the documentary *Becoming*, Michelle Obama captures the essence of intergroup contact when she says, "If we can open up a little bit more to each other and share our stories, our real stories, that's what breaks down barriers."

Peer Group Influence

◊ The influence of group norms can be powerful. When individuals identify with an in-group, that in-group will be more influential on their beliefs. Identifying allies and inclusive multiculturalists, providing them with training on influence skills, encouraging them to be forthright about their personal attitudes, and ensuring that they are represented in appropriate forums extend peer influence.

Stereotype Replacement

◊ This strategy replaces stereotyped with nonstereotyped responses. It requires the individual employee to complete a series of steps: recognition "that a response is based on stereotypes, labeling the response as stereotypical, and reflecting on why the response occurred." The individual then "considers how the response could be avoided in the future and replaces it with an unbiased response."[107]

Table 5-2

The simple question that needs to be asked about each tool is "Given our organization's unique circumstances and the specific attitudes we wish to change, what initiatives should we undertake to implement the particular tool?"

Debiasing Talent Systems

W. Edwards Deming, the father of total quality management, estimated that 94 percent of defects result from systems and processes and only 6 percent are caused by people.[108] Deming's ideas have proved extremely powerful. Incorporation of Deming's ideas into Japanese manufacturing after World War II propelled Japan from a producer of low-quality goods to a highly differentiated, high-quality manufacturer. The purpose of total quality management is to reduce the number of defects in a product or service. Bias is simply a defect in talent judgments.

No wonder organizational bias has been so intractable. Organizations are focusing on the 5 or so percent of the problem that is about fixing people when the far more fruitful opportunity is fixing the talent processes that make judgments about people, including recruiting, hiring, development, evaluation, compensation, and advancement processes.

Unfortunately, no systemic approach for debiasing talent processes currently exists. Drawing upon the well-proven tools and methods of total quality management and multidisciplinary research on bias-free decision-making, a four-step methodology for debiasing human capital decisions is offered below (figure 5-3).

Bias Mitigation Process

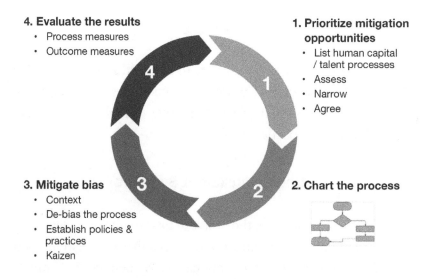

4. Evaluate the results
- Process measures
- Outcome measures

1. Prioritize mitigation opportunities
- List human capital / talent processes
- Assess
- Narrow
- Agree

3. Mitigate bias
- Context
- De-bias the process
- Establish policies & practices
- Kaizen

2. Chart the process

Figure 5-3

Step 1: Prioritize mitigation opportunities

◊   *List*: A talent process improvement leadership group composed of key stakeholders should be established. That group creates a list of the talent decision-making processes that are most salient for their organization. A comprehensive starter list of processes is offered below (table 5-3). Processes can be actual decision-making processes, such as hiring and compensation, or they can be processes that support decision-making, such as employee information systems and analytics and talent branding.

The Talent System: A Starter List of Processes

Planning

- Human capital strategy
- Workforce planning
- Employee information and analytics

Hiring

- Employee requisition
- Sourcing and advertising
- Recruiting
- Applicant information
- Interviewing
- Employee testing
- Selection
- Hiring
- Relocation
- New-employee orientation
- On-boarding

Compensation and Benefits

- Compensation
- Benefits
- Work–life
- Recognition and rewards

Development

- Mentoring
- Sponsorship
- Coaching
- Career development
- Supervisory effectiveness
- High-potential designation
- Leadership effectiveness
- Learning and development

Advancement

- Promotion
- Succession planning
- Employee certification

Separation

- Leave of absence
- Retirement
- Termination
- Layoff

Evaluation

◆ Individual objective setting
◆ Performance assessment
◆ Feedback
◆ Supervisory effectiveness

Other

◆ Employee communication
◆ Talent branding
◆ Competency management
◆ Employee relations
◆ Climate measurement, including employee satisfaction and engagement
◆ Organization effectiveness
◆ Suggestion system
◆ Diversity, equity, and inclusion

Table 5-3

◇   *Assess/Narrow:* Two methods are effective for identifying talent decision processes that are most biased: an assessment, and the four-fifths rule of adverse impact—a legal definition of selection bias. These methods can be used to narrow the list of human capital decision processes down to eight to ten.

An assessment can be either qualitative or quantitative or a combination of the two. In a qualitative approach, members of focus groups and interviewees are asked, "Which of our talent processes are most biased?" In a quantitative assessment, questions about the organization's talent processes are incorporated into the employee survey or a diversity climate survey.

An assessment determines how employees *perceive* the functioning of selection processes. The four-fifths rule is used by the US Equal Employment Opportunity Commission to determine whether a selection process *actually* has a biased or adverse impact on a protected group:

> To determine whether a selection procedure violates the "four-fifths" or "80 percent" rule, the selection rate . . . for the group with the highest selection rate is compared to the selection rates of the other groups. If any of the comparison groups do not have a passing rate equal to or greater than 80 percent of the [selection] rate of the highest group, then it generally is held that evidence of adverse impact exists for the particular selection procedure.[109]

For example, suppose that 182 people apply for positions at an organization: 128 are White, and 54 are people of color; 18 of the White people (14.1 percent) are hired and 5 of the people of color (9.3 percent). Because 9.3 percent is only 66 percent of 14.1 percent (9.3 percent/14.1 percent), adverse impact has occurred. While a court might order further statistical testing to determine whether adverse impact really did occur, the four-fifths rule is an excellent standard for prioritizing biased processes and measuring improvements in debiased processes.

The challenge in applying the four-fifths rule to each talent process is having enough cases and capturing the data required to make the calculation. If one or only a few people are hired for a position, then an adverse-impact calculation will be either impossible or unreliable. If an organization does not have the data, then the first step is to build a data-gathering process into the human capital information system.

◊ *Agree:* As a component of strategy formulation, the results are usually presented to the top management team or diversity council, which further narrows the list and agrees on two to four processes on which the organization will work over the next year or so. Once bias in these processes has been adequately reduced, additional priorities can be established.

Step 2: Chart the Process

◇ This chart is a simple flowchart (see figure 5-4 for an example) in which inputs and outputs are represented by a circle or oval, activities are represented by a rectangle, and judgments about people are represented by a diamond.

◇ Creating a flowchart is a highly inclusive process in which the stakeholders of the process—including those with expertise about the process, customers of the process, owners of process components, talent/HR leaders, diversity leaders, and line leaders, and those who will be tasked with implementing changes—are engaged and represented. The goal of flowcharting is to represent the process as it actually operates, not how it ideally or prescriptively should operate. The facilitator first establishes the inputs and outputs of the process, called the process boundaries. Then, starting after the original input, the facilitator guides those assembled through successive activities and decisions until the final output is reached. Decision-making about process steps is by consensus, surprisingly easier than many anticipate.

◇ Flowcharting directions are readily available on the internet. The one distinction between traditional flowcharting and bias-mitigation flowcharting is how decisions are rendered. In traditional flowcharting, decisions are typically binary, yes/no decisions. In bias mitigation, judgments or decisions are often binary but may have multiple outcomes. Take, for example, the credentials-review activity in a recruiting process. The decisions emanating from a review of credentials may include inviting the candidate for an interview, requesting the submission of additional documents, retaining documents for future openings, or rejection of the candidate.

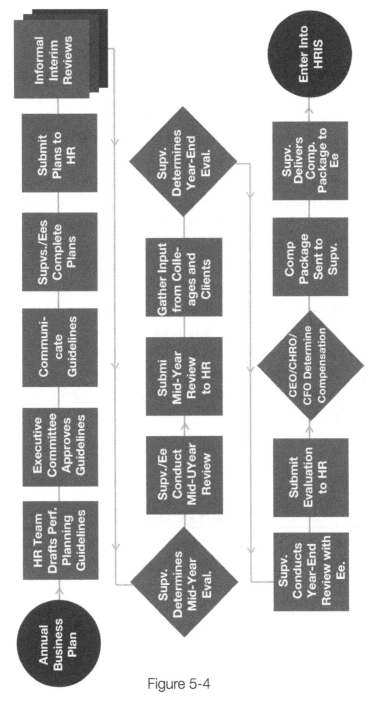

Performance Evaluation Process Example

Figure 5-4

Step 3: Mitigate Bias

◊   *Context:* Talent decision processes do not stand alone; they are surrounded by a changing external environment, organizational priorities and culture, improving knowledge about how to design and implement processes, and other talent decision processes. The influences on the process should be considered first and, if possible, addressed. For example, a promotion process is dependent on succession planning, top-talent designation, leadership development, career planning, and especially performance management. If the performance management process is highly biased against people of color, then performance outcomes considered in a promotion will also be biased.

◊   *Debias the Process:* Through extensive research I conducted across numerous disciplines, three leverage points for mitigating bias in talent decisions were identified: having the right judges, employing the right information, and putting in place the right safeguards. Each is described below (table 5-4).

Righting the Process

RIGHT JUDGES	
Group	◆ A judgment that is made by a group is less likely to be biased than a judgment made by an individual.
Key stakeholders	◆ Stakeholders, including experts, internal and external customers, function and line representatives, process owners, and improvement implementers, should be identified and included.

Self-aware
♦ Those involved in making judgments should be aware of their own tendencies toward bias, especially unconscious bias. Evidence of self-awareness comes from participation in bias awareness training, completion of the implicit association test (IAT), and soliciting and receiving feedback from trusted colleagues.

Diverse
♦ The 15 percent rule, although not proven, is a good rule of thumb. It holds that at least 15 percent of the judges should be members of underrepresented groups.

Experienced
♦ The more experienced a judge is in making a particular decision, the less likely it is that bias will enter.

Outsiders
♦ Judgments that include an outsider's perspective are less likely to be biased. If a true outsider, ideally an expert in the process, is not available, then at least one of the internal judges should take an outsider's perspective.

RIGHT INFORMATION

Eliminate poor information
♦ Determine what information is being utilized to support the process.
♦ Assess the information for what is irrelevant, unreliable, or invalid and eliminate it.

Identify weaknesses and determine additional relevant, reliable, and valid information to be sought	◆ Assess weaknesses in current information and what vital information has not been sought, used, or shared. One person should play the "devil's inquisitor" who asks the "What might . . . ?" question, seeking relevant information outside the boundaries of awareness.[110] ◆ Determine what additional information should be sought, and make and execute a plan to seek that information. ◆ Drive out WYSIATI.*

RIGHT SAFEGUARDS

Maintain a diverse pipeline and pool	◆ A robust and representative pipeline, stretching back to the beginning of recruitment, should guarantee a labor pool from which to draw sufficient underrepresented candidates.
Be inclusive	◆ In all aspects of the process, ensure that key stakeholders and candidates are included. The degree of inclusion should fit the judgment being made, although overinclusiveness is rarely a problem except when time is extremely limited.

---

* A critical feature of ensuring the right information is the concept of WYSIATI (what you see is all there is), an acronym coined by Daniel Kahneman, Nobel Prize winner in economics. The term describes the tendency of decision makers to come to conclusions using only the information they already possess or have readily at hand. Kahneman advises decision makers to ask the meta-question "What obtainable information is necessary to make this decision as effectively and efficiently as possible?"

Provide adequate time	♦ To the degree possible, eliminate time pressure. The further in time the judgment is from its consequences, the better.
Choose among multiple candidates	♦ Always have at least two candidates from whom to choose. Having even two candidates significantly improves judgments.
Consider the opposite	♦ View judgments from opposing perspectives. For every judgment, someone should play the role of the devil's advocate who argues opposing viewpoints.
Consistently apply objective criteria	♦ Ambiguous criteria or criteria irregularly applied increase bias. Judgments should be based on criteria that are clear, objective, and consistently applied. Apply one criterion across all candidates before moving on to the next criterion.
Build in accountability	♦ When judges know that their judgments are open to scrutiny, they tend to be less biased.
Embed warning signs	♦ Alert judges to the potential presence of bias in a judgment they are about to make.

Incorporate checklists	◆ Develop formal, written checklists for making talent decisions. At minimum, checklists should identify common types of bias that might enter decision-making, such as confirmation bias (the tendency to seek information that confirms an individual's own assumptions or beliefs), and the actions that decision makers should take to reduce bias (e.g., always having at least one candidate from an underrepresented group for every hiring decision). Checklists should be reviewed by everyone involved in a talent decision prior to entering the decision-making process and be kept present and used during execution of the process.
Drive out "fit"	◆ The question of whether a person is a "fit" for the culture or the team should be eliminated, if possible, or discussed at the end of the judgment process. Fit is a code word for someone who is just like the people who are already on the team, in the organization, or in leadership roles, a sure way to replicate a nondiverse organization.
Make judgments blind	◆ To the degree possible, remove information about the race, ethnicity, gender identity, sexual orientation, age, physical status, veteran status, etc., of the individuals being judged.

Table 5-4

To right a process, the stakeholder team should consider each input, activity, and judgment in order. The arrows in the flowchart represent the time between steps, which should also be considered. Transit time or in-box time between steps can often be shortened, freeing up more time for actual judgments, which reduces bias.

Once mitigation strategies have been identified, programs, policies, and procedures should be established to hardwire the mitigation strategy into the talent decision process. For example, if a particular decision point in the process is identified as overly subjective, a procedure of objective criteria followed consistently might be established.

◊ *Kaizen*: This is a Japanese term for creating a culture in which everyone in an organization is involved in continuous improvement of operations. It is the logical extension of inclusion. Continuous improvement is aimed at improving organizational efficiency and effectiveness, reducing waste, and eliminating non-value-added activities. Continuous improvement of talent decision-making processes should become an everyday component of an organization's culture.

Step 4: Evaluate the Results

Evaluation of a process has two components: process measures and outcome measures. Typically, process measures indicate whether the organization is *doing things right*, while outcome measures indicate whether the organization is *doing the right things*. Process measures gauge whether the organization is doing the things to which it has committed to reduce bias, including the proportion of underrepresented people in the pool of those who are considered and whether mitigation programs, policies, and procedures (the circles and rectangles in the flowchart of a debiased process) are actually followed.

Outcome measures determine whether judgments (the diamonds in the flowchart of debiased processes) and the collection of judgments that make up the entire talent process have moved the needle toward reduced bias, including measures of representation, self-report, and the four-fifths rule. Representation refers to the proportion of members of targeted underrepresented groups at each level of the organization, similar to figure 2-1. Self-reports are measures derived from questions on employee or diversity climate surveys or from interviews and focus groups relating to the functioning and fairness of the various decision processes. The four-fifths rule, a legal standard discussed above, determines whether the selection process resulted in an adverse impact on one group or another.

Outcome measures should not just examine whether the judgments are fair toward underrepresented people; ideally, they should also measure whether the judgments are improving the quality of talent. Talent quality, however, can be difficult to measure. Talent quality asks, "Did we hire, develop, and promote the right person for the job, and did the best performer receive the highest evaluation?" This question can be difficult and expensive to answer.

The gold standard for answering this question is whether the people who were selected after debiasing are more successful than those selected before the process was debiased or whether the person selected performed better than the person who wasn't selected. Of course, when the selection is for a job, those who weren't selected cannot be measured on their performance in the job. Measuring successful performance in a job requires determining actual performance, a potentially highly subjective undertaking. Measuring actual performance is best done by a panel of knowledgeable leaders with extensive data on the actual performance of an individual, using objective performance criteria.

To keep costs down, the focus should be on the outcome of a talent process, such as performance evaluation or top-talent designation, and a random sample should be selected from the entire set of process applications (e.g., if an organization does one thousand performance evaluations in a year, review their performance records, sample ten that ranked high, ten that ranked in the middle, and ten that ranked low, review their performance in great detail, and determine whether the ratings were fair).

TARGETED SOLUTIONS

Unconscious Bias

The first step in solving unconscious bias is helping employees to be aware of their own biases (figure 5-5). The most reliable and valid measure of an employee's unconscious bias is direct observation, through a 360-degree or similar type of assessment. Another useful technique for surfacing an individual's own bias is the Implicit Association Test (IAT). Several versions are available, including race, gender, age, disability, sexuality, and religion. All can be accessed for free by Googling *Harvard IAT* and clicking on *Take a Test*. Which test is appropriate depends on the identity issues surfaced in the organizational assessment. The IAT is not without controversy as some scholars believe that its methodology is flawed. However, the widely used IAT, which is free, has high validity and reliability, and requires little time to complete, is currently the best self-report assessment of unconscious bias available.

How an individual responds to their own self-assessment of unconscious bias depends on the degree to which they value being unprejudiced. For those who don't, the response to self-awareness tends to be inertia. They can either be forced to value being unprejudiced or be more subtly influenced. Force through punishment or the establishment of behavioral requirements is unpredictable. It may suppress the bias, contain the bias, or even amplify the bias. Because of this unpredictability, force or other forms of pressure should be avoided.

Evidence suggests that more subtle influence can be achieved through rational arguments, training on the benefits of being without prejudice, and peer influence. Influence is most effective in the hands of informal leaders (i.e., employees without formal authority who have outsized influence over their peers). Informal leaders are not necessarily the top performers but rather those employees who are self-aware, act the same in public as they do in private, are often charismatic, have a strong ethical core and integrity, are inclusive, and are willing to put the organization's interests above their personal interests.

The response to self-awareness in those who do value being unprejudiced is usually feelings of guilt. Guilt reduces an employee's motivation to address their unconscious bias unless they have a strategy to ameliorate that bias. Google, for example, offers employees four strategies with specific tools for responding to unconscious bias (table 5-5).

Unconscious Bias Solution Methodology

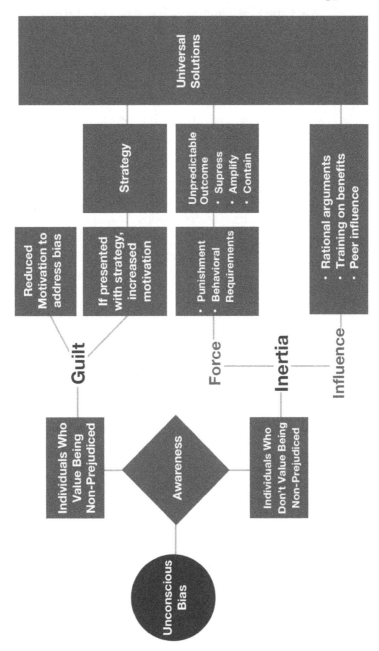

Figure 5-5

Google's Strategies for Addressing Unconscious Bias	
Use Structure and Criteria	Talent decisions should follow an agreed-upon structured process that can be represented by a flowchart. The process should have clear and consistent criteria for what constitutes a successful decision.
Collect Data and Measure Decisions	Google encourages employees to utilize three measures: the outcomes of decisions for members of underrepresented and well-represented groups; how unconscious bias affects employees' beliefs, attitudes, and experiences through a climate assessment; and the impact of interventions to combat unconscious bias.
Evaluate Subtle Messages	Employees should be aware that an individual's sense of belonging and self-worth and, therefore, performance can be influenced by the cumulative effect of subtle messages such as microinequities (actions that marginalize the recipient), underrepresentation of an individual's social group in forums that matter, or the physical environment (e.g., conference room names that are all male, or women sitting in cubicles with men sitting in offices). Employees should stand up when they are a bystander to an act of subtle bias.
Hold Everyone Accountable	Everyone is accountable for taking action to reduce unconscious bias. Google provides action guides for conducting a debiasing workshop and for starting conversations about unconscious bias.

Table 5-5

The two universal solutions—attitude change and debiasing—are both effective at reducing unconscious bias. Debiasing is particularly effective because it focuses on talent decision systems and process rather than fixing the individual.

Favoritism

Favoritism, although positive, is perhaps more insidious and widespread than bigotry. What's wrong with selecting people who you know and like, who have characteristics similar to yours, who come from the same neighborhood and attended the same schools as you, went to church or camp with you, or who seem to be a "fit" for your organization? An extensive review of research literature by Anthony Greenwald and Thomas Pettigrew argues that favoritism rather than hostility is actually "the *prime* cause of American discrimination."[111] Similar results have been found in Germany, France, Great Britain, and the Netherlands.[112]

The challenge of favoritism is that it is completely natural. A significant, often unconscious, driver of favoritism is the well-proven principle of *homophily*: people connect more with people who are similar to them—or, more simply, birds of a feather flock together. An early study in which homophily was uncovered started with the administration of a twenty-six-item attitude questionnaire. The subjects were called back two weeks later and asked to judge a person they didn't know. Each was given that person's "answers" to the same twenty-six questions as the sole basis of their evaluation. Unknown to the subjects, they were given one of four questionnaires that systematically varied the responses along a continuum from exactly the same responses as the subjects' to exactly the opposite responses. Positive evaluations of those judged to have similar attitudes were significantly higher than the evaluations of those with different attitudes.[113]

Homophily is even evident among young children. Preschool

children aged four and five were given T-shirts, half of which were blue and half red. The children wore the T-shirts every day for three weeks. T-shirt colors were never mentioned during those three weeks, nor were the children ever grouped by T-shirt color. The children never divided themselves by T-shirt color. After the three weeks, when asked which color team was better to belong to, which was smarter, or which team might win a race, the children chose their own color. The reds never showed hostility toward the blues. "It was more like, 'Blues are fine, but not as good as us.'"[114]

Favoritism can be addressed by either reducing it, giving underrepresented people the same access and organizational privileges that favoritism affords, or both. Reducing favoritism can most effectively be achieved through the two universals: changing attitudes, and bias-proofing talent decision-making processes and specific rules and procedures that prevent favoritism.

Providing equal access to favoritism is largely a matter of enhancing the internal and external networks of underrepresented employees. A significant "body of empirical research shows evidence of the central role networks play in the career development process."[115] Networks directly provide access to mentoring, development opportunities, and jobs and to the information needed to successfully complete work tasks, and they play an indirect role in "socialization and identity development" processes.[116] McDonald's, for example, has established a range of networks for its employees, franchisees, and suppliers, especially for people of color and women.[117]

For networks to be effective, they must combine both psychosocial benefits (supports "that enhance an individual's sense of competence, identity, and effectiveness in a professional role") and instrumental benefits (task and career supports). Social supports are further enhanced by the closeness of relationships. In addition, they must have sufficient range (a diverse group of connections which provides access to a wide range of information and resources) and status (which provides connections with individuals of higher status).[118]

Homophily plays a large role in determining the success of networks. It limits the access of underrepresented people to high-status network contacts, since they tend to be White men, and limits relationship closeness, since people have closer relationships with those who are more like them. Members of underrepresented groups should have two distinct networks—a social network of people with similar characteristics for psychosocial support and an instrumental network of well-placed individuals for task and career support. White men need only one network. It is no wonder, then, that members of underrepresented groups tend to perceive networking as less effective than White males perceive it to be.[119]

To be successful, network building must meet the following criteria:

◇ Provide both social and instrumental benefits
◇ Enhance the closeness of relationships
◇ Increase the range of connections
◇ Connect employees with high-status individuals
◇ Overcome the resistance that some members of underrepresented groups have toward networking

Network building can be achieved in numerous ways. Here are some examples that meet one or more of the criteria for benefiting underrepresented employees:

◇ Establish employee resource groups, if you don't already have them, and very aggressively recruit both underrepresented employees and allies, especially high-status allies, to the groups.

◇   Encourage employee resource groups to sponsor networking events with clients and customers of the same underrepresented group.

◇   Develop an on-boarding initiative that pairs new hires both with employees from their in-group and with allies.

◇   Provide both in-group and ally mentors to high-potential underrepresented employees.

◇   Train on the benefits of networking and the skills required to be an effective networker.

◇   Provide career self-management training.

Leaders should do the following:

◇   Sponsor an employee resource group composed of employees from a group outside their own social group.

◇   Establish and lead an initiative to identify high-potential underrepresented people and develop and implement career plans for them.

◇   Become a mentor or, better, a sponsor of employees from different social groups.

◇   Support and join the boards of civic and community organizations where connections with well-placed members of underrepresented groups will be made.

◇   Support and join the boards of organizations that educate and develop leaders from underrepresented communities.

Overall, organizations should evaluate employees' existing networks, employing organizational network-analysis tools, and provide feedback to employees and their managers on each individual's network performance. The data from network analyses can be aggregated to assess the organization's progress on networking.[120]

Self-Based Bias (Internalized Oppression)

Internalized oppression occurs when a person from an underrepresented group believes and takes action on the stereotypes propagated by an outside, usually dominant, group. Stereotype threat, called "subconscious self-handicapping,"[121] is a well-documented form of internalized oppression that significantly affects educational and job performance. It occurs when an individual perceives that she is at risk of confirming that a stereotype is characteristic of her. For example, in a test of math achievement, a woman may perceive that she is at risk of confirming the stereotype that women are not as proficient as men in mathematics. The impact: she actually performs worse than her math aptitude would predict. When stereotype threat is removed, women perform equal to men on mathematics tasks.

Several conditions set the stage for the emergence of stereotype threat:

1. A stereotype is at large in the surrounding social milieu (e.g., the stereotype that women are not as good at math and science as men or that White men are not as good at basketball as Black men).
2. A complex task is being undertaken in a domain that is relevant to that task and in which the stereotype is likely to operate (e.g., an engineering team [domain] that is assigned to develop a new production process [task]).
3. Performance on the task is measured and evaluated.
4. Identity and self-esteem are dependent on task performance.
5. A fear of confirming the stereotype is present.

Stereotype threat is further exacerbated when the person is a "token" representative of their stereotyped group; has a heightened, chronic expectation of being stereotyped; works in an organization that is rigid and hierarchical; and the workforce in general is more highly prejudiced.

The impact of stereotype threat on organizations is severe, including underperformance, unwanted turnover, absenteeism, tardiness, disengagement, lowered receptivity to feedback, and avoidance of careers salient to stereotyping.[122]

Research on mitigating stereotype threat is in its infancy and has tended to concentrate on educational environments. As the focus shifts to workplaces, expect the principles recommended below (table 5-6) to evolve rapidly.

Principles for Mitigating Stereotype Threat	
Strategy and skill development	Works on the complexity of task condition by closing the distance between the difficulty of the task and the knowledge and skills required to complete the task. Employees often react to stereotype threat by working harder when what they need are better strategies and skills for completing the task.
Stereotype threat awareness	From their research on stereotype threat, Loriann Roberson and Carol Kulik note, "Telling employees that you know stereotype threat can happen, and that they should be aware of it, gives them a different attribution for their anxiety"[123] *(It's not me; it's the stereotype threat).*
Provide role models	A same-social-group role model who is highly proficient in the task domain can alleviate stereotype threat. Even stories of effective role models have been successful at reducing stereotype threat.[124]

Principles for Mitigating Stereotype Threat	
Value positive attributes	Emphasize positive stereotypes. For example, for women in a negotiating task, emphasize the importance of empathy and communication (relative strengths of women) for negotiating task success.
Value commonalities that transcend demographic identity	Emphasize the importance of characteristics that transcend identity. For example, in a negotiating task, highlight "the power of career aspirations, education, and work experience in predicting negotiating success."[125]
Self-affirmation	A method of insulating individuals from stereotype threat is self-affirmation, in which employees are encouraged "to think about their characteristics, skills, values, or roles that they value or view as important."[126]
Affirmation	Leaders make it clear that they have high standards for task performance and affirm that the individual at risk of stereotype threat is quite capable of meeting those high standards.

Table 5-6

Systemic Bias

Systemic bias is a process that establishes a hierarchy of power that significantly determines which social groups will receive the greatest social, political, educational, and economic benefits and fewest negative consequences from society. The process is defined by four interrelated steps:

1. People quite naturally separate themselves into groups based on common characteristics, such as race, religion, gender, political affiliation, taste in music, or style of dress. Social group members do not bear hostility

toward members of other groups, although they do show favoritism toward members of their own group.[127]

2. When members of one group perceive members of another group to be competitors or threats, they tend to ascribe negative traits to them in such areas as intelligence, personality, and morality (e.g., Black men are more likely to be violent criminals). When ascribed traits have no or little rational or scientific basis, they form prejudice, stereotypes, and conspiracy theories. Black men are arrested in greater proportion, but the reasons are more likely poverty and racism than the inherent criminality of Black men (e.g., in a US Department of Justice study of nonfatal violent victimization, poor urban White people had slightly higher rates of violence than poor urban Black people).[128] A century ago, in many of our large cities, it was Irish people who were the subjects of stereotyping, prejudice, unconscious bias, and overt discrimination; consider the roots of the term *paddy wagon*. Demagogues find potent accelerants of animosity and rancor in stereotypes, prejudice, and conspiracy theories.

3. Under the guise of protecting society, these stereotypes, prejudices, and conspiracy theories spawn laws, policies, judicial and extrajudicial actions, institutions such as the Ku Klux Klan, disenfranchisement, threats, harassment, falsehoods, intimidation, humiliation, and violence against the social group they believe is competing against or threatening them, giving them power over that social group. Examples related to law enforcement include qualified immunity, which limits the ability of an aggrieved individual to bring a civil suit against the police; the "blue wall of silence," an informal agreement among police officers to not report police misconduct; and

police union contracts that frustrate accountability for police actions. Perhaps the most striking and horrendous example of an extrajudicial action that confers power is lynching. The dominant social group gains supremacy on the power hierarchy. Isabel Wilkerson, in her book *Caste*, metaphorically describes the power hierarchy as "the wordless usher in a darkened theater, flashlight cast down the aisles, guiding us to our assigned seats." This hierarchy is the essence of White supremacy or male supremacy.

4. Supremacy on the power hierarchy confers unearned privileges on the dominant group of which its members are often unaware (e.g., White privilege means that if you are stopped for speeding, you will know that it wasn't because of the color of your skin, you will be able to remain in your car while your violation is processed, you need not keep your hands held high on the steering wheel or out the window, your car will not be searched for drugs and weapons, and you can be confident you will survive the stop).

Power is always necessary to maintain privilege and can be exercised in many ways. It is, therefore, not sufficient to attack prejudice, stereotypes, supremacy, and bigotry without also working to dismantle the power structure that animates them. Those who enjoy privilege and do not take action to reduce systemic bias and the power hierarchy that maintains it are complicit.

Thinking Strategically about Combating Systemic Bias

For each step in the formation of systemic bias, a strategic framework for thinking about remedies is offered below. Organizations can play a finite role in remedying systemic bias by educating and influencing their own employees, embedding a diversity philosophy, and contributing their voices and actions to efforts to eradicate systemic bias. Most remedies, however, require resources beyond the scope of any one organization and are often outside their direct control. As a result, remedies will often require partnerships or coalitions of organizations to pool resources or advocate with government entities that are more likely to have the resources and the legislative and judicial leverage to address systemic bias. In developing remedies, organizations should also consider the impact of the unique characteristics, situation, and environment of the organization.

The first strategic framework is to reduce perceptions of difference through attitude change (see "Attitude-Change Tools") and the elimination of favoritism. The most proven method of attitude change is intergroup contact. Contact among different social groups tends to break down the walls between them by offering lenses through which members of one social group view members of other social groups as more like than unlike themselves.

Eliminating favoritism requires that hiring managers recuse themselves when they have a personal relationship with a candidate and not try to otherwise influence the hiring decision. Two of the most insidious ways organizations play favorites, often unconsciously, is when they consider "fit" in hiring and advancement decisions or pay bonuses to employees who recommend candidates who are eventually hired. These reinforce favoritism and end up replicating the organization's current racial and ethnic makeup. "Fit" should be eliminated and bonuses paid only when employees recommend candidates from targeted underrepresented groups who are hired and retained for a specified period.

Second, challenge or join others in challenging the ascription of negative traits to underrepresented groups. Support the gathering and analysis of data on the ascription of negative traits, incorporate this in training, and publicize the results widely. For example, an organization could support gathering, analyzing, and disseminating data on whether immigrants who have crossed the southern border of the US are more violent, more likely to be infected with COVID-19, more likely to receive welfare support, or likely to take jobs away from citizens.

Third, contribute to or participate directly in efforts to eliminate the laws, policies, judicial and extrajudicial actions, institutions, disenfranchisement, and other mechanisms that enforce the power hierarchy. This requires that individuals learn about how they participate in the enforcement mechanism of the power hierarchy—especially how their individual behaviors reinforce the hierarchy and the role that organizations in which they participate play in enforcing the social hierarchy. In addition, institutions can support organizations that aim to eliminate the mechanisms of the power hierarchy, such as the Southern Poverty Law Center, the League of Women Voters, the Brennan Center for Justice, or the American Civil Liberties Union.

Fourth, act to mitigate the effects of White privilege. Most people are unlikely to relinquish their privileges, even if they could. Because privileges are conferred, often unknowingly, by the social hierarchy, in most cases they cannot simply be given up. Further, asking people to give up their privileges is likely to be met with strong resistance. The goal of mitigating White privilege should be to provide equal privilege. The starting place for mitigating privilege is to create the conditions for achieving awareness and personal acknowledgement of privilege. Organizations can increase privilege for all by supporting and advocating for educational, financial, judicial, housing, voting rights, and anti-poverty legislation or by getting directly involved in those and similar efforts.

The final step is for the leadership team to create an action plan to address systemic bias. Below are actions, internal and external to the organization, that leaders might consider or which might stimulate their own signature initiative to address systemic bias.

Internal

Although leaders should aggressively endeavor to eliminate the negative ideology and power differentials that produce disempowering hierarchy in organizations, this is extremely challenging when power hierarchy is firmly entrenched and highly active in the surrounding culture.

Perhaps the place to start is to tilt the organizational playing field more to the benefit of underrepresented people, with the goal of reducing unequal outcomes, while being conscious of local, state, and federal laws. For example, provide greater educational opportunities to those at the bottom of the organizational hierarchy, or offer leadership development, career development, mentoring, and sponsorship opportunities specifically for members of underrepresented groups but not to the exclusion of well-represented employee groups.

External

Top leaders can support or lead efforts to advocate for legislation that advances toward leveling the playing field. For example, leaders might advocate for the Equal Rights Amendment, especially if headquartered in one of the states that have not ratified it (a constitutional amendment requires ratification by three-quarters of the states) or one of the states that are attempting to rescind their previous ratification. In addition, organizations should encourage their legislators to extend the deadline for ratification. Or they could support HR 40, which establishes the Commission to Study and Develop Reparation Proposals for African Americans, a bill to examine slavery and discrimination from 1619 to the present and recommend appropriate remedies. Or organizations could support comprehensive immigration reform.

Often, by the time employees reach the doors of an organization, inequality has already wreaked its havoc. Inequalities in education, housing, economics, and healthcare can limit the careers of underrepresented employees before they have begun. Leaders might work on education, housing, healthcare, economic, and other reforms that equalize the playing field at the entrances to their organizations.

Three additional modes of external influence, although they do not address ideology or power directly, offer organizations some leverage to reduce systemic bias:

1. Community partnerships in targeted educational subsystems—for example, science, technology, engineering, and mathematics (STEM) education and early-childhood education.
2. Legislative, executive, and judicial advocacy in support of targeted systems and subsystems, or *amicus curiae* briefs in support of legal actions supportive of diversity
3. Vendor diversity programs and standards

Community Partnerships

Community partnerships range from making significant contributions to systemic initiatives to serving on the boards of community organizations to providing internships and other development opportunities to members of underrepresented communities. Organizations are best served by determining one sector they wish to influence and then concentrating their resources on the chosen sector. ExxonMobil, for example, has a longstanding commitment to STEM education. It is a member of Change the Equation, a collaboration of over 100 businesses that focuses on expanding the numbers of highly qualified STEM teachers and attracting students to STEM careers. ExxonMobil is a founding sponsor of the National Math and Science Initiative, a nonprofit to which they have contributed $125 million. With golfer Phil Mikkelson, they founded the Mikkelson ExxonMobil Teachers Academy, which trains 500 third-to-fifth-grade teachers in the knowledge and skills needed to motivate students to pursue STEM careers, and with Bernard Harris, the first African American to walk in space, they created the Bernard Harris Summer Camps to prepare and encourage lower-income students to pursue STEM careers.

Organizations need not invest $125 million in a community partnership. They can sponsor community organizations, their leaders can serve on the boards of those organizations, and their employees can provide pro bono consulting to those organizations and volunteer direct service to their clients.

Community partnerships not only influence systemic bias but also often connect organizational leaders to highly placed members of underrepresented groups. As leaders serve on boards and committees of community organizations and national initiatives, they are more likely to establish networks with members of underrepresented groups who can connect them with prospective underrepresented job candidates.

Organizations with the means should consider establishing signature initiatives, like ExxonMobil's STEM commitment, to focus their resources in a way that makes a significant difference and brands the organization's diversity initiative.

Legislative, Judicial, and Executive Advocacy

Most large organizations and many small and medium organizations advocate for their own institutional, industry, and sector interests. Those same mechanisms can be employed to advocate for targeted underrepresented populations. Sixty-five prominent companies, for example, signed an *amicus curiae* brief in support of the University of Michigan in the Supreme Court's Grutter decision on using racial preferences in admissions decisions. Numerous businesses, nonprofits, and professional and trade organizations banded together in an *amicus curiae* brief to the Supreme Court in its Defense of Marriage Act (DOMA) decision.

Vendor Diversity Programs and Standards

Vendor diversity programs earmark a percentage of their annual spending to diversity-owned and certified businesses. The National Minority Supplier Development Council estimates that the 11,978 American firms it has certified as 51 percent or more owned by Black, Hispanic, Asian, and Native American people have created 2.25 million jobs and generate $138 billion in salaries and benefits and $49 billion in tax revenue on over $400 billion in sales.[129] Vendor diversity programs provide significant positive impact on the community at very low cost to the organization and make the organization's supply chain more competitive and resilient.

Organizations can also promulgate vendor diversity standards that all suppliers must meet as a condition of doing business. Think of the impact just one large company could have if it established diversity standards for its vendors. Take, as a possibility, Pfizer, which already has a strong supplier diversity program. Consider the leverage its $500 million annual spending could have with its 2,500 suppliers in encouraging them to become more serious about diversity. Imagine the impact if several large companies and institutions banded together to establish and encourage the achievement of diversity standards.

The Baldrige Excellence Framework offers a model on which diversity standards could be based. Administered by the National Institute of Standards and Technology in the US Department of Commerce, the framework promulgates standards for the systemic improvement of quality and provides awards every year to those demonstrating highly successful implementation of the framework. The impact of the framework on US competitiveness has been profound.

The standards would measure achievement in a series of evidence-based categories, which might include leadership, strategy, equity, inclusion, measurement, accountability, and representation. The standards would need to be simple and robust enough to account for a wide range of unique diversity strategies and approaches. Standards developed under Section 342(b) of the Dodd-Frank Act provide a simple, flexible framework for assessing diversity.[130]

Conscious Bigotry: The Intersection Between Conscious and Negative Bias

At their most virulent, those at the intersection between being conscious of their bias and negative toward other identities are conscious bigots. Luckily, those who are consciously bigoted tend to shun organizations that are committed to diversity and inclusion and "gravitate toward jobs that enhance group hierarchy and defend the status quo."[131] Organizations that are aggressively committed to increasing the proportion of underrepresented employees and stamping out bias, and have the flatter organizational characteristics of inclusive organizations, tend to discourage the most bigoted.

For those organizations not willing to depend on self-selection by the bigoted or who have not progressed far enough on diversity and inclusion to discourage those who are bigoted, deselection is highly useful and most effective at the point of recruitment. Recruiters and hiring managers should be on the lookout for two distinctive characteristics that are most highly associated with bigoted people: right-wing authoritarianism (RWA) and social dominance orientation (SDO).[132]

RWAs "believe strongly in submission to authorities and the social norms those authorities endorse. They also believe in aggressing against whomever these authorities target."[133] SDOs "not only believe some people were meant to dominate others, they personally want to do the dominating. Winning is the only thing for them. They want power and relish using it, to the point of being relatively ruthless, cold blooded, and vengeful."[134] Together, RWAs and SDOs account for "50% of overall prejudice."[135] The only other factor that is substantively associated with bigotry, one that cannot be considered in employment decisions in the US, is gender—men score higher on social dominance orientation than women.[136]

The RWA and SDO positions are relatively extreme, and prospective employees will likely be wary about expressing them. Besides simply being aware of these positions, how can interviewers get at them? When direct questions are likely to be avoided, an indirect approach is useful. For RWAS, inquiries concerning attitudes about obeisance to organizational leadership (authority), people who challenge rules and policies, employees who think for themselves, and self-managed work teams may indirectly reveal RWA attitudes. For SDOs, questions about equality in its many forms are revealing. Recruiters may wish to administer the thirty-two item right-wing authoritarian and the fourteen-item social dominance orientation scales to screen prospective employees for conscious bigotry.[137] Legal counsel should review the questions developed and the scales to ensure that they do not violate applicable regulations and laws.

Identity Bias

Social group identity, the demographic group memberships that define underrepresented people, is especially relevant to intergroup bias. The social psychologist Henri Tajfel determined that through a completely natural process of social categorization, people put themselves and others into groups. The group to which an individual belongs is the in-group, the other the out-group. People characterize certain aspects of out-groups as negative and exaggerate the differences between groups, all to enhance their own feelings of self-esteem and pride.

All bias is rooted in identity bias. Thus, every tool and method designed to combat other dimensions of bias also combat identity bias. Two additional aspects of identity bias that need to be addressed are how to determine which, if any, identities an organization should focus on (identity salience), and understanding the intersections between underrepresented identities (intersectionality) that are extremely difficult crossroads at which to reside.

Identity Salience

Determining which identities are most salient to a particular organization requires an examination of identity discrimination from two perspectives: business or organizational need and geography.

Business need encompasses both the talent and product/ service markets, the markets in which organizations compete for talent and customers and clients. If an organization needs well-educated, entry-level employees, then women, who receive more advanced degrees than men in most countries of the world, would likely be a prime identity group to attract and retain. If an organization is in the pharmacy business, then it might also have a focus on women, who, as of 2012, constituted 55 percent of all pharmacists and 65 percent of pharmacy program graduates.[138] If a company wishes to sell products in Vietnam, then it needs Vietnamese employees in product development and design, marketing, and sales, and it needs distribution channels and communications expertise in Vietnam.

The identities salient to a particular geography vary. For example, in the US, people who are Black and Latino experience significant discrimination, while in Europe, Roma people and immigrants are widely discriminated against. The experience of discrimination for a Black person residing in Detroit is different from that of a Black person residing in Soweto, a township of Johannesburg, South Africa.

The intensity of discrimination can vary across countries and regions. Take, for example, discrimination against the LGBTQ+ community. Sweden, which decriminalized homosexuality in 1944, is considered safe and welcoming for the LGBTQ+ community. Although discrimination does exist in Sweden, it is far less intense and consequential than discrimination in Nigeria, which passed the Same Sex Marriage (Prohibition) Act in 2014 that made being gay a criminal offense punishable by up to fourteen years in prison. Even those who advocate for LGBTQ+ people in Nigeria face imprisonment.

Decisions about which identities are most salient from a business point of view should ideally be made by business unit leadership and those from a geographical point of view by country or region leadership. The analysis on which to make these decisions can be aided by the analytic categories and topics in the identity group salience analysis template (table 5-7).

Identity Group Salience Analysis	
History	History of the identity group in the nation or region, its story, key historical moments and heroes, and power relations with other identity groups
National and Organizational Cultures	In the surrounding national and organizational cultures, the predominant attitudes toward and beliefs about the group, norms of behavior toward the group, myths about the group, and how hierarchy and privilege are maintained
Government	Understanding of key statutes, regulations, and judicial decisions to prevent discrimination toward the identity group and those that discriminate against the group, such as Nigeria's Same Sex Marriage (Prohibition) Act, apartheid in South Africa, and Jim Crow laws in the US
Market	The dependence on particular identity groups to staff key functions and roles and to provide expertise about product and service needs, desires, requirements, purchase habits, and usage patterns of their own identity group

Table 5-7

Two considerations about identity and related decisions should be made at the top management level of the organization. The first is how to handle pariah countries like Nigeria. If your organization has strong values about fair and just treatment of LGBTQ+ people or important business and talent interests in the LGBTQ+ community or are simply a moral leader, then whether and how to do business in Nigeria is an important top management consideration.

The second consideration is whether to focus on a single identity group. For many companies, women resoundingly achieve business and geographic salience on a global basis. Professional services firms, educational institutions, and consumer goods, retail, and healthcare companies, for example, are highly dependent on the talent of women. Women are half the world's available workers and are rapidly growing to become the world's most educated workforce. They drive most of the world's consumer goods purchases and make up a majority or near-majority of its nurses, pharmacists, biological scientists, and administrative and legal services workers. Many firms exclusively or nearly exclusively prioritize the women's identity group. Is this the right thing to do, when so many other identity groups do not receive fair and just treatment? Every leader must decide.

Intersectionality

Intersectionality occurs when identities interact with each other to create even greater barriers to equal opportunity. For example, Native American women are likely to bear greater bias than either Native Americans or women. Kimberlé Williams Crenshaw, a professor of law at Columbia and UCLA, coined the term *intersectionality* when she recognized that multiple identities may require unique solutions: "In 1976, Emma DeGraffenfield and several other black women sued General Motors for discrimination, arguing that the company segregated its workforce by race and gender. Blacks did one set of jobs and whites did another. This was of course a problem in and of itself, but for black women the consequences were compounded. You see, the black jobs were men's jobs, and the women's jobs were only for whites."[139]

While discrimination on the basis of race or gender is unlawful, apparently discrimination on the basis of race *and* gender is not; the federal district court "dismissed their claims" because it "believed that black women should not be permitted to combine their race and gender claims into one."[140]

Crafting Solutions to Identity Differences

Because identity differences are omnipresent, they are addressed by many of the solutions presented in this chapter, oftentimes intentionally, sometimes unintentionally. To ensure that identity is intentionally addressed when crafting a solution to any form of bias, consider the characteristics of each identity involved, how that solution will work across identities, and how the solution should be adapted to the different identities. In considering how identity and solutions interact, the different voices of those identities should be represented, engaged, and heard in answering questions such as the following:

◊ How biased and inaccurate is intergroup understanding among the different identity groups involved (*hint*: often shockingly stereotypical)?

◊ What features of group identity (e.g., norms of behavior, basic assumptions, moral beliefs, family values, individualistic or collectivistic culture, distribution of power, assertiveness, orientation toward uncertainty, locus of control, gender equality, and leadership style) are relevant to the proposed solution, and how should these features play into crafting the solution?

◊ Does the solution speak to the intersectionalities among identities?

◊ How should intergroup understanding be made more accurate and unbiased?

◊ How should the solution be adapted to identity differences?

COMPETENCY 6:

Instituting Inclusion

"You do not take a person who, for years, has been hobbled by chains and liberate him, bring him up to the starting line of a race and then say, 'You are free to compete with all the others,' and still just believe that you have been completely fair."
Lyndon B. Johnson, President of the United States
Commencement Address, Howard University, 1965

THROWING OFF THE CHAINS OF inequality that hold back underrepresented people is not enough. Getting through the door to the organizational starting line and even having fair and just processes and judgments for advancement are not enough if all employees are not able to bring their full value to the table. To bring that value they must meet the following criteria:

◇ Believe that they truly belong
◇ Be able to bring their authentic selves to the workplace
◇ Have their strengths spotlighted
◇ Have their voices heard and considered
◇ Work in an environment that stimulates and supports them
    to their highest level of performance

◊   Have leaders who will stand up against even the slightest
     hint of prejudice and discrimination

Such an inclusive workplace is not only good for
underrepresented employees: it is quite possibly the rising tide
that lifts all boats.

Inclusion must leverage the differences among employees to
achieve a performance advantage. Leveraging differences is not
about finding the "secret sauce." It is about the fundamentals
of discovering the unique strengths, experiences, perspectives,
knowledge, attitudes, and other talents associated with those
differences and unleashing them to achieve a performance
advantage. When individuals are excluded from work groups,
conversations, meetings, assignments, or even from being their
true selves and exercising their greatest strengths, their unique
value is obscured or lost altogether.

Achieving a performance advantage through inclusion is not
straightforward. Exactly which leadership and organizational
practices provide a performance advantage has been a matter
of extensive scholarly and practitioner study and debate, with
many studies showing a positive relationship between particular
practices and performance and others questioning those same
relationships. The debates are largely a matter of methodology—
questions of definition, experimental design, statistics, and
competing consulting models. Yet out of this haze of research
and practice, consensus on aspects of what leverages difference
for performance advantage has been emerging. That consensus
focuses on five elements of inclusion: core principles, talent
enablement, employee participation, inclusive leadership,
and standing up against prejudice (figure 6-1). No one-size-
fits-all methodologies exist for realizing these elements. Each
organization must craft its own model from the elements of
inclusion presented here and elsewhere and incorporate them
into the strategic choices they make.

The Elements of Inclusion

The core principles—belongingness and authenticity—constitute the gateway to inclusion through which all inclusion initiatives must pass. *Core principles* are the province of employees. Without each employee shepherding belongingness and authenticity, inclusion is only an aspiration.

Elements of Inclusion

Figure 6-1

Enabling the talents of employees and enabling employee participation are, respectively, concerned with unleashing the assets of employees and ensuring meaningful involvement of employees in decision-making. *Talent enablement* and *employee participation* are the province of managers. *Inclusive leadership* and *standing up* are the domains of leaders. Inclusive leadership encompasses the practices that predict organizational performance and especially make a difference for underrepresented employees. Standing up is the obligation to be powerful and public in facing and resisting prejudiced behavior. Although all employees should aspire to inclusive leadership and lead in standing up, leaders must carry the ball. Taken together, the five elements of inclusion, if practiced assiduously and skillfully, forge a performance advantage that contributes mightily to a sustainable competitive advantage.

CORE PRINCIPLES

The core principles of belongingness and authenticity are central to leveraging differences.[141] Without a sense of belongingness and the freedom to be authentic, inclusion would be severely stunted, if not impossible. The core principles are particularly relevant to underrepresented people, who are considerably more likely to perceive themselves to be disconnected from their work group and unable to bring their true selves to the workplace.[142]

Belongingness

Belonging is *a fundamental psychological need of all humans to form strong bonds and a deep sense of connectedness with other people.* Belongingness is not individuals' perceptions of whether or not or to what degree they belong to a work group but their perceptions of the degree to which the group is signaling that they belong. Those perceptions are fostered by whether group members make individuals believe that they belong to the group, fit in, are an insider, and are liked, appreciated, and cared about.

Some cultures acknowledge the fundamental significance of belongingness. In greeting each other, Zulu people acknowledge belonging with the greeting *Sawubona*, literally "I see you."

Sawubona is far deeper than a simple hello; it is an appreciation of the essential humanity of the other person, demonstrating that the person has been understood, showing respect, and recognizing the other person's dignity. The response to Sawubona is *Ngikhona*, which means "I am here," communicating that the humanity of one person derives meaning through the humanity of others—thus the Zulu saying "Umuntu ngumuntu ngabantu," which means that a person is a person because of their interconnection with other people.

A sense of belonging is strongly correlated with employee engagement[143] and mental and physical health,[144] and serves as a buffer against depression and anxiety.[145] "Uncertainty about social belonging" can cause people to monitor their environment and negatively "color interpretations of ambiguous events . . . further eroding feelings of belonging."[146]

In a survey of over 14,000 LinkedIn members, the single most important factor for making an employee feel like they belong was "Being recognized for my accomplishments" (59 percent), followed by "Having opportunities to express my opinions freely" (51 percent), "Feeling that my contributions in team meetings are valued" (50 percent), "Transparent communication about important company developments" (48 percent), and "Feeling like my team/company cares about me as a person" (46 percent).[147]

Promising practices that managers can apply to promoting belongingness are summarized in table 6-1. In addition, several of the inclusive leadership practices conveyed below reinforce belongingness.

Promising Work Group Practices for Promoting Belongingness

Be Welcoming	A vital component of on-boarding, welcoming is not just important in the early stages of employment but should also be an everyday practice. All members of the work group, not just the supervisor, should strive to be welcoming. While being welcoming will seem like a "no-brainer" to many, consider how frequently and robustly you have been welcomed to new groups you are joining.
	With new employees, introduce yourself and then introduce them to others; or, better, the others should reach out and introduce themselves. When in conversation with one person or a group of people, don't let others shuffle around outside the conversation circle. Invite them in and mention what is being discussed. In every social or work gathering or meeting, be prepared to greet everyone warmly, the metaphorical equivalent of welcoming a guest to your front door with a glass of champagne. In one-on-one conversations, inquire about the other person's likes, interests, motivations, families, etc., without conducting an inquisition. A good rule of thumb is that they should talk more than you. In considering how to welcome employees, Maya Angelou's insight is an excellent guideline: "I've learned that people will forget what you said, people will forget what you did, but people will never forget how you made them feel."

Promising Work Group Practices for Promoting Belongingness	
Recognize Accomplish-ments	Recognition is perhaps the most important action managers and work group members can take to encourage belongingness (and authenticity), and it is also the easiest to do. Take every opportunity to recognize employees for their accomplishments. "Catch" them doing something extraordinary. Be sure to ask employees whether they are comfortable with public recognition; many are not.
Tell Stories of Belonging	Have employees share stories of belonging, as well as experiences of nonbelonging. Stories that are specific about what happened and what the employee learned from the experience are best. Many listeners will empathetically enter into the story, identifying with the speaker. After everyone in the group has told their story, facilitate a conversation about the principles of belongingness that can be gleaned from the stories. These principles can provide a guidepost for creating a belonging workplace.
Expand Your Inner Circle	Encourage employees to bring a team member who is different into their inner circle—the people with whom they eat lunch and socialize outside of work.
Track Be-longingness	By tracking belongingness, leaders are able to determine whether their interventions are effective and, if not, what specifically they can do to improve belongingness. A good measure is the Perceived Group Inclusion Scale[148] (sixteen items), which measures the strength of the bond between the individual and the group and whether that bond is positive or negative. Eight of the sixteen items measure authenticity. The General Belongingness Scale (twelve items) measures the degree of inclusion and exclusion that an employee is experiencing.[149]

Table 6-1

Authenticity

Authenticity is *the ability of employees to act in a way that is consistent with their true selves and their most deeply held values and beliefs.* Authenticity stands in contrast to assimilation—conforming to the values, beliefs, mores, and behaviors of the dominant group—and covering, which is playing down critical aspects of one's own special uniqueness. Authenticity is a significant piece of what makes a person different, and differences cannot be leveraged if they are washed away or hidden below the surface.

Authenticity is composed of four factors: awareness, unbiased processing, behavior, and relational orientation.[150]

◇ *Awareness* is "possessing and being motivated to increase knowledge of and trust in one's motives, feelings, desires, and self-relevant cognitions." Awareness focuses on knowledge about and acceptance of the many, often contradictory aspects of one's self. For employees to engage deeply in self-examination, they must be motivated to know who they are and have the time and opportunity to uncover their true selves. Motivation comes from leaders who are themselves role models of self-exploration and who create an environment that supports and makes it safe to engage in self-exploration. Knowing yourself is the result of self-examination through the methods of introspection and external feedback from respected and respectful individuals and instruments such as 360-degree assessments. Leaders can support self-examination by providing access to the methods of self-examination and embodying Socrates's admonition, "The unexamined life is not worth living."

◇ *Unbiased processing* of self-relevant information is about being objective in one's self-assessment "with respect to one's positive and negative self-aspects, emotions, and other internal experiences, information, and private knowledge." For employees to conduct unbiased, objective self-examination requires that they allow themselves to be vulnerable. To be vulnerable is to expose oneself to the emotional risk of shame. Being authentic, expressing the real self, opens a person to shame if that real self is rejected. Embracing vulnerability requires the courage to be imperfect and the compassion to be kind to yourself.[151] Leaders can best support vulnerability by allowing themselves to be vulnerable and standing behind employees who show their vulnerability, making them feel safe and secure enough to be objective in their assessment of their true selves.

◇ *Behavior* refers to "behaving in accord with one's values, preferences, and needs as opposed to acting 'falsely' merely to please others or to attain rewards or avoid punishments."

◇ *Relational orientation* "involves valuing and striving for openness, sincerity, and truthfulness in one's close relationships. In essence, relational authenticity means being genuine rather than fake in one's relationships with close others."

To determine whether employees are behaving in consonance with their selves, assessments are useful. In addition to the Perceived Group Inclusion Scale, additional work-related measures of authenticity are the Individual Authenticity Measure at Work[152] (IAM Work—twelve items) and the Authenticity Inventory[153] (forty-five items). The former measure assesses the degree to which employees perceive that the group allows and encourages them to be authentic, while the latter measures assess employees' perceptions of their own authenticity. The Authenticity Inventory assesses awareness, unbiased processing, behavior, and relational orientation.

No one is completely authentic or inauthentic; it is a matter of degrees. Authenticity partly comprises what the individual brings to the table and partly whether coworkers, managers, and organizational climate and culture encourage authentic behavior. To some degree, authenticity is situational. Authenticity does not mean complete honesty and transparency at every moment. Being authentic does not mean being self-revelatory in a way that hurts and damages others unnecessarily. Nor should all aspects of oneself be put on the table in every situation. As Jean Tomlin, former HR director at Marks and Spencer, a leading British retailer, noted, "I want to be me, but I am channeling parts of me to context. What you get is a segment of me. It is not a fabrication or facade—just the bits that are relevant for that situation."[154]

Authenticity is particularly challenging for underrepresented people for whom assimilation and covering can be pathways to being hired and advanced. The "dress for success" imprimatur, for example, is about covering up in the clothes of the leadership group, mirroring them and forgoing the stylishness that expresses individuality. Authenticity comes at the price of sacrificing the structure and comfort that conformance provides. Yet that conformance flies in the face of many of the benefits of diversity, such as innovation and improved problem-solving.

Authenticity is associated with numerous other benefits, such as job satisfaction, in-role performance, and work engagement[155] ("a positive, fulfilling, work-related state of mind that is characterized by vigor, dedication, and absorption"[156]); work ability and intrinsic motivation;[157] and life satisfaction, well-being, and positive affect.[158] The inability to be authentic can cause depression, burnout, stress, negative affect, irritation, and symptoms of physical illness.[159]

Where the rubber of authenticity meets the road of organizational life is for people with hidden disabilities, gender identities, and sexual preferences. They must make choices about whether to present their true selves—choices which may significantly impact their careers. Institutional supports for authenticity will not be effective until the true composition of the workforce is known. To be heard, included, and supported, all employees, especially those with hidden disabilities, gender identities, and sexual orientations, require an anonymous and confidential vehicle to reveal aspects of themselves that may be threatening and uncomfortable for others. Engagement, employee, and client surveys and internal reporting forms offer the best vehicles for employees' authentic selves to be counted while remaining anonymous. An excellent example of an internal reporting form that allows people to confidentially disclose a disability is the federal government's Standard Form 256: "Self-Identification of Disability." The form can easily be adapted to other social group identities.

Belongingness and authenticity together are the gateways to inclusion. If one or both are weak, the gateway to inclusion will close, and inclusion will be only an aspiration.

Belongingness and authenticity should be readily understandable and achievable by all employees. Even the kindergarten, first, and second graders at Davis Elementary School in Bedford, Massachusetts, get the importance of authenticity and belongingness—as reflected in the chorus of their school song (sung to the tune of Pharrell's "Happy"):

> Because Davis is the place
> Welcome every face
> No one left behind
> Because Davis is the place
> Where I can be me
> We are all unique

TALENT ENABLEMENT

The essence of inclusion is to amplify the unique talents and maximize the performance of each employee. Yet the predominant approach to acquiring and managing talent in organizations more often than not diminishes that talent and minimizes performance. To truly enable talent, a new approach to talent management is needed.

Talent management today is role driven, conflict inducing, and deficit focused. Roles, or positions, emerge out of organizational structure; they are the boxes on an organizational chart. Roles are also a vital component of the rationale for adding a new employee. Employees are hired to fulfill a job description that elaborates the responsibilities and qualifications for the role. Once hired, employee performance is managed to the role. Development is usually focused on remediating role deficiencies, deepening role competencies, or preparing the employee for advancement to a new role.

While an individual's *assigned* role or position is fixed until the next formal lateral move or promotion, the *actual* role the individual is performing fluctuates. Changes in an organization's external environment, driven by such conditions as global competition, technological change, transforming markets, disruptive innovation, and all-too-frequent catastrophes, force changes in organizational priorities, which in turn drive changes in assigned roles and responsibilities. As the roles and responsibilities of multiple team members change, often in a haphazard, unplanned manner, they begin to overlap, creating conflict. In over thirty-five years of consulting, by far the most frequent organizational problem I have encountered is overlapping roles and responsibilities among team members and the resulting conflicts they produce. Indeed, a popular organizational development tool called the responsibility or

RACI chart (responsible, accountable, consulted, informed) was developed to address this problem.

When an employee underperforms in his role, ordinarily the causes are assessed, improvement areas identified, and performance improvement plans developed. This system of performance management has received significant criticism (among other criticisms, it is often highly biased), and for some organizations, that criticism has driven real change.[160] Nevertheless, one aspect of performance management that has not seen much change is its deficiency focus. Performance managers are taught to start performance reviews with the positives, then move on to "areas of growth" or "areas in need of improvement" (euphemisms for deficiencies), and performance improvement plans.

The experience of many employees and supervisors alike is that the strengths part of the discussion goes rapidly and smoothly, as the employee nods approval, while the deficiency part of the discussion is often interminable, with the employee trying to provide context and explanation and both supervisor and employee becoming increasingly defensive. To stop this motivation-deadening interchange, the manager shifts the conversation to the performance plan. Frequently, what drives this process is the need to fill a folder with an evaluation and a performance plan, a folder that is rarely looked at again until performance deteriorates badly or downsizing is required. Too often, this deficiency focus actually undermines performance and supervisors' credibility. An overfocus on roles, all-too-frequent conflicts among those roles, and employees' deficiencies in those roles disable instead of enabling talent.

The antidote is to shift to a strengths-based system of performance management that is able to address the persistent changes that confront most organizations today while improving performance. "When employees know and use their strengths, they are more engaged, have higher performance, and are less likely to leave" the organization.[161] Roles should not be abandoned. They should simply be moved to the background while strengths are moved to the foreground.

As a leader, consider how you would manage a high-stakes work team where the average annual salary is nearly eight million dollars and where your performance and the work team's performance are widely scrutinized on a daily basis. That is the job of Joe Mazzulla, the interim coach of the Boston Celtics, and Brad Stevens, the general manager and president of Basketball Operations, who employ strengths-based performance management to ensure their team excels. Stevens does the "hiring" of basketball players. Although the traditional roles of point guard, shooting guard, small forward, power forward, and center are considered, they take a back seat to the strengths, versatility, and adaptability of the player. Stevens seeks versatile players who have an array of strengths and the potential to expand existing and development new strengths. He seeks strong characters, a high basketball IQ, exceptional leadership ability, athleticism, and players who excel at multiple basketball competencies, such as lateral quickness, vertical leap, ambidexterity, ball handling, and, of course, shooting. Stevens also seeks adaptable players who are flexible, highly coachable, willing to play an assigned role and sacrifice for the team, and have a strong work ethic.

Mazzulla's job is to maintain adaptability, broaden and deepen versatility, and meld players' strengths into a winning team. He emphasizes a developmental mindset to expand versatility, teaching every day and assigning an assistant coach to develop and expand the strengths of every player. He identifies roles based on strengths and then works with players to accept their roles and play them to perfection. Specialized coaches work with players on physical strength, flexibility, and conditioning. With new competitors to go up against virtually every day, Mazzulla may switch the roster to optimize the strengths of his players versus the competition.

While NBA basketball is merely a metaphor for strengths-based performance management, the correspondence with standard organizations rings true. Roles are formulated by aligning employees' strengths with the tasks at hand. Employees are selected for their strengths, versatility, and adaptability, and then they are extensively developed to maximize their strengths and expand their versatility.

Formulating Strengths-Based Roles

As strategic and operating objectives shift to respond to changes in the organizational environment, those objectives should be deployed to the team level and translated into the tasks the team should accomplish to support strategic and operating objectives (figure 6-2). Most organizations have a process to make this translation. If not, then a deployment process should be developed. Without a deployment process, the work team will accomplish tasks that do not necessarily support the organization's strategy and operations.

Formulating Strengths-Based Roles

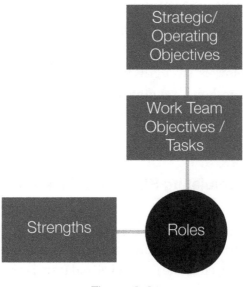

Figure 6-2

Once strengths have been identified, they are matched with the tasks at hand to define roles.

Identifying Strengths

Strengths, areas in which the employee is highly competent, are virtually always on a developmental continuum with room to improve. In this sense, strengths are really potentialities, always open to further refinement and perfection. Strengths fall into numerous categories, such as fundamental values and beliefs, functional expertise, personality characteristics, and general knowledge, skill, and practice areas. The latter include planning, communicating, interpersonal skills, strategic thinking, critical thinking, problem-solving, decision-making, and the robustness of the employee's network.

While strengths are a component of every performance evaluation, most employees would be hard-pressed to state what their supervisor believes their strengths to be. Furthermore, even if clarity about strengths does exist, it is likely that most employees are unable to state how their strengths relate to job assignments.

Strengths must become a near-obsession for the organization and should be a major part of the discussion on employee evaluations and assignments. Strengths should be discussed frequently not only between the employee and supervisor but also between the employee and her peers. Every employee and her supervisor must have clarity about the employee's strengths and use those strengths for making job assignments and as a basis for development. Imagine that every day you go to work, your strengths and those of all team members are an intensive topic of daily conversation. You discuss where the external environment is driving the organization and what new strengths will be needed, what new strengths you should develop and which existing strengths to deepen, whether you have untapped strengths that the organization could profit from, and whether your strengths are well understood and effectively applied by your leaders.

One methodology that is often used to assess strengths as well as weaknesses is the 360-degree assessment, which utilizes performance feedback from an individual's manager(s), peers, and, where that person is a manager of people, his direct reports. A 360-degree assessment can be as simple as requesting feedback from those people who have observed the individual in action, or it can be a formal set of questions with opportunities for open-ended responses submitted by observers at every level.

Two useful, strengths-focused, generic 360-degree assessment instruments are the CliftonStrengths from Gallup and the Echospan 360 assessment. The CliftonStrengths identifies an employee's strengths on thirty-four different personality characteristics, including responsibility, self-assurance, harmony, discipline, and consistency. Echospan offers a set of competencies from which the assessment administrator can draw, including accountability, analytical thinking, change leadership, collaboration, conflict management, integrity, and recruiting. Echospan can be customized for specific purposes, and organizations may add their own competencies. Organizations that have the resources should consider creating their own strengths assessment.

A strengths-based system of management rests on two pivotal pillars: adaptability and versatility.

Adaptability

Adaptability is *an employee's ability to anticipate and adjust to changes in the work environment, strategy and goals, and task requirements.* Adaptability is largely about anticipating changes, a willingness to adjust to those changes, and the skill to make adjustments. A synthesis of the literature on employees' adaptive characteristics identified six categories: personality, future orientation, positivity, learning orientation, interpersonal skills, and cultural characteristics (table 6-2).[162]

Characteristics of Adaptive Employees	
Personality	◆ Conscientiousness (compliance with organizational and group norms and rules) ◆ Extraversion (desire to interact with others) ◆ General cognitive ability (ability to learn and process information) ◆ Self-efficacy (an individual's confidence in their ability to execute actions to achieve defined outcomes)

Characteristics of Adaptive Employees

Future Orientation	◆ Proactive (maintaining performance by self-adjusting to changes in work) ◆ Anticipatory (anticipating and recognizing changes in the external environment and how those will impact work)
Positivity	◆ Resilient (ability to recover from negative emotions or situations) ◆ Optimistic
Learning Orientation	◆ Seeking out feedback and learning opportunities ◆ Relentless pursuit of learning for self-improvement ◆ An orientation to experimentation and ability to learn from failures ◆ Openness to novel experiences and motivation to adapt ◆ Experience adapting to novel situations ◆ Curiosity ◆ Ability to disengage from old work requirements and adapt to the demands of a new set of tasks
Interpersonal Skills	◆ Ability to adapt to new relationships ◆ Capability to build task and interpersonal networks ◆ Team player (willingness to sacrifice for the team and is an effective collaborator) ◆ Emotional control
Cultural	◆ Ability to speak the language ◆ Understanding of laws and politics ◆ Knowledge of the new culture and adjustment to it

Table 6-2

Creating an environment of autonomy, mutual support, innovation, and a clear change vision and providing the necessary resources facilitate employee adaptation.

A truly inclusive and empowering approach to adaptability is job crafting. Job crafting occurs when employees reframe and reimagine how their jobs are designed to make their jobs more personally meaningful. Components of job crafting that are vital for adaptation are the crafting of tasks (what they do) and relationships (with whom the employee works to accomplish tasks). Role adaptation is a more constrained use of job crafting than is usual in that the focus is on selecting and agreeing upon the tasks the employee will undertake rather than crafting the tasks themselves. Nevertheless, inclusive organizations should be open to employees designing their own slate of tasks, especially through team collaboration. A useful tool is the Job Crafting™ Exercise, available from the Center for Positive Organizations at the Ross School of Business of the University of Michigan.[163]

Versatility

Versatility is *the possession and application of a wide repertoire of relevant competencies and the commitment by the employee and the organization to continuously deepen and expand them*. Relevant competencies are knowledge, skills, and behaviors that address the new and altered tasks that organizational changes have wrought. It is of no value to simply possess a competency if it goes unapplied. Research on versatility has concentrated on leadership versatility. The focus here is on the versatility of the entire workforce.

Versatility is usually a team sport, where the team has objectives and employees undertake tasks to fulfill those objectives. Team members are either assigned tasks by the team leader, or, more inclusively, the team leader facilitates a collaborative process to identify and sometimes craft the range of tasks and allocate those tasks among team members according to their strengths and passions. The latter approach models inclusion.

Role-driven organizations seek I-shaped employees who have great depth in the core role. Versatile organizations seek

T-shaped employees who have depth in the prescribed role but also have a wide repertoire of other relevant competencies or the capability and motivation to acquire new competencies or deepen existing ones.

To foster versatility, the T-shaped employee, leaders, and the organization must embrace a developmental mindset. A developmental mindset includes anticipating changes to the internal and external environments and how these changes will affect strategy and operations; identifying new tasks and changes to old tasks that will arise from strategic and operational changes; understanding the new competencies required to successfully achieve emerging tasks; and the relentless acquisition of new competencies and the deepening of still-relevant existing competencies through such modalities as cross-training, coaching, formal training and development, and experience. Leaders should assign tasks to employees or facilitate teams to allocate tasks to employees, and provide enthusiasm, budget, time, and opportunity for employees to gain new and deepened competencies. The organization must create policies and programs and provide resources to encourage competency acquisition.

In addition to being adaptive, T-shaped, and having a developmental mindset, versatile employees have several other important characteristics (table 6-3).

Additional Characteristics of Versatile Employees	
Strategic Perspective	◆ Able to see how the puzzle pieces of tasks fit together to achieve an objective
	◆ Sees the forest first, but also the trees
	◆ Oriented to the relationship between present activities and future trends

Collaborative	◆ Willing to sacrifice personal passion for the good of the team ◆ Works effectively across silos ◆ Willing to openly contribute information and knowledge they possess ◆ Has wide network and makes connections for self and others ◆ Relationship oriented
Open Minded	◆ Asks conversation-advancing, open-ended questions ◆ Empathic ◆ Listens attentively and deeply
Knowledge Creator	◆ Experiments with different pathways to achieve tasks ◆ Creative problem solver ◆ Documents and communicates learnings to other team members

Table 6-3

No matter the strengths of employees and their adaptability and versatility in the face of continuous change, those capabilities are useless if not utilized. The next section, "Employee Participation," demonstrates how leaders can mobilize employee strengths across and up and down the organization.

EMPLOYEE PARTICIPATION

Employee participation is ordinarily thought to be a vertical process of a manager allowing or encouraging direct reports to participate in decision-making. However, participation is a much broader concept. It encompasses permanent teams of direct reports and temporary teams brought together solely to address a particular decision to be made or problem to be solved. Participation may also encompass those who have a stake in the decision but do not report to a single manager. Participation, especially with teams, can be as much side to side, often called collaboration, as it is up and down.

Employee participation in decision-making has a multitude of meanings. Participation may mean that employees are either fully empowered to make decisions or empowered only to make input into decisions. It can be formal or informal; a short-term team activity, such as a quality circle, or the way decisions are made in all situations; or decisions ranging from an employee's own work to strategic, organization-wide decisions.

The degree and nature of participation is contingent upon the decision to be made. Participation in decision-making is not giving up power and control but fitting the amount of delegated power and control to the decision. Not all decisions warrant a high level of employee participation. A higher level of participation is justified when decisions are highly relevant to employees' lives, when employees have unique expertise that informs decision-making, when organizational commitment to the decision being made is vital for successful implementation, and when innovative outcomes are sought. The stronger these justifications, the greater the level of participation in decision-making should be.

The Decision-Making Hierarchy

The decision-making hierarchy (figure 6-3) breaks decision-making into four levels of involvement: decide and inform, collect input and decide, achieve a consensus, and delegate.

Decide and Inform

At this lowest level of participation, the leader seeks no input from stakeholders and simply makes a decision and informs those who need to know about the decision. Decide and inform is relevant in situations where the leader has all the relevant information and expertise required to make the decision and where commitment is not required for implementation to succeed or in emergency or combat-like situations.

Collect Input and Decide

At this level, the leader sets the desired outcomes and process or agenda, assembles the stakeholder group (usually in a meeting format), and facilitates a discussion of the decision to be made. At minimum, leaders should open the meeting by seeking the group's agreement on the outcomes sought and on the agenda for reaching those outcomes.

Input may be collected one-on-one or in a group setting. Group settings have a higher level of participation since the group wields more influence collectively than individuals do alone.

Collect input and decide makes sense in situations where stakeholders have vital information and expertise but their involvement in implementation is minimal, or where the leader wields considerable power. A presidential cabinet meeting is an example of collect input and decide.

Achieve a Consensus

This level of decision-making is reserved for situations in which the group has the information and expertise and where high commitment to the outcomes is required for implementation to be successful. Consensus is not everyone agreeing on the decision but everyone agreeing to support the decision made. When their voices have been heard and considered, group members are more inclined to support the decision made even if they disagree with it. In consensual and delegated decisions, the leader has the right to overrule the decision if she can't accept it, a right that should be used sparingly and cautiously.

Delegate

Delegating makes sense in situations where the leader has little to add, little or no relevant expertise, or does not have the time to be involved. The leader also has the right of refusal in delegated decisions. An example of delegate might be solving an engineering problem about which the leader knows little. The leader determines the decision to be made and makes her desired outcomes and expectations explicit before delegating.

Determining the level of decision-making is the province of the leader. The leader should always announce the level of decision-making at the outset of the participation process. Employees rarely, if ever, argue with the level of decision-making.

Decision-Making Hierarchy

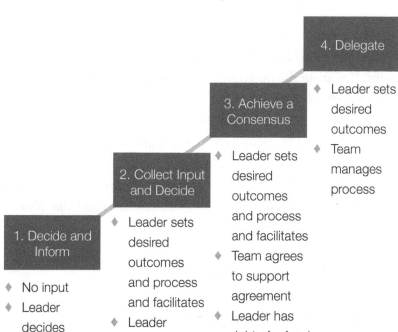

Figure 6-3

Participation in decision-making has multiple benefits. Employee perception of control of their own work environment has important positive effects, including high levels of job satisfaction, employee commitment, performance, and motivation, and reduction in physical symptoms, emotional distress, role stress, absenteeism, intent to leave, and actual turnover.[164]

The Participative Mindset

The greatest challenge in expanding the use of participation is that most managers, even if they know when to use participation, have little idea of how to be participative and, worse, poor self-judgment of their participation skills. Managers often confuse participation with asking questions until the subject of questioning comes up with the answer that the inquirer already had in mind—more an interrogation than positive inquiry into the subject's opinions, ideas, or point of view. For positive inquiry to occur, leaders must develop a participative mindset that reframes the pathway to action, assumes a beginner's mind, ensures that understanding precedes persuasion, demonstrates vulnerability, and views participation as strategic.

Reframe the Pathway to Action

Reframing the pathway to action is extremely challenging for leaders. Moving an individual employee or group to action is the core of the leader's job. How can a leader embrace participation when it seems to slow action? The answer is that it doesn't slow anything down. While participation often extends the time to make a decision, it also increases support for the decision by those whose voices have been genuinely heard and considered, shortening the total time to action when decision-making *and* implementation are considered together. The pathway to action can best be thought of by the mantra "Go slow to go fast."[165] As a general rule of thumb, decision-making, especially about diversity matters, should err on the side of participation.

Assume a Beginner's Mind

To embrace a participative mindset requires leaders to genuinely be interested in, or even fascinated by, others' ideas, opinions, and points of view, to be in a genuine state of wonderment about what employees are thinking. Brugh Joy called this state the beginner's mind: "that unencumbered, open, allowing, alert, receptive state of consciousness that experiences any and all things with the freshness usually directed only to the totally new."[166]

Ensure Understanding Precedes Persuasion

Participation results from acts of inquiry. The wonderment of a beginner's mind leads to questions to uncover the object of wonderment, just as a child, full of wonder upon becoming conscious of the stars above, unleashes an array of questions. The danger in questioning is that it can turn into a courtroom drama where the leader is the prosecutor and the stakeholder is the defendant. When inquiry becomes fraught with angst and emotion, it tends to shut off the richness of the response that comes when an employee is treated as wise and knowledgeable. What shuts off this richness is when the leader inquires to persuade the employee to accept or support his interests. Leaders can overcome this loss by always ensuring that inquiry for understanding precedes persuasion, that questions are for the pure purpose of understanding and learning. Persuasion comes later.

Demonstrate Vulnerability

Participative leadership requires rethinking power and control. Leaders are ultimately judged on the success of a decision, less on whether they came up with the decision or idea themselves. To be genuinely open to the ideas, beliefs, and opinions of others, leaders should allow themselves to be vulnerable—to step away from power and control, to ask open-ended questions to which they don't know or might not like the answers, to be open to feedback, to expose their weaknesses, and to risk uncertainty and failure. To be vulnerable is not to be "weak or submissive";[167] on the contrary, to be vulnerable is to be courageous.

Vulnerability is built on a foundation of authenticity, transparency, self-confidence, and courage. Authenticity, as discussed above, is the willingness to be one's true self. Transparency is to operate at the furthest reasonable limits of personal openness without being hurtful and insensitive. Self-confidence is positive esteem toward oneself, not hiding fears of inadequacy behind bluster and self-puffery. It is what social work professor Brené Brown calls a "profound sense of inner worthiness."[168] Courage is the willingness to risk failure in standing up for what is right. As Nelson Mandela put it, "I learned that courage was not the absence of fear, but the triumph over it. The brave man is not he who does not feel afraid, but he who conquers that fear."

Vulnerability invites group members into the conversation. It promotes "social connection—a sense of 'oneness' between staff and manager,"[169] advances collaboration and connections among colleagues, engenders trust and respect, and facilitates creativity.

View Participation as Strategic

Participation is not a tactic. Participation embodies a strategic perspective. To be participative is to assess and understand the current state, to visualize the future state, and to articulate the process of getting from the current to the future state. It is to identify stakeholders, understand their interests, and include them in the decision-making process in a way that fulfills those interests. It is to step into a forest of ambiguity, assumptions, paradox, and complexity and find a passage to resolution.

To address the strategic nature of participatory decision-making requires a process and methods to make that process work. The next section offers a process for leaders to follow to create a participatory workplace and additional templates and tools to make it work.

Leading Participation

The medium of participation is the meeting. The meeting can be one-on-one, a small group, or a large gathering; a formal meeting or a chance hallway meeting; or a single meeting or a series of linked meetings. Effective participation processes follow five fundamental phases: understand, generate, focus, decide, and act, as depicted in figure 6-4.

Understand

Participants in the conversation must understand the purpose of the dialogue and what problem is being solved or decision made. One or more desired outcomes—precisely what the participation process will achieve—should be stated. Usually, the desired outcomes are the leader's prerogative, although at the beginning of the participation process, she should seek the agreement of the individual or group as to the outcomes.

In many situations, data will need to be gathered and an analysis undertaken to better frame the problem or decision. Ideally, this data should be gathered by the group members. Sometimes, the assessment will require substantial expertise, such as survey design, experimental design or advanced statistics, or an objective perspective, in which case an outside resource is required. The group should agree on the outside resource before the resource is engaged.

In the understand phase, a goal should be set for the number of objectives to be established or actions to be taken. For example, if the desired outcome is to establish a diversity strategy for an organizational unit, then a goal of two or three actions might be appropriate. Setting a maximum is vital, since too many objectives or actions can abuse available resources and undermine focus and attention. Generally, it is difficult to manage more than five actions or objectives at any one time. If it is necessary to go beyond five, then they should be split between timeframes (e.g., three actions should be achieved in the first six months and three actions in the succeeding nine months). A core responsibility of the leader in the understand phase is to align the desired outcomes of the decision-making process with the strategic objectives of the organization.

The Participation Process

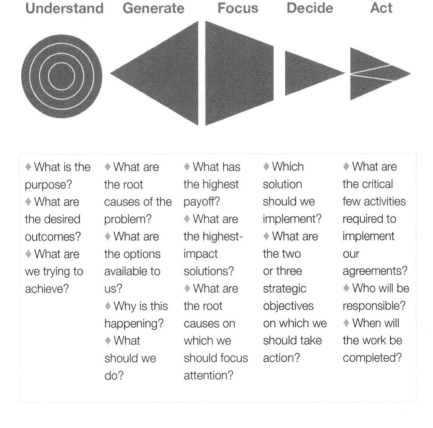

Understand	Generate	Focus	Decide	Act
♦ What is the purpose? ♦ What are the desired outcomes? ♦ What are we trying to achieve?	♦ What are the root causes of the problem? ♦ What are the options available to us? ♦ Why is this happening? ♦ What should we do?	♦ What has the highest payoff? ♦ What are the highest-impact solutions? ♦ What are the root causes on which we should focus attention?	♦ Which solution should we implement? ♦ What are the two or three strategic objectives on which we should take action?	♦ What are the critical few activities required to implement our agreements? ♦ Who will be responsible? ♦ When will the work be completed?

Figure 6-4

Generate

Generate is the phase where the rubber meets the road. It provides the opportunity for everyone to participate in the most robust way possible. The leader's responsibility is to ensure the broadest participation, to make sure every voice with a contribution is heard and that each idea is documented. In a group situation, the leader should systematically move around the group, soliciting ideas and input, until generative capacity has been exhausted. Or the leader can use "popcorn style," which is to let anyone at any time throw out an idea as long as they don't step on the input of other group members. The advantage of a systematic approach is that it ensures everyone participates. The advantage of popcorn style is that it allows group members to build more immediately on the ideas of others.

During the input process, there should be no evaluations or critiques of the ideas presented. That comes in the decide phase. Generation is best when it is nonjudgmental, encouraging the widest range of input from the greatest number of people.

The leader should appoint an individual who is not a group member to document ideas. In one-on-one dialogue, the leader should ordinarily do the documentation. For group idea generation, documentation works best on a flip chart if all participants are together, or with collaborative decision-making software or a simple digital whiteboard if participation is virtual. This allows everyone to observe a record of ideas as they are presented and the person who presented an idea to determine whether what is recorded is faithful to the idea she presented.

Focus

Focus reduces the bulk of ideas from the generate phase to a smaller number. The exact number is dependent on how much consensus already exists among decision makers. A technique for focusing is N over three (N/3). In N/3, the total number of ideas generated in the generate phase is divided by three. The result is the number of votes each member of the decision-making group is given. The leader should label each idea presented with a capital letter. The leader then takes the group through every idea recorded, asking, "Who votes for 'A,' who votes for 'B,'" etc. They can place no more than one vote at a time on any one idea. So, if N/3 equals seven, then each individual may place up to seven votes on seven different ideas. The reason for lettering rather than numbering is to prevent confusion between the label and the number of votes each idea receives. It is often surprising in N/3 to see just how much consensus already existed.

N/3 is not the end of decision-making. It simply provides a feel for the level of consensus among group members and focuses the conversation on those actions on which there is high consensus.

Decide

In the decide phase, group members debate and ultimately determine which ideas to take action on. As a first step, group members should determine criteria for selecting the options or ideas on which action will be taken.

Many techniques exist. The simplest method of deciding is to achieve consensus on the ideas to act on. The number of ideas that will make the action list is the number designated in the desired outcomes. The decide phase should not be oversimplified by selecting the ideas that received the highest votes in the focus phase. The number of votes is a good place to start the conversation, not to end it. The facilitator or leader should state, for example, something like "Idea 'D' received the most votes. Should that be an idea on which we take action?" Then, the facilitator or leader lets dialogue and consensus take over. Once it has been determined whether or not idea D is on the action list, the facilitator or leader guides the group to idea A, which received the second most votes. And so forth until the minimum number of actions designated by the desired outcomes has been achieved.

Finally, the facilitator or leader should ask, "Are there any other ideas that didn't make the action list that should be on it or that are on it and shouldn't be there?" This is the "Speak now or forever hold your peace" statement. It opens the door to anyone with strong feelings to be heard one last time, ensuring that not only their ideas and arguments have been heard but also the strength of their belief in an idea. It is useful to quickly mention to the group the teleplay, and later theatrical production and movie, *Twelve Angry Men*, the story of a murder trial in which one juror, played by Henry Fonda, changes the minds of eleven jurors who are ready to convict the defendant and which demonstrates how vital it is to ensure that a lone, strongly held voice is heard. Ask, "Is there a Henry Fonda here?" It is surprising how often the "Henry Fonda" in the group successfully argues to have their idea, which didn't receive many votes, added to the action list.

A more formal and rigorous method of deciding, although it overlaps with the N/3 process, is the decision matrix. In the decision matrix process participants establish decision criteria, assign relative weights to each criterion, consensually assign ratings to each criterion for one idea or objective at a time on a scale of one to five (or another scale), multiply each rating by the criterion weight and record in the matrix, and sum the weighted ratings for each idea or objective. The top-scoring ideas or objectives are selected for action. The internet contains many examples of decision matrices.

Act

The act phase is intended to establish who has lead responsibility and accountability for the selected action, idea, or objective, to identify what tasks need be completed to achieve the action, to identify who has responsibility, and to set milestones for the accomplishment of each task. An action plan should be established for each action or objective (table 6-4).

Action Plan

Action/Objective:
Lead:
Completion Date:

Task	Task Lead	Others with Responsibility	Milestone or Completion Date

Table 6-4

The assignment of the lead and the completion date for each action is the responsibility of the leader. The assignment of task leads, team members, task responsibilities, and task completion dates is the responsibility of the designated lead. The leadership team should identify the tasks required to achieve effective action with affirmation from action and task leads. Often, leaders will want the prerogative of making action leadership assignments after the meeting. In those cases, the action assignments and milestones will have to wait a day or two. Of course, leaders should monitor task completion and quality and hold those responsible accountable.

INCLUSIVE LEADERSHIP

Inclusive leadership is composed of eleven competency areas: empowerment, network facilitation, integrity, respect, coaching, career development, succession planning, transparency, safety and security, work–life integration, and intercultural capability. The competency areas are neither collectively exhaustive nor mutually exclusive. They were selected from the extensive research on high-performance organizations regarding the strength of the relationship between the competency and high performance and how closely the competency is linked to leveraging human differences in organizations.

Not all the competencies are relevant in every organization. To determine relevance, organizations should consider the business strategy, national and organizational cultures, diversity climate, industry and competitive characteristics, and labor force characteristics.

Applying the competencies is, in the final analysis, about individuation—the process of considering the individual's background, characteristics, and capabilities and shaping and applying the competencies to enable employees to perform at their highest potential.

Empowerment

Empowerment is *leadership behavior that is characterized by "delegating authority to employees, promoting their self-directed and autonomous decision-making, coaching, information sharing, and asking for input."*[170] Empowerment can be observed from two perspectives: the employees' perceptions of leadership behaviors—empowering leadership—and employees' perceptions of their own behavior—psychological empowerment. The focus here is on empowering leadership, although it is important to consider psychological empowerment since it is dependent on leadership behaviors and mediates between empowering leadership and its benefits. More formally, "Empowering leadership is the process of influencing subordinates through power sharing, motivation support, and development support with intent to promote the . . . self-reliance, motivation, and capability to work autonomously within the boundaries of overall organizational goals and strategies."[171]

Within the three categories of power sharing, motivation support, and development support are eight specific empowering behaviors (table 6-5).[172]

Empowering Behaviors		
Power Sharing	**Delegate**	Not just participation in decision-making but delegation of authority. Delegation should not be abandonment.
	Coordinate and Inform	Coordinate task objectives so employee and manager have the same objectives and information about overall goals and the work itself.

Empowering Behaviors		
Motivation Support	**Encourage Initiative**	Encourage employees to be proactive in initiating and completing work and going above and beyond what is requested.
	Encourage Goal Focus	Encourage employees to establish personally empowering goals that align with organizational goals and their personal values and beliefs and actively work to achieve those goals.
	Support Efficacy	Efficacy is the ability to produce an impact. Leaders who support efficacy listen to employees, recognize their strengths and weaknesses, and encourage them to use their strengths.
	Inspire	Inspiring leaders create a sense of optimism.
Development Support	**Model**	Leaders serve as role models by repeatedly and clearly demonstrating effective leadership competency.
	Guide	Leaders help employees to move from dependence to independence by teaching and providing coaching, encouragement, and support.

Table 6-5

In instituting empowerment, attention should be given to the predominant management style within the organization. If the style is more command and control oriented, an estimated 50 percent of managers will be incapable of making the transition to an empowered model of leadership.

Culture also has an impact on the effectiveness of empowerment, although researchers disagree on the direction of that impact. Individual receptivity to empowerment depends on whether employees are from high- or low-power-distance cultures.[173]

High-power-distance cultures are characterized by hierarchy and centralization and respect for status and privilege, while low-power-distance cultures emphasize equality and decentralization and frown upon privilege and status symbols. Employees from high-power-distance cultures tend to have a lower receptivity to empowerment than those from low-power-distance cultures.[174]

Examples of high-power-distance cultures are the Russian Federation, Peoples' Republic of China, and the Arab countries. Those with lower power distance are the US, Netherlands, Australia, and Britain. Denmark has the lowest power distance. Power distance is relevant not only to country or regional cultures but to organizational cultures as well.

Another study of the effects of empowering leadership on employee task performance showed that empowerment had greater impact on the performance of routine tasks in Eastern as opposed to Western cultures. The disparate findings suggest that while employees in Western cultures are more receptive to empowerment, in Eastern cultures empowerment has a greater effect on actual task performance.[175] Nevertheless, empowerment has a positive effect on task performance regardless of culture and especially strong impacts on creativity and mutual support behaviors.[176] Other benefits of empowerment include job satisfaction, employee engagement, work effort, improved team performance, intention to stay, and reduced employee strain.[177]

An array of validated measures is available for assessing empowering leadership. The eighteen-item Empowering Leadership Scale[178] developed by Stein Amundsen and Øyvind Martinsen covers power sharing, motivation support, and development support. The seventeen-item Leader Empowering Behavior Questionnaire (LEBQ)[179] measures delegation of authority, accountability, self-directed decision-making, information sharing, skill development, and coaching for innovative performance. The thirty-eight-item Empowering

Leadership Questionnaire (ELQ) measures leading by example, participative decision-making, coaching, informing, and showing concern/interacting with the team.[180]

Network Facilitation

Organizations contain formal and informal networks for accomplishing work. Formal networks follow the chain of command, are governed by rules and policies formulated by management, and have delineated roles. They may be inside the organization or outside—for example, in procurement and sales. At the same time, informal networks arise out of the day-to-day interactions among employees. They are self-directed and governed by norms. Informal roles emerge out of the give-and-take of network interactions. Informal networks connect people to others who can provide work, career, and personal resources. Leaders who are network facilitators encourage these connections to happen.

Informal networks are the essence of inclusion and a major pathway to being hired, successfully completing work tasks, receiving increased compensation, and advancing in organizations. The currency of networks is social capital: ties to those with status and power who provide information, resources, and opportunities.[181] However, research demonstrates "that women and minorities have limited access to or are excluded from organizational networks."[182] The result is that not only are they excluded from vital relationships, but they are also less inclined to network.

The more diverse an individual's network, the more advantageous.[183] Herminia Ibarra points out, "People whose network contacts extend beyond their required workflow interactions, immediate work groups, or immediate work units tend to be perceived as more powerful."[184] Women and people of color, especially African American women, have less diversity in their networks.[185]

Leaders who are network facilitators provide access to their own networks and encourage and support their direct reports to engage in and build three interlocking networks: task, career, and psychosocial.

Task Networks

Task networks are those that support employees in completing their work at a high level. They encompass the information, expertise, political support, professional advice, and access required to effectively perform work. The primary network for accomplishing tasks is the value chain, the connections required to provide an output to an internal or external customer and the supply and support systems required to sustain those tasks. Supply systems provide the products and services to which an employee will add value. For example, suppose the employee makes deliveries. Her suppliers include those who pick the product and manage logistics. Or suppose the employee is a social worker. His suppliers include those who assign cases and manage intake. Support systems include human resources, IT, and other support functions and departments. Every employee plays a role in one or more value chains. The value chain comprises, at minimum, the connections to immediate suppliers and customers and often connections to numerous stakeholders along the course of the chain. Usually, an employee's supervisor or a manager further up the chain of command helps employees make connections with key stakeholders along their value chain. Individual employees ultimately have the responsibility for building and maintaining their value chain network relationships.

Career Networks

Career networks are connections with those who can advance an individual's career. They can be formal or informal mentors who advise an employee over a period of time on task and career topics; sponsors who actively seek to advance an individual's career; an advisory board that the employee establishes herself; or other career vehicle. Career networks exchange information, expertise, and advice and provide advocacy and access.

Psychosocial Networks

Psychosocial networks are those that provide support in navigating the twists and turns of everyday organizational life. Psychosocial networks are particularly important for underrepresented employees, whose race, ethnicity, gender identity, ableness, sexual orientation, or other characteristics may provide particular challenges in adjusting to and navigating organizational life. For example, in cross-gender mentoring, "misunderstandings and tensions are commonplace, causing the relationship to be less stable."[186]

Furthermore, underrepresented employees have a smaller pool of people, especially more senior leaders, with similar life experiences from whom to draw support. Because psychosocial support is usually best provided by people with a common identity, underrepresented people require a separate psychosocial network, while White men usually receive psychosocial support from their task and career networks.

In general, underrepresented people may be excluded from participating in a network or deriving maximum benefits by network homophily, the birds-of-a-feather metaphor that describes how people of similar identities tend to band together. Common group identity "increases ease of communication, improves predictability of behavior and fosters relationships of trust and reciprocity."[187]

Building psychosocial networks requires contacts and contact time. Leaders should provide employees with opportunities to hang out together, which provides greater closeness than time spent working together and talking.[188]

Underrepresented employees benefit from leadership facilitation that increases their comfort with the idea of networking, expands participation in networks, and fosters connections to key network participants. Leaders should also support and encourage, if not require, employees to be proactive in five types of networking behavior: maintaining contacts, socializing, engaging in professional activities, participating in the community, and increasing internal visibility.[189]

Providing leaders with measures of the diversity, status connections, and reach of employees' networks provides motivation to leaders and employees to ensure that networks are robust. A variety of social-network-analysis software tools exist for visualizing employee, manager, and leadership networks. They visually characterize networks in terms of nodes (people) and lines (demonstrating connections and interactions). Numerous social-network-analysis tools are open source and available online. The Networking Behaviors Scale,[190] a self-report measure, provides a good overview of whether employees are taking the actions that build networks, and the eighteen-item Short Networking Behavior Scale[191] focuses on building, maintaining, and utilizing internal and external networks.

Integrity

Integrity is *the quality of having moral principles and acting consistently with them.* In diversity, moral principles are the values and beliefs expressed in the organization's diversity philosophy and the leader's personal case. If a leader hasn't completed a personal case, then she should consider her diversity values and beliefs and document them to create a personal reference. The leader should communicate those values and beliefs to those they lead.

Consistency is the core of integrity. Consistency is acting the same regardless of the situation or context, even as psychological research indicates that "situational factors are often better predictors of behavior than personal factors."[192] For example, acting consistently with the moral principle of respect for differences means demonstrating that respect in public and private contexts, no matter the identity of the person being considered.

Consistency is vital in an organization's programs and policies. Take, for example, work–life programs and policies. In a global study of six countries, both developed and emerging, over 80 percent of leaders responded that work–life programs and policies are "important" or "very important" to recruiting and retaining top talent, employee satisfaction, and employee productivity. Yet when employees avail themselves of work–life programs and policies, a quarter to a half of leaders are concerned that employees won't be accessible when needed, and they won't know whether work is getting done, others may have to pick up that work, service to customers will be negatively affected, and it will require them to put in additional time, all inconsistent with their professed beliefs.

About half of leaders in emerging countries and over a quarter in developed countries believe that those who utilize work–life programs and policies "will not advance very far" in their organizations. Only 5 percent of leaders in emerging countries and 25 percent in developed countries have no concerns about work–life programs and policies. This inconsistency sends a mixed message to employees: "We strongly believe in the business case for employee work–life integration. However, if you make use of those programs and policies, you won't be successful here."

Consistency is a choice. Making the morally consistent choice is often an act of courage, especially when in the company of compatriots acting toward or discussing people who are different. Consistency is demonstrating the same diversity values and beliefs in day-to-day management as at the country club, in the boardroom, in the conference room, or in private conversation.

To act with integrity, leaders must first communicate the organizational diversity philosophy and their personal beliefs, making them clear and understood. Then, all that is left to do is to act consistently with those values and beliefs.

Integrity can be measured in different ways. Questions may be included in the employee or diversity survey. A minimum of two questions should be asked, one about whether the person's supervisor or boss has explicit values and beliefs about diversity and the other about whether that manager acts or behaves consistently with those values. A third question might be whether the employee is inspired by their supervisor's diversity values and beliefs. Unless the individual's supervisor can be identified by the survey, then supervisors cannot receive personal feedback on how their integrity behavior is perceived by those who report to them. Nevertheless, this information can be used at an organization-wide level to assess the state of integrity and develop policies and programs to foster integrity. If the organization conducts 360-degree assessments of its leaders, then questions such as those above should be asked about the leader's integrity.

Respect

Respect emanates from leaders and peers. Respect can be granted as a right of organizational membership or it can be earned. In its simplest form, respect is simply living the golden rule, "Do unto others as you would have them do unto you." But the golden rule does not account for individual needs, so the platinum rule takes over: "Do unto others as they would want done to them." In the workplace, a good working definition of respect is *employees perceive they are respected when their work experiences and their interactions with leaders and peers communicate to them that they are worthy, included, recognized, and valued for their skills, knowledge, abilities, ideas, work efforts, and especially for their differences.*

Respect from peers and especially from leaders is vital for high performance. Being respected by those they lead is a *sine qua non* of effective leadership. As Aretha Franklin, whose rendition of Otis Redding's song "Respect" is an American anthem, so aptly described in a *60 Minutes* interview, "Everyone wants respect, everyone needs respect, from the young to the very old and in the middle; male, female, we all want respect, and we all want to be appreciated."

Receiving respect from leaders is more important than recognition, an inspiring vision, useful feedback, and learning, growth, and development opportunities.[193] When they receive respect from their leaders, employees experience, "56 percent better health and well-being, 1.72 times more trust and safety, 89 percent greater enjoyment and satisfaction with their jobs, 92 percent greater focus, and 1.26 times more meaning and significance. Those that feel respected by their leaders were also 1.1 times more likely to stay with their organizations than those that didn't."[194]

It is shocking, then, that 54 percent of employees reveal "that they don't regularly get respect from their leaders."[195] Incivility is on the rise. For example, fifty percent of research subjects in a 2011 study "said they were treated rudely at least once a week—up from a quarter in 1998."[196] Of particular concern here, "Women and people of color are more likely to experience disrespect or incivility than White [men].[197]

Disrespect or incivility is one of the most potent negative forces that leaders can possess. Uncivil behaviors include being rude and inconsiderate, using abusive language, and applying coercion. These behaviors can be as simple as a leader treating someone as they might treat a child, not noticing a coworker in a setting outside of the office, and talking over an employee in a meeting or excluding them altogether. In a study of 800 employees across seventeen industries, researchers discovered the following statistics among employees who are subject to disrespect:[198]

◊ 48 percent intentionally decreased their work effort.
◊ 47 percent intentionally decreased time at work.
◊ 38 percent intentionally decreased the quality of their work.
◊ 80 percent lost time worrying about the incident.
◊ 63 percent lost time avoiding the offender.
◊ 66 percent said that their performance declined.
◊ 78 percent said that their commitment to the organization declined.
◊ 12 percent said that they left their job because of uncivil treatment.
◊ 25 percent admitted to taking their frustration out on customers.

One study found that those behaving uncivilly are "three times as likely to be of higher status than the target" of their incivility and over two times as likely to be male than female.[199]

Respect has two sides: unconditional and achieved.[200] Unconditional respect is the respect that is accorded every member of the organization. Achieved respect is the respect accorded to an employee based on their achievements, behavior, and character.

Unconditional respect is conveyed through an organizational climate that consistently demonstrates esteem for employees, where leaders show them consideration, treat them with dignity, solicit their input and listen to it, and value their diversity and individuality.[201] Unconditional respect is largely the province of top leadership. To foster unconditional respect, leaders should be clear about the meaning of respect, ensure respect is incorporated into the diversity philosophy, be explicit in their communications about the importance of respect, serve as role models of respect, and ensure that respect is measured on employee surveys. To create a climate of unconditional respect, leaders should assume respect in all relationships where respect need not be won, only lost.

Employees earn achieved respect by *achieving, behaving,* and *being* consistent with a prototypical employee. Most organizations do not specify the prototypical employee, at least not publicly. Rather, the prototype emerges from the haze of the organizational culture, from its norms, values and beliefs, heroes, and myths. *Achieving* is assessed by whether the employee fulfills her work role, meets performance objectives, and behaves during the fulfillment of her work role in accord with the prototypical employee. *Behaving* is judged on whether the individual acts in accordance with prototypical organizational values and norms. *Being* is the degree to which the individual employee's character traits match the prototypical employee. Important character traits for earning respect include independence, persistence, giving back to others, and being a go-getter.[202]

Organizations should consider explicitly defining the prototypical employee. On the positive side, a definition is helpful in hiring decisions as well as ascertaining achieved respect. On the negative side, a definition may reinforce prejudice and stereotypes. Care should be taken to remove consideration of social identity (e.g., race, ethnicity, and gender) in any form from the conception of a prototypical employee, whether explicit or implicit including especially code words that connote a person from an underrepresented group.

Leaders should also seek feedback on whether they are behaving respectfully through 360-degree assessments and by asking for feedback from peers and the employees who report to them. Employee surveys should contain at least one item on whether employees feel respected by their supervisors. Ideally, it should contain three questions: whether employees feel respected by their peers, by their supervisors, and whether the work climate supports and encourages respect.

Coaching

Google, through its Project Oxygen, conducted a series of rigorous studies and analyses to identify what its best managers do. The number one characteristic of its best managers was being "a good coach."[203]

Coaching comes in many forms (e.g., executive coaching, life coaching, peer coaching, and managerial coaching). Coaching may be provided by an external resource, usually called executive coaching, or by an internal resource, typically an employee's supervisor or a peer. Here, coaching is defined as *a continuous process conducted by leaders with their direct reports to develop employees' knowledge and skills for the purpose of unlocking their full potential and improving organizational performance.* Effective coaching maximizes strengths and minimizes weaknesses, focuses on learning and development to improve day-to-day work performance, and is largely nondirective. Coaching is not mentoring, which tends to be career focused, although mentoring may incorporate coaching.

Coaching offers a vast array of benefits to organizations. It contributes to high levels of motivation; improves employee performance, working relationships, employee satisfaction, organizational commitment, and organizational performance; and reduces costs and intention to leave the organization.[204] Employees "experience higher levels of confidence and self-esteem, purpose, respect, goal achievement, enhanced skills, results, recognition, involvement in decision-making, and creativity."[205] Leaders who exhibit coaching behaviors are more likely to be regarded as effective managers by their bosses and are more likely to be promoted.[206]

Despite its broad value, only 27 percent of leaders usually or always coach, and 53 percent usually or always possess the necessary skills to be effective coaches.[207] Ninety-three percent of HR leaders and professionals believe that managers need more training on how to coach employees.[208] If developing leaders' coaching skills and behaviors is to be effective, a series of prerequisites must be satisfied.

Prerequisites

Capability and Motivation

The leader doing the coaching must have the capability to be an excellent coach (see "Coaching Behaviors and Skills" below) and the motivation to undertake coaching. With spans of control increasing and leadership roles expanding in the name of efficiency, learning coaching skills and having the time and motivation to apply them is often challenging.

Supportive Organizational Culture

Another prerequisite is that organizational norms must encourage and support coaching. While coaching norms are strong in some organizations, in others they are weak, nonexistent, or they may offer tacit approval for de-emphasizing coaching. Top managers have the greatest influence over norms. To influence norms, they must be aggressive toward demanding coaching and must be role models themselves.

Feedback Environment

Coaching is kindled by feedback, which itself is based on an evaluation or assessment of the employee. Coaching requires a feedback environment in which an individual's orientation to feedback and the organizational culture align to create a workplace in which feedback is a priority and is energetically practiced. In a feedback environment, "individuals continuously receive, solicit, and use formal and informal feedback to improve job performance."[209]

Characteristics of an individual who is positively oriented to feedback include "(1) liking feedback, (2) having a propensity for seeking feedback, (3) possessing an ability to process feedback mindfully [in a careful, deliberate manner], (4) being aware of others' perceptions of oneself, (5) believing in the value of feedback, and (6) feeling accountable to respond to or act on the feedback."[210]

Individuals lean toward either a mastery orientation or a performance orientation. Mastery is far more conducive to coaching. Those with a mastery orientation focus on competence, on acquiring the knowledge and skills to perform at a high level. They tend to see feedback as learning and an opportunity for improvement. Those with a performance orientation "often compare their performance to that of others."[211] When they perceive that the feedback they receive doesn't stand up well to others, they tend to regard themselves as failing.

In feedback cultures, organizations support feedback by providing "nonthreatening, behaviorally focused feedback, coaching to help interpret and use the feedback, and a strong link between performance improvement and valued outcomes."[212]

Strong Interpersonal Relationship

Coaching also occurs in the context of an interpersonal relationship between coach and coachee. Interpersonal relationships that are positive, empathic, and learning and development oriented, as opposed to teaching oriented, facilitate effective coaching.

Researchers have identified four variables that predict the quality of coaching relationships (table 6-6):[213]

Predictors of Coaching Relationship Quality	
Genuineness of the Relationship	The leader and employee have mutual respect, and the leader truly cares about the employee and is committed to the employee.
Effective Communication	The leader is a good listener, easy to talk to, and an effective communicator.
Comfort with Relationship	The employee is comfortable speaking with the leader about their job performance, feels content to discuss their concerns and troubles with the leader, and feels safe being open and honest with the leader.
Facilitating Development	The leader is strengths focused. She helps the employee identify their assets and build on them, supports the employee's development, and works to help the employee develop her full potential.

Table 6-6

Coaching Skills and Behaviors

While the prerequisites provide the catalyst for exemplary coaching, to really excel, coaches must master a series of skills and behaviors (table 6-7).

Coaching Skills and Behaviors

Goal and Expectations Setting	◆ At the outset of coaching, the coach and coachee should establish goals for the coaching process. They should start with no more than three goals. Additional goals should be held for the next round of coaching. Goals should be measurable or observable so that the coach and coachee can agree when goals have been achieved. ◆ Expectations are the requirements the coach has for the coaching process. The coach should make clear at the outset any expectations he has. Expectations should be reserved for critical issues and should stay far away from micromanagement.
Inquiry	◆ Inquiry is questioning in the service of learning and development. Effective inquiry is based on understanding the context, the situation, and the individual. The best coaching questions are open-ended, exploratory questions that empower the coachee's response. They don't have a yes or no answer. They are not aggressive, are not a source of accountability, do not put the coachee on the defensive, and signal that the coach is genuinely interested in the answer. Compelling inquiry neither presumes to know the answer to the question being asked nor comes from an advocacy position. ◆ Exceptional inquiry skills facilitate the coaching process by surfacing the data on which many of the other coaching skills rely.

Coaching Skills and Behaviors

Listening
- Listening is active, not passive. Without competent inquiry, listening is difficult. The coach should demonstrate that he is attending to the coachee through eye contact (without burning a hole in the coachee) and reflecting back what the coachee is saying.
- In coaching, listening is for understanding and insight, not for evaluating and judging what has been said or the person saying it.
- Interruptions send a message that what is being heard from the coachee is less important than what is being messaged or who is coming through the phone or the door. Great listeners spend far more time listening than talking. An aphorism that captures the value of listening is "Knowledge talks, but wisdom listens."

Reframing
- Reframing is viewing the current situation, person, or relationship from another point of view. It is useful when patterns of behavior, often repeated over and over, are not productive or when the coachee is stuck. The frame through which people view the world is based on their attitudes, beliefs, and values. Reframing can challenge unproductive attitudes, beliefs, and values, changing the meaning of the situation for the coachee.
- At the root of many situations where reframing is needed is when the coachee views himself as lacking control over the situation. The coach's role is to help shift the frame from out of control, from being the victim of the situation, to being the in-control, empowered master of the situation.

Coaching Skills and Behaviors	
Solution Focused	◆ Coaching that focuses on solutions rather than problem analysis and identification is more effective.[214]
	◆ A solution-focused approach identifies goals and constructs solutions that achieve those goals, while a problem-focused approach is concerned with discovering the root causes of an employee's work challenges. Finding the root cause can be so complex and difficult that it becomes a waste of effort.
	◆ Coaching that focuses on solutions has a number of positive effects, including increased positive feelings, decreased negative feelings, higher self-confidence, and greater orientation toward goal achievement.[215]

Table 6-7

Three valid and reliable measures capture the quality of the coaching relationship, many of the skills and behaviors of effective coaching, and the feedback environment: the twelve-item Perceived Quality of the Employee Coaching Relationship (PQECR),[216] the thirty-item Coaching Behaviors Inventory,[217] and the twenty-item Feedback Orientation Scale.[218]

Career Development

Career development seems simple and straightforward—just formulate a career development plan, update it occasionally, and implement it. While having a career development plan and keeping it updated are vital, career development is a dynamic, complex process in which bias is rampant, requiring a more nuanced solution.

The context in which career development occurs is undergoing rapid change. What was once a predictable career progression through a single or a few organizations has morphed into a series of jobs across a variety of organizations. Loyalty has declined while job changes have increased. This trend appears to be accelerating, especially among the younger generations. For the five years after leaving college, "people who graduated between 1986 and 1990 averaged about 1.6 jobs, and people who graduated between 2006 and 2010 averaged nearly 2.85 jobs."[219]

As career mobility has accelerated, the demand for career development has grown. Employers have not responded effectively. Eighty-seven percent of millennials say that career growth opportunities are very important.[220] Yet only "12% of college-educated employees feel their employers aid them in their career development."[221] Seventy percent of employees are "dissatisfied with future career opportunities,"[222] setting the stage for turnover.

For women and employees of color, the career picture is even grimmer. Women experience discrimination in compensation, promotion prospects, assignment to career-advancing tasks, the authority to do their job, and opportunities for "developmental relationships with mentors, sponsors, and peers."[223] Employees of color receive less favorable performance evaluations than Whites, especially when their supervisors are White, "restricted advancement opportunities," and are too often dissatisfied and frustrated with their own careers. Employees who experience "restricted opportunities ultimately lower their aspirations and commitment and engage in behaviors that reinforce negative opinions about their potential contributions to an organization,"[224] creating a self-fulfilling prophecy that limits their careers.

To address these challenges, organizations must find their way through a thicket of ideas, solutions, and challenges. While the business case and the evidence about what works are underdeveloped, in a seeming paradox, the practice of career development is replete with ideas and solutions. Ideas such as career anchors and the protean career are giving way to careers as experiences and boundarylessness. Solutions range from networking, coaching, mentoring, sponsorship, and succession planning to career self-management and mass career customization.

The responsibilities for career development reside at three levels: individual employee, supervisor, and organization. Although employees often look to their supervisors and organizations for career development, the ultimate responsibility resides with employees themselves. The role of the supervisor is to support and guide employees to reach their full potential, while organizations' primary responsibility is to support employees and supervisors in their roles and ensure a pipeline of future leaders.

Individual Role

Long careers with a single organization are declining, in many cases precipitously. The days of a thirty-to-forty-year career on a factory floor or entering as a management trainee and working toward the executive suite are largely gone. Given this stark reality, employees must take charge of their own careers. For those underrepresented employees who are subject to discrimination, taking charge is even more imperative.

While every employee should have a career development strategy and keep it updated, of even more vital importance is managing their network connections. In the career development literature, network connections are called the developmental network,[225] which is defined as "the set of people a protégé [person who benefits from the network] names as taking an interest in and action to advance the protégé's career by providing developmental assistance."[226] Developmental networks incorporate people who provide counsel and guidance to the employee in accomplishing work tasks, provide psychosocial (personal) support, and support career advancement. The measures of the quality of a developmental network consider the diversity of the network and the strength of the developmental relationships within the network.[227] Although research on the relationship between networking and career advancement is sparse, in general, networking has been shown to be positively related to total compensation, promotions, and perceived career success.[228]

The Boston University Medical Center has developed a useful resource, "Building Your Developmental Network," for helping employees define, analyze, and advance their networks.[229]

In addition to developing their own career development strategy and managing their developmental networks, employees should take leadership in advancing their own role (see job crafting above). If the role an individual is playing does not fit their interests and assets, then they should consider proposing a role that is more consistent with their interests and assets. In making the case for a role change, employees should consider how their current roles fit the evolving business environment and the organization's strategy, explore emerging roles in their industry that relate to the work they do and better fit them, document their assets and specify their interests, and work with their supervisor to create a proposal for a new role. While many leaders might look askance at the idea of employees pushing their own formulations of roles, the alternative is likely to be turnover.

Supervisor Role

Leaders in supervisory roles are caught in a career development conundrum. On the one hand, employees, especially millennial employees, demand support for career development, and that support pays off for the organization. On the other, supervisors lack clarity about their career development role and often have limited tools and resources to support employees' career development and limited leverage over the careers of those who report to them. What role should supervisors play in developing the careers of employees who report to them?

Supervisors do have a developmental role. While career development should be provided to all employees, organizations should place a special emphasis on the career development of underrepresented employees. In guiding career development, as in all their managerial activities, managers should be aware of their stereotypes, especially stereotypes about the leadership potential of diverse employees. In general, supervisors should undertake the following:

◇ Welcome employees into the organization, connect them with colleagues and other managers who can provide psychosocial support, and help them perform work and advance their careers.
◇ Make employees aware of key organizational norms and politics.
◇ Provide support, including input and feedback, for employees' career goals and plans and for formulating next steps toward reaching those goals.
◇ Allow employees to take calculated, well-vetted risks, and defend them if those risks go bad.
◇ Ease the way for employees' ideas and proposals for improving the functioning of the organization.[230]

More specifically, supervisors have four pivotal career development roles: facilitating developmental network connections, coaching, ensuring that each direct report has a realistic career development plan, and facilitating employees' career goals. The first two are inclusive leadership competencies and are covered above; the latter two are covered below.

Ensuring a Career Development Plan

A prerequisite to the other three roles is that each employee should have a career development plan. A typical career development plan follows a cycle that includes the following:

◊   An assessment of the individual's current values, interests, abilities, and strengths
◊   An assessment of relevant future career opportunities and risks presented by the internal and external business or organizational environments
◊   The establishment of career goals in line with the employee's current values, interests, abilities, and strengths, and with career opportunities and risks
◊   Development of a plan to build on strengths and abilities and, where realistic, to close the gaps between the current values, interests, and abilities and the career goals
◊   Implementation of the plan
◊   Revision by repeating the cycle, starting with a new assessment

Facilitating Career Goals

To facilitate employees' careers, supervisors should help employees obtain the developmental assignments and educational experiences they need in order to build on strengths and abilities, close gaps, and otherwise advance in their careers. The facilitator role is particularly important for underrepresented employees, who have greater difficulty accessing developmental assignments and educational experiences. Because an estimated 90 percent of learning and development occurs on the job (OTJ), supervisors must ensure that all employees have equal opportunity for OTJ developmental experiences.

Many supervisors perceive that if they provide strong support for career development, they run the risk of seeing their top performers promoted and therefore losing them. Leaders should manage this perception by creating a process of identifying and monitoring key talent that includes, but is not dependent upon, supervisors and by ensuring that supervisors who report to them are providing the developmental assignments and educational experiences necessary for advancement, especially for underrepresented employees.

Leadership Role

Leaders play four distinct roles in career development: creating a developmental culture, establishing key policies, encouraging effective career development practices, and holding managers accountable for bringing underrepresented employees into the pipeline to leadership.

Developmental Culture

If it is to be effective, career development must be supported by the organization's culture. Organizational support cannot simply be a series of organizationally required policies and practices, since "employees' perceptions of organizational policies and practices are a more proximal [central] predictor of employee behaviors than are the actual policies themselves."[231] A culture that influences perceptions requires leadership that walks the talk.

Cultures are characterized by behavioral norms that arise from the everyday interactions among employees. Though leaders do not control culture, through their own behavior they are the single greatest influence on culture and the perceptions of culture. In reinforcing the renowned developmental culture at GE, Jack Welch, its former CEO and chairman, stated that he spent 50 percent of his time on employee development, largely through GE's succession-planning process and participating in leadership development training at the GE Learning Center at Crotonville, New York. He set a powerful example that was replicated throughout GE. Besides time spent focusing on such areas as succession planning, mentoring, and learning and development, the diversity imperative for leaders is to commit quality time to seeking out and developing top prospects from underrepresented groups, modeling these behaviors for all managers and supervisors.

Because supervisors play such a pivotal role in career development (e.g., doing most of the mentoring and ensuring that career plans have been developed and implemented), they should also walk the talk. When supervisor behaviors contradict the behaviors of more senior leaders, they negate the actions of those senior leaders. Leaders from the supervisory level to the executive level should be held accountable for productive actions to support and participate in career development.

Key Policies

A vital policy for increasing career opportunities for underrepresented employees is to require that some number or percentage of the pool for all open positions, especially higher-level positions, be composed of underrepresented employees. Beware, however, that such a policy was instituted by the NFL, called the "Rooney rule," and it has had marginal success. Pressed by Dan Rooney, former owner of the NFL's Pittsburgh Steelers, the Rooney rule requires all NFL teams to include "ethnic minority" candidates in the pools for head coach and senior football operations positions. Although the number of head coaches rose to eight at the beginning of the 2018 season, it had fallen back to three at the start of the 2019–2020 season. This backward progress encouraged the NFL to improve the Rooney rule by requiring the person in charge of hiring to participate in the interviews of ethnic minority candidates, requiring more thorough documentation of the hiring process, and establishing the Career Development Advisory Panel that maintains a list of qualified ethnic minority coaches. Of the nine head coach openings for the 2022–2023 season, only two were filled by underrepresented candidates, leaving the total at five out of thirty-two franchises. This occurred in a league where around 70 percent of the players are Black.

The epitaph of the Rooney rule may be the recent discrimination lawsuit filed by Brian Flores against the NFL and several of its teams. Flores, who is African American, has accused teams of conducting bogus interviews in which they interviewed Flores for coaching jobs that had already been decided. The fundamental concept of the Rooney rule is still sound, but leaders adopting a Rooney-type rule must ensure that it is followed with integrity.

Another possible policy, also with pros and cons, is to require every employee to have a career development plan and to hold their supervisor accountable for that plan. Any policy that requires everyone to produce a document runs the risk of being rotely followed, undermining the spirit of the policy; at the same time, making individuals responsible for their own career plan and supervisors accountable for reviewing the plan with the employee and signing off on the plan largely ensures that plans will be developed and a career dialogue with the supervisor will at least occur.

All open positions should be posted internally and everyone encouraged to apply. Those who apply should, at minimum, receive acknowledgement that their application has been received and notice when the position has been filled. Some organizations provide feedback to employees who were not selected about the reasons why.

Practice: Leadership Development of High Potentials

A high-potential leadership development program is an important element of advancing the careers of underrepresented employees. As for all talent processes, the first step is to establish a debiased process for selecting high-potential employees. A target number for the proportion of the candidate pool that should be underrepresented employees can mirror the proportion of underrepresented employees in the overall labor pool from which the candidate pool is selected.

Leadership development activities aimed specifically at high-potential underrepresented people, although a violation of the principle of inclusiveness, may be necessary to provide those employees with an opportunity to address in an unrestrained manner the leadership barriers and challenges which only underrepresented employees face.

Practice: Mentoring and Sponsorship

Among the leading barriers to advancement for underrepresented people is not having a mentor or sponsor.[232] Mentoring is typically "a relationship between an older, more experienced mentor and a younger, less experienced protégé for the purpose of helping and developing the protégé's career."[233] Mentoring can also be peer-to-peer or reverse mentoring in which the more junior person mentors the more senior person (e.g., mentoring on the use of social media or on managing millennial employees). Mentors provide career guidance, advice, and support to protégés. Anyone in an individual's developmental network can be a mentor, whether inside or outside the organization.

Formal mentoring relationships are those that are initiated by the organization, while informal relationships result from the actions of sponsors and protégés. In general, informal relationships are more effective than formal relationships.[234] The executive search firm Heidrick & Struggles surveyed over 1,000 professionals in North America who have had a mentor and found that only 9 percent of mentoring relationships result from formal programs. Most mentoring relationships (60 percent) are with supervisors. People of color are less likely to have a supervisor as a mentor and more likely to find a mentor on their own. Men tend to have male mentors and women female mentors.[235]

Mentoring pays off. A study found that "employees with mentors report higher levels of job satisfaction, organizational commitment, compensation and promotions."[236] Mentoring predicts "a wide range of outcomes, including psychological health and well-being, job and career attitudes, career success, and relationship satisfaction."[237] Although mentoring pays off for all gender identities, men receive more advantage from mentoring than women, and the same is likely true when race and ethnicity are considered. For example, although men and women are equally likely to have a mentor, men who are mentored are more likely to start their first job post-MBA at a higher level and receive higher compensation and more promotions than similarly situated women.[238]

Why the difference? Catalyst, a global nonprofit dedicated to the advancement of women, found that among the reasons are that men have more highly placed mentors than women and are more likely to have same-sex role models available as mentors. A powerful difference is that men are more likely to have mentors who are sponsors. Sponsors add advocacy to the advice and guidance provided by the mentor. Sponsors are high-status individuals who advocate for protégés to obtain pay increases, promotions, and developmental assignments that are high profile, and they link protégés to their own networks.

Sponsorship works best when it is provided in response to a specific challenge, helps protégés develop knowledge and skills that support their advancement, and assists protégés to gain visibility.[239] Successful sponsorship requires high-status sponsors, active advocacy by the sponsor for the protégé, an emphasis on informal relationships, high quality of relationships, effective matching of sponsors and protégés, and a culture that encourages mentoring and sponsorship. Because most senior roles are occupied by White males and most sponsors gravitate toward protégés from their social group, underrepresented employees have difficulty finding appropriate high-status sponsors. The talent or diversity organization must step in to make sure appropriate matches are made between members of different social groups.

The talent or diversity organization should not only promote formal sponsorship initiatives but also conduct an internal campaign on the benefits of informal mentoring and sponsorship relationships, how to identify a sponsor or protégé, how to initiate a relationship, and how to establish ground rules and otherwise maintain and nurture the relationship. Where sponsorship relationships between top leaders and underrepresented employees are not forming in adequate numbers, organizations should consider holding senior leaders accountable for sponsoring underrepresented employees or, at minimum, should provide encouragement and visibility to those senior leaders who serve as cross-social group sponsors.

The quality of the relationship between sponsor and protégé is of vital importance. High-quality formal relationships are usually more effective.[240] However, the skills and behaviors that predict high-quality relationships have been inadequately researched. One small study found that the characteristics of high-quality sponsor–protégé relationships are trust, honesty, communication, and commitment.[241] In addition, researchers have hypothesized that the following skills and behaviors are essential to quality relationships: empathic listening, personal learning, self-reflection, emotional intelligence, compassion, authenticity, and vulnerability.[242]

The evidence about what makes a successful mentor–protégé match is also limited. What is known about making successful matches is that mentors and protégés with similar personality traits, including openness to experience and conscientiousness, make more successful matches. Other factors to consider in making matches include expectations; complementarity (the degree to which both mentor and protégé have knowledge, skills, guidance, etc., valued by the other person); common interests; the developmental needs of the protégé; mentor knowledge, skills, and job level; and the potential to develop a deep professional relationship.

In most formal mentoring and sponsorship initiatives, matches are made by a program administrator or advisory board. In either case, it is critical to involve the mentor and protégé in the formal matching process.

Accountability

Career development makes a substantial contribution to inclusion. Although career development is in high demand, especially by millennials, it is difficult to find the time and wherewithal for career development and the tools and skills to adequately support employees, much less to ensure that career development is carried out equitably. Besides policies, practices, and programs aimed at career development, leaders, especially those who manage people, must be held accountable for ensuring that employees actually receive career development and that what they receive is assigned with fairness.

An upward or 360-degree appraisal of leaders' and managers' support and skill for career development can easily be built into any employee survey as long as the survey identifies the respondent's supervisor. Furthermore, managers and leaders can be held accountable for such metrics as the following:

◇   The proportion of diversity candidates receiving promotions compared to the proportion of diversity candidates in the labor pool

◇   The proportion of diversity candidates receiving promotions compared to the proportion of White, non-Hispanic males receiving promotions

◇   The proportion of diverse direct reports who progress two levels beyond their current level (i.e., which managers are most effective at developing employees who progress beyond the manager himself)

◇   The proportion of candidates in every selection pool that come from underrepresented populations

◇   The proportion of employees with career development plans developed or revised within the previous twelve to twenty-four months

Managers' own personal performance plans should include goals for developing their direct reports and for ensuring their own fairness in making developmental assignments. Furthermore, metrics like those above should be included in promotion and bonus decisions.

Succession Planning

Succession planning is *the process, often highly complex, of identifying high-potential successors to executives, leaders, and other key personnel who leave or are removed from their positions, and developing their leadership skills in preparation for succession.* Complexity results from the numerous interdependencies with other talent processes and activities that must be well managed for succession planning to work effectively, including employee backgrounds and records, individual performance evaluations, human capital planning, talent management, the business strategy, selection for developmental assignments, the selection of high potentials, promotions, and executive selection. Of particular importance for expanding diversity are the following:

◊ Debiasing the succession-planning process and associated processes, particularly the performance evaluation, high-potential designation, promotion, and executive selection processes
◊ The conceptualization of succession planning
◊ The designation of high potentials
◊ Leadership development

Debiasing Succession Planning

Pivotal to the decisions that surround succession planning is the performance evaluation process, which has been shown to be biased against underrepresented people. Many organizations use the nine-box evaluation method to identify those with high potential to advance (figure 6-5). The nine-box method ranks employees on current performance and potential. One challenge of the nine-box for underrepresented people is the higher probability of discrimination in assessing current performance[243]—thus the importance of debiasing performance evaluation before tackling succession planning. The other challenge of the nine-box mode of thinking is that it is based on a projection of potential performance in the future.

Projecting the future requires an assessment of the future and an assessment of how an individual will perform in that future world, both highly speculative undertakings. It's better to substitute adaptability and versatility for potential. Adaptability and versatility can be described behaviorally and therefore be observed and evaluated in the here and now—considerably simpler to assess than potential to succeed in an unknown future. These qualities are more consistent with the need for leaders to meet changing social, political, and economic environments and, because they are more straightforward to assess, are less subject to bias.

Revised Nine-Box Method

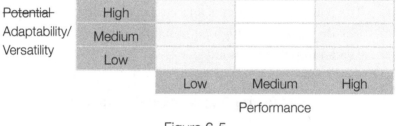

Figure 6-5

The Conceptualization of Succession Planning

Succession planning is conceived of in two ways: the identification of an "heir apparent" or the identification of a pool of successors. The identification of an heir apparent, called replacement planning, lacks the flexibility that may be required by changing conditions and may lead to "damaged morale and potential turnover of leadership talent not targeted for succession."[244] Identification of a pool of successors that includes at least one underrepresented individual is usually a superior approach.

Designation of High Potentials

Designation as high potential is ordinarily a gateway to leadership development and other development opportunities, which in turn lead to advancement to executive roles. In the US, women and people of color tend to be judged as less suitable for leadership roles.[245] An excuse I have often heard from White executives as to why women and people of color are not advancing is that they do not come to the organization with leadership skills and capabilities equivalent to White men.

The evidence indicates that men and women are equally effective leaders.[246] A key distinction in judgments of the suitability for leadership between men and women is the ascription of leadership style, the "relatively stable patterns of behavior that are manifested by leaders."[247] Men are seen to have a more autocratic and directive *agentic* style that is described as "assertive, controlling, and confident," while women are ascribed a more participative, democratic *communal* style, characterized by "a concern for the welfare of people."[248] A problem arises when the female gender role (communal) is incongruous with how the leadership role or prototypical leader is conceived (typically agentic), creating "prejudice toward female leaders and potential leaders [that] takes two forms: (1) less favorable evaluation of women's (than men's) potential for leadership because leadership ability is more stereotypic of men than women and (2) less favorable evaluation of the actual leadership behavior of women than men because agentic behavior is perceived as less desirable in women than men."[249]

Research on race and ethnicity and leadership is limited. What is known is that African Americans are less likely to be judged as fitting the leadership prototype,[250] typically based on White males, and that those judging leadership potential tend to make judgments based on their own cultural norms.[251]

Judgments of leadership potential at the intersection of race/ethnicity and gender are also troubling. The assumption is often made that the challenges for women in attaining leadership designation are the same across all races and genders. White women and women of color have different leadership styles. African American women, for example, are socialized to possess both agentic (autonomy, independence, and self-confidence) and communal characteristics (supportive, caring, and considerate) as distinct from White women, who generally display communal styles. The possession of dual styles may actually provide a competitive advantage since those with both agentic and communal characteristics are more readily able to shift styles when the situation demands.

Underrepresented people can internalize the perception that they are not good leadership material, possibly causing them to view themselves as less capable leaders. The consequence is likely to be lowered aspirations for leadership, creating a self-fulfilling prophecy.

An important consideration in the designation of high potentials is whether to inform employees of their designation. Besides the importance of transparency, other benefits accrue when employees know of their selection. Employees tend to reciprocate when their organizations invest in them, leading them to "accept increasing demands to do their job well," support strategic priorities and build competencies that support those priorities, and identify with the organization in which they work, all of which contribute to their self-esteem and self-motivation and facilitate cooperation across the work unit.[252] It is particularly important, then, for underrepresented people to be aware of their designation as high potential, since it may very well prevent them from leaving the organization and provide a motivational platform for them to demonstrate their true leadership potential.

Leadership Development

Leadership development is *a planned series of learning activities and experiences that prepare high-potential employees to be effective leaders.* Following the designation of high potentials, leadership development is focused on the development of either specific leadership competencies or more generic leadership knowledge and skills, including negotiating, influencing, networking, personal branding, interpersonal relations and communications, collaborating, intelligent risk-taking, leading high-performance teams, and strategic thinking. These activities are usually bounded by an assessment on the front end, an individual development plan, and executive coaching during and after the development process.

Leadership development that is focused on competencies begins at the organizational, operating unit, or functional unit level with the identification of the leadership behaviors, knowledge, and skills or competencies that are critical to the success of the organizational or unit strategy. Although outside experts might guide the articulation of competencies and then design and construct developmental activities, it is usually best for those activities to be facilitated by senior leaders of the organization. Top leadership facilitation offers a number of benefits for all high potentials that accrue especially to underrepresented high potentials: top leaders get to observe high potentials in action, develop relationships that foster mentoring and sponsorship, learn what's on the minds of future top leaders, and demonstrate through their words and actions their commitment to leadership development.

The development of underrepresented high-potential employees for leadership raises unique considerations: whether underrepresented employees should receive specialized leadership development or the same leadership development activities and experiences as everyone else in the organization, how a competency focus can undermine diversity advantage, and the advantages of experience-based leadership development for advancing diversity.

Specialized Leadership Development for Underrepresented High Potentials

If underrepresented people have unique leadership characteristics, either strengths or gaps, then a specialized leadership initiative should be considered. For example, top leaders may believe or have evidence that for women in their organization to be effective leaders, they must become more assertive and better negotiators and influencers (which are, incidentally, all-too-frequent tropes of discrimination against women). Since the set of issues to be addressed are unique to a particular social group, development in these areas should be conducted in a homogeneous group, in this case all women employees. Homogeneous groups offer the opportunity for more open and inclusive dialogue and psychosocial support from same-social-group peers.

For leadership issues that are the same across all social groups, heterogeneous groups should be used. Heterogeneous groups offer a "contact hypothesis" advantage, building acceptance and collaboration across social groups. In general, then, with leaders from underrepresented groups, a mixed model, with some homogeneous and some heterogeneous groups, should be employed.

The Case against Overreliance on Competencies

The foundation for leadership development is usually a set of leadership competencies. These competencies are often either abstracted from competency lists developed by consultants or professional groups or crafted from a careful examination of the competencies of the organization's most successful leaders. The danger of competencies and similar leadership requirements is that they tend to drive a mindset of one right way to lead, narrowing the variation among leadership styles. When those competencies are derived from successful leaders of the past, they may end up replicating the races, ethnicities, and genders of past leaders, in some cases precluding underrepresented people.

In open systems theory, the principle of equifinality establishes that ends can be successfully achieved through a variety of means or, in this case, a variety of leadership styles. The focus of leadership development for a diverse workforce should be on adaptability and versatility. High potentials should have a demonstrated commitment to and facility with learning; maintain an evolving grasp of changing labor pool, environmental, and market conditions and the ability to adapt to them; hold the core values and beliefs of the organization, including especially the diversity philosophy, in their embrace and act consistently with them; and possess an inclusive leadership style.

The Centrality of Experience

Globally, organizations spend billions on leadership training and development.[253] At best those development efforts receive a positive reaction from participants and lead to real learning and modest behavior change. Yet, within days, knowledge and skills become foggy and new behaviors revert to the old way of doing things. Improvements are nowhere to be found after a few weeks.

There are two significant reasons for the low return on leadership development investment:

◊   Leadership is largely contextual.[254] To be effective, leaders must understand and adjust their leadership style to the unique characteristics of the situation, the nature of the people led, and the surrounding environment.

◊ A significant element of leadership development is concerned with the acquisition and employment of soft skills, such as emotional intelligence, communications, managing performance, and leading innovation.[255]

The classroom, where much leadership development is conducted, is inadequate for addressing context and soft skills. Leadership is most effectively forged in the crucible of experience. Experience includes on-the-job training, special projects, short-term assignments, job rotation, and interactions with key managers. Research suggests that "'experience' should consist of 70 percent challenging assignments, 20 percent other people . . . and 10 percent programs"; those "other people" tend to be either "excellent or terrible bosses and senior executives who, more often than not, were neither good coaches nor mentors."[256]

The most significant learning results from challenging experiences. The factors that make "an experience challenging— the unexpected, high stakes, complexity, pressure, novelty, and so on—is what makes it a potentially powerful learning experience."[257] In addition to being challenging, learning experiences should ideally be real work that advances organizational priorities. Team experiences should follow the rules of intergroup contact. Assuming that diversity is a true organizational priority, then implementation of strategic diversity objectives and resolving critical diversity challenges can be important components of leadership development experiences.

Learning requires reflection, which is unlikely to occur if leaders don't have the opportunity to reflect on their experience. Coaching, mentoring, and classroom learning, when constructed to reflect upon a challenging experience, facilitate reflection and, thus, learning.

Unfortunately, underrepresented people are unlikely to have equal access to the kinds of leadership experiences that result in learning and advancement. For example, "women have less access to challenging work assignments and are less likely to be given assignments that are high risk to the company."[258] Even if an underrepresented person has been selected for leadership development, she may still not have access to the myriad informal opportunities that are not subject to debiasing (60 to 80 percent by some estimates).[259] Managers must be aware of whether their gatekeeping of access to informal leadership development experiences is contributing to bias.

Transparency

Transparency—the disclosure of relevant information—incorporates several dimensions, including organizational, employee, and customer information transparency. Organizational information typically includes financials, operating data, compensation, strategic and tactical decisions, and employee satisfaction, engagement, and diversity climate surveys. Employee information usually encompasses individual performance. Customer information covers everything from details about consumers to the results of market surveys and sales.

Transparency offers numerous benefits, including trust, productivity, effectiveness, innovation, accountability, and collaboration. With respect to managing across differences, in addition to increased organizational and interpersonal trust and improved collaboration across differences, transparency democratizes information and cuts down on bias in decision-making. Information is a source of power. Transparency democratizes information by creating information equity across social groups and status groups. Bias in decision-making is reduced when decision makers believe that their decisions and the processes used to make those decisions will or even may see the light of day.

Categories of information extend from general and business information to diversity-specific information. Diversity-specific information of consequence usually includes results of diversity assessments, pay, diversity strategies and tactics, company demographics, diversity spending, diversity-related lawsuits and their outcomes, and performance on diversity initiatives. Transparency has the potential to drive positive change. For example, pay transparency may encourage pay equity if it is viewed openly and equitably across the organization.

The critical issue of transparency is the degree of information disclosure, from completely open (radical transparency) to completely opaque. Today, a handful of companies are practicing radical transparency. With few exceptions, they make everything about the organization and its people transparent. Qualtrics, a leading provider of research and experience measurement software, discloses individual performance on quarterly objectives and results achieved, "performance reviews, ratings, and bonus structures," tidbits from each individual's weekly goals, individuals' "career history at Qualtrics," and "noted successes and failures."[260]

One size does not fit all. While radical transparency may work for some organizations, others may need to be more nuanced. For example, consider pay equity. Pay equity should be relatively straightforward: just be radically transparent about every employee's pay. Leaders will work hard to ensure equal pay for equal work to avoid the conflicts that arise when all employees can see each other's pay. Nuance enters when consideration is given to the finding that employees often perceive that they perform better than they actually do, potentially creating conflicts between what they think they should be paid and what others are paid. A study of 700 engineers showed that "nearly 40 percent felt they were in the top 5 percent. About 92 percent felt they were in the top quarter."[261] Furthermore, perceptions that peers are paid more "decreases effort, output, and retention."[262]

Verve, a mobile marketing technology company in the UK, has attempted to address this challenge by making pay determination considerably more objective. Verve bases pay solely on job scope and market value.[263]

How should an organization determine where to stand on a continuum of radical transparency to total opacity?

Transparency Strategy

Transparency strategy has a number of components: an assessment of the transparency situation, the objectives of information transparency, the information to be dispersed, the stakeholders or audiences to whom it is dispersed, the quality of the information, an assessment of the risks and unintended consequences of dispersing the information, the costs of assembling and dispersing the information, a decision on degree of transparency, and a plan for disseminating the information. Table 6-8 presents the questions to be asked and elements to be considered in formulating and implementing a transparency strategy. The components are not so much steps as issues to be considered in formulating a transparency strategy.

Transparency Strategy	
Transparency Assessment	◆ Where does transparency present a barrier to diversity?
	◆ How can transparency aid in achieving strategic diversity objectives?
	◆ What aspects of diversity do employees seek greater transparency about?
	◆ Where is too little or too much transparency about diversity a problem?

Transparency Strategy	
Strategic Transparency Objectives	♦ What transparency issues and concerns should we focus on? ♦ What results do we plan to achieve through transparency management?
Information Packages	♦ For each strategic transparency objective, what are the packages of information (discrete groupings of information) on which we should focus? ♦ What are the boundaries for each information package (i.e., what, if anything, should explicitly be excluded and included)?
Stakeholders	♦ To what stakeholder or stakeholder groups should the information be directed? ♦ Should every stakeholder receive the same information?
Quality of Information	♦ For a given stakeholder or stakeholder group, how can we ensure that the information is understood, accurate, and timely?
Risk Assessment	♦ What are the risks, especially the unintended consequences, of being transparent about an information package? ♦ What does the research say about transparency for this particular information package?
Cost	♦ What are the financial costs of making the information transparent, including assembling and dissemination of the information?
Transparency Strategy	♦ In summary, what are the costs and benefits of radical transparency for each transparency objective? ♦ How transparent on a scale of radical transparency to total opacity should the organization be about each information package?

Transparency Strategy	
Dissemination Plan	◆ For each stakeholder or stakeholder group, what is the message to be conveyed and the best medium to convey it? ◆ What is the action plan (activities, accountable people, and completion dates) for creating and conveying messages?

Table 6-8

The table above is meant to be exhaustive in considering every aspect of transparency and to aid in walking the fine line that is often required in transparency decisions. Not every question needs to be asked in every situation. At a bare minimum, strategic goals, information packages, stakeholders, risks, and the transparency strategy for each strategic objective should be considered.

Safety and Security

Providing a safe and secure workplace is not only vital for creating inclusion but also the law in many jurisdictions, including the US. The benefits of creating a safe and secure workplace are the avoidance of legal actions and the creation of an inclusive workplace that substantially contributes to high employee engagement. What, then, is a safe and secure workplace, what is the law and what does it require, and what is the role of leaders in responding when harassment does occur and in creating a safe and secure workplace?

A Safe and Secure Workplace

Creating a safe and secure workplace is not about protecting employees from work-related injuries and illnesses or making the workplace secure from intruders, although these are important. Here, safe and secure refers to *a workplace that is free from psychological and physical harassment*. The US Equal Employment Opportunity Commission defines harassment as

> Unwelcome conduct that is based on race, color, religion, sex (including pregnancy), national origin, age (forty or older), disability or genetic information. Harassment becomes unlawful where 1) enduring the offensive conduct becomes a condition of continued employment, or 2) the conduct is severe or pervasive enough to create a work environment that a reasonable person would consider intimidating, hostile, or abusive. Anti-discrimination laws also prohibit harassment against individuals in retaliation for filing a discrimination charge, testifying, or participating in any way in an investigation, proceeding, or lawsuit under these laws; or opposing employment practices that they reasonably believe discriminate against individuals, in violation of these laws.

> Offensive conduct may include, but is not limited to, offensive jokes, slurs, epithets or name calling, physical assaults or threats, intimidation, ridicule or mockery, insults or put-downs, offensive objects or pictures, and interference with work performance.[264]

Employers are liable for supervisory harassment that results in a negative tangible employment action, including hiring, termination, failure to promote, demotion, undesirable reassignment, or significant alteration in compensation or benefits.

The best way to address harassment is to prevent it in the first place and to address it thoroughly and expeditiously when it does occur. Harassment prevention should include the following elements:

◇   A description of applicable national, state or regional, and local laws against discrimination, harassment, and retaliation

◇   Explicit descriptions of prohibited harassment and bullying behaviors (sexual harassment should be described separately)

◇   Who the policy covers, including customers, suppliers, and relevant others

◇   How the organization handles reporting, investigation, and response

◇   To whom to report harassment and bullying (everyone should have at least two reporting channels)

◇   Protections for those who report harassment

◇   The consequences of violating the policy

A good example of a comprehensive, clear, and explicit policy is Johnson & Johnson's "Position on Providing a Safe and Harassment Free Workplace."[265] Johnson & Johnson's position calls for the prohibition of any act of bullying, the prohibition of harassment, preventing harassment from nonemployees, providing training and education, providing a safe mechanism for reporting harassment, investigating reports of harassment, the prohibition of retaliation, and upholding freedom of association.

An additional aspect of safety and security is job stability, the degree to which an employee is secure from termination or reduction in compensation and benefits. Though organizations manage for stable growth and profitability, they cannot always guarantee employment. Economic conditions change, and organizations must adapt effectively, which may mean layoffs or redundancies. In the face of such actions, the truth for employees will be how the organization handles these situations. Is the organization transparent? Is the termination process respectful? Does the organization provide good termination packages? Does the organization discriminate against underrepresented groups? Many layoffs or redundancies are conducted on a "last in, first out" basis (i.e., those hired most recently are the first to be laid off). In many situations, because of a history of discrimination and other factors, underrepresented groups are often the most recently hired.

Work–Life Integration

Work–life integration, or balance, is *the degree to which employees are able to manage their work and personal lives to an acceptable level of well-being.* Work–life integration has repeatedly been shown to have a positive relationship with employee satisfaction and engagement, reduced stress and burnout, increased customer satisfaction and loyalty, higher productivity, and improved attraction and retention.[266] In human capital survey after human capital survey, work–life integration is at or near the top of employee satisfaction factors, often ahead of compensation and benefits.

Despite its vital importance to employee well-being and organizational performance, most organizations do a poor job of supporting employees to manage the integration of their work and personal lives. A 2018 survey of 1,200 employees shows that only 30 percent are satisfied with their work–life balance, down from 45 percent on the same survey just three years previously.[267]

The COVID pandemic has had a mixed impact on work–life integration. A 2022 survey conducted by Pew Research shows that 64 percent of those working from home have found it "easier to balance work and personal life." Those working from home tend to be professional and managerial workers, while those face-to-face are likely to have an overrepresentation of people from underrepresented groups. The Pew study also found, however, that 60 percent of employees believe they are less connected to coworkers.[268] Connectedness is a major factor in employee engagement.

The program components of a work–life strategy, including flexible work arrangements, dependent-care supports, and employee services, are well understood. Why, then, is there such low satisfaction with work–life integration? Three primary obstacles are blocking high satisfaction with work–life: a nonstrategic, programmatic approach, leadership that offers lip service instead of commitment, and supervisors who are ill prepared to manage work–life.

Strategic Approach

Most organizations that adopt work–life benefits focus on the implementation of best-practice program initiatives. Many organizations conduct work–life surveys to determine what practices their employees want or need. Then, their work–life professionals go to conferences and learn about what top companies are doing in the areas of need, and they adapt and implement those programs. Occasionally, a senior leader will hear about an exciting program that a leading company is offering and ask their work–life professionals to implement it. The danger is that the work–life initiative will become a series of programs, which individually may provide some benefits but collectively often work at cross purposes, do not enjoy the synergies and cost savings that strategic initiatives offer, and are not well integrated with business and corporate direction other than in the most general way.

A strategic approach should differentiate the organization from talent and product/service competitors as a component of a competitive strategy. Like a diversity strategy, it should incorporate change management, have top management commitment, be based in values and beliefs, be aligned with organizational and human capital strategy, have measures tied to organizational objectives with accountabilities, provide comprehensive policies, and implement a broad-based communications plan.

Leadership Commitment

All too frequently, top leaders send mixed messages to employees. They communicate their support for work–life flexibility, even extolling its business benefits. At the same time they communicate expectations—verbally and nonverbally—that employees, especially those who work directly for them, should be available when they need them. When their direct reports comply with these expectations, much of the organization receives an anti-work–life message, sowing confusion about whether or not they should utilize flexible work benefits.

Top leaders often use work–life benefits informally; they do what they need to do to support their personal lives outside of the organization's formal work–life structure. For example, one executive told me that after returning from two weeks in China, he took the afternoon off to attend his daughter's soccer game, telling only his executive assistant. Furthermore, high-earning, top leaders have more resources to manage their personal lives and more often have a nonworking spouse or partner. In summary, company-supported work–life balance is often less important to top leaders,[269] although they have significantly higher access to work–life benefits.[270]

The antidote is that top leaders must understand the sometimes contradictory messages they send and their own differential use of work–life benefits and the unique advantages their higher statuses and income provide. They must communicate their commitment to work–life and then walk the talk of their communications.

Supervisor Preparation

Supervisors are the ones who must negotiate the who, why, and when of work–life benefits, a scenario rife with potential discrimination. They must address who will pick up the slack when an employee avails himself of work–life benefits and respond to resentments when usage is imbalanced.

First, organizations should develop work–life utilization policies and ensure that supervisors are adequately educated on how to apply them. Second, most supervisors assume it is their responsibility to dole out work–life benefits, leaving the process subject to their own biases and preconceptions. A participatory approach, in which the work group itself addresses the needs of its members, is much more effective. In a participatory approach, within the boundaries of company goals and policies and internal and external customer requirements, employees make their work–life needs clear and identify the currently unknown requests—such as dependents' sick and snow days and employees' medical appointments—that are most likely to arise in the future. Then, the team members, facilitated by the team leader, work through each request and possibility, establishing schedules and policies as needed.

The team leader should have right of refusal but should be extremely cautious in using it. The whole process requires about a half day of total time. One result is that resentments virtually disappear, acceptance of decisions rises, and substantial slack is often identified. Third, the debiasing methodology should be applied to work–life usage decisions.

Intercultural Capability

The capstone of inclusive leadership—that unifies and synthesizes the other leadership practices—is the capability to lead across cultural or social group differences in an organization.

A culture is the common values, beliefs, behavioral norms (rules of behavior), and assumptions that a group of people hold in common, which Marvin Bower, the former managing director of McKinsey and Co., colloquially defined as "the way we do things around here." A culture is manifested in its artifacts, rites and rituals, heroes, and myths.

Artifacts are the visible creations of the culture, such as buildings, values statements, and uniforms. At IBM, for example, a policy letter on equal opportunity, written in 1953 by former chairman and CEO Thomas J. Watson, Jr., is a frequently cited, highly revered document.

Rites and rituals express the culture through action. They describe the workplace and how work is accomplished. The anthropologist Edward T. Hall described rites and rituals as the "dance of culture." For example, Google's hiring process has become a ritual.

Heroes are those who are afforded special status on the basis of their acts and statements. J. Irwin Miller, who marched with Martin Luther King, Jr., is regarded as a diversity hero at Cummins.

Myths communicate the culture of the organization through words. Occasionally apocryphal, they are stories that articulate the values, beliefs, norms, and assumptions held by the members of an organization. A common myth in organizations is that an emphasis on diversity will lower the quality of the workforce. The myth emanates from the belief that the organization will lower its standards of recruitment and promotion to hire and advance underrepresented people, effectively discriminating in favor of underrepresented people. Not only is this myth an affront to underrepresented people who have worked hard, perhaps even harder than well-represented people, to achieve their positions, but in the US discrimination on the basis of race, color, religion, national origin, sex, age, and disability in employment are for the most part illegal.

Artifacts, rites and rituals, heroes, and myths are the visible, observable elements of culture. They are the gateway to the subterranean world of assumptions—"what to pay attention to, what things mean, how to react emotionally to what is going on, and what actions to take in various kinds of situations."[271] Collectively, the assumptions organization members hold form mental models that substantially govern their behavior.

Cultures and the mental models they spawn are not ordained by a statement of desired or even required diversity values and beliefs, although such a statement can influence cultural formation and change. Mental models form over time through the everyday interactions and behaviors of people in groups. For example, organization members who have witnessed quarter after quarter of growth that is supported by an established, ritualistic recruitment process will come to believe that the recruitment process is a key ingredient of the secret sauce that has made the organization successful. As a result, once established, the mental model of recruitment is deeply shared by organization members and therefore extraordinarily difficult to change.

Mental models surrounding difference are among the most deeply embedded. They are driven by the prevailing national as well as the organizational culture. They are reinforced by segregation and other isms; inadequate and inaccurate historical representations, frequently learned in schools; the myths that surround particular social groups; and the privileges they confer. To successfully lead across differences, then, unsupportive mental models that underlie culture must be changed.

Leaders who are successful at intercultural leadership— crossing cultural differences—possess four capabilities: multicultural perspective, cultural self-knowledge, intercultural knowledge, and effective intercultural leadership behaviors. A multicultural perspective is the embodiment of embracing and valuing differences, especially—but not exclusively—social group or cultural differences. Cultural self-knowledge is the ability to understand one's own cultural influences and how they influence mental models and behavior. Intercultural knowledge is understanding the values, beliefs, and norms of relevant social and cultural groups other than one's own. Intercultural behaviors are those that have proved successful in crossing cultures, including trustworthiness, openness, empathy, curiosity, empowerment, and respect.

Skillful practice of these four leadership capabilities improves cross-cultural leadership and alters the mental models of leaders, which reinforces positive change in the culture and the mental models of all employees.

Multicultural Perspective

To successfully cross differences, leaders must first value cultural differences, a perspective called multiculturalism. Affirming the business case is vital but not sufficient for multiculturalism. Two barriers to multiculturalism—assimilation and colorblindness—must be recognized and overcome. Multiculturalism means that *all cultures are valued equally, including the majority or dominant culture.* Assimilation is *the belief that for a society or organization to function effectively, individual cultures must be subservient to the dominant culture and all members must adopt its values, beliefs, and norms.*

Those who embrace assimilation often believe that it creates unity among the members of various cultural groups. This is why questions of "fit" are so often ubiquitous in hiring decisions. The dominant group frequently perceives that multiculturalism excludes them,[272] so multiculturalism has "generated significant backlash. This backlash is manifested at the individual level in biased language, discrimination, silence regarding inequities, avoidance of difference, and discrediting ideas and individuals and at the organizational level in discriminatory human resource policies and practices, cultures of silence, and delays in diversity initiatives."[273]

Assimilation suppresses the very cultural differences that contribute to innovation and improved decision-making. On the other hand, "multiculturalism can . . . have positive implications for interracial interaction, engagement, performance, and detection of discrimination."[274]

The solution to the barrier presented by assimilation is to create a synthesis of assimilation and multiculturalism. Borrowing from Jean Piaget's theory of cognitive development, a process of adaptation provides that synthesis. Adaptation is the interplay between assimilation and accommodation. The antithesis of assimilation is accommodation, in which the dominant group alters its values, beliefs, norms, and mental models to accommodate critical features of the nondominant cultures represented in the organization. The process of adaptation is a never-ending dialogue composed of eight conversations (four for assimilation and four for accommodation).

The Eight Conversations of Adaptation

All conversations should include members of the dominant culture and members of nondominant cultures in such numbers that neither dominates the conversation. The goals of the four conversations of assimilation are (1) clarity about the current culture, (2) determination of which elements of the current culture are sacrosanct, (3) the behaviors of organizational members and groups that are reinforced by the current culture, and (4) which behaviors should be retained.

The clarity conversation—about the values, beliefs, norms, and especially mental models of the dominant culture—is best facilitated by data from surveys, focus groups, interviews, and exercises designed to elicit views of the current culture.

The second conversation revolves around the question of what elements of the dominant culture are most vital for achieving business or mission success. Which play most prominently in creating employee engagement and job satisfaction? Which are viewed as most valuable to employees themselves?

The third conversation surfaces the behaviors that are reinforced by the current culture. Given the cultural elements identified in the first conversation, what behaviors do you observe, especially behaviors involving nondominant groups, that appear to emerge from the values, beliefs, norms, and mental models of the current culture?

The fourth conversation considers, given the sacrosanct elements of the current culture, which behaviors should be retained (i.e., which behaviors strongly contribute to organizational success) and which can be abandoned without damaging the organization.

The goals of the four conversations of accommodation are a mirror of the assimilation conversations: (1) elaboration of the key cultural elements of nondominant cultures, (2) consideration of the sacrosanct elements of the nondominant cultures, (3) identification of the behaviors reinforced by the nondominant cultures, and (4) which behaviors are both most vital to the identity of the nondominant group and of greatest value to the organization.

The elaboration conversation should not simply be addressed to protected differences, such as race, ethnicity, gender orientation, sexual preference, religion, physical or mental ability, and age or generation, but to other critical differences as well. For example, at most high-technology companies, the dominant group is often White male engineers. It is equally important to understand the cultural influences of engineering viewpoints as it is to understand White male viewpoints. This conversation is also best facilitated by data and exercises.

The other conversations are the same as the assimilation conversations, except that they should occur for each nondominant culture.

The purpose of the eight conversations is not to resolve the questions underlying adaptation; these are open-ended conversations designed for participants to understand and learn from each other and, ultimately, to integrate assimilation and multiculturalism in the consciousness of those participants. The role of the leader is to facilitate the conversation without judgment or favoritism and to adhere to the following ground rules, to which they should ask the group to agree and perhaps add before entering the conversation:[275]

◇   Maintain confidentiality.
◇   Participants speak for themselves, not for a particular group or interest.
◇   Show respect for others by being open and nonjudgmental, listening, letting them express their views without interruption, and seeking the value in other viewpoints, even if you disagree.
◇   Treat all participants as equal—leave role, status, and stereotypes at the door.
◇   Speak your discomfort by sharing what is bothering you during group interaction.
◇   Be aware of taking up more than your share of the conversational space.
◇   Maintain an atmosphere in which it is safe for each participant to express their own thoughts and feelings.

Cultural Self-Knowledge

Cultural self-knowledge is *awareness, understanding, and interpretation of one's own patterns of thinking, feeling, and acting in relation to those from different social groups.* For example, cultural self-knowledge includes the following:

◊   Awareness of early learning about and formative experiences with those who are different
◊   How the individual has behaved in cross-cultural situations, particularly those involving conflict, and how these situations have been interpreted
◊   The individual's personal identity and how it was formed
◊   Attitudes toward people of difference and how these attitudes color behavior directed toward people who are different
◊   Openness to learning about one's intercultural thoughts, feelings, and behaviors and willingness to change

Self-knowledge can be beneficial, with "evidence from various settings [demonstrating] an association between self-awareness and managerial success and leadership effectiveness. High self-awareness has been found to be associated with higher performance ratings in various settings."[276] Alternatively, "people with low self-awareness are more likely to ignore or discount feedback about them, suffer career derailment, and have negative attitudes towards work."[277]

Though no definitive pathway to cultural self-knowledge is known, three are suggested below to initiate and deepen the conversation with self. These are attitudes toward those from underrepresented groups, 360-degree feedback, and self-assessment.

Attitudes toward Underrepresented Groups

Determination of your baseline attitudes toward those from protected groups, including different races, sexual orientations, gender identities, ability groups, religions, and age groups, can be done easily by completing the Implicit Association Test. Simply Google *IAT*, click on *Take a Test - Harvard University*, click on *I wish to proceed* in blue at the bottom of the page, and select the test you would like to take. I suggest starting with the test on race and proceeding through the others that are relevant. Be sure to record your score.

Questions you should ask yourself are as follows:

⋄   Were you surprised by the results? If yes or no, how come?
⋄   Why do you think you achieved those particular results?
⋄   If your score was not where it should have been or where you wanted it to be, what do you plan to do to improve?

360-Degree Feedback

Sometimes called multirater or multisource feedback, 360-degree feedback is *a process for gathering and reporting to a designated leader the self, peer, direct report, and supervisor feedback that facilitates performance improvement.*

Feedback is not as straightforward as might be imagined. Although feedback is generally effective, in 38 percent of the cases in one leading study, feedback actually resulted in lower performance.[278] When feedback focuses on the personality of the individual, which is largely immutable, instead of improvable behaviors, the effects of feedback are often detrimental.[279] Furthermore, feedback does not result in improved performance unless it provides information on a process by which the behavior can be improved.[280]

To be effective, 360-degree feedback should focus on improvable behaviors, limit raters only to judging behaviors to which they have a direct line of sight, be concerned with development and not evaluation, provide assistance and resources to employees to interpret and respond to the feedback, and be repeated on a regular basis, such as annually or biennially.

Questions on 360-degree feedback instruments should be directed to a specific leader, with reference, as needed, to his specific work group, and should cover, at minimum, the following concerns:

◊   Whether work group candidate pools always contain members of underrepresented groups and whether the leader makes hiring decisions and assigns development and advancement opportunities equitably
◊   Whether behaviors underlying the diversity philosophy are being demonstrated by the leader
◊   Whether supervisor behaviors are consistent with multiculturalism, including belongingness, authenticity, focus on employee assets, employee participation in decision-making, empowerment, network connections, integrity, respect, coaching, career development, transparency, work–life integration, leading across cultures, and standing up

Self-Assessment

Assessing yourself can be a complicated matter, especially assessing your own interpersonal and managerial abilities, two of the abilities most likely to affect intercultural work.[281] People overestimate themselves; they "typically do not possess all the information required to reach . . . accurate self-assessments," and though "ironically, people state that they are more likely than their peers to provide accurate self-assessments that are uncontaminated by bias,"[282] in fact peers tend to predict an individual's behavior better than the individual herself.

Furthermore, people "who received feedback that was more negative than expected valued the feedback less than did those for whom feedback was more positive than expected." As feedback becomes increasingly negative, recipients are more likely to distort the feedback, view the content of the feedback more negatively, and disagree with the person providing feedback.[283]

Even when individuals receive accurate feedback that they have accepted, "accumulating evidence indicates that nearly all individuals, and particularly those who score highest on measures of psychological adjustment, exhibit a pervasive tendency to view the self and their world in a more positive way than can realistically be justified."[284] Individuals who are self-assessing should be made aware of their natural tendency to be overly positive in their self-assessment.

Numerous measures are available to assess an individual's general intercultural capability. Among the most prominent are the following:[285]

◇ The Intercultural Development Inventory (IDI), a fifty-item survey that assesses an individual's ability to shift among cultural perspectives and adapt their behavior to cultural differences
◇ Cross-Cultural Adaptability Inventory (CCAI), a fifty-item survey that assesses "an individual's effectiveness in cross-cultural interaction and communication"
◇ Intercultural Sensitivity Inventory (ISI), a forty-item survey that measures an individual's "ability to modify behavior in culturally appropriate ways when coming into contact with diverse cultures"

To self-assess the ability to lead across differences, answering the following questions is suggested:

◊   What role does your race, gender identity, sexual orientation, physical ability, religion, or age play in your own identity (i.e., how you think about who you are)?

◊   Have you ever behaved differently or used different language in cross-difference conversations than in no-difference conversations?

◊   What roles, no matter how minute, do you play in racism, classism, sexism, anti-LGBTQ+ bias and homophobia, ageism, and religious discrimination?

◊   What are examples of times where privilege has played a role in achieving your career goals?

◊   How do you incorporate anti-bias and inclusion work into your role as a leader?

Intercultural Knowledge

Several years ago, I facilitated a leadership development workshop for a large US multinational. The participants came from recent acquisitions in the UK, Germany, Japan, and France. A few hours into the workshop, it became clear that a lack of intercultural understanding was impeding the group's progress. I broke them into their four country groups and asked them to write down on flip chart paper, out of view of the other groups, the five chief characteristics of another national culture in the room and then the chief characteristics of their own culture. When the flip charts were turned around to reveal what had been written, each group discovered a complete disconnect between their self-defined cultural characteristics and those ascribed to them.

This lack of intercultural knowledge or, worse, the presence of intercultural misinformation is as significant when considering national subcultures as it is when considering differences across national cultures. For example, consider the challenges of understanding African American subculture:

African American cultural psychology is necessarily multidimensional in at least three ways: First is the joint function of Africa-originating cultural effects and the adaptive, reactionary mechanisms demanded by slavery and the experience in the Diaspora. Second, the social structure of slavery created multiple levels of African American society first distinguishing slave from free, then among slaves, the field and house slaves. Third, the regional context presented additional dimensions for divergence including North and South distinctions as well as variations caused by western expansion.[286]

The writer Touré described the challenge of uncovering African American identity: "The number of ways of being black are infinite . . . the possibilities for an authentic black identity are boundless . . . and what it means to be black is so staggeringly broad, unpredictable, and diffuse that blackness itself is indefinable."[287]

If truly knowing another culture is possible, how can leaders meet the challenge of gaining accurate knowledge of other national cultures and subcultures? For starters, numerous online services provide learning programs for understanding specific national cultures. These are usually aimed at employees taking expat assignments and their families. Programs like GlobeSmart® and Country Navigator provide country knowledge, compare an employee's workstyle to the predominate workstyle of a country, provide coaching, and offer cultural training to employees and their families. Language training is widely available online from such leading companies as Pimsleur®, Rocket Languages, and Babbel. Free language training is available from Duolingo and the Foreign Service Institute.

A widely used method of intercultural knowledge is total immersion in another culture—living and working in another culture, occasionally with modest or no support. Total immersion may occur in arenas ranging from college semesters abroad to cross-cultural team problem-solving assignments to the Peace Corps to expatriate work assignments. Unfortunately, short of recruiting employees with prior cultural immersion experiences, total immersion is often impractical. Finding meaningful immersive assignments can be difficult, and immersion requires time and is expensive. Furthermore, many programs exist for immersion in national cultures, but little exists for immersion in the subcultures of one nation. For example, in the US, other than life experience, personal initiative, and college curricula and housing that focus on a subculture, it is difficult to identify subculture immersion experiences, such as between Latinx and African American subcultures.

Another approach is applying models of intercultural understanding. Based on research, the best of these models identify the key dimensions that distinguish among cultures.[288] The most practical of these is Hofstede and Hofstede's five dimensions: power distance, individualism–collectivism, masculinity–femininity, uncertainty avoidance, and long- and short-term orientation.

Power Distance

Power distance is "the extent to which the less powerful members of institutions and organizations within a country expect and accept that power is distributed unequally."[289] Smaller-power-distance cultures are distinguished by decentralization, fewer supervisors, narrow salary differences between the top and bottom of the organization, and managers who look to themselves and their subordinates for direction. In these cultures, "privileges and status symbols are frowned upon," and all work has equal status.

Large-power-distance cultures, on the other hand, are distinguished by centralization, smaller spans of control, wide salary differences, and managers who look to their superiors and to formal policies and plans for direction. In large-power-distance cultures, "privileges and status symbols are normal and popular," and knowledge work is more highly valued than physical work.[290]

Individualism–Collectivism

In individualistic cultures, "the ties between individuals are loose: everyone is expected to look after himself or herself and his or her immediate family."[291] Individualistic cultures are defined by greater job mobility; an employee contract that stresses a balance between the employer's and the individual's interests; hiring and advancement decisions based only on knowledge, skills, and roles; and the beliefs that the role of management is managing individuals and that task is more important than relationship.

In collectivistic cultures, "people from birth onward are integrated into strong, cohesive in-groups, which throughout people's lifetimes continue to protect them in exchange for unquestioning loyalty."[292] Collectivistic cultures are defined by lower mobility, a contract that focuses on the interests of the subgroup of which the individual is a member, hiring and promotion decisions that take an employee's subgroup into account, and the beliefs that the role of management is to manage groups and that relationship is more important than task.[293]

Masculinity–Femininity

In masculine cultures, gender roles are distinct, with the expectation that men "are supposed to be assertive, tough, and focused on material success, whereas women are supposed to be more modest, tender, and concerned with the quality of life."[294] In a feminine culture, gender roles overlap.[295]

Uncertainty Avoidance

Uncertainty avoidance is "the extent to which the members of a culture feel threatened by ambiguous or unknown situations."[296] In cultures with weak uncertainty avoidance, people change jobs more frequently, seek minimal rules, have a high tolerance for ambiguity, believe in common sense, are focused on strategy and the decision process, are more inventive, and have high achievement motivation. In cultures with strong uncertainty avoidance, employees stay in jobs longer; seek the security of rules, clarity, and stability; believe in expertise; focus on daily operations and decision content; and are motivated by security.[297]

Long- and Short-Term Orientation

Long-term orientation is "the fostering of virtues oriented toward future rewards—in particular perseverance and thrift. Short-term orientation stands for the fostering of values related to the past and the present—in particular, respect for tradition, preservation of 'face,' and fulfilling social obligations."[298] In cultures with a short-term orientation, people value "freedom, rights, achievement, and thinking for oneself" and the bottom line and immediate profits. In short-term cultures, workers and managers have different interests and aspirations, and "employees' personal loyalties vary with business needs."[299] In long-term cultures, people value "learning, honesty, adaptiveness, accountability, and self-discipline," market position, and long-term profitability. Workers and managers have common aspirations, and people invest in "lifelong personal networks."[300]

These dimensions are useful for uncovering the mental models of employees, customers, and those in the supply chain. Understanding others' mental models provides leaders with the ability to modify their own assumptions, expectations, and behaviors to accommodate the cultural orientations of others.

Effective leadership behaviors that transcend all forms and levels of national and in-country culture provide a potent means for effectively bridging differences.

Effective Intercultural Leadership Behaviors

Leadership is contingent upon the culture or cultures in which it is embedded. How leadership is defined, valued, and practiced varies across cultures.[301] Nevertheless, nine dimensions of effective leadership transcend culture (table 6-9). They apply in most national cultures and, by extension, most subcultures.

These attributes come from the ten-year Globe Leadership and Organizational Behavior Effectiveness (GLOBE) Research Program, a survey of more than 17,000 managers in 951 organizations across sixty-two societies.[302]

Positive Leader Attributes that Transcend Culture[303]	
Integrity	Is trustworthy, just, and honest
Visionary	Has foresight and plans ahead
Inspirational	Encouraging, positive, dynamic, motive arouser, confidence builder, motivational
Benevolent	Dependable and intelligent
Decisive	Resolute
Diplomatic	Effective bargainer and win-win problem solver
Administratively Competent	Skilled at accomplishing administrative tasks
Team Integrator	Communicator, well informed, coordinator and collaborator, team builder
Performance Oriented	Oriented toward excellence

Table 6-9

Effective inclusive leadership is fundamentally about grasping and affirming the essential humanity of every employee and then responding to that understanding through the following methods:

◇   Appreciating each employee's essence
◇   Acknowledging their higher needs
◇   Recognizing their competence
◇   Hearing their deepest thoughts and concerns
◇   Empowering, connecting, coaching, and developing them
◇   Creating a workplace of respect, integrity, transparency, safety and security, and intercultural competence
◇   Supporting and encouraging their most extraordinary performance

Although the social groups to which employees belong are fundamental to leading across differences, difference in the final analysis will only be transcended when employees are understood and led as individuals in their full complexity and uniqueness.

STANDING UP

If authenticity and belongingness are the core of inclusion, then the foundation of inclusion is "standing up," *never allowing an act of bias, discrimination, stereotyping, or prejudice to go unchallenged*. Perhaps no one has been more inspirational in standing up than the late civil rights leader John Lewis, who said, "When you see something that is not right, not fair, not just, you have a moral obligation to do something, to say something."

Challenging prejudicial statements and behaviors generates individual and group benefits. When confronted, perpetrators are more aware of their biases and less likely to exhibit prejudicial behavior in the future.[304] Of women bystanders who observe prejudiced interactions and systems and respond assertively,

71 percent were more satisfied with their response than the 31 percent who were satisfied by their nonassertive response.[305] The cumulative effect of standing up is that it may influence the organization's social norms in a more equitable direction, influencing not just behavior but attitudes too. However, when challenges are more hostile in confronting an "individual's favorable self-concept, reactions are likely to be negative" toward the confronter.[306] And they are more negative when the confronter is Black in the case of racial bias, or a woman in the face of sexist behavior,[307] intensifying the argument for those who are not in the target's social group to be particularly proactive in standing up.

Bystanders often do not stand up. Most bystanders have positive intentions toward intervening, but a much smaller number actually intervene. In a study of experiences of discrimination over a one-week period, while "75 percent of female participants considered an assertive response, only 40 percent actually made one."[308] Another study, focused on heterosexism, found that respondents considered an assertive response in 68 percent of incidents and acted on them 53 percent of the time.[309] Often, when either a target or bystander does not confront a perpetrator, they may experience "negative intrapersonal consequences,"[310] such as guilt, feelings of unworthiness, and even self-loathing.

A number of obstacles prevent bystanders from standing up. Witnesses to acts of discrimination may simply not know how to respond effectively. Members of a social group are more likely to stand up for those similar to them than for members of outside social groups. Bystanders are less likely to stand up when they believe there is personal risk in taking action, such as jeopardizing relationships with peers and leaders, retaliation, or loss of status. The lack of effective organization cultural norms that support intervention also creates barriers, along with "perceptions that intervening would be ineffective" and the assumption that the situation is "none of [their] business."[311]

Standing up requires a balance "between communicating discomfort and maintaining interpersonal relations."[312] Being challenged typically engenders defensiveness in the perpetrator. The following interventions are useful for challenging prejudiced behavior while mitigating the defensiveness of perpetrators:[313]

◇   Ask questions, as unloaded as possible, such as "Why do you say that?" Avoid admonishing the perpetrator.

◇   With perpetrators who espouse equity, raise the contradiction in what they said by stating, for example, "I'm surprised to hear you say that because I've always thought of you as someone who is very open-minded."

◇   Tell perpetrators the feelings their statements arouse in you rather than your judgments about them. For example, "It makes me uncomfortable to hear you say that" rather than "You shouldn't say that."

◇   Many perpetrators will defend themselves by saying that they were only joking. Rather than saying something to the effect that their attempt at humor wasn't funny, ask, "Can you see how [the target] might have taken your humor differently than you intended?"

◇   Control anger toward the perpetrator, even if it is well founded. Anger and hostility, especially toward an individual with a self-concept of equity and fairness, often results in a highly negative reaction, undermining the interpersonal relationship. Nevertheless, high-anger responses are likely to reduce the perpetrator's proclivity toward prejudice in future interactions.

◇   All employees should be knowledgeable about what constitutes prejudiced (racist, sexist, heterosexism, etc.) behavior and cognizant of the damage done by bigotry.

◇   Leaders, especially top leaders, must be unequivocal "that any form of racism [or bigotry of any kind], no matter how 'minor' or 'jovial,' is unacceptable"; furthermore, leaders should model effective responses to prejudiced behavior and emphasize that confronting prejudice is everyone's responsibility.[314] Finally, leaders should ensure that all employees have the skills and motivation to intervene when they observe prejudiced behavior.

Effective training to encourage bystanders to stand up provides an understanding of the organization's cultural norms about prejudiced behavior and standing up as well as practices for applying guidelines for responding to incidents of prejudice. Response guidelines should include when and how to confront the perpetrator and the imperative to involve bystanders, provide support to the target of racism, report the incident, and involve a person in power.[315]

Conclusion

The elements of inclusion—belongingness and authenticity, talent enablement, employee participation, inclusive leadership, and standing up—can only be perfected in a climate of humility from which self-importance, arrogance, and hubris have been banished. Leaders create the climate. They must embrace humility in the spirit of the art critic, artist, and social commentator John Ruskin, who wrote, "I believe that the first test of a great man is his humility. I don't mean by humility, doubt of his power. But really great men have a curious feeling that the greatness is not of them, but through them. And they see something divine in every other man and are endlessly, foolishly, incredibly merciful."[316]

Engineering Sustainable Diversity Competitive Advantage

"If you don't have a competitive advantage, don't compete."
Jack Welch

ORGANIZATIONS COMPETE IN TWO DISTINCT diversity markets: the diversity product/service market and the diversity talent market. Competition in the product/service market is concerned with attracting and serving underrepresented consumers, clients, businesses, and allies of underrepresented people. Underrepresented people have significant buying power (see "Competency 2: Constructing a Business Case for Diversity"), and the market for the business of allies of underrepresented people is largely unknown, but initial evidence suggests that it is sizable.

Competition in the talent market is about recruiting and retaining the top talent, no matter the gender, race, ethnicity, sexual orientation, gender identity, ability, religion, or age of that talent. For those organizations not competing effectively for the talents of underrepresented people, the situation is bleak. In organizations hoping to attract employees who are currently employed by other organizations, 58 percent of those employed are underrepresented people.[317] If an organization is competing for the unemployed, 65 percent are underrepresented people.[318] And if the organization is considering its future or hires directly out of school, about 73 percent of the bachelor's degrees, 79 percent of the master's, and 72 percent of the doctorates go to underrepresented people.[319]

Perhaps Jack Welch's statement above should read, "If you don't have a competitive diversity advantage, you're missing a huge opportunity."

What, then, is sustainable diversity competitive advantage? How can an organization achieve that advantage in product/ service and talent markets? What is the role of the diversity organization in capturing those markets?

Sustainable Diversity Competitive Advantage

Diversity competitive advantage in the product/service market follows three distinct strategic paths: cost leadership, differentiation, and focus[320] (figure 7-1). *Cost leadership* is a company's strategic decision to have the lowest overall cost of any competitor in the market. Only one company can hold the cost leadership position.

Competitive Product-Market Diversity Strategies[321]

	Cost Leadership	Differentiation
Market-Wide Focus		
Market Segment Focus		

Figure 7-1

Differentiation is distinguishing product/service offerings in a market from those of competitors on the basis of one or more features or benefits that underrepresented consumers, customers, clients, and allies seek, such as a product or service unique to the purchaser's life state or heritage. If those features and benefits are superior to those of competitors and the price is commensurate with the value provided, a competitive advantage is created.

Differentiating a product/service is not just about altering an existing or creating a new product/service; it can also be about creating the perception in the buyer's mind that the product fulfills their unique needs, a practice called positioning. Positioning is a communications methodology for establishing the features, benefits, or brand image in the mind of the consumer or client in a way that distinguishes the product or service from the competition. Procter and Gamble's "My Black is Beautiful" advertising campaign, for example, was intended to position the P&G brand in the minds of African American women as a "celebration of the personal and collective beauty of African American women" and to encourage them "to define and promote a beauty standard that is an authentic reflection of their spirit," according to Najoh Tita Reid, P&G multicultural marketing director.[322]

Focus is the choice to compete through either cost leadership or differentiation in a segment of the total market. An example of a segment is the hair care market for African American women. In this lucrative market segment, African American women spend three times as much on hair care products as other women. However, care must be taken to avoid seeing demographic segments as monolithic. For example, African American women may desire a wide range of different hairstyles, suggesting different products for different hairstyles.

Competitive advantage in the market for diverse talent contains essentially the same elements as competitive advantage in the product/service market. The exception is that in the talent market, cost advantage is replaced by compensation advantage, the highest pay and benefits and often equal pay for equal work. Parallel to cost advantage, only one competitor can have the compensation advantage in any industry.

Differentiation and segmentation are not just for profit-making organizations. They can work for nonprofits, NGOs, and government organizations as well. Take, for example, a nonprofit drug rehabilitation program with a capacity of 100 beds. The organization receives funding for each person it treats, so if beds are empty, revenue dips, jeopardizing the mission of the organization. Segmentation of the suppliers of clients into MDs, psychologists, social workers, individuals, and other rehabilitation organizations that don't provide inpatient services and are referral sources and then positioning communications to each of those segments is a focus strategy to differentiate the organization in each market segment to fill empty beds.

Sustainability is achieved through creating barriers to entry, obstacles that an organization creates to discourage competitors from competing against them. In the product/service market, barriers to entry include economies of scale (more customers over which to spread costs), brand identity, and the costs of buyers switching to another competitor. In the talent market, barriers include employer brand, innovation, and the diversity of the workforce (the more diverse the workforce, the more diverse workers are likely to join and stay).

SUSTAINABLE DIVERSITY COMPETITIVE ADVANTAGE IN THE PRODUCT/SERVICE MARKET

The role of diversity leaders in the product/service market is not to take charge of sustainable diversity competitive advantage but to identify opportunities in the diversity marketplace and collaborate with marketing, business development, sales, and other relevant functions to bring those opportunities to market. Typically, those opportunities require segmenting diversity markets and then differentiating within those markets. Merck and IBM have followed that path to significant business results.

As described in "Competency 4: Mastering Diversity Strategy," Deb Dagit, former chief diversity officer at Merck, was able to seize the fact that patients often did not take the medications prescribed (adherence) and turn it into a health benefit for diversity communities, as well as a significant business opportunity for Merck, by focusing on adherence challenges in certain underrepresented communities.

When IBM stood up eight task forces of underrepresented leaders to invigorate its diversity initiative, those leaders were asked to answer four questions. One of those questions—"What can the corporation do to influence your constituency's buying decisions so that IBM is seen as a preferred solution provider?"— proved particularly prescient. The answers to that question in the eight diversity segments that the task forces represented led to the identification of an abundance of business opportunities. They were so successful that IBM established the Market Development organization, a group focused on growing the market of multicultural and women-owned businesses in the United States.[323] Between 1998 and 2001, Market Development's revenues grew from $10 million to over $300 million by addressing the needs of underrepresented business segments.[324]

One of those opportunities was identified by the people with disabilities task force. Section 508 of the Rehabilitation Act of 1973 applies to US federal agencies and their contractors "when they develop, procure, maintain, or use electronic and information technology." Section 508 requires that all disabled employees and members of the public have access to electronics and information that is comparable to the access of all people.[325] The people with disabilities task force guided IBM into a leadership role in Section 508 compliance. Today, IBM's Human Ability and Accessibility Center has locations in seven countries, including Japan, China, and Brazil. In addition to taking a leading role in accessibility research, IBM ensures its products are accessible and offers or is developing a host of accessibility products, including such offerings as cognitive eldercare, accessible transportation, and mobile navigation. It hasn't been lost on IBM that universal accessibility—meaning everyone can effectively use the product or service no matter what their ability is—means a considerably larger marketplace.

Identifying Business and Service Opportunities

Affinity groups or employee resource groups are often the best source of business or service opportunities. They bring a cross-functional group of people with a deep understanding of their own social group, a perfect team to identify opportunities among segments of underrepresented people. Opportunities are as much about positioning existing products and services in new communities or markets as about developing new products.

As at IBM, the identification of opportunities should be part of every affinity group's charter, which should also identify a process for bringing those opportunities to market. In some cases, opportunities will spontaneously emerge from the affinity group. Affinity groups should constantly scan for opportunities, perhaps establishing a subcommittee to drive opportunity identification. In other cases, a more formal process of opportunity identification will be required.

The first step of a formal process for generating product/ service opportunities is to understand the needs of the market and how that market might be successfully segmented. It is often useful to identify segments based on common needs and then to identify opportunities that emerge out of those specific segments. Affinity groups will typically have a good feel for marketplace needs and which segments are underserved or unserved. Partnering with the internal market research group is often the best place to start. Obtaining data from outside research firms can also be useful and relatively inexpensive, although that data will be available to competitors. Conducting a from-scratch market research project is usually expensive and requires research design and analytical sophistication or external resources.

Consideration should be given to whether an organization offers products/services to other organizations (business to business or organization to organization) or to individual customers (business to consumer or organization to client). While similar in many ways, the two markets differ significantly. Products/services offered to businesses and organizations are usually far more complex than those offered to individuals, and because they are complicated, purchase decisions are often group decisions, sometimes including outside consultants. Communication strategies to reach business and consumer segments vary greatly.

Once opportunities have been identified, they should be prioritized and the top one, two, or three pursued through the bring-to-market process. Criteria for prioritization include the following:

◇   Investment requirements
◇   Projected cost to produce the product/service
◇   Projected selling price and margin
◇   Projected ROI, internal rate of return, whatever is standard for measuring investment performance in the organization
◇   Projected growth rate of the segment
◇   Level of competition
◇   Value chain advantages
◇   Differentiation potential

Differentiation in the product/service market is predominately based on some element or elements of the value chain, which describes the process and component activities for designing, developing, producing, marketing, distributing, and servicing products or services in a business unit and the ancillary functions, such as human capital and IT, that support the process. A generic, high-level product/service value chain is pictured in figure 7-2. Different products or services may have their own value chains.

Differentiation can be based on any activity or set of activities in the value chain. For example, Starbucks differentiates on several value chain activities:

◇ All procurement is done by Starbucks' internal experts and procured directly from coffee farms rather than intermediaries.

◇ Starbucks exercises tight control over the production of coffee in its stores, ensuring high quality.

◇ Starbucks invests heavily in customer service. If service has been slow or a customer is dissatisfied, employees are quick to give them a gift card for a free coffee or other Starbucks product.

◇ Marketing and sales are based more on product quality and customer service than large investments in advertising.

◇ A focus on human resources ensures low turnover and satisfied employees who, in turn, provide exemplary customer service.

Unfortunately, with its failed "Race Together" campaign and the arrest of two African American men waiting for a friend in a Philadelphia store, Starbucks has inadvertently established a negative brand image in many African American communities.

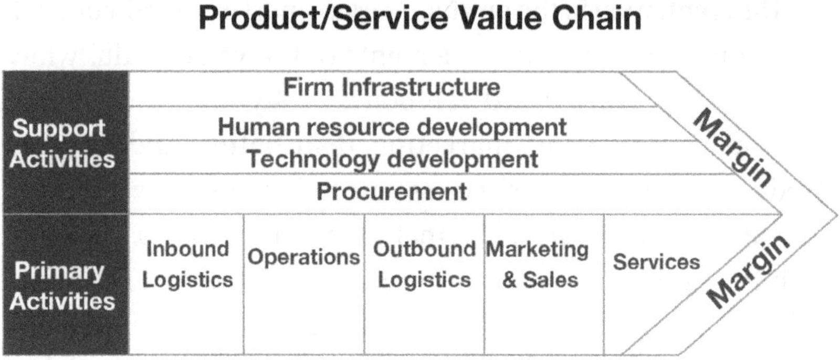

Product/Service Value Chain

Support Activities	Firm Infrastructure				
	Human resource development				
	Technology development				
	Procurement				
Primary Activities	Inbound Logistics	Operations	Outbound Logistics	Marketing & Sales	Services

Margin

Reprinted from Michael Porter, *Competitive Advantage*, New York: The Free Press (1985),37.

Figure 7-2

Advancing Business and Service Opportunities

Diversity leaders who wish to advance product and service ideas, assuming that they are not able to pursue them on their own, will need to influence their service delivery, marketing, distribution, and business development organizations. While they ordinarily won't need a business plan, they will need to provide good (not perfect) answers to the questions those organizations are likely to raise. Questions they should be prepared to answer include the following:

◊   What is the product/service offering?

◊   Who are the customers and what are their unmet needs?

◊   Is the product/service offering new or is it a repositioning of an existing offering?

◊   Will this product/service offering take sales from the organization's other products and services (a process called cannibalization)?

◊   What is the size of the market? Is the market growing?

◊   What are the factors that drive growth in the market and the risk factors that could inhibit market growth?

◊   Who are the competitors? How are they likely to respond to the new or repositioned offering?

◊   How will the offering be differentiated from competitive offerings (i.e., why would a customer of a competitive offering switch to the new offering)?

◊   How will the offering be developed, produced, and distributed to the market, and what will be the associated cost factors?

◊   Will the new offering need to be serviced? What are the cost and resource implications of the customer service required?

◊   What organizational units have a stake in the offering? How will you influence those departments to support the offering?

◊   What existing organizational resources will the offering need to utilize? What are the opportunity costs (costs of not using those resources on other products and services or other activities)?

◊   Once this offering has been established, what barriers to entry will discourage competitors from making competitive offerings?

These questions can also provide additional criteria for prioritizing product/service options.

SUSTAINABLE DIVERSITY COMPETITIVE ADVANTAGE IN THE TALENT MARKET

Competitive advantage in the market for diverse talent is achieved through either compensation and benefits leadership and pay equity, differentiation, or focus, leading to four strategy alternatives (see figure 7-3). Sustainability is achieved through various sources, including innovation and diversity execution, knowledge, and communication. In general, the model for diversity talent competitive advantage is the same as for talent competitive advantage.

Diversity Talent Competitive Market Strategies

	Compensation Leadership	Differentiation
Market-Wide Focus		
Market Segment Focus		

Figure 7-3

The diversity talent market is typically the bailiwick of either the talent organization or the business unit or organization to which the targeted employees will report and which makes hiring, evaluation, and advancement decisions—or both. Affinity groups or employee resource groups can also be key players in diversity talent advantage. The role of diversity leadership will largely be to assemble and facilitate these employment stakeholders through a collaborative process that ensures sustainable competitive advantage in the market for diverse talent.

To formulate a competitive strategy for a diversity talent market that is sustainable over the long run, organizations should consider the following:

◇   What strategic diversity opportunities, both explicit and implicit, are presented by the business and functional strategies of the organization, as well as from aspirational statements such as the diversity philosophy

◇   Whether those opportunities demand a market-wide or segment focus

◊   Whether they demand a compensation or differentiation approach

◊   How the strategy can be designed to ensure sustainability

Identification of Strategic Diversity Opportunities in the Talent Market

The first step is to identify what strategic diversity opportunities emerge from superordinate strategies, including corporate, business, institutional, and human capital; talent and/ or human resources strategies; and the diversity philosophy or other high-level people-related commitments.

Superordinate strategies should be analyzed and discussed to determine whether any imply or offer explicit business or organizational directions that the diversity strategy should take. For example, suppose that the business strategy of the AZN accounting firm calls for 20 percent year-over-year growth. Even though women are not mentioned in the strategy, achieving it would be extremely difficult without attracting women since, for experienced hires, 60.6 percent of accountants and auditors in the US are women,[326] and for new hires, 51.1 percent of the bachelor's degrees in accounting awarded in 2018 went to women.[327] It's no wonder that all the Big Four accounting firms (Deloitte, KPMG, PwC, and E&Y) focus extensively—although not exclusively—on the women's segment of the diversity labor market. The superordinate strategy for AZN implies a talent segment strategy focused on women with degrees in accounting.

Suppose that AZN's business strategy calls for asserting leadership in workplace diversity within the accounting industry, calling for equal pay and boards of directors and staff that mirror the proportions of underrepresented people who are certified public accountants. This business strategy calls for a market-wide (all underrepresented people) focus.

Market-Wide or Segment Focus?

The superordinate strategy will virtually always answer the question of whether there should be a market-wide or segment strategy. When the superordinate strategy doesn't provide an answer, then the organization should back up to the question "What social identity segments, if any, are critical to organizational success?"

Answering this question is a two-step process. The first step is to determine whether there are critical talent pool segments on which an organization is dependent for strategic success. For example, several trends are driving the importance of pharmacists to success in the retail pharmacy industry, such as growing customer expectations for one-on-one attention and the increase in the proportion of specialty drug sales. Variables useful for identifying segments that are critical to organizational success are identified in table 7-1.

Talent Pool Segmentation Variables	
Competency	The ability to perform an act efficiently and effectively, including analytical thinking, conflict resolution, interpersonal relations, and writing
Discipline	A branch of knowledge, such as botany, chemical engineering, or psychology
Education Level	The highest level of education completed, including high school diploma, years of college, associate degree, bachelor's degree, master's degree, and doctoral degree
Generation	The group that is born in the same time period, including baby boomers, Generations X, Y, and Z, and the emerging alpha generation (born between 2011 and 2025)

Talent Pool Segmentation Variables	
Language and Culture	The language spoken or the social norms and mores of a talent pool
Level	Organizational status—for example, entry level, supervisor, middle manager, director, and executive
Occupation	A wide range of these job categories exist, such as marketing and sales manager, compliance officers, computer network architects, cooks, and carpenters. In the US, the Bureau of Labor Statistics offers a breakdown of gender, race, and ethnicity by occupation.[328] Occupations may be further segmented by years of experience.
Personality Trait	The Big Five personality traits derived from in-depth psychological research: openness, conscientiousness, extraversion, agreeableness, and emotional stability[329]

Table 7-1

The second step is to determine whether any underrepresented social identity groups comprise a large proportion of the identified critical success talent segment or bring special skills and capabilities. This is largely determined by data, such as a nation's census and labor statistics or international statistics from the International Labor Organization (ILO) or the Organisation for Economic Co-operation and Development (OECD), and analytics. It might be a labor pool dominated by a particular social group, such as women accountants, or with the language and cultural skills to compete more effectively in a global market, such as speakers of the Yue dialect when setting up a joint venture in Guangdong Province.

Most of the pharmacists that are a critical success talent factor for pharmacies are women: in all regions of the world except Africa, the vast majority of pharmacists are women, approaching 70 percent in the US and Europe and 60 percent in the Eastern Mediterranean, Southeast Asia, and the Western Pacific.[330] In the US, 62 percent of first professional pharmacy degrees in the 2017–2018 school year went to women.[331]

Compensation or Differentiation Strategy?

Once diversity talent markets have been identified, the next step is to determine whether to take a compensation leadership or differentiation strategy. If a differentiation strategy is chosen, then the next step is to work out the details of how differentiation will be accomplished.

Compensation Leadership Strategy

Compensation leadership as a strategy is severely limited. First, it is difficult to sustain since any talent competitor can match or beat another competitor's compensation leadership at any time simply by raising compensation. Furthermore, a compensation strategy approach is difficult in the diversity world, since US federal law (the Equal Pay Act) and the laws of some other countries require equal pay for equal work across gender, race, color, religion, national origin, age, and disability. Equal work is defined as equal skill, effort, responsibility, and working conditions within a single institution.

Compensation leadership makes sense if it is recast as compensation equity (equal pay for equal work). Because women, people of color, people with disabilities, and people who are LGBTQ on average receive lower pay,[332] the promise of pay equity can be a formidable talent strategy. However, pay equity leadership suffers from the same competitive challenge that faces compensation leadership: it can easily be matched. Attaining pay equity across all social groups is considerably more difficult than compensation leadership. It requires defining the terms of pay equity (equal skill, effort, responsibility, and working conditions), measuring those differences fairly, and bringing pay into equality.

Differentiation

Differentiation in a talent market results from eliciting a perception in employees' and prospective employees' minds of a distinctive and appealing employee experience that distinguishes an organization from its talent competitors. Differentiation in the market for diverse talent, as in the product/service market, is derived from the value chain, in this case the diverse talent value chain (DTVC). The DTVC (figure 7-4) has four components:

◇ The critical experiences that employees have in equity and inclusion and in each of four core activity areas: recruiting, retaining, advancing, and exiting diverse talent

◇ The human capital administrative supports for employee experiences and the information and analytics that drive the design, development, accountability, and continuous improvement of those experiences

◇ The diversity climate (i.e., employee perceptions of their experience in the organization, segmented by social group membership)

◇ The outcomes of employees' organizational experiences: the employer diversity brand and diverse employee engagement, which are significant factors in determining the organization's social group diversity

Differentiating the employee experience to appeal to underrepresented employees should not come at the expense of social groups that are not underrepresented. The employee experience should appeal to all talent pools. Differentiation merely refines and calls out those aspects of the employee experience that appeal to a particular segment of the population and then ensures that those aspects are included in the employee experience. The intention of differentiation is to expand the universe of talent, not to narrow it to one social group or another.

The Diverse Talent Value Chain

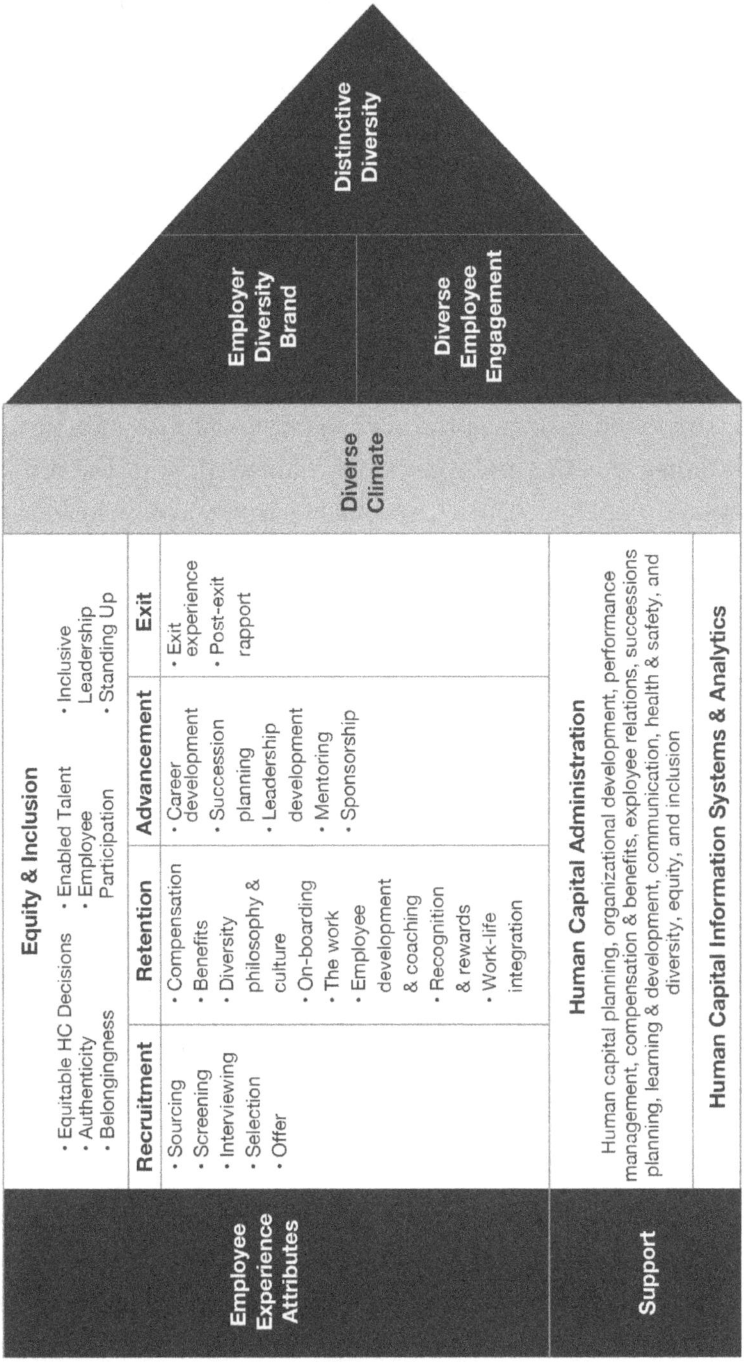

Distinctive Diversity

Employer Diversity Brand

Diverse Employee Engagement

Diverse Climate

Equity & Inclusion
- Equitable HC Decisions
- Authenticity
- Belongingness
- Enabled Talent
- Employee Participation
- Inclusive Leadership
- Standing Up

Recruitment	Retention	Advancement	Exit
• Sourcing • Screening • Interviewing • Selection • Offer	• Compensation • Benefits • Diversity philosophy & culture • On-boarding • The work • Employee development & coaching • Recognition & rewards • Work-life integration	• Career development • Succession planning • Leadership development • Mentoring • Sponsorship	• Exit experience • Post-exit rapport

Human Capital Administration

Human capital planning, organizational development, performance management, compensation & benefits, employee relations, successions planning, learning & development, communication, health & safety, and diversity, equity, and inclusion

Human Capital Information Systems & Analytics

Employee Experience Attributes

Support

Figure 7-4

Critical Employee Experiences

Recruitment, retention, and advancement of top talent form the core of most talent strategies. How employees are shown the exit is often not included in talent strategies. However, the experience of exiting an organization, whether voluntary or involuntary, can have significant impact on how an organization's employer brand is perceived in the talent marketplace—especially in this era of social media—and also on the engagement of the employees who remain. As a result, *exit* has been added to core differentiating experiences.

The critical employee experiences that have been selected for this model have all shown a moderate or substantial relationship with employee performance. Most of the critical employee experiences are subsumed by equity and inclusion and discussed elsewhere in this text. So as not to be redundant, the focus here is on the employee experiences that have not been deeply addressed, are most critical for achieving differentiation, and lead to improved employer diversity brand, diverse employee engagement, and, ultimately, demographic diversity.

Much of the recruitment, retention, advancement, and exit processes are invisible to the eye of the employee or prospective employee until a decision has been made. When underrepresented people are rejected or simply not included in these processes, they often experience the process as biased, diminishing the quality of their experience. This section considers both how to enhance the prospect's or employee's experience and decision-making about employees and prospective employees.

Recruitment

While the data demonstrates that larger American companies are doing reasonably well at recruiting educated, diverse, professional employees (see figure 2-5), numerous studies show that bias still exists in recruiting processes, especially in screening.

To eradicate bias in recruiting, organizations are increasingly turning to artificial intelligence, machine learning, and gamification in all aspects of talent recruitment. These technologies have the potential to reduce bias significantly. The algorithms forming the foundation of these technologies can be designed to make more accurate decisions, free from discrimination and bias. Algorithms are scalable, make decisions at a faster pace, adhere to a defined decision-making process, and do not lose focus when reviewing a high volume of applications. Algorithms, unlike many human decisions, leave an evidence trail that allows evaluators to determine whether decision-making is discriminatory and, more precisely, what aspect of the decision-making process is biased. However, they are not a panacea. Algorithms require data inputs, such as work experience, grades, schools attended, and test scores, which might themselves be biased. Also, many of the algorithms are based on the cognitive and emotional traits of current employees, which tend to replicate the existing workforce.

At the London-based consumer goods company Unilever, recruiters are using gamification to expand beyond the small number of schools where they traditionally recruit, in order to make recruiting more efficient and to drive bias out of the decision-making process. Men and women and White, Black, and Hispanic people play games in roughly the same proportion (49 percent).[333]

To start, Unilever placed targeted advertisements on such websites as Facebook, WayUp, and the Muse. Clicking on the ads led prospective employees to a site where they could apply to entry-level jobs and internships with just a few clicks. Their application pulled resume information from LinkedIn, which was compared to job requirements, and screened in 50 percent of the applicants. Those selected were invited to complete "a set of twelve short online games designed to assess skills like concentration under pressure and short-term memory."[334] The third who were screened in by the games were invited to submit a video application via HireVue.

In the US and Canada, this process identified 300 candidates to be interviewed for 200 positions. Unilever believes that the process reduced costs, streamlined the recruitment process, and significantly expanded the number of schools from which it draws junior employees. Unilever has not yet been able to determine the effects of gamification on long-term employee success and on reducing racial, ethnic, and gender bias.[335]

SOURCING

Sourcing is one of the most unconsciously biased talent processes. Organizations often recruit from the same schools from which they have always recruited, use the same recruiting firms that have been successful in the past, pay bonuses to employees who recommend candidates who are eventually hired, and look for "cultural fit" in new employees. These approaches tend to perpetuate the status quo, resulting in new hires that look like old hires.

Take, for example, recruiting for engineers. Returning to the same schools often leads to a limited pool of diverse engineers. If, however, an organization wishes to attract African American engineers, it should start with North Carolina A&T State University, Georgia Tech, and Morgan State. If it wishes to recruit Hispanic engineers, the organization should be building relationships with career placement officers at such schools as the University of Puerto Rico at Mayaguez, Florida International University, and the Polytechnic University of Puerto Rico. These schools turn out the largest numbers of African American and Latino engineers, respectively.

Recruiting firms tend to follow a similar path of least resistance. I have observed organization after organization ask their recruiting firms to find them qualified diverse candidates, only to have recruiters come back a few months later saying, "We couldn't identify any [or more than an inadequately small number of] qualified diversity candidates." Why? They are sourcing candidates in the same old way they always have, often through networks that are not representative. Although many recruiting firms are getting the diversity message, organizations must be firm with recruiters, communicating something like "Bring us highly qualified candidates of color or we will not do business with you in the future," forcing them to expand their networks. In addition, the number of firms that specialize in recruiting women, people of color, and other underrepresented people or that are women- or minority-owned is growing rapidly.

Many growing organizations offer bonuses to employees who recommend candidates that are eventually hired. This presents a conundrum. While this approach tends to replicate the existing workforce, often discouraging diversity, it does offer benefits. These referrals are more effective than other sources of talent. Referred employees are three times more likely to stay three years or more, and the hiring process is much faster.[336] The solution to the conundrum: pay higher bonuses to employees who recommend successful candidates from targeted underrepresented groups. An added benefit is that employees are encouraged to develop and maintain networks in diverse communities.

Sourcing is moving onto the internet. Seventy-nine percent of job seekers utilize internet resources.[337] Men (44 percent) are slightly less likely than women (46 percent) to apply for a job online, and Black people (56 percent) are more likely than White and Hispanic people (each 43 percent) to apply for a job online.[338] This is heartening when consideration is given to the statistics on internet usage: 92 percent of White people use the internet compared to 85 percent of African American people and 86 percent of Hispanic people.[339]

Sourcing is extraordinarily competitive when there is only a small group of qualified underrepresented people in the labor pool. For example, while according to the Census Bureau women are slightly over 50 percent of the US population, they earned less than 20 percent of degrees in engineering.[340] In these cases, the further back in the talent pipeline—even before college entry—an organization reaches, the more likely it is to encourage qualified, underrepresented candidates and build relationships with them. Internships are the gold standard, but considerable effort must be put into ensuring that interns have a positive, meaningful experience. All interns should have a senior-level mentor or sponsor who is not their supervisor to support their learning, as well as to ensure they have an exceptional experience and have visibility.

Stimulating the labor supply in underrepresented fields can be an excellent differentiator. An example is IBM's Technology Camp for Girls at its Research Triangle Park campus in North Carolina. The program has not only encouraged young women to enter technology careers and made IBM a desired career destination, but it has also burnished IBM's image in the local community.

SCREENING

Glassdoor, the recruiting and company evaluation website, reports that corporations receive an average of 250 resumes for each job opening, while Forbes reports that 118 people apply for every job opening.[341] Whatever the number, it is often significant. Research using eye-tracking technology revealed that recruiters spend an average of six seconds scanning a resume to screen each candidate—essentially, an invitation to bias.[342] If an organization spends scant time reviewing resumes, the need for a technologically based solution is almost a given.

Organizations need to understand the process recruiters are using to screen resumes and how rapidly they are being screened. Where that process is inadequate, nonexistent, or not followed, then that process needs to be designed or redesigned, debiased, and enforced.

When screening moves at a fast pace or where the screening process is inadequate, the candidate with "pull" or influence is more likely to pass the screen. Pull, since it favors the well connected, is likely to engender bias. Arguments can be made that pull is beneficial, insofar as it provides additional, relevant information. Furthermore, attempts to eliminate pull are likely to drive it underground. If organizations are reluctant or unable to eliminate pull in identifying candidates, then they might consider conducting an initial screening—without the involvement of the actual hiring manager or group—that follows a defined, debiased process that does not allow external influence. Once the preferred candidate pool has been identified, then hiring managers can select only from that list.

This two-step process encourages the hiring manager or group to be explicit about job requirements, experience, and competencies. This would at least ensure some level of fairness in the process and that any candidate with pull will be qualified without undermining the hiring authority of managers. Ideally, pull should be eliminated altogether from the recruitment process.

INTERVIEWING

In addition to reducing the reality of bias through debiasing, differentiation can be achieved by eliminating the perception of bias in interviewing. Even if two people experience the exact same interview process, the one who has a lifetime of being discriminated against will be more likely to perceive discrimination.

The first step in establishing a perception of fairness is to establish a structured interview process to which all interviewers comply, asking the same questions in the same order. Interviewees in many instances are likely to know other interviewees and will compare notes after their interviews. If each experienced the exact same interview process, the likelihood of actual bias and the perception of bias is reduced.

A number of other actions can reduce the reality and perception of bias in interviews:

◇   Focus on discovering the candidate's strengths and ability to excel at the work or tasks to be done in the position rather than their past experiences and education.

◇   Ideally, the interviewers should be as diverse as possible without falling into tokenism.

◇   To the degree possible, make the interview blind to social group membership.

◇   Always follow up. Organizations damage their brand when candidates are left to wonder whether their applications were even considered.

SELECTION

Selection is replete with opportunities for bias, standing as it does at the intersection of numerous data sources and previous decisions. Data sources that may be biased, both positively and negatively, include test results, interviewing, screening, performance evaluation, and recommendations. Biases include human biases, such as supervisor bias, and cognitive and social biases, including stereotyping, confirmation bias, expectation bias, selective perception, status quo bias, and in-group bias. To eliminate these sources of bias, there should be a standardized selection process that has been debiased. The decision makers for each position should be as consistent as possible. For example, in the military all promotions for a particular position (e.g., colonel or brigadier general) are made by a single panel of officers.

ENGINEERING SUSTAINABLE DIVERSITY

Unfortunately, in organizations without standardized roles and levels, this is more difficult.

Preparation materials for the selection process should include a description of how and where bias can enter decision-making as well as recommendations for overcoming these sources of bias. Furthermore, if the selection is a group decision, the leader or facilitator should make it clear that it is an organizational priority to make bias-free decisions. Finally, once the selection process is complete, a message should be sent to each candidate, thanking them for their application and providing additional pertinent information.

In considering application materials and interviews to make the selection decision, one question with implications for diversity that is often raised is "Does this person fit our culture?" As mentioned above, the question of cultural fit or fit, whether consciously or unconsciously asked, can end up being code for "Hire people that look and act like the people who are already here." Fit should be eliminated from the search conversation. If this isn't possible, then the fit discussion should be moved to the end of the decision process. Make the hiring decision first, and then test it for fit. If the individual doesn't fit, then move on to the candidate next in line.

OFFER

A critical component of the offer is the compensation. Salary and wage gaps between men and women and between non-Hispanic White people and other races and ethnicities persist, even when comparisons are controlled for such factors as differences in hours worked, occupation, education, industry, location, and job experience.[343] This pay gap begins with the offer.

Women and people of color receive lower starting salaries than White men. An important factor in these pay gaps for women, although not unequivocal, are that they are less likely to negotiate job offers than men.[344] Also, those managing the offer have the expectation that African American applicants will be less likely to negotiate. When these expectations are violated, African Americans who negotiate receive lower salaries than White people who negotiate. Furthermore, when the negotiator is prejudiced, the outcome is even worse.[345]

In addition to debiasing the offer process, other differentiators might include the following:

◊ Pay equity accountability, including analysis of total starting compensation by position and demographic group, individual manager, and department, and rewards and recognition to those who directly contribute to moving the needle on equity in compensation

◊ Educate hiring managers on unconscious bias in compensation and the differences between men and women and among White people and people of color in how they negotiate compensation and how hiring managers' expectations shape those negotiations.

◊ Make explicit that offers are open to negotiation. While this may sound like leaving the candy store unattended, research has demonstrated that when openness to negotiation is unambiguous, there are no differences between the willingness of men and women to negotiate.[346]

Retention

Many of the retention differentiators have been covered in "Competency 6: Instituting Inclusion." Diversity philosophy and culture, a key factor in employer brand and an important differentiator, is addressed in "Competency 3: Envisioning a Diversity Philosophy." Here, the focus is on the work itself and recognition and rewards.

THE WORK

In his classic description of the division of labor in a pin factory in *The Wealth of Nations*, Adam Smith describes how a single man with no special skills might struggle to produce a single pin in a day, but that ten unskilled men, each taking on a small component of the total production process, could produce thousands of pins in a day.[347]

The division of labor that Smith described was the foundation of the industrial revolution and even today describes production in many industries. In developed countries, the effects of education, technology, and the economic evolution toward service and knowledge work has turned the division of labor on its head. The nature of work has fundamentally changed and continues to change at a rapid pace—toward, for example, virtual work and contract work.

In its current state, work has been found to have three design components that strongly correlate with job satisfaction and, to some degree, retention: job, social, and physical components (see table 7-2).[348] These components can be managed to create a meaningful, engaging, and productive work experience. At the same time, however, implicit in each component is the potential for bias, a reality that must also be managed. For example, bias can enter into the assignment of autonomy through prejudices about reliability, integrity, and follow-through. The determination of the components of a job should be made within the structure of a defined and debiased process rather than in a one-off manner at the discretion of a single manager.

Components of Work[349]

JOB COMPONENTS

Autonomy	The degree of freedom an employee has to fulfill the requirements of the job. Specifically, three aspects of autonomy are salient: the freedom the employee has to schedule the work, to determine work methods and procedures, and to make decisions.
Skill Variety	The variety of skills that are required to do the job
Task Variety	The variety of tasks the employee is expected to fulfill
Meaningfulness	The degree to which fulfillment of the job requirements contributes to the lives of others both inside and outside the organization
Comprehensiveness	The degree to which the individual can complete all the elements of a single task
Feedback from Job	The degree to which the job itself provides evaluative feedback

SOCIAL COMPONENTS

Feedback from Others	The degree to which other employees provide evaluative feedback
Interdependence	The degree to which completion of the job is dependent on others and the work of others is dependent on the job
Social Support	The degree to which employees are provided with input, encouragement, and resources from their managers and colleagues to successfully complete job assignments

PHYSICAL COMPONENTS

Physical Demands	The physical requirements of the job
Work Conditions	The degree to which the health and safety of the employee is at risk

Table 7-2

The social components have the most significant relationship with retention. Because most social science research is conducted at a single moment in time, it is impossible to determine whether specific behaviors actually contribute to retention, since retention occurs after the study is over. Researchers substitute a question about intention to leave—whether the research subject is planning to leave the organization within some defined period of time, usually one year. So, the intention to leave is what the social components have a strong relationship with.

Underrepresented people are at greater risk of turnover, especially in the early years of employment. Thus, it is crucial for leaders to ensure that underrepresented employees receive supports for developing critical interdependencies, unbiased feedback from others, and the input, encouragement, and resources to do their jobs effectively.

RECOGNITION AND REWARDS

Though they are often spoken of contemporaneously, recognition and rewards are really two different approaches to the management of employee motivation and behavior. Rewards are instrumental in nature, serving as a means to obtain specific behaviors. They motivate extrinsically and focus on compliance and meeting goals and standards. Rewards are based on an agreement or contract made before the actual targeted behavior occurs and typically have a financial component.

Recognition is aimed at intrinsically motivated behaviors, such as engagement, initiative, collaboration, encouragement, support, and innovation. Recognition happens after the targeted behavior occurs and typically has no or little additional cost. Rewards tend to be tactical, while recognition is more strategic. Recognition is more linked to behaviors that can differentiate the organization in the talent marketplace.

Rewards and recognition have downsides. When behaviors

become instrumentally linked to rewards, those behaviors tend not to be performed in the absence of a reward.[350] Recognition must be genuine and sincere, or it will be perceived as manipulation and become more like extrinsic motivation. Effective recognition provides employees with "positive information about their self-competence."[351]

Rewards and recognition impact diversity in two ways: differences in how rewards and recognition are distributed among demographic groups, and rewards and recognition for behaviors that advance the cause of diversity. Like any talent decision process, data should be recorded regarding how rewards and recognition are distributed among demographic groups. Since rewards are typically tangible, including money and promotions, and awarded in a systematic manner, they are usually straightforward to track. Where inequities exist, the rewards process should be debiased, and the improved process should become the standard for rewards. In addition, prompts about preventing bias in decision-making should be provided to decision makers before rewards are determined.

Recognition is usually intangible and often informal; therefore, systematic data is unlikely to be available and prompts unrealistic. Because recognition is a more powerful differentiator in the talent market, a debiased, standardized process should be developed for ensuring equitable recognition, and the recognition process and practices should be an important part of any diversity training for managers.

For behaviors that advance diversity, formal rewards should be offered in alignment with accountability measures. Rewards should not be offered for individual acts of leadership but rather should be available to all employees for achieving diversity objectives or meeting other standards. Singling out one or a few individuals to receive monetary rewards can often have an across-the-board negative impact ("Why didn't I receive a reward?").

Recognition for advancing diversity should come from peers. Peer recognition fosters inclusion and is less likely to be perceived as biased since any employee can nominate a peer. A survey by the Society for Human Resource Management found that "HR professionals are [at least three times] more likely to rate their employee recognition program as 'good' at organizations where any employee is able to nominate or recognize a peer, compared with those who had supervisors/managers, senior-level executives or HR give recognition."[352]

Advancement

The components of advancement—career development, succession planning, leadership development, mentoring, and sponsorship—are covered in "Competency 6: Instituting Inclusion."

Exit

Though the pace and demands of organizational life often give rise to a "gone and soon forgotten" mindset about former employees, how employees are escorted to the exit (exit management) and how the organization maintains relationships with former employees (post-exit rapport) are critical for employer brand management, allaying lawsuits and the potential for violence, and building future business and finding future employees.

Employees exit for a variety of reasons—some voluntary, some involuntary. Reasons for electing to leave include a new job, retirement, dependent-care responsibilities, the supervisor, and working conditions. Reasons for involuntary departures include layoffs or redundancies, firing for nonperformance, and firing for cause (e.g., violation of sexual harassment policies and unethical behavior). Managing these different reasons for exiting often require different approaches. The next section on exit management discusses how to create an exit process that leads to positive outcomes while calling out information that is relevant to managing specific reasons for exiting. The final section on post-exit rapport examines the rationale for maintaining relationships with former employees, particularly those from underrepresented groups, and offers some strategies for managing relationships with alumni.

EXIT EXPERIENCE

The degree of difficulty for creating a positive exit experience is usually greater for those whose exits are involuntary. Furthermore, because of past experiences of discrimination, underrepresented employees may be more likely to perceive the exit experience as negative and unjust.

Four factors typically account for positive exit experiences: prior employee engagement, procedural justice, palatability of the reason for termination, and termination decision ownership.[353]

Prior Employee Engagement: Employee engagement is *the degree of passion employees feel for their organization, their willingness to go the extra mile for it, their emotional attachment to it, and their identification with it*. A history of being engaged tends to insulate exiting employees from negative feelings. High employee engagement contributes significantly to the sustainability of competitive advantage.

Procedural Justice: Procedural justice is *the perception by exiting employees of whether the decision process leading to their exit was fair and effectively handled*. Actions that organizations can take to ensure exiting employees perceive procedural justice include providing valid reasons for termination; having a fair, debiased, and transparent process for identifying those to be terminated; treating exiting employees with dignity and respect; and providing frequent, high-quality, and transparent communication.[354]

Palatability of the Reason for Termination: Palatability refers to *the degree to which exiting employees perceive the reason for termination to be consistent with the psychological contract they hold with their organizations.* The psychological contract is implied and is the *employee's perceptions of the reciprocal obligations between herself and the organization.* Psychological contracts typically include such elements as employees' expectations about training and development, advancement, company loyalty, the job, job security, and compensation expectations in exchange for organizations' expectations about job requirements, loyalty, work effort, and performance.

To make involuntary exits more palatable, leaders should consider offering severance payments, career coaching, job search support, and recommendations in behalf of departing employees. Psychological contracts tend to emphasize different elements for people of different genders and cultures, and presumably different races and ethnicities. In managing palatability, it is important to understand how different social groups perceive their psychological contracts and to shape palatability actions to those differences.

Termination Decision Ownership: Termination decision ownership refers to *the degree to which an employee perceives that they have control over their exit.* Exiting employees will often shape the narrative of their exit more positively than is perhaps warranted by the real circumstances of their departure. Organizations can shape this narrative by ensuring the exit experience is as respectful and empowering as possible and by providing exiting employees with as much control as possible, such as control over how they will make their physical exit or decisions about severance payments or use of job and career resources.

POST-EXIT RAPPORT

Post-exit rapport is *the development and maintenance of high-quality relationships with employees after termination.* Post-exit rapport is significant for several reasons, both positive and negative:

◊   Former employees can be excellent sources of business leads and recommendations of candidates for employment.

◊   They can be rehired. The costs of hiring a former employee are half those of finding a new employee, and former employees are 40 percent more productive in the first three months of re-employment.[355]

◊   They can influence the employer brand.

◊   On the negative side, former employees may bring lawsuits against organizations for discrimination and wrongful termination. Underrepresented people are more likely to sue.

◊   Unhappy former employees, insofar as they have relationships with those who remain, can have a substantial negative impact on employee morale.

By a significant margin, the biggest factor in predicting the quality of the post-exit relationship—stronger even than economic considerations or the employment experience prior to termination—is the experience of the former employee at the moment of termination.[356] Thus, effective management of procedural justice, palatability, and decision ownership are especially critical.

For underrepresented people, their perceptions of procedural justice and palatability at the moment of termination may be shaped by prior instances or perceptions of bias and discrimination. Furthermore, because of discrimination, underrepresented people are disproportionately among the last hired, and therefore when a downturn hits they are among the first laid off. To manage the exit process, then, it is especially important to understand whether the exit experiences of underrepresented people are different from those of White men.

Exit interviews can be a vital source of data for improving the exit experience overall and especially for understanding and improving the exit experiences of different social groups. However, exit interviews are notoriously inaccurate.[357] An old saying goes, "Employees don't burn bridges," meaning they pull punches in their exit interviews. Exit interviews can be perfunctory and incomplete as human resources personnel rush to complete an overload of exit paperwork. The antidote is to conduct post-exit interviews or surveys six months or so after an employee departs. Third parties who specialize in post-exit interviews are more likely to be given trustworthy information by former employees.

At minimum, exit interviews or surveys should examine procedural justice, palatability, and decision ownership, reason for leaving (if resignation), contain questions on the exit experience and the relationship since exit, and have demographic questions to identify the underrepresented group of which the employee is a member. The latter allows the data to be examined for differences in social groups.

Once the door to a continuing relationship has been opened, it must be maintained. Many tools are available for maintaining relationships. For general rapport, invitations to social and organizational events, newsletters, and alumni networks are effective. To build business, organizations will want to ensure that former employees are up to date on new products and services and organizational plans. Employee resource groups can sponsor gatherings with alumni from their social group and even invite alums to bring guests who would be interested in the products and services the firm offers or who might be or know high-quality job candidates.

To receive talent referrals, organizations should communicate job postings and perhaps provide bonuses to those who refer underrepresented candidates who are eventually hired. A tool that can be borrowed from sales and marketing is customer relationship management (CRM), which is used to maintain and enhance relationships with current and former customers. Usually heavy on analytics, CRM systems can provide valuable information to improve the employee experience.

Human Capital Support

The three components of human capital support—centers of excellence, human capital business partners, and human capital shared services—are the activities that enable the employee experience. Centers of excellence or expertise (CoE) are typically responsible for program, policy, and process development and oversight; conducting research; fostering best practices; providing training and development; and vendor management. Some are more organized around business issues, such as mergers and acquisitions, growth, and innovation, while other CoEs are more organized around talent issues, such as organization effectiveness, learning and development, and diversity, equity, and inclusion. Managing the employee experience is a collaborative exercise across CoEs, since different CoEs are likely to own different aspects of the employee experience. The diversity CoE may not directly own most aspects of the employee experience but should play an influential role in how those experiences are tailored to different social groups.

Human capital or human resource business partners (HCBP) are strategic partners with the business, helping the business to meet its strategic talent needs and integrate the business with the CoEs. HRBPs are like senior partners in a consulting firm, bringing deep knowledge of the needs and requirements of the business and the human capital resources available to fulfill those needs, and serving as senior project managers to coordinate the various players in formulating and implementing business solutions.

HCBPs, like the line leaders they serve, are under tremendous pressure to solve business problems related to bottom line success. Diversity, equity, and inclusion may not be a top priority in many businesses. Therefore, it is necessary, to the degree possible, to ensure that HCBPs are deeply committed to diversity, equity, and inclusion at minimum and at best are advocates for diversity.

Human capital shared service (HCSS) organizations are responsible for delivering human capital benefits to employees and for administration of human capital programs. They often include case managers who assist employees with questions and challenges. That point of contact is replete with opportunities for bias, requiring that the case management process be debiased and monitored for bias. HCSS is also usually responsible for human capital data and analytics, a critical function in determining where to deploy resources to improve diversity, equity, and inclusion.

Diversity Climate

Diversity climate is the *collective perceptions of how underrepresented employees experience equity and inclusion; recruitment, retention, advancement, and exit; and human capital support.* Although perceptions are not reality, they are highly salient because they have a strong influence over behavior. In the diverse talent value chain, a measure of diversity climate provides the perfect summary of how diverse employees experience the organization and gives leaders the knowledge to prioritize the deployment of resources to improve the diversity experience for underrepresented, as well as well-represented, employees.

In addition to summarizing the employee experience, a diversity climate measure can be used diagnostically, to determine what aspects of diversity employees believe require improvement, and evaluatively, to determine the effects of interventions to improve diversity. An organization's diversity climate measure is a significant component of the internal assessment in the strategy process and is central to the formulation, implementation, and evaluation of its diversity strategy.

A climate measure can be a survey or a series of individual and group interviews of employee perceptions—or a combination of the two. Surveys provide quantitative data, which allow precise comparisons between the perceptions of well-represented and underrepresented people and between the organization and its competitors, are more credible with quantitatively oriented leaders, and allow for sophisticated statistical analysis. On the other hand, focus groups and interviews are useful in organizations experiencing "survey fatigue," can be rolled out more quickly, are usually less expensive, signal inclusion, and determine root causes more effectively.

Diversity Climate Survey

Three pathways exist to fielding a diversity climate survey: an existing employee survey, an existing diversity climate survey, and the development of a custom or largely custom survey. An organization's existing employee survey, while not really designed to measure diversity climate, can be a good half measure as long as it asks demographic questions about race, ethnicity, gender identity, sexual orientation, disability, and age. If the organization is large enough, then the data can be sliced by underrepresented group and then compared to determine whether one group is less satisfied than another.

Many existing diversity climate measures already exist and, although not tailored to an organization's unique work environment, can provide adequate assessments of diversity climate. Two well-validated and reliable measures of organizational climate are the eighty-two-item Organizational Climate Measure[358] developed by Malcolm Patterson et al., and the forty-seven-item Organizational Climate Survey developed by the Hay Group.[359] These can assess and evaluate diversity climate as long as demographic data is collected so underrepresented groups can be compared with well-represented groups.

A prominent diversity climate instrument that is more focused on issues of diversity and has been used in several studies is the sixteen-item Diversity Perceptions Scale.[360] It includes four scales, including the organizational fairness factor, the organizational inclusion factor, the personal diversity value factor, and the personal comfort factor. Because it has few questions, this instrument's usefulness is limited for diagnostic purposes.

The optimal but more time-consuming and costly approach is to develop a custom climate survey. The custom climate survey measures perceptions of how executives, managers, and colleagues are performing on the employee-experience attributes of the diversity talent value chain, including equity, inclusion, recruitment, retention, and advancement. This approach is optimal because it measures performance on the attributes that drive sustainable diversity competitive advantage. Exit should be measured by post-exit interviews or a survey.

The climate survey should also include a short measure or index of employee engagement. Employee engagement has been shown in numerous studies to predict organizational performance. A short index of employee engagement questions allows each question about an employee-experience attribute to be correlated with the engagement index. The size of the correlation indicates how strongly the question is related to employee engagement and, therefore, to organizational performance.

Validated and reliable measures are available from consulting firms and from academicians. Amy Richman and her colleagues at WFD Consulting (the author's former firm) developed a well-validated seven-question measure that can be included in any of the three climate survey options.[361] A widely used scholarly measure is the nine-question Utrecht Work Engagement Scale that is available for free as long as it is not used for commercial purposes (i.e., the using organization does not charge for it) and the raw score results and ages and genders of the respondents are provided to the developers to be added to their database. Neither the names of employees nor the organization are required. They would like general information on the organization, including its size, occupations covered, language, and country.[362] Both surveys have acceptable levels of validity and reliability.

How frequently to administer the diversity climate survey depends on the organization's situation. Many organizations administer the survey annually. When leaders are concerned that employees are being surveyed on diversity and other topics too frequently, the survey can be administered every two or three years. Some organizations use the pulse survey method, administering the climate survey every month or quarter to a sample of employees. For organizations with aggressive strategic diversity plans, pulse surveys allow them to track on a continuing basis how strategy implementation is affecting diversity climate. A good rule of thumb is to, at a minimum, administer the survey at the initiation of a new round of strategic diversity planning.

Employer Diversity Brand

Whether they wish to or not, organizations project an employer brand: *how current, prospective, and former employees perceive the value of the experience of working in an organization.* To influence the perception of the employer brand and to attract employees, organizations advance an employee value proposition (EVP), *the valued experiences an employee will receive from working in an organization, and, in some cases, what the employee will give in return for that value.* The employer brand is the perception of the actual work experience—the reality— while the EVP is a combination of reality and aspiration. The employer diversity brand is how members of underrepresented groups perceive the employer brand. The diverse employee value proposition is the EVP targeted to the specific needs and requirements of various diverse employee groups.

An attractive employer brand offers several benefits in talent competition. Organizations with attractive employer brands are able to source talent from 60 percent of the labor market, while organizations with ineffective employer brands are only able to source from 40 percent of the market.[363] In organizations with poor employer brands, only 9 percent of new hires have high levels of commitment. For organizations with attractive employer brands, 38 percent of new hires have high commitment.[364] When the employer brand is unattractive, a 21 percent increase in average compensation is required to attract a new employee versus 11 percent when an organization has an attractive employer brand.[365] Employer brand correlates positively with the quantity of applicants (0.42).[366] Organizations that deliver on their employee value proposition can see as much as a 69 percent reduction in annual turnover.[367]

The employee value proposition is central to the management of the employer brand. The EVP is the core message that organizations use to shape how talent markets perceive the employer brand. Creating an EVP is replete with challenges. Because an organization must attract multiple segments of the talent market (e.g., scientists, engineers, and salespeople; entry level and experienced; different national cultures; well represented and underrepresented), the EVP must be consistent across all markets as well as resonate with the needs and requirements of each talent market to which it is targeted. Furthermore, the EVP must be anchored in reality so that what the EVP says employees will receive is consistent with the employer brand. The EVP for an underrepresented group is central to how the employer diversity brand and ultimately the diversity brand are perceived.

If an individual from an underrepresented group joins an organization based in some part on a diversity EVP (the employee experience promise) and finds the employer diversity brand (the reality) inconsistent with that diversity EVP, then they will usually end up dissatisfied. If the diversity EVP misses the mark on the needs and requirements of the social group to which it is targeted, then it will lose its power to recruit and retain. If the diversity EVP is at odds with the organization's talent strategy, top management's strategic priorities, or the diversity philosophy, then it risks creating competitive advantage in unimportant areas.

To address the conundrums above, the creation and continuous improvement of the employer diversity brand should follow a five-step process: (1) employer brand assessment, (2) global employee value proposition development, (3) diverse employee value proposition formulation, (4) communication strategy, and (5) employer brand evaluation. The steps are slightly different for the original formulation of the global and diversity employee value propositions than for subsequent iterations of the process to improve the perception of the employer brand and the effectiveness of the employee value propositions.

Step 1: Employer Brand Assessment

The purposes of a strong employer brand are to increase the engagement and retention of current employees, to attract prospective employees, and to turn alumni into brand ambassadors. To achieve these purposes effectively and efficiently requires sound data. Those developing and improving the employee value proposition and the diverse employee value propositions should understand how the employer brand is perceived and what attributes target populations seek in an employer, the organization's and competitors' strengths and weaknesses on those attributes, and how competitors are positioned on those attributes. The communication strategy requires knowledge of which media and communication channels and what kinds of messages are most salient to each target population. Regrettably, only 52 percent of companies always or frequently use data to drive employer branding.[368]

The first action in the EB assessment is to undertake the following:

◇   Determine the types of employees that are the highest priority and their key characteristics.

◇   Assess the relevant labor markets to determine the supply of qualified candidates now and in the future.

◇   Determine the level of competition among those competitors, and their competitive strategies.

◇   Identify where these candidates are likely to be found (e.g., colleges and universities, high schools, vocational programs, unemployment rolls, other employers).

The second action is to gather the information needed to fulfill the three purposes. This requires three data-gathering instruments: the climate survey of current employees, market research on prospective employees, and a post-exit survey or interviews with alumni.

The climate survey determines the quality of the employee experience, the central organizational attributes that contribute to the quality of that experience, how the organization is performing on those attributes, how employees view the employer brand, and whether the employer brand and the EVP are consistent.

Market research assesses how the organization's diversity brand and those of its talent competitors are perceived by prospective employees, the central attributes prospective employees seek, the channels they use to gather information and apply for jobs, and how to bring prospective employees from awareness to application. If the organization has an EVP, market research should also gauge whether prospective employees are aware of the EVP, how they view the EVP relative to competitor EVPs, and the communication channels they used to learn about the EVP. However, market research can be expensive. A less expensive—although not as robust—substitute is to survey new hires before their perceptions are influenced by life in the organization.

Post-exit surveys and interviews are aimed at understanding the experience of alumni during their employment and exit experiences, how they view the employer brand and its consistency with the employee value proposition, and whether and how they wish to continue their engagement with the organization. Respondents should be segregated by reasons for leaving, including poor performance, violations of policies and ethical guidelines, layoff, and voluntary resignation, and whether they were employees the organization wished to keep (unwanted turnover). If only a trickle of employees is leaving, attempts should be made to interview every former employee. To help ensure participation, the post-exit interview can be written into the severance agreement. A payment for participating in the post-exit process might also be offered. Exit interviews are more fully discussed in the "Exit" section above.

Websites such as Glassdoor and Comparably offer low- or no-cost employee reviews of organizations, analysis of those reviews, and comparisons with competitors. Although the information provided is often general, these websites can provide competitive comparisons of employer brands.

The culmination of the assessment process should be a set of objectives based on the assessment data that is aimed at strengthening the experience of diverse employees, improving the diversity EVP and its reach, and any other objective that will have a positive impact on the perception of the employer brand by prospective, current, and former underrepresented employees. Each of these objectives should be measurable so they can be assessed during evaluation. Performance on these objectives will be a key component of the evaluation of the employer diversity brand process.

Step 2: Global Employee Value Proposition Development

Building an effective employee value proposition is a highly collaborative and inductive process with numerous data inputs and considerations. The first action is to assemble a team or task force to create the EVP. For most organizations, groups that should be included are stakeholders, representing senior management; business unit leadership; the diversity, human resources/human capital, talent, marketing, and communications/public affairs organizations; and employee resource groups or representatives of the various underrepresented groups.

Next, relevant data from the three instruments should be assembled and presented to the task force. Of particular importance are the following:

◊   The categories of employees that are the highest attraction and retention priorities for achieving strategic success
◊   The attributes of the employer that are most desirable to these employees
◊   The strengths and weaknesses of the organization relative to its talent competitors on those attributes

All this needs to be understood in the context of talent market realities, such as supply and demand in key categories and environmental trends, including technological, governmental, economic, cultural, and demographic factors. Much of this information is likely to have been gathered in the course of the organization's talent strategy process.

The task force members should understand the organizational strategy, organizational values, the diversity philosophy, and the branding of the organization's products and services, as well as the talent strategy. Then, the task force should construct a strong draft of the EVP, keeping these organizational imperatives in mind. The EVP should be global (i.e., consequential across geography and demography). Beyond the global EVP, organizations may wish to establish local EVPs, of which diversity EVPs are an example.

The EVP should establish a core positioning—the critical few attributes that resonate globally with the employees whose capabilities and qualities are most sought after. In some instances, a supplementary positioning may be useful, but it should not be a substitute for the hard work of agreeing on a core position. The EVP should contain attributes that are based on organizational strengths and some attributes to which it can realistically aspire. A good rule of thumb is the 70/30 rule: 70 percent based on reality, 30 percent on aspiration. Effective EVPs meet several additional criteria:

◇ *Authentic*: credible and true to what the organization really stands for and offers to its employees
◇ *Attractive*: attributes that have a strong pull toward the organization and counteract attributes, such as compensation and status, that push employees away from the organization
◇ *Distinctive*: differentiates the organization from its talent competitors ("58 percent of surveyed HR leaders believe that differentiation is the biggest challenge" to talent attraction)[369]
◇ *Simple*: clear, straightforward, and unembellished

◇   *Sustainable*: focuses on attributes that are difficult to replicate and which the organization has the wherewithal to defend and advance over time

Once established, many organizations create a tagline, a succinct, catchy expression of the most vital components of their EVP. The final action is to review the EVP and any tagline with employees before going public. These reviews are best conducted in focus groups of employees and, ideally, prospective employees and alumni. Focus groups may be heterogeneous or homogeneous, conducted for different social groups or target groups, such as engineers, salespeople, and research scientists, or students and experienced employees.

Many examples of great EVPs and taglines can be found on the internet. For example, Avalara, a company that develops and sells automated sales tax solutions, offers an EVP that captures many of the criteria above:

> Avalarians wear orange. We're optimistic. Curious. Adaptable. We are intensely committed to making the difficult simple for our customers—which is really hard, but really rewarding. Some say we're a little quirky, but that's a good thing, right? We welcome and value unique people and insights, and we believe our winning culture sets us apart. We recognize, cherish, and hire to that conviction every day.

> Through the years we've identified a few key traits that are common among our most successful employees. Ranging from passion and urgency to ownership, fun, and optimism, these traits form the basis of our culture and we hold them in highest esteem. In the end, it's a simple proposition: At Avalara we are not only good at what we do, we are also proud of how we get things done.[370]

Two distinctive taglines are L'Oreal's "Lead the future of Beauty. When you love your work and the people you work with, amazing things can happen," and Nike's "We are the people that do. We lead. We invent. We deliver. We use the power of sport to move the world." The trouble is, I found in a review of over a hundred EVPs and taglines that they can most easily be found in the marketing of the consulting firms that helped create them. They are difficult to find on employer websites and in other communications. An effective communications strategy is critical.

This development process creates a global EVP that applies to every current, prospective, and former employee regardless of their gender, race, ethnicity, or membership in another underrepresented group. Should the global EVP contain a general diversity attribute, or should local EVPs be developed around the attributes sought by each underrepresented group? The next step examines whether and how to create local EVPs targeted to underrepresented groups.

Step 3: Diverse Employee Value Proposition Formulation

Although 85 percent of the world's most attractive employers indicate that hiring for diversity is a high priority, their EVPs don't reflect it. Less than half (37 percent) include diversity in their EVPs. And of all companies, only 12 percent include diversity as a key attribute.[371] One solution to this disconnect is to simply include diversity in the global EVP. Another is to develop local EVPs targeted to the attributes that individual underrepresented groups seek with communication strategies designed specifically for the channels that group uses to gather information about employers.

Whether to develop local diversity EVPs depends on whether different underrepresented groups seek substantially different attributes in an employer. The evidence from a massive study of 58,000 employees in ninety global organizations suggests that those of different genders, races, and ethnicities do not seek different attributes and do not use distinct communication channels to access information about employers. Evidence does suggest that there are differences in the attributes sought by those in different countries and in how they access information. The study also found that younger workers (twenty-three to twenty-nine) prefer moderately different attributes than older workers (fifty to fifty-nine).[378]

For organizations that are able to gather internal and external data on candidates, employees, and alumni, determining whether distinct EVPs are needed for diverse groups is a straightforward matter of reviewing whether significant differences exist in the attributes those groups seek and how they access information about employment. For those organizations that do not have access to data, the best approach is to go along with the general data, as limited as it might be, and incorporate diversity into the global EVP. Building an EVP focused on a particular underrepresented group follows the same action steps as building the global EVP.

Step 4: Communications Strategy

The process for developing a communications strategy for an EVP is similar to the process for creating any diversity-related communication, as covered in "Competency 10: Talking the Walk: Top Leadership Communications."

For each global and local EVP, the following should be undertaken:

◇   An audience should be chosen.
◇   Goals should be established for the chosen audience.
◇   Media or communication channels should be selected.
◇   The messages or content developed and transmitted through the media and channels should be selected.

AUDIENCE

The question of audience simply relates to whether the target of communications is prospective, current, or former employees.

GOALS

In general, the goals of marketing communications are to create awareness, interest, desire, and action. Regarding the prospective employee, the employer's purpose in creating awareness is to channel their attention to the organization. Under the umbrella of interest, the candidate becomes aware of the attributes of working in the organization and how those attributes might apply to them. In the area of desire, the candidate makes a favorable connection between the attributes, the requirements of a particular job, and their own strengths and interests. In action, the candidate applies for the job and, if invited, shows up for the interview. Done effectively, the process should lead the candidate to self-qualify for the job. Qualified candidates are more likely to have the capabilities and qualities the organization desires and are more likely to accept a job if offered, to stay, and to speak favorably about the organization.

For current employees, the employer's ultimate goal is to encourage their commitment to the organization and have them promote the employer brand and recommend the organization to others. Awareness as it applies to current employees means they understand that the organization is looking to them to be a brand ambassador. Interest involves understanding how to promote the organization. Desire refers to their seeing that the expectations they had upon joining the organization correspond with their actual employee experience. This is no small challenge. Glassdoor, the recruiting and employee-experience review company, found that 61 percent of employees say the realities of their new jobs differ from their expectations when they started their jobs. The goal of action is fulfilled when employees actively promote the employer brand.

For former employees, the goals are the same as for current employees, although harder to attain since there was a reason, often negative, that the employee left. The exit experience is a critical component of whether the former employee will be a brand ambassador or brand denigrator.

MEDIA/COMMUNICATION CHANNELS

Depending on the audience and the goal, a wide array of communication channels are available, from traditional advertising to the internet and intranet. Different stages in the marketing process may also require different media. For example, awareness might be achieved through organization websites, articles about the organization, and advertisements.

MESSAGE

Content should vary by the audience, goal, and stage of the marketing process and be tailored to the medium. Messages are not only conveyed through words. Images have advantages. They are processed faster and remembered longer, they communicate more clearly, and they transmit emotions better than words. But images can be double edged. When they communicate an EVP that is not borne out by the employer brand, they increase the negative impact. For example, one popular way to convey commitment to diversity is to show pictures of underrepresented employees. But if the reality is that the organization has few underrepresented employees, then it is likely to lose prospective underrepresented employees somewhere during attraction and retention. And those prospects and employees will have a negative view of the organization.

As a communications channel, employees are great advocates for their organizations, but they need to know what specific actions they are expected to take. Employees need to be encouraged to be better advocates, as "more than 80% of candidates believe that current employees are credible sources of information about organizations; however, fewer than 24% of employees actively advocate for their organization in the labor market."[373] The message should communicate the actions it expects from employees.

Given the credibility employees have with the talent market, it makes sense to engage them in crafting messages. This can run from testimonials tied to the EVP to photographs taken by employees. A group of employee brand ambassadors can be formed to focus on communication of the EVP and advocacy for the organization.

Step 5: Employer Brand Evaluation

The employer brand evaluation is distinct from the employer brand assessment. The brand assessment is diagnostic and formative, identifying objectives that should be undertaken to produce and improve outcomes. The employer brand evaluation assesses how the organization is performing on those objectives. It can be as simple as a single measure or a dashboard of measures intended to direct the organization toward the objectives.

Employer brand evaluation can be a core dashboard of three measures or an expanded dashboard with additional measures (figure 7-6). The results on all measures should be broken out by the underrepresented groups the organization is targeting.

Employer Brand Dashboard

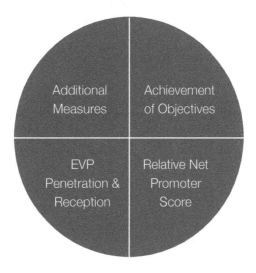

Figure 7-6

CORE DASHBOARD

The most straightforward and important measure is the degree to which employer brand objectives have been achieved. Achievement of objectives not only summarizes the improvements to the employer brand but also sets the stage for the next round of assessments by identifying what employee experiences need additional improvement and what new diagnostic questions should be asked.

A second measure that captures the value of the employer brand is the net promoter score (NPS). The NPS contains a single question: "How likely are you to recommend employment at [name of organization] to a friend, relative, or colleague?" The answer is scored on a zero-to-ten scale with zero labeled *Not at All* and ten labeled *Extremely Likely*. The scores are summarized into three categories:

◇   Detractors, the percentage who gave a rating of six or lower
◇   Passives, the percentage who gave a rating of seven or eight
◇   Promoters, the percentage who gave a rating of nine or ten

The percentage of detractors is then subtracted from the percentage of promoters for a score of negative 100 to a high of 100. Bain & Company, the global management consulting firm and originator of the NPS, suggests the following scale for interpreting NPS:

◇   Above zero is good
◇   Above twenty is favorable
◇   Above fifty is excellent
◇   Above eighty is world class

The NPS can also be compared to other organizations. Several benchmarks are available.

The third measure is how deeply the EVP has penetrated the labor market and how well it has been received. Penetration is an important measure of prospective employees. It can be measured during market research to test awareness of the EVP among targeted employee markets. Though not as robust, the number of clicks on the portion of the website that contains the EVP can be measured. Reception to the EVP by prospective employees can also be measured with market research.

ADDITIONAL MEASURES

All of these additional measures should include comparisons between members of well-represented and underrepresented groups:

◇ *Absenteeism*: The average days of absence per year is likely to decline when the employer brand is strong.

◇ *Compensation*: A strong employer brand should reduce average compensation at time of hire.

◇ *Cost/Hire*: If the employer brand and EVP are compelling, the cost of hiring should go down. Cost of hire is calculated by dividing total internal and external recruiting costs by the number of hires.

◇ *Diversity of Hires*: The proportion of hires in targeted underrepresented groups should improve year over year.

◇ *Employee Commitment at Time of Hire*: Organizations with a strong EVP attract employees that are more highly committed at the time of hiring.

◇ *Quantity of Applicants*: A robust employer brand can increase the number of applicants, particularly the number of passive applicants (individuals who are currently not looking for a new job).

◇ *Retention*: The average length of time targeted employees remain in the organization should grow. Since underrepresented people often leave earlier in their careers, another way of looking at retention is percentage of hires who are retained for three years.

Care must be taken not to overattribute the results of positive movement on the additional measures to the employer brand or the EVP. While employer brand and EVP can have a significant impact on these outcomes, the additional measures have many other drivers. Supervisory behavior, compensation, work–life benefits, and several other factors all impact on retention. Thus, it is difficult to say with any certainty that employer brand or EVP is the reason turnover declines.

Diverse Employee Engagement

The construct of employee engagement is still in its relatively early stages of development. While practitioners have developed a number of tools for measuring employee engagement (see "Diversity Climate Survey" above), shown strong relationships between employee engagement and individual and organizational performance, and identified a number of factors that contribute to employee engagement, many scholars are concerned that an agreed-upon definition of employee engagement doesn't currently exist. A 2014 employee engagement research review found fourteen different definitions of employee engagement.[374] Nevertheless, scholars do acknowledge the gains that practitioners have made in developing employee engagement, and they acknowledge that employee engagement is of such importance that it is worth the time and resources to operationalize it. Though imperfect, employee engagement is the best measure available to link work experience to performance.

Employee engagement is defined as *the degree of passion employees feel for their organization, their willingness to go the extra mile for it, their emotional attachment to it, and their identification with it.* The following sections examine what leaders can do to drive employee engagement, the beneficial impacts of high employee engagement, and the engagement levels of underrepresented groups.

The Drivers of Employee Engagement

In a review of twelve research studies on the drivers of employee engagement, the Conference Board identified twenty-six different drivers.[375] Of those, consensus was found on eight broad drivers, which are consistent with the findings of more recent studies. The five elements of inclusion and the components of achieving a sustainable diversity competitive advantage address most of those drivers (see "Competency 6: Instituting Inclusion" and "Competency 7: Engineering Sustainable Diversity Competitive Advantage").

Of the five elements of inclusion, the core principles of authenticity and belongingness, talent enablement, employee participation, and inclusive leadership—especially empowerment, integrity, respect, and transparency—are vital for employee engagement. Of the employee-experience attributes in the diversity talent value chain, the work itself, employee development and coaching, recognition, and career development are strong drivers of employee engagement. Four other factors, not included elsewhere, are important drivers of employee engagement: relationships, pride, resources, and alignment with organizational purpose and imperatives (see table 7-3).

Additional Drivers of Employee Engagement	
Relationships	The quality of employees' relationships with their direct manager and with their colleagues
Pride	The sense of pride, prestige, and stature employees experience as a result of their association with their employer
Resources	The degree to which employees have the resources, including tools, support, and access to networks, they need to excel at their work
Alignment	Employees' clarity about how their personal work goals align with the strategic imperatives of the organization and whether their values and beliefs are a fit with organizational purpose

Table 7-3

The Impact of Employee Engagement

High employee engagement has been linked to improvements in the performance of individuals and organizations. However, the direction of causality remains in question. Does employee engagement lead to higher performance, or does higher performance lead to employee engagement? For example, high-performing companies may be in a better position to afford and implement the kinds of progressive human resource practices that lead to better employee engagement. The following are just a sample of the studies on the impact of high employee engagement:

◇   The probability of departure is 87 percent lower in high-engagement than low-engagement organizations. For every 10 percent improvement in engagement, employee performance increases 2 percent. Moving employees from disengaged to highly engaged "can result in a 57 percent increase in discretionary effort."[376]

◇   A study conducted from 2008 to 2012 among ninety-four global companies demonstrated a "strong correlation" between employee engagement and sales growth in the following years. For every 1 percent of employees who became engaged, sales grew an additional 0.6 percent.[377]

◇   At New Century Mortgage, highly engaged account executives and loans officers outperformed those who were disengaged or moderately engaged by 28 percent and 23 percent respectively.[378]

◇   A study of 36,000 hourly to senior management employees in the US found that as employee engagement went from low to high, customer focus nearly doubled, revenue growth went from nearly 2 percent below industry average to almost 1 percent above industry average, and those actively seeking another job went from 23 percent to 2 percent.[379]

⬦   A study of 7,939 business units in thirty-six companies found
    significant relationships between employee engagement and
    improved customer satisfaction and loyalty, profitability,
    and productivity, and reduced lost days and turnover (both
    voluntary and involuntary).[380]

⬦   Research on 360,000 employees in forty-one countries
    demonstrated that over a three-year period, high-
    engagement companies had operating margins and net
    profit margins that grew 3.74 percent and 2.06 percent
    respectively, while in low-engagement companies, operating
    margins declined 2.01 percent and net profit margins
    declined 1.38 percent.[381]

⬦   Companies with above-average employee engagement had
    87 percent higher company performance than companies
    with below-average employee engagement.[382]

⬦   Companies in which 60 to 70 percent of employees were
    engaged had total shareholder return (TSR) of 24.2 percent,
    while companies in which 49 to 60 percent of employees
    were engaged had a TSR of 9.1 percent, and companies in
    which less than 25 percent of employees were engaged had
    a negative TSR.[383]

⬦   A study of thirty-nine companies over a five-year period
    demonstrated that high-engagement companies achieved a
    TSR that was seven times greater than lower-engagement
    companies.[384]

Differences in Employee Engagement Among
Underrepresented Groups

Employee engagement can be influenced by demographic
differences among employees. However, research on differences
in employee engagement among underrepresented people, except
for gender differences, is extremely limited:

◇   Differences in employee engagement among men and women are not definitive, with women slightly to significantly more engaged than men in most studies. Differences appear to relate to national culture and the unique aspects of different organizational environments.[385]

◇   Though research on racial and ethnic differences is sparse, one major study of 500,000 employees across 8,700 organizations found that in the US, Latinx employees were the most engaged, followed by White employees, and then, in order, Asian, Native Hawaiian or other Pacific Islanders, Native American or Alaskan Natives, multiracial individuals, and Black employees. In some organizations I have studied, Black employees were the most engaged. Again, the unique organizational environment appears to be a factor.[386]

◇   New employees are more engaged than longer-term employees, engagement increases with rank, salaried workers are more engaged than hourly workers, and those workers over the age of sixty-six are the most engaged.[387]

◇   Employee engagement has a more positive impact on job satisfaction for heterosexual employees than it does for LGBTQ+ employees.[388]

◇   In a limited qualitative study, the evidence suggested that the employment of people with disabilities could increase overall employee engagement by promoting a more trusting and psychologically safe work environment.[389]

Distinctive Diversity

The outcome of the diverse talent value chain (DTVC) is *distinctive diversity*. Diversity is the equitable representation of all groups, especially historically underrepresented groups, at all organizational levels. The DTVC leads to diversity that is distinctive in two ways—first, in the high quality of employees it attracts, retains, and advances through bias-free, merit-based talent decisions and inclusive practices that amplify the unique talents and maximize the performance of each employee. The exceptional quality of employees creates sustainable competitive advantage in the markets in which the organization sells products and provide services. In nonprofits, exceptional employees and the high-performing organizations they enable create competitive advantage in raising funds and attracting and serving clients.

Second, distinctive from talent competitors, the DTVC differentiates the organization by providing an extraordinary work experience for underrepresented employees that is difficult to duplicate and onerous to surpass. The DVTC expands the talent marketplace to the nearly 58 percent of the US workforce that is underrepresented[390] and the over 89 percent of the global workforce in Africa, Asia, Latin America, Eastern Europe, and the Arab States.[391] An extraordinary work experience establishes an exceptional organizational climate and highly engaged employees, improving the work experience for all employees.[392]

Designing a Diversity Management Structure

"There is no such thing as a good or bad organizational structure; there are only appropriate and inappropriate ones."
Harold Kerzner
Senior Executive Director, International Institute for Learning

CRAFTING THE APPROPRIATE INFRASTRUCTURE FOR a diversity initiative requires resolving four design considerations: reporting relationship, separate versus blended diversity organization, differentiation/integration, and degree of centralization. *Reporting relationship* addresses the question "To whom should the chief diversity officer and the diversity office report?" *Separate versus blended* resolves the dilemma of whether diversity should be a wholly separate organization or be blended with an existing organization, such as human resources or talent. *Differentiation/integration* determines the division of diversity labor, its specialties or functions, and the mechanisms and authority to ensure coordination and consistency among those divisions. *Degree of centralization* is concerned with where diversity functions such as compliance, diversity knowledge, and measurement should be placed along a centralization–decentralization continuum.

Reporting Relationship

Generally, chief diversity officers (CDOs) report to the chief executive officer (CEO), the chief operating officer (COO), the chief human resources or human capital officer, the chief talent officer, or the chief administrative officer. The key considerations are the degree to which the officer to whom the CDO reports is in a position to empower them to successfully fulfill the diversity mandate and the degree to which that person is committed to diversity. Obviously, reporting to the CEO offers the greatest empowerment potential. Furthermore, because the CDO has a highly cross-functional role, reporting to the CEO or COO makes sense. Just as obviously, an indifferent CEO affords little chance of empowerment. Working out the reporting relationship is a critical conversation for the CEO and the incoming CDO to have before the CDO begins. In numerous conversations with CDOs, I have found that the number one reason they leave an organization is because of an uncommitted CEO.

Separate versus Blended Diversity Organization

Whether to create a separate diversity organization or blend it into the human resources, human capital, talent, or another organization depends on where it can be most effective. A blended organization will almost always be more efficient than a separate organization and is therefore tempting. However, more important than efficiency is effectiveness. Will blending the two organizations diminish the effectiveness of either or both? Will it undermine the focus or authority needed to achieve diversity objectives? Will the new organization have the resources to accomplish both its existing and new objectives?

A blended model that has proven effective at Goldman Sachs is to have the chief diversity officer report directly to the executive office, composed of the CEO and COO. Diversity is carefully integrated into their global talent development process and is overlaid on each of the process components, including career development, succession planning, and promotions. Recruiting, training, and on-boarding of underrepresented people is integrated into the human capital management organization. The diversity organization undertakes a small number of targeted initiatives. Each year, a diversity planning process identifies two or three firm-wide objectives, which each division and region translates into their own objectives, according to their own unique context and situation. Every senior leader is accountable for the diversity objectives of the organization they lead and is reviewed on diversity progress.

Differentiation and Integration

Differentiation determines the specializations or functions required to achieve diversity goals. Organizations should determine their own unique division of labor. Typical functions include diversity, equity, and inclusion strategy; compliance; resourcing/budgeting; diversity, equity, and inclusion knowledge and content; data gathering and analysis; assessment and evaluation; reporting; program development and operations; internal communication and marketing; and external communication and marketing.

Once diversity functions have been established, mechanisms must be created to ensure that they are coordinated and working toward the same ends. Key integrating mechanisms typically include the diversity strategy, the chief diversity officer, a diversity center of expertise, and the diversity council. In large organizations, a program-management function can integrate business units, functions, and regions across a single program category, such as work–life or diversity training and development.

DIVERSITY STRATEGY

The establishment of strategic diversity objectives, measures, and targets that are cascaded throughout the organization provides an integrating mechanism. Instead of having to negotiate everyone's diversity activities, employees are able to look to their unit's diversity objectives, measures, and targets to determine the objectives and activities that make sense at their level and for their responsibilities. Diversity strategy goes a long way toward integrating all activities around the same objectives. However, it does not go far enough toward ensuring consistency among the activities of all units and employees.

DIVERSITY OFFICE

The diversity office is composed of the chief diversity officer and those reporting to her and is responsible for diversity objectives and activities—be it direct ownership, an advisory role, or oversight. However, the authority of the diversity office to accomplish those activities has limits. The diversity office derives its authority from the CEO or other C-suite executive and through its own influence. Both the amount of bandwidth the CEO or other executive can devote to diversity and the natural limits of the diversity office's influence place limitations on the authority and therefore on the integration capability of the diversity office. The diversity office requires a mechanism that extends its authority and influence.

DIVERSITY COUNCIL

The diversity council is the keystone of integration, enabling diversity strategy formulation and implementation and empowering the diversity office. An amalgam of C-suite, line, and diversity leaders, the diversity council has the authority, influence, and reach to ensure a high level of consistency across diversity activities and organizational functions. When effectively constructed, the diversity council is also a critical component of the diversity change process (see "Competency 12: Leading Change").

DIVERSITY ADVISORY COUNCIL

The advisory council is composed of external diversity experts and successful practitioners. While it can extend the influence of the diversity office, its primary integrating role is between the external environment and the organization. The advisory council identifies effective practices and the latest scientific evidence from the external world that can be incorporated into the formulation of diversity activities, raising the credibility of the activities and making them more robust for achieving diversity objectives. Ideally, the advisory council membership should comprise CDOs from other organizations, scholars of diversity, and practitioners. Practitioners should be drawn from diversity research and think tank organizations rather than consulting firms. If consultants are selected, firm ethical boundaries should be drawn between their advisory-board and consulting roles.

Degree of Centralization

In more complex multidivisional, multifunctional, and global organizations with a wide range of different diversity challenges and needs, some diversity functions may need to be pushed further out and deeper down into the organization. Centralization helps ensure a higher level of integration and drives consistency throughout the organization, ideally creating economies of scale. On the other hand, centralization engenders resistance and a one-size-fits-all approach that can struggle to accommodate local differences. To determine which functions should be centralized and which decentralized, four factors should be considered: complexity, oversight, local differences, and knowledge requirements (table 8-1).

Factors Determining Degree of Centralization	
Complexity	In organizations with a simple structure and a single core business, centralization is efficient and effective. In organizations with numerous functions and divisions, especially divisions that are highly differentiated from one another, the activities that will be most effective in achieving strategic objectives will vary greatly across the organization, requiring greater decentralization.
Oversight	Diversity oversight functions, such as compliance and measurement and evaluation, should ordinarily be centralized. Since oversight functions are the roots of accountability, they need to be protected from the self-interest and resistance that ordinarily arises when people are being judged. Centralization of oversight also ensures that judgments are consistent across the organization.

Factors Determining Degree of Centralization	
Local Differences	Local differences, such as culture, government, and language, often reflect wide-ranging diversity laws and regulations, attitudes, ways of interacting, and management styles. They require unique responses, especially in the legal sphere, that are difficult for centralized diversity functions to execute.
Knowledge Requirements	Functions that require extensive expertise, such as strategy formulation, evaluation, and program development, will tend to be centralized. Knowledge of diversity methods must be balanced with knowledge of local conditions.

Table 8-1

Naturally, insofar as they are accountable for the achievement of strategic objectives, most diversity leaders will seek greater control and centralization of diversity functions. Care must be taken to create a diversity office that seeks not to control diversity in disparate organizational functions and units but rather to understand how it can support those functions and units in achieving a diversity agenda that is developed collaboratively.

DIVERSITY BUSINESS PARTNER

In large and highly complex organizations, most notably those with highly decentralized infrastructures where diversity expertise is far removed from where objectives, activities, and measures are being formulated, the above mechanisms may not offer enough bandwidth to achieve effective integration. At the same time, the unique national cultures, laws and regulations, functions, and business specialties of dispersed organizational units may demand distinct solutions. The challenge is to integrate diversity expertise with local conditions.

For these complex, decentralized infrastructures, the best—although not the least expensive—solution may be a new role: the diversity business partner (DBP). Akin to the role of human resource business partners, DBPs bring centralized diversity knowledge and expertise, such as strategy formulation, diversity training, and measurement and evaluation, to regional and divisional levels. Diversity business partners should check the following boxes:

◊   Work with one or more operating units, as needed
◊   Be well versed in the various diversity functions and knowledge areas and the strategic diversity process
◊   Have excellent facilitative and influence skills
◊   Be highly collaborative
◊   Be skilled and experienced trainers
◊   Be well networked in the diversity community
◊   Have a high degree of business acumen

Though they cannot be fully accountable for diversity outcomes in operating units and non-diversity functional units, they should nevertheless be on the line for their client units' diversity achievements.

The Power of Place

Miles's law, formulated by Rufus Miles, Jr., former assistant secretary of the Department of Health, Education and Welfare, states, "Where you stand depends on where you sit." Miles's law points to a truth of organizational life: your position in the organizational structure shapes your point of view. In keeping with Miles's law, members of the diversity organization will likely advocate for greater employee and especially leadership involvement in diversity initiatives, larger diversity budgets, and aggressive programs, practices, and policies. On the other hand, line leaders may resist diversity not because of bigotry, although that may be the case, but because they see diversity as a distraction from achieving business goals. As each component of infrastructure is designed, consider how that design will influence the organizational point of view and self-interest of diversity stakeholders who will play roles in that infrastructure. The infrastructure should be designed in such a way that it fosters diversity success.

COMPETENCY 9:

Measuring for Accountability

"However beautiful the strategy, you should occasionally look at the results."
Winston Churchill

WHILE MANY WILL REGARD CHURCHILL'S above admonition as a truism, research shows that less than 20 percent of organizations "have a method for measuring the impact of [their] diversity practices." Even in organizations with 500 or more employees, only 34 percent have a method for measuring diversity's impact.[393]

Measurement is ubiquitous in diversity strategy. It determines effectiveness, establishes the foundation for accountability, links strategy formulation to implementation, and shapes behavior. Because measurement plays such a broad role, it is also ubiquitous throughout this book. Measurement is implicit in "Competency 2: Constructing a Business Case for Diversity" as measures largely make the business case. In "Competency 4: Mastering Diversity Strategy," the section on diversity assessment identifies improvement opportunities as a basis for formulating strategic diversity objectives and can also serve as a measure of progress when repeated over time. Competency 4 also discusses how to create measures for individual strategic objectives by linking them to the programs and policies that will fulfill the strategic mandate. The topics of equity, inclusion, and sustainable competitive advantage in competencies 5 through 7 are all based on measurement. This chapter brings together these and other measures into an integrated tool of strategy implementation: the diversity dashboard.

The Diversity Dashboard

Measurement is both *evaluative*, focusing on the outcomes of diversity initiatives, and *formative*, pointing toward actions that should be taken to produce those impacts and outcomes. Most measures serve both formative and evaluative purposes; however, the assessment is the primary tool of formative measurement, and the diversity dashboard is largely evaluative.

The purpose of the diversity dashboard is to give diversity leaders the evaluative information they need to determine the effectiveness of the diversity strategy and to form the foundation for accountability. The diversity dashboard is composed of strategic objectives in four areas: (1) equity, (2) inclusion, (3) sustainable diversity competitive advantage—largely in product/service markets, since talent markets are generally captured through equity and inclusion—and (4) strategy implementation, including infrastructure, measurement, communications, leadership, and other vital strategy operations. Those objectives, coupled with program and policy initiatives and targets, move the organization toward increased representation of underrepresented people at all organizational levels (figure 9-1).

The Diversity Dashboard

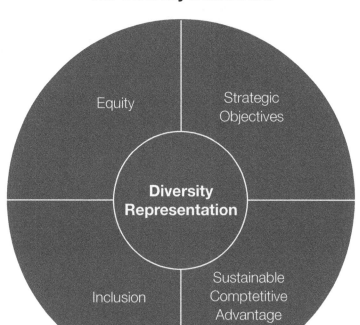

Figure 9-1

In some cases, organizations may wish to add vendor diversity to the core elements of the diversity dashboard. Vendor diversity has the potential to have an extraordinary influence on representation and the economic advancement of underrepresented people.

FEATURES OF EFFECTIVE DASHBOARDS

Effective diversity dashboards incorporate four essential features: they blend leading and lagging indicators, consider unintended consequences, are built on a model of diversity, and are linked to a vehicle for consolidating and communicating results.

Blend Leading and Lagging Indicators

Measures can be leading, predictive of an outcome, and lagging, after the outcome occurs. For example, a leading indicator of sexual harassment is whether women employees perceive that the organizational culture tolerates sexual harassment (i.e., "complaints are not taken seriously, it is risky to complain, and perpetrators are unlikely to be punished"),[394] while a lagging indicator might be incidents of sexual harassment. The power of leading indicators is that if a behavior or an action can be predicted, there is a good chance it can be prevented. An organization that is perceived by a substantial number of employees to tolerate sexual harassment predicts that actual harassment will occur—if it isn't already occurring.

The value of lagging indicators is that they indicate what actually occurred and can usually be measured with precision. Ideally, measures should be a blend of leading and lagging indicators.

Consider Unintended Consequences

An old saying goes, "What gets measured gets done." In other words, measurement drives accountability and therefore behavior. The danger is that the behaviors that result may not be the ones intended. Before instituting a measure, consideration should be given to possible unintended consequences.

Guidelines for considering unintended consequences were presented in "Competency 4: Mastering Diversity Strategy." Anytime a measure is used, those guidelines should be applied and unintended consequences considered.

Build on a Model of Diversity Action

A simple model of action should frame the diversity dashboard. The model connects diversity strategy to diversity representation at various levels of the organizational hierarchy through measures, targets, results, and program and policy initiatives (figure 9-2). Basing action on a model integrates the various measures and, when targets are assigned to individuals, establishes the basis for accountability.

The strategic objectives emerge from the diversity strategy formulation process, stating what the organization will do in the areas of equity, inclusion, sustainable diversity competitive advantage (SDCA), and implementation to improve representation. *Measures* demonstrate how the organization will know that its strategic diversity objectives and core programs and policies have been successful, while the *targets* are the level of the measure that the organization should achieve in a specified time period. *Actual* communicates what was actually achieved on the measure relative to the target. For example, imagine that the strategic diversity objective is to improve leadership commitment to diversity. One measure for the objective is where the leader stands, as judged by peers, on a five-point scale of leadership commitment. The target might be an average of level 4, while the actual might be 4.2, which would indicate that the leader has exceeded his target. Core programs and policies are the tools an organization uses to achieve strategic objective targets.

Diversity Dashboard Action Model

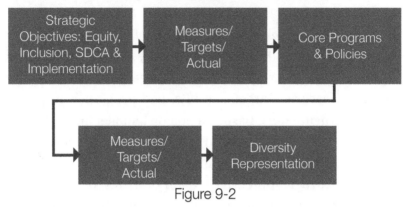

Figure 9-2

Consolidate and Communicate Results: The Dashboard Heat Chart

A particularly useful and straightforward method for consolidating and communicating dashboard results is the heat chart (table 9-1). By characterizing each target—in stoplight fashion—as green (achieving or making substantial progress toward achieving the target), yellow or caution (some progress is being made, but additional progress is required), or red (progress has been inadequate), attention is focused on the areas most critically in need of continuing improvement or change.

The dashboard heat chart incorporates measures for each strategic objective. While the dashboard should balance equity, inclusion, strategic diversity competitive advantage, and implementation, strategies for different time periods may emphasize only one or two of the four strategic elements. The strategic objectives may overlap with each other. This should not be a matter of concern as long as the measures of overlapping objectives do not drive behavior in contradictory directions.

The heat chart includes all the components of the diversity dashboard action model, including strategic objectives, core programs and policies measures, targets, actual results, and representation measures. Also included is a baseline, which establishes the beginning or current state of the measure. Where appropriate, measures should be broken out by underrepresented and well-represented groups so comparisons can be made.

The dashboard heat chart is intended to be comprehensive. Not all measures will make sense for all organizations, or they might wish to add additional measures. Organizations that elect to create their own action model may wish to develop a heat chart that corresponds to their model.

The dashboard heat chart depicted below has nine categories, represented by column headings:

1. *Row Number*

The row numbers simply facilitate dialogue about the chart, allowing discussants to refer to rows of interest.

2. *Objective*

An objective is an endpoint toward which action is directed. Through the diversity strategy process, strategic objectives for equity, inclusion, sustainable diversity competitive advantage, and implementation are established.

3. *Measure*

Each objective and core program and policy has a measure or measures that indicate whether it has been successfully achieved.

4. *Target (Quarter) Baseline*

The target is the goal for the measure: where the organization wants the measure to be in a specified period of time.

Quarter, which refers to the end of the designated quarter, is the specified period of time. When targets are being tallied at multiple points in time, such as in the rollout of a training program, the quarter is designated as "rolling." The baseline is the current state of the measure (i.e., where the measure is when the heat chart is originally constructed). When the strategy, programs, and policies are established, often no baseline exists. If a heat chart is created before a baseline is established, *NB*—"no baseline"—should be inserted in place of a baseline until one has been established.

5. *Actual*

Actual is what was really achieved on the measure in the prescribed time period.

6. *Core Programs and Policies*

This simply refers to a program, such as a training or mentoring program, or a policy, such as "Flexible work arrangements are available to all employees," that is intended to move the objective toward its target. This answers the question "What can most effectively and efficiently be done to achieve the target during the course of the strategy?"

7–9. *Measure, Target (Quarter) Baseline, and Actual*

The final three columns are the same as the previous similarly named columns except that they refer to the program or policy instead of the objective.

The heat chart below (table 9-1) is an example of a comprehensive, fully articulated dashboard heat chart.

Dashboard Heat Chart with Examples

▨ yellow   ▨ green   ▨ red

ROW NO.	STRATEGIC OBJECTIVES	MEASURE	TARGET (QUARTER) BASELINE	ACTUAL	CORE PROGRAM OR POLICY	MEASURE	TARGET (QUARTER) BASELINE	ACTUAL
1	Improve diversity climate	Average percent of underrepresented employees who agree/ strongly agree on diversity climate survey questions	90% (Q4) 72%	86%	Develop and roll out awareness and behavioral training	Percent trained	100% (Q3) 0%	95%
2					Develop and roll out awareness and behavioral training (cont'd)	Average percent agree/ strongly agree that training was effective	85% (Q4) 0%	91%
3					Develop and roll out on-boarding program focusing on intergroup contact	Percent of new employees participating	100% (Rolling) 0%	92%
4					Implement diversity philosophy communications initiative	Percent of departments participating	100% (Q2) 0%	100%
5	Increase leadership commit-ment level	Average leadership commitment level	3 (Q3) 2.1	2.5	Develop and implement leadership training	Percent of leaders trained	100% (Q3) 0%	72%

Table 9-1

yellow ■ green ■ red

ROW NO.	STRATEGIC OBJECTIVES	MEASURE	TARGET (QUARTER) BASELINE	ACTUAL	CORE PROGRAM OR POLICY	MEASURE	TARGET (QUARTER) BASELINE	ACTUAL
6					Develop and implement leadership training (cont'd)	Average percent agree/strongly agree that training was effective	90% (Rolling) 0%	92%
7					CEO communication of business case/personal case	Percent exposure of all employees	100% (Q3) 0%	100%
8					Develop strategic diversity objectives at EVP, division president, vice president and director levels	Percent with successfully completed objectives	100% (Q4) 0%	84%
9	Grow business in Black and Hispanic consumer markets	Market share	50% (Q4) 12%	29%	Develop and roll out products targeted to Black and Hispanic communities	Percent of total sales from targeted products developed in last twenty-four months	40% (Q4) 18%	27%
10					Conduct social media campaign targeted to Black and Hispanic communities	Display click-through rate	4% (Rolling) 0%	3.2%
11					Conduct social media campaign targeted to Black and Hispanic communities (cont'd)	Conversion rate for click-throughs	2.75% (Rolling) 0%	1.3%

Table 9-1 (continued)

yellow ▮ green ▮ red

ROW NO.	STRATEGIC OBJECTIVES	MEASURE	TARGET (QUARTER) BASELINE	ACTUAL	CORE PROGRAM OR POLICY	MEASURE	TARGET (QUARTER) BASELINE	ACTUAL
12					Hire additional Black and Hispanic sales personnel	Percent of sales force that is Black or Hispanic	18% (Q2) 6%	14%
13					Hire additional Black and Hispanic sales personnel (cont'd)	Percent of Black and Hispanic sales force achieving sales goal	90% (Q4) 73%	62%
14					Increase distribution in Black and Hispanic communities	Number of distributors	200 (Q4) 179	181
15	Increase spending with underrepresented and standards certified vendors	Percent of spend with underrepresented vendors and vendors who meet minimum diversity standards	15% (Q4) 13.7%	16%	Create and implement procurement program for underrepresented vendor segments	Percent of total spending with underrepresented vendors	15% (Q2) 8%	16%
16					Develop vendor diversity standards and certify vendors	Percent of vendors meeting diversity standards	25% (Q4) NB	32%

Table 9-1 (continued)

MEASUREMENT ERRORS

Many organizations, especially those that are science and engineering oriented, prefer quantitative measures. For the most part, numbers are favored because of their presumed accuracy and precision. But numbers can deceive. They often require assumptions that may be inaccurate or colored by subjectivity and are often statements of probability (e.g., election polls that give a candidate's predicted percentage of the vote at plus or minus 4 percent). Care should be taken to avoid overinterpreting quantitative results.

In the cause of diversity action, the trustworthiness of the reporter, the presenter, or author of the measurement report is also vital. If those reviewing the measures have even an inkling of belief that the reporter is deceptive, acting in her own self-interest, or taking an advocacy position, the data as a stimulus of diversity action will be diminished and the diversity initiative damaged. Trustworthy reporters are conservative in their assumptions, transparent about their methodology, and direct about the deficiencies in their data.

COMPETENCY 10:

Talking the Walk: Top Leadership Communications

"The single biggest problem in communication is the
illusion that it has taken place."
George Bernard Shaw

AS THE TWENTY-SOMETHING CHIEF EXECUTIVE
of a nonprofit serving people with disabilities, I faced my first
personnel crisis—a poorly performing, problematic staff member.
After a period of improvement plans and coaching—or, at the
time, what I thought was coaching—her performance had not
improved and her behavior had deteriorated further. With
trepidation, at the end of the workday, I sat her down and fired
her. Finding my communication illusory, the next day she showed
up for work. I had to fire her again.

Misunderstanding

Misunderstanding of diversity communications—both
internal and external—has multiple causes. In addition to the

traditional causes of miscommunication, such as mistrust, imprecision, and language differences, those especially relevant to diversity miscommunications include conflicting mental models, disregard for stakeholder beliefs and interests, and disconnects between communication and action and between explicit and implicit communication.

CONFLICTING MENTAL MODELS

According to the American Psychological Association, a mental model is "an internal representation of the relations between a set of elements."[395] All mental models are internal to an individual, are based on life experiences, and have the capacity to affect how a person acts. Considering the broad range of life experiences with people who are different, influential attitudes of significant others about those differences, media experiences focusing on differences, and other elements, it is no wonder that the mental models of diversity that employees hold can vary so greatly. Mental models are particularly relevant in diversity where the need for change is so critical and where mental models can be a significant source of conflict and an anchor inhibiting change.

Leaders must be aware of the capacity for differing mental models and the effects that they have on diversity action. Further, they must encourage employees to surface and think about their own implicit mental models of diversity and examine the evidence and assumptions that underlie those models.[396] Finally, they must craft and communicate an organizational mental model of diversity that provides the foundation for effective and consistent diversity action. Communicating a common mental model of diversity is one of the most significant actions a leader can take to foster a culture of diversity, equity, and inclusion.

DISREGARD FOR STAKEHOLDER BELIEFS
AND INTERESTS

Presidential candidate Elizabeth Warren took a DNA test (it showed that she probably had a Cherokee ancestor several generations ago) and issued a news release to address her claim that she was part Cherokee. It backfired. Besides the capitulation to the racist "one-drop rule" that having even one ancestor from sub-Saharan Africa (one drop of Black blood) makes a person Black, her comments missed the point. Citizenship in the Cherokee Nation is "rooted in centuries of culture and laws, not DNA tests," as a spokesperson for the Cherokee Nation declared.[397]

Had she reached out to members of the Cherokee Nation, the central stakeholders in the conversation, she would have known that her communication would be poorly received. While members of employee resource groups usually do not want to be put in the position of speaking for their entire social group, they are an excellent sounding board for diversity communications. Leaders should also reach out to leaders of advocacy groups for underrepresented people for advice and input.

DISCONNECT BETWEEN COMMUNICATION
AND ACTION

Communication quickly turns to hypocrisy when words are inconsistent with actions. Theodore Levitt of Harvard Business School famously noted, "The best way to kill a bad product is good advertising." The better and more rigorously an organization that is ineffective at diversity communicates its "wonderful" diversity accomplishments to its internal and external constituencies, the more cynical that constituency will become.

An all-too-frequent example of this disconnect is inclusion. While an organization's values, its diversity philosophy, and the speeches of its executives call for greater inclusion, leaders' behaviors may belie their communications. How frequently do we observe the proponents of inclusion making decisions without stakeholder input, expounding without inquiring, or inquiring for the answer they already possess? The behavior of organizational members and especially its leaders must be strenuously consistent with their communications; they must walk the talk. In turn, their communications strategists must talk the walk.

If communications professionals are not able to communicate reality, they should push back and become advocates for greater transparency. In particular, this means that communications about the results of diversity surveys must be transparent and not merely designed to accentuate what is positive.

DISCONNECT BETWEEN IMPLICIT AND EXPLICIT COMMUNICATION

The words that leaders speak (explicit communication) convey only a limited proportion of the message heard. Nonverbal communication (implicit communication) is a powerful component of spoken messages. According to researchers,[398] nonverbal communication in the form of body language (posture, facial expression, hand and head movements), vocal variety (tone, inflection, rate of speech), space and distance, touch, physical appearance, and objects and artifacts account for over 50 percent of the meaning conveyed by a communication. When verbal and nonverbal communications conflict, nonverbal communications win out.[399]

In elaborating on the power of observing nonverbal communication, Sherlock Holmes, in *A Study in Scarlet*, observes, "By a man's finger-nails, by his coat-sleeves, by his boots, by his trouser-knees, by the callosities of his forefinger and thumb, by his expression, by his shirt-cuffs—by each of these things a man's calling is plainly revealed." Unsurprisingly, women are considerably better observers of nonverbal communication than men.[400]

Nonverbal communication is a significant part of communicating emotions, which play strongly in diversity communications. When leaders' implicit diversity communications contradict their explicit diversity communications, at best their earnest messages will fail, and at worst, they will endanger the perceived veracity of all their diversity communications.

Developing a Strategic Communications Plan

For the diversity, equity, and inclusion strategy to be successful, it must be supported by a communications strategy that prepares employees and vendors for effective participation in the diversity initiative, integrates all diversity communications, and aims to ensure that all stakeholders know and understand the diversity initiative and are prepared to participate in its success.

The strategic communications planning template (table 10-1) provides a framework for working through a strategic communications plan. The first step is to establish internal and external communications goals, followed by determining the audiences that must be reached to fulfill each of those goals, the appropriate media through which to communicate with each audience, and the message that each medium will convey.

Strategic Communications Planning Template

	Goal	Audience	Medium/Channel	Message
Internal Communication				
External Communication				

Table 10-1

GOALS

Internal communication goals are aimed at employees, board members, and other internal constituencies relevant to achieving strategic diversity objectives, while external goals are targeted toward candidates for employment, customers and clients, vendors, and the broader organizational community.

Internally, the central goal for leaders is to communicate the answers to five questions employees often have:

◇ What does "diversity" mean in this organization? (the language of diversity)

◇ Why are we making diversity a priority? (the business case and the diversity philosophy)

◇ Why are our leaders personally committing time and energy to diversity? (the personal case)

◇ What are our goals for diversity and how will we achieve them? (the diversity strategy and vision)

◇ What is my role in achieving our diversity goals? (clarity about role and accountability for individual diversity objectives)

Other goals, both internally and externally oriented, typically fall into five categories: branding, awareness, education, transparency, and public relations, although organizations may wish to identify additional or other categories. The categories are not so much a structure for the goals as heuristics to generate goals.

Branding

The purpose of branding is to introduce the employer brand and establish it in the minds (and, ideally, hearts) of employees, board members, customers and clients, vendors, other internal and external stakeholders, and the broader community.

Awareness

Fundamentally, awareness is about raising the consciousness of employees and other stakeholders about the causes of bias (e.g., the forms of bias, including unconscious bias, favoritism, microinequities, microaggressions, stereotype threat, injustice, and exclusion) and its consequences.

Education

Education incorporates numerous goals aimed at understanding a host of diversity topics. It educates about the diversity philosophy, business case, and strategy; diversity programs and policies; vendor initiatives and standards; and the knowledge, skills, and tools for the effective practice of diversity.

Transparency

Transparency goals focus on providing open and honest feedback about the results of assessments and the results of diversity initiatives that are intended to address the assessment results.

Public Relations

Public relations is concerned with sharing diversity initiative successes both internally and externally through a variety of media for the purpose of creating a positive impression of the organization and its diversity accomplishments.

AUDIENCE

Determining the right audience is simply a process of identifying the audience that must be reached to achieve a communications goal. Consideration should be given to whether the audience is really a single audience with common needs and interests or whether segments of the audience have different needs and interests that require distinctive media and messages.

MEDIUM

The medium is the communications channel through which the audience or audience segment can most effectively be reached. Sometimes, more than one medium is required to adequately reach the audience and achieve the communications goal.

A wide variety of media exist. For internal communications, speeches, meetings, newsletters, and intranet content are typical. Media for external communications include speeches, especially from top management; social media; articles in journals and the popular press; conference presentations; and awards ceremonies.

In selecting media, attention should be paid to the message conveyed by the medium itself. As Marshall McLuhan, the influential communications theorist, cautioned, "The medium is the message."

MESSAGE

Creating effective messages is more craft than science. Different audiences and media require different styles. All messages should begin with a solid understanding of the audience and should be written from the audience's point of view.

A professional copywriter can be very helpful in crafting a message. However, many copywriters are taught to write in "marketing speak," a style that rings more of assertion, exaggeration, and equivocation than truth. Be sure to see some writing samples before enlisting a copywriter. Test all messages with stakeholders before going public.

COMPETENCY 11:

Walking the Talk: Top Leadership Commitment

"If you don't believe it, it won't come out of your horn."
Charlie Parker
Jazz Saxophonist and Composer

PLAYING OFF THE TOP THREE criteria for real estate investment, "Location, location, and location," the three top criteria for the success of a diversity initiative are top leadership commitment, top leadership commitment, and top leadership commitment. Commitment is more deeds than words—thus, walking the talk. However, if a leader's commitment is insincere, then their deeds will not be believed and their leadership notes will sour. Even as those sour notes are bathed in exquisite language, employees will still grasp their noxiousness.

In numerous meetings, I have asked top executives, "Are you committed to diversity?" Every hand in every room rose. Then, I showed them the ladder of diversity commitment (figure 11-1) and asked, "Where do each of you predominantly stand on the ladder?" I say predominantly because most leaders have characteristics of all four or at least the three bottom levels. Their

The Ladder of Diversity Commitment

4. Lead

- Makes diversity a priority for the organization he/she leads
- Has articulated a compelling personal commitment to diversity
- Models inclusion and diversity values (walks the talk)
- Takes a specific diversity leadership role, such as chairing the diversity council or task force or chairing an employee resource group
- Leads the formulation and implementation of a diversity strategic plan with objectives and measures, regularly reviews achievements against objectives, and holds line and staff leaders accountable for achievements
- Communicates personal commitment, diversity definition, values/ philosophy, strategy, business case, and achievements to external forums
- Engaged with at least one organization serving a diverse population

3. Manage

- Communicates diversity definition, values/philosophy, strategy, business case, and achievements to organization which she/he manages
- Has zero tolerance for prejudice and discrimination
- Holds reports accountable for achieving diversity strategic objectives and performance goals
- Provides resources to diversity initiative

2. Support

- Encourages/requires reports to participate in diversity activities
- Gives employees time off for training
- Endorses diversity initiatives
- Includes diversity information in presentations to reports
- Participates in diversity training and mentoring programs

1. Acquiesce

- Does not oppose diversity efforts
- Attends presentations and trainings
- Does what is required by more senior managers

Figure 11-1

answers on average placed them at rung two, bordering on rung three. What many leaders believe is strong commitment is, in the eyes of employees, mostly lip service, training, and dollars.

The value of the ladder is not that it precisely characterizes a leader's commitment. Most organizations will want to create their own ladder with their own language and the leadership behaviors that matter to them. The value is that it demonstrates to leaders that they are not so much leading the diversity initiative as, at best, beginning to manage it. Furthermore, the ladder is cumulative, so it serves as a pathway of behaviors for those aspiring to diversity leadership.

To truly lead a diversity initiative requires a belief—based on the diversity philosophy and the business and personal cases—that a diversity initiative is a valuable undertaking for the organization and a high priority. Not just valuable in its own right, but a priority versus other uses of the same resources. A diversity initiative, no matter how tightly conceived and well run, will always compete with important revenue-raising and mission-fulfilling activities. It must take its place alongside critical business and organizational priorities and supplant others.

Leaders must also walk the talk of the leadership rung on which they stand. If their commitment is not honest and crisp and clear, then employees will hear the sour notes. Insincere leadership pronouncements engender the DuHICA response (Duck, Here It Comes Again), the penchant of employees to wait out what they don't perceive to be vital to the welfare of the organization until new leadership changes direction.

Assessing Commitment

An assessment is often required to make leaders aware that the commitment they evidence is not the commitment level required to successfully lead an organization toward effective diversity outcomes. The assessment can be as simple as asking leaders to rate themselves, as I did above, or incorporated into a more formal assessment. Formal assessments can be self-assessments or assessments by direct reports, peers, and managers. A formal assessment would turn the above behaviors into a short survey that asks respondents, "Which of the four sets of behaviors most closely describes [the leader]?" Or the commitment ladder could be converted into a survey, with a few modifications, and administered to all or a sample of employees or turned into an upward appraisal or 360-degree assessment.

A survey might ask on a standard scale of "strongly agree" to "strongly disagree" whether the leader is behaving consistently with each of the commitment behaviors. Minor modifications should include a "don't know" box, since many employees will not have enough evidence on which to make a credible response. Split questions with multiple components into separate questions. For example, "Communicates diversity definition, philosophy, strategy, business case, and achievements to external forums" should be five different questions for definition, philosophy, strategy, etc. This provides specific information about leadership gaps, giving improvement efforts more precision.

Building Top Management Commitment

Many chief diversity officers and others charged with implementing diversity initiatives find themselves without genuine support from their immediate manager or from the chief executive. Without top management support, diversity leaders are forced to take a more tactical approach and introduce a variety of programs, such as training and mentoring, which, although they give the appearance of progress, usually do not lead to meaningful increases in equity, inclusion, sustainable diversity competitive advantage, and diversity representation. Offered below are several strategies for influencing top managers to move up to the "lead" level.

IGNITE A BURNING PLATFORM

The burning platform has become a metaphor for galvanizing people to action. The diversity assessment is the burning platform of top leadership commitment. When an assessment reveals that underrepresented people have low commitment to the organization, that they feel disrespected, mistreated, and otherwise oppressed, have low levels of employee engagement, and, in general, are dissatisfied in their jobs, feelings that are often shared by their well-represented peers, leaders are faced with a stark choice—jump into action or slowly fry on the flame of a dissatisfied workforce. As Jack Welch, the quotable former chairman and CEO of GE, warned leaders who are facing unfavorable circumstances, "Lead change before you have to."

ENCOURAGE LEADERS TO CRAFT A PERSONAL CASE

The development of a personal case requires consideration of life experiences that include underrepresented people and exploration of personal values and beliefs and upbringing. Crafting a personal case is only part of stimulating commitment. Even more important is for the senior executive to communicate her personal case to employees or to the general public. When what a person authors is going to be seen and judged by an important audience, she puts more careful thought and heartfelt consideration into the writing, stimulating her own commitment.

IMMERSE LEADERS IN DIVERSITY EXPERIENCES

Most White senior leaders have limited experience with people who are different from them. Few have an underrepresented person in their inner circle. Encourage top leaders to join a board that is populated with underrepresented leaders of similar stature to themselves. Or have them lead an employee resource group composed of people who are different from them or reverse mentor a person from a different group, where the more junior person mentors the more senior person. Bring in outside speakers who are members of underrepresented groups and are top diversity experts, advocates, or top leaders themselves. Make sure uncommitted executives share a meal with the speaker. Orchestrate experiences for leaders to build relationships with high-status diversity leaders.

SPEAK EXTERNALLY

Nothing gets an executive more serious about diversity than giving a speech to a significant external audience. Aggressively seek invitations for the CEO or other top executives to speak at conferences, awards banquets, and other diversity-related venues. Not only will the process of crafting a speech cause leaders to solicit input from their top diversity staff and to think deeply about diversity, but also speaking at a large diversity gathering will bring them into contact with other top diversity leaders.

Ineffective Commitment Strategies

Some commitment strategies are usually ineffective. Having a top executive direct those in her chain of command to get committed to diversity will often have the opposite effect.

Business and financial arguments rarely work—not because they aren't powerful but because most top leaders have many superior business opportunities in front of them.

While the commitment of top leaders is critical to the success of a diversity initiative, what is most critical for diversity is that commitment be sustained, not only for the individual leader but across leaders over time. The next chapter, "Change Leadership," and the final chapter, "Legacy," demonstrate how to keep commitment alive across careers and generations.

COMPETENCY 12:

Leading Change

"There is nothing more difficult to take in hand, more
perilous to conduct, or more uncertain in its success,
than to take the lead in the introduction of a new
order of things."
Niccolò Machiavelli
Italian Statesman and Philosopher

IF THERE IS ONE CONSTANT in achieving an equitable
and inclusive workplace and more diverse workforce, it is change.
When the current work climate, leadership approaches, talent
processes and policies, and diversity practices are not producing
the diversity outcomes sought, they must be changed. A single,
large-scale change rarely succeeds in diversity; rather, what
moves an organization toward being equitable, inclusive, and
more representative of the communities in which it operates is
a continuous cycle of assessment, improvement, and evaluation.
For leaders, that continuous process of change requires new
skills, knowledge, and attitudes. As Machiavelli reminds leaders,
change also requires the acceptance of risk. This chapter offers
a series of principles regarding how that risk can be ameliorated
and success more confidently pursued.

Principles of Change Leadership

The nine principles below are derived from studies of organizational change and change leadership and adapted to the realities of leading strategic diversity change.[401]

1. PROMOTE A CHANGE VISION

The change vision, like the organizational vision, describes the outcomes the diversity initiative is intended to achieve (i.e., what success will look like). Coca-Cola's diversity vision is tightly tied to its business imperatives:

> Be as inclusive and diverse as our brands, unleashing the power within our associates to drive innovation and sustainable system growth.

Apple's diversity vision is elegant, focusing on inclusion:

> **Open.**
> Humanity is plural, not singular. The best way the world works is everybody in. Nobody out.

At the American Red Cross, the diversity vision is straightforward and down to earth:

> The American Red Cross empowers people in America to perform extraordinary acts in the face of emergencies and disasters.
>
> ◊ To ensure full benefit of this experience by all, we deliver our products and services in a culturally sensitive and appropriate manner to all we serve.

◊ We fully embrace and promote inclusion across our
people, products and services, and we integrate diversity
into our business strategies and decisions.

Diversity visions should, as the three visions above do,
reinforce the diversity brand. To be of value internally, the
vision must be communicated frequently and widely, and the
meaning of the vision should be openly discussed at all levels.
Employees should consider how it applies to them and their jobs.
Communicating the diversity vision should be one goal of the
communication plan.

2. INSPIRE URGENCY

A number of vehicles have been discussed through which to
create commitment to diversity among all employees, including
an assessment, the business and personal cases, and awareness
education. Inspiring urgency takes commitment to the next level,
at which employees not only are committed but also understand
that the organization needs to move forward on diversity at high
speed and with full force.

The sense of urgency should not be manufactured; it must
be real, or employees will see through it in a moment. Like the
business case, urgency must be local. Even the most powerful
information about the external diversity world will not produce
urgency within the organization.

Aggressive diversity leadership and assessments are the most
powerful tools for creating urgency. Aggressive leaders push
diversity every day. They ask about progress on diversity activities
at every opportunity and hold their direct reports accountable,
always challenge stereotyping and discrimination when they see
it (and of course never engage in stereotyping and discrimination

themselves), review the diversity pipeline and succession plans frequently, and speak about diversity in every forum.

Assessments include not only workforce and climate assessments but also surveys of the organization's clients, customers, and consumers. In product/service markets, these surveys examine what influences the purchase and participation decisions of underrepresented consumers, what features they prefer, how they use the organization's products and services, what their emerging needs and interests are, and how they perceive the diversity of the organization. In talent markets, surveys consider the experiences of underrepresented people who have joined and declined to join the organization and those who have left the organization voluntarily, the most effective channels and recruiting communications to reach prospective employees, and what the perceived employer brand is. In addition, a survey should look at whether the employee experience is consonant with the marketing communications of the organization and at employees' intentions to leave the organization.

3. ESTABLISH A DIVERSITY LEADERSHIP GROUP

A diversity council or committee that is inclusive of all internal stakeholders should guide the diversity initiative. The top management team, especially the CEO, COO, CFO, CMO, CHRO, CLO, and, of course, the CDO, should be members of the leadership group. In addition, a cross section of underrepresented groups, oftentimes the leaders of employee resource groups, should also be members. The diversity council should have decision-making authority, contingent upon approval of the CEO. Decision-making should be by consensus.

4. COMMUNICATE RELENTLESSLY

Organizations that are successful at diversity, equity, and inclusion overcommunicate. Leaders not only utilize every communications medium at their disposal—speeches, newsletters, memos, and one-on-ones—but also aggressively seek opportunities to communicate about their diversity initiative. In particular, leaders should focus on communicating the diversity definition, diversity philosophy, diversity strategy, diversity vision, business case, and their personal case.

5. ENLIST THE INCLUSIVE MULTICULTURALISTS

As defined in chapter 7, inclusive multiculturalists have both inclusive characteristics, such as inquiring for understanding, listening skills, a collaborative instinct, and empathy, and multiculturalist characteristics, such as entering relationships with respect, valuing and reaching across differences, and cross-cultural understanding. Inclusive multiculturalists who, in addition to the characteristics above, are perceived as high-potential organizational leaders make the best diversity leaders and role models for the organization. In addition, open-minded high potentials who are not yet identifiable as inclusive multiculturalists also make good diversity leaders. Their experiences leading elements of the diversity initiative will, coupled with their open-mindedness, bring them into greater contact with underrepresented employees, evolve their understanding and attitudes, and be a positive force in their growth as advocates for diversity. Many become inclusive multiculturalists.

6. MOBILIZE THE MIDDLE

When asked about the greatest challenge he faced as CDO of the US Navy, Captain Ken Barrett pointed to himself, remarking that middle managers like himself were the greatest barrier to the implementation of diversity. Middle managers are truly in the middle. They are the linchpin at the interface between strategy and operations in the successful implementation of diversity strategy, bearing significant responsibility and accountability. At the same time, they are concerned that diversity might undermine their authority to make employment decisions and lower the quality of their workforce. They are concerned that diversity will be a distraction from their real job, on which their rewards are largely dependent. They are the front line in managing the pushback and skepticism that frequently accompany diversity initiatives. And they are subject to the same stereotypes and prejudices as others. No wonder so many middle managers are resistant to diversity initiatives.

Overcoming the resistance of middle managers and raising their awareness and commitment to diversity strategy occurs through their inclusion at every critical stage in the strategic process: assessment, formulation, evaluation, and implementation. Waiting until implementation to engage middle managers is simply too late; they are likely to be lost.

In the assessment stage, middle managers provide their perceptions of the current state of diversity, equity, and inclusion at the middle and operating levels of the organization. Surveys represent all middle managers, while focus groups represent the views of select groups. Care should be taken to draw a focus group sample of middle managers who are opinion leaders among their peers.

Middle managers, if they are adequately represented on the diversity council, provide a critical perspective on assessment results and innovative solutions. They are more likely to come up with pathways to addressing results and achieving solutions that are practical and grounded. Middle managers are integral to strategy evaluation. Their operating view breathes reality into the strategy.

In strategy implementation, middle managers play the critical role of deploying the diversity strategy into day-to-day operations. The consistency of their behavior with the intent of the diversity philosophy and strategy sends a vital "walking the talk" leadership message to employees. Insofar as they have been heard in previous stages, middle managers will adapt the strategy to on-the-ground realities in ways that are consistent with strategic intent.

Finally, middle managers are the key to understanding resistance to the strategy, particularly since much of the resistance might be their own, and key to determining ways to overcome that resistance.

7. HOLD EVERYONE ACCOUNTABLE

Everyone, from the chief executive officer to the line worker, should have diversity objectives. Strategic diversity objectives should be cascaded down through each level of the organization, with each employee accountable for achieving diversity objectives that drive the strategic diversity objectives of their organizational unit. At minimum, everyone from director above should have diversity objectives tied to the diversity strategy. To give accountability teeth, those eligible for bonuses should have a meaningful share of their bonus tied to the achievement of their diversity objectives. Furthermore, achievement of diversity objectives should be a factor in promotion.

Although linking accountabilities to compensation is a powerful motivator, the reality is that few companies actually make the linkage. Of the 3,000 companies studied by compensation consulting firm Pearl Meyer, only 78 tied CEO compensation to diversity objectives.[402] This offers a diversity competitive advantage to organizations that are bold enough to tie meaningful top leadership compensation and advancement to diversity objectives.

8. PRODUCE QUICK WINS

Creating quick wins builds momentum and motivation, signaling both seriousness of intent and successful progress. A useful approach to developing quick wins is for the strategy to consciously contain one or two "low-hanging fruit" strategic objectives or programs that can be implemented quickly, are visible, and have a high probability of success.

9. LEAN TOWARD INCLUSION

Inclusion creates consensus, the willingness to support decisions with which you might not even agree. Inclusion means genuinely hearing and considering others' voices in the decision-making process. When leaders lean toward inclusion in decision-making about diversity, they create the conditions for support for diversity and for overcoming resistance to it.

Even the most exquisitely led diversity initiative does not guarantee long-term success. Over time leaders leave and are replaced by others who may not be as committed to diversity. New leaders may be genuinely uncommitted or may want to signal that they are moving the organization in a different direction from their predecessor. The next chapter examines the power of a legacy of deep commitment to diversity that can sustain organizational commitment over leadership generations.

EPILOGUE:

Forging a Legacy

"The great use of life is to spend it for something that will outlast it."
William James

A LEGACY OF DIVERSITY, EQUITY, and inclusion requires creating not just a leadership persona that outlives a leader but also a diversity initiative that, though always evolving, has sustainable momentum and impact. Legacy is forged in two ways: sustainable change within the organization and an outsized influence on the world without. Neither is accomplished without a leader who transcends the daily rush of life and organizational responsibility to create a legacy and a sustainable diversity initiative that outlasts her.

Outlasting Legacies

Two leaders—J. Irwin Miller of Cummins and Ted Childs, Jr., of IBM—are exemplars of the transcendent leader. They are paragons of both strategic institutional leadership and strategic diversity leadership.

J. IRWIN MILLER

J. Irwin Miller, the man Martin Luther King, Jr., called "the most socially responsible businessman in the country," was born to affluence in small-town Columbus, Indiana. After graduating from Yale and receiving a master's degree from Oxford, Miller joined the Navy Air Corps, seeing action in the Pacific during World War II. The US government asked Miller to return home to lead his family's company, Cummins Engine, a supplier of diesel engines to the war effort.

During his tenure as chairman and CEO, he took a company that hadn't made a profit for sixteen years to a highly profitable industry leader (in 2020, Cummins revenues were $19.8b with net income of $1.8b). But it was not only financial success that Miller achieved; he also became a civil rights pioneer and established a deep commitment to diversity at Cummins.

Cummins, through the foundational efforts of Miller, has a long and winning commitment to diversity. Among its numerous diversity awards, Cummins was listed as one of the top fifty companies for diversity by DiversityInc for twelve straight years. Miller's commitment is best characterized in his own words, which hang on factory walls and conference rooms throughout Cummins: "Character, ability and intelligence are not concentrated in one sex over the other, nor in persons with certain accents or in certain races or in persons holding degrees from some universities over others. When we indulge ourselves in such irrational prejudices, we damage ourselves most of all and ultimately assure ourselves of failure in competition with those more open and less biased."

Miller's commitment to equal rights in the world outside Cummins was certainly outsized. As a founding member and the first lay leader of the National Council of Churches (NCC), an ecumenical organization devoted to social justice, he worked with Presidents Kennedy and Johnson toward passage of the Civil Rights Act, guided the NCC to become one of the sponsors of the historic 1963 March on Washington, and through the NCC's Commission on Religion and Race took on a number of anti-segregation initiatives, including bailing out activists, participating in demonstrations and interracial worship services in the Deep South, and troubleshooting in areas of racial tension. Despite having a 20 percent share of the South African diesel market, he pulled Cummins out of South Africa to protest apartheid and supported legislation imposing economic sanctions on South Africa.

THEODORE "TED" CHILDS, JR.

Ted Childs has been called "perhaps the most effective diversity leader on the planet." At the root of his effectiveness are the following:

◊   An unrelenting fierceness about fighting for the underdog and opening the circle of leadership to people of all races, gender identities, ethnicities, sexual orientations, cultures, abilities, faiths, and economic stations

◊   A resolute sense of fairness engendered by his father, his best friend, who instructed his son to look down on no man

◊   Respect for the individual, a traditional IBM value and his anchor in decisions about employees' lives

◊   A belief that a tsunami of people of color is approaching and that those who do not heed it will be left in its wake, their ability to compete for talent and business flattened

◊   The practicality of a businessperson, seeing diversity as a competitive business strategy and facilitator of organizational success

Born in Springfield, MA, Childs recalls, "In kindergarten, there was a handful of Black people, but I don't remember anything that was hostile of any kind." His first recollection of being in a public place that wasn't integrated was at age five, riding in the "colored" car on a train heading to his mother's hometown of Durham, NC. At age twelve, Childs had to be carefully extricated by a friend when Ms. Emma, his Durham grandmother, sent him to the store and, with the Black store closed, he went to the White store, inadvertently entering through the "Whites only" entrance.

Childs joined IBM out of West Virginia State University, an historically Black land-grant university. Integrated after the Brown v. Board of Education decision that separate is inherently unequal, WVSU was a school of separate lives, with Black students living in dorms and White students commuting by day, their paths rarely crossing except in class. Homecoming at WVSU was a largely Black event with only about six White couples attending the homecoming dance. In his senior year, Childs accepted the appointment from the student body president to be social chairman on the condition that they would integrate student activities. Working with three other students, he set about integrating homecoming. He convinced the university president to allow an admission fee for the homecoming dance, which Childs's team used to hire two bands: the Esquires, to appeal to White students; and Martha and the Vandellas for the Black students. Six hundred White couples attended that year. When Childs told that story to an IBM recruiter, he was hired the same day.

After serving in a number of positions in IBM's human resources organization, Childs was appointed vice president for global workforce diversity, a position from which he retired in 2006 after fifteen years of vaunted changes within IBM and an enormous influence in the broader diversity community. In 1983, Childs took an eighteen-month social service leave to serve as executive assistant to Benjamin Hooks, then executive director of the NAACP. Although IBM had a long history of commitment to diversity, when Lou Gerstner joined IBM as chairman and CEO in 1993, he determined that the senior management team did not adequately reflect the diversity of its employees or customers. Gerstner and Childs set out to forge "a significant philosophical shift—from a long tradition of minimizing differences to amplifying them and to seizing on the business opportunities they present."[403]

To launch this shift, they established eight constituency-based task forces, including one for White men, composed of executives who were constituency members. The task forces were co-chaired by two or more carefully selected executives, who were also constituency members, and were assigned an executive sponsor, a member of the Worldwide Management Council (WMC), IBM's top leadership group. Executive sponsors were responsible for "learning about [their] constituency's concerns, opportunities, and strategies and with serving as a liaison to top management."[404] Each task force was given six months to research and answer four questions:

1. What is required for your constituency to feel welcome and valued at IBM?
2. What can the corporation do, in partnership with your group, to maximize your constituency's productivity?
3. What can the corporation do to influence your constituency's buying decisions so that IBM is seen as a preferred solution provider?
4. And which external organizations should IBM form relationships with to better understand the needs of your constituency?

The answers to those questions created significant business opportunities for IBM and initiated a series of diversity initiatives that led to historic demographic changes in IBM's workforce. The work of the women's task force and others led to the creation of the Market Development Group, which focuses on business development in small and mid-sized diversity markets. In just three years, as noted in the section on sustainable competitive diversity advantage, the business development efforts of the Market Development organization grew from $10 million to over $300 million in revenue. The work of the people-with-disabilities task force helped to open up the adaptive technology market to IBM, a US market that is estimated to exceed $58 billion in 2020.

Whether at the very beginning of a diversity initiative or to reinvigorate it, task forces reinforce several change-leadership principles. They inspire urgency as they raise opportunities and concerns, establish the foundation of a leadership coalition, can produce quick wins, and are highly inclusive vehicles. Task forces educate and cross-pollinate executives who are critical to the success of the diversity initiative and can provide the burning platform that mobilizes the organization for change.

Under Childs's leadership, IBM developed globe-leading initiatives to respond to employees' work–life and dependent-care needs, creating benefits inside and outside of IBM. Childs and his team partnered with childcare experts to create the resource-and-referral industry, a system of organizations that provide referrals for child- and eldercare and other supports for family caregivers and work to build the availability and quality of dependent-care services. IBM's Global Work/Life Fund (GWLF) was a $50-million multiyear commitment to increase the supply of services in communities where IBM employees live and work, create global initiatives to improve the quality of dependent care, support the development of innovative childcare programs, and invest in over 300 childcare centers worldwide in which IBM employees receive priority.[405]

In addition to providing a cutting-edge array of services to its own employees, the GWLF has created numerous innovations in dependent care and flexible work arrangements that have been replicated by companies across the globe. Each year, Working Mother Media announces its hundred best companies based on their achievements in parental leave, family support, availability of employee resource groups for parents and users of flexible work, flexible work programs and policies, and in the representation of women at all levels. By 2020, IBM had made the hundred-best list for thirty-five straight years.

In addition to resource and referral, Childs played a major role in creating the infrastructure for the advancement of dependent care. He was an early and strong supporter of Catalyst, a global nonprofit that strives to create "workplaces that work for women"; the Families and Work Institute, which conducts research that advances work–life integration; and WFD, a consultancy that has pioneered numerous innovations in organizational work–life and dependent-care services. Childs was the impetus behind the American Business Collaboration for Dependent Care, a collaboration of leading US companies which invested over $135 million to ensure access to quality dependent-care programs and services for their employees.

Today, Childs heads his own consultancy, Ted Childs LLC, that provides strategic diversity advice. He is a frequent speaker at company and industry meetings. For his work, Childs has received a long list of awards:

◇ The National Association of Child Care Resource and Referral Agencies' Lifetime Achievement Award (1998)
◇ The Human Rights Campaign Corporate Leadership Award (2003)
◇ "The Captain Charlie Tomkins Award," presented to a civilian by the United States Navy to recognize the individual's contributions to making the Navy a better place for all its personnel

◇   The Families and Work Institute's Work/Life Legacy Award (2004)

◇   Omega Psi Phi Fraternity's Omega Century Award of Excellence

◇   And others

To honor his life's work, Working Mother Media created the Ted Childs Life/Work Excellence Award, given annually to an individual who has made a distinctive contribution to the integration of personal life and work.

The pedestal on which legacy creators like Miller and Childs stand is composed of an amalgam of the sheer force of their passion, commitment, discipline, and will. Each venerated the humanity of people different from themselves. Each transcended their race, gender, and other boundaries prescribed by their lives. Each rooted their actions in enlightened, deeply held values. Each was relentless. Each embedded diversity into the cultural fabric of their organizations. Each closely linked diversity to organizational and business goals. Leaders like Miller and Childs often influence the next generation of leaders to follow suit. And even the next and the next. But what about the generations after those?

The legacies these two men have created are extraordinary. Yet even their remarkable achievements may not be enough to create the momentum and ongoing commitment required to sustain positive diversity change. As a sign that momentum might be dissipating, neither company appeared on the 2019, 2020, or 2021 DiversityInc Top Fifty Companies for Diversity lists after long runs on that annual list.

Sustaining Diversity

Establishing a legacy requires the sustainment of a deep commitment to diversity over leadership generations. Childs believes that it is difficult to sustain change longer than the terms of two CEOs as new leaders bring new ideas, competing organizational interests and priorities arise, the business cycle turns down, organizational fortunes decline, or diversity objectives are not achieved.

No panacea exists to ensure sustainment. To sustain a diversity initiative first and foremost requires enculturating every employee to the diversity philosophy. Additional leverage points that can help sustain diversity include inclusive leadership networks, the composition and structure of the board of directors, signature initiatives, and vendor diversity.

ENCULTURATING EMPLOYEES TO THE DIVERSITY PHILOSOPHY

Sustaining diversity through multiple generations requires that each employee is enculturated with the values, beliefs, assumptions, norms, and mental models that compose the diversity philosophy. Enculturation is *the process through which employees learn the organization's diversity philosophy and adapt their own behaviors to it.* Enculturation has four dimensions:[406]

1. *Behavior*: choices of who is in an employee's inner circle, involvement in voluntary diversity activities, and language used and ideas expressed when with individuals of the same social group
2. *Values*: beliefs about gender identity, race and ethnicity, and sexual orientation
3. *Knowledge*: understanding of the history of race relations in an individual's country; concepts such as racism, sexism, anti-Semitism, ableism, and homophobia; and different cultures

4. Identity: beliefs about and attitudes toward one's own identity and the identities of those from other social groups

Enculturation to the diversity philosophy aligns leadership generations by establishing shared purpose, common goals, and ways of behaving that integrate behavior across functions, specialties, and changes to the business and organizational environments. Cultures provide stability in a world of constant adaptation. Thomas Watson, Jr., former chairman and CEO of IBM, famously said about culture,

> I firmly believe that any organization, in order to survive and achieve success, must have a sound set of beliefs on which it premises all its policies and actions. Next, I believe that the most important factor in corporate success is faithful adherence to those beliefs. And finally, I believe that if an organization is to meet the challenges of a changing world, it must be prepared to change everything about itself except those beliefs as it moves through corporate life.[407]

The starting point is the diversity philosophy, an aspirational philosophy that states the organization's diversity values, beliefs, and assumptions. Enculturation to the diversity philosophy can be achieved through the application of a series of management practices—including selection, advancement, training, communications, and behavioral management—that align the behavior, values, knowledge, and identity of employees to the diversity philosophy.

INCLUSIVE LEADERSHIP NETWORKS

As mentioned above, most leaders have few relationships in their networks that cross social group differences. Leaders should ask themselves just how many people of different races, ethnicities, abilities, religions, and genders are members of their inner circle (i.e., their closest group of friends and colleagues). Too often the answer is few or none.

This inner circle is the source of job referrals (an estimated 80 percent of jobs are found through personal referrals). A White male with a demographically limited inner circle cuts himself off from the 66 percent of the civilian working population that is neither White nor male. Perhaps worse, he cuts himself off from the learning and empathic understanding that comes from close relationships with people who are different.

Leaders should make it a priority to bring people who are demographically different from themselves into their work and personal inner circles. They should sit on at least one board where they are the underrepresented group. They should sponsor an employee resource group of people who are different from themselves, and they should formally or informally mentor a rising star or two from a different social group. And they should insist that those who report to them do the same.

COMPOSITION AND STRUCTURE OF THE BOARD OF DIRECTORS

Boards sit at the pinnacle of organizational power. They select, advise, evaluate, determine compensation for, and, when necessary, fire executives. They approve the corporate strategy and significant asset purchases. They establish performance targets and are the voice of the owners or the mission.

When the board reflects employee and customer populations and the demographic makeup of society, members are more likely to be connected and open to top candidates of difference, offer role models who show underrepresented employees that they can get ahead, communicate to prospective employees that there are unlimited opportunities, and pressure management to diversify leadership. Thus, diversity begets diversity.

At one nonprofit organization on whose board I used to serve, I observed a change from a predominately White, male board to a highly diverse board. The energy, excitement, and vibrancy of the board and staff picked up substantially, a woman of color was appointed chief executive, the staff overall became more diverse, and the organization embraced racial justice in their work.

Insofar as boards plan for and select new executives, they have the ability to ensure that the commitment to diversity is sustained across leadership generations. Besides their demographic makeups, boards should establish a standing diversity, equity, and inclusion committee and ensure that diversity is on the agenda and a topic of discussion at every board meeting. Board demography and practices can go a long way toward institutionalizing the commitment to diversity.

SIGNATURE INITIATIVES

Signature initiatives are activities the organization undertakes in the community or marketplace to establish its identity and commitment to diversity. Signature initiatives that sustain diversity must be long-lived, surviving multiple executive leadership generations, or better yet, permanent. Efforts that require funding every year or so or for a limited time do not meet the sustainment standard. Initiatives must also be associated with the strategic diversity objectives and philosophy of the organization.

For example, consider VMware, which offers a suite of technical services to fully digitize businesses. In 2016, they provided $1.5 million to the Clayman Institute for Gender Research at Stanford University for the Seeds of Change project, an educational research initiative that "aims to provide young women and girls with the frameworks, knowledge, and skills to find and strengthen their own voice and to navigate critical transitions such as starting college and entering the workforce."[408] In 2018, they endowed the VMware Women's Leadership Lab, which partners with corporations to create inclusive workplaces for women and to empower change agents for the advancement of women. By endowing the Leadership Lab, VMware has created a lifetime association that encourages its future leaders to keep attention on women's advancement and has put its name in front of many prospective customers who are concerned with more equitably advancing women.

A yawning gap in the diversity enterprise is the dearth of comparative diversity data. The Equal Employment Opportunity Commission (EEOC) by statute gathers representation data for private industry, unions, state and local government, elementary and secondary education, and the federal sector for a variety of different jobs and levels, but it largely covers only race, ethnicity, and gender. More comprehensive data that also includes LGBTQ+, age, and disability and is open to scholars and organizations is needed.

A superb legacy would be to band together with other organizations to establish a nonprofit organization to which members would voluntarily submit confidential data for a central database. An excellent model is the Profit Impact of Market Strategy (PIMS) database that currently gathers data from 4,200 strategic business units. The database offers intra- and inter-company comparisons across a rich array of process and outcome metrics and enables companies to determine the performance impact of various strategies. This would contribute immensely toward professionalizing diversity management.

VENDOR DIVERSITY

In 2018, nearly 27 percent of vendor diversity leader AT&T's spending went to certified diverse suppliers, vendors whose ownership is majority diverse. What about the other 73 percent? Organizations have a huge opportunity, an opportunity that could remake the diversity landscape if they also focus attention on nondiverse vendors who are neither minority nor woman owned. Requiring nondiverse vendors to meet prescribed diversity standards as a precondition of receiving their business could exponentially expand the universe of commitment to diversity. In effect, requiring vendors to meet diversity standards heightens their business case for diversity.

The asset management industry provides a perfect example of how diversity standards can work. Pension funds, especially public pension funds, often demand that the asset management firms with whom they do business meet diversity standards. The California Public Employees' Retirement System (CalPERS) issued *Governance & Sustainability Principles* that ask the companies with which they invest to consider board diversity. Although they use a broader definition of diversity than just underrepresented people, they ask companies to undertake the following: disclose how they evaluate board talent, identify attributes they seek in board members, stipulate director tenure limits, and publicly disclose their demographic information, including the racial, gender, and ethnic makeup of their workforce by job category and level.

In setting diversity standards, organizations should not stipulate what vendors should do but rather determine the categories in which they expect their vendors to establish policies and practices. An excellent example of standards, albeit in the area of quality management, is the Malcolm Baldrige National Quality Awards, which ask award applicants to describe in precise terms the actions they are taking in seven categories, including leadership, strategy, measurement, workforce empowerment and inclusion, and the outcomes they are achieving. A good starting point for vendor diversity standards categories is leadership, diversity representation, equity, and inclusion.

A powerful way to sustain diversity is for each leader to set a goal of establishing a personal diversity legacy. Legacy is not necessarily about becoming a revered diversity hero, like Miller or Childs, although that would be wonderful, but rather about being one ripple in a mighty current flowing across leadership generations.

Dangers on the Path to Legacy

The road to diversity legacy is strewn with dangers. Robert F. Kennedy, in his 1966 anti-apartheid speech, "Day of Affirmation," delivered in Cape Town, South Africa, identified and named those dangers: expediency, timidity, comfort, and futility. Leaders who aspire to legacy must come to terms with each of those dangers and establish pathways to overcome them.

EXPEDIENCY

A leader must constantly weigh and determine priorities in order to achieve the relentless focus necessary for an organization to succeed. The pure short-term pragmatics of profit, growth, and mission, the pressures coming up and down the line, and the day-to-day personnel challenges all can drive diversity down the list of priorities.

I have asked many senior leadership teams whether diversity is a priority in their organizations. The vast majority say, "Yes." Then, I ask them where diversity ranks on their priority list. Is it in third place, fifteenth place, thirtieth place, or even further down the list? They have trouble answering the second question. Great organizations focus on the critical few objectives and address significant unexpected events, often leaving scant space for diversity on the executive agenda.

Robert Galvin, the CEO and chairman of Motorola who the *New York Times* called "one of America's most visionary entrepreneurs," was a leader in Six Sigma quality. He was reported to have said, "Quality was always on the executive team's agenda, but we never quite got to it. When quality became a priority, we never quite got to anything else." When top leaders make diversity a serious topic at every executive team meeting, when they are held accountable for achieving results on strategic diversity objectives, when they stand up to injustice, and when they engage rather than avoid diversity in employee forums, all employees will understand that diversity has become a priority.

Diversity is not a sure thing, especially over the long term. It takes time and investment to succeed, and it engenders pushback and resistance all along the way. Diversity requires leaders to have the vision, courage, and steadfastness to rise above the moment and invest in the future of the organization and its people.

TIMIDITY

Timidity means hesitance, fear, and indecision in the face of risk. Timidity is inaction in the face of an act of racism, sexual harassment, or other unethical or illegal behavior. The antithesis of timidity is moral courage, the willingness to do what is right in behalf of others and in the face of personal risk.

Acting with moral courage requires that leaders have moral principles and that they act in accordance with those principles when faced with risk. Though top leaders can state those principles in a diversity philosophy, they cannot assure they will be embraced and pursued. Leaders will have the greatest influence on morally courageous behavior when they themselves display moral courage. They must be willing to step into the arena of moral ambiguity and conflict and demonstrate principled action. Theodore Roosevelt described this morally courageous leader in his "Citizenship in a Republic" speech, often referred to as the "Man in the Arena" speech:

> To the man who is actually in the arena, whose face is marred by dust and sweat and blood, who strives valiantly, who errs and comes up short again and again, because there is no effort without error or shortcoming, but who knows the great enthusiasms, the great devotions, who spends himself for a worthy cause; who, at the best, knows, in the end, the triumph of high achievement, and who, at the worst, if he fails, at least he fails while daring greatly, so that his place shall never be with those cold and timid souls who knew neither victory nor defeat.[409]

COMFORT

Perhaps the most insidious of the dangers inherent in achieving legacy is comfort, for those who are lucky enough to enjoy it. Those resting in comfort have little motivation to take the bold actions and risks that are the genesis of legacy.

Comfort in the face of inequality and exclusion is a gift of privilege. Privilege means that a person enjoys freedoms, advantages, and opportunities that are available to members of his social group and not readily available to other social groups. Privilege is manifested in numerous ways of which the privileged are often unaware—a job referral from a friend of the family, a mentor who looks like you, an invitation to the inner circle, or the latitude to integrate work and personal life.

The word *privilege* has a similar effect on the privileged as *affirmative action* has on those who are discriminated against. People of privilege do not want to hear that their successes are based on their privilege rather than their individual talent and hard work, just as people who are objects of discrimination do not like to be told that their successes are based on affirmative action. When their privilege is unmasked, privileged people typically act to preserve their innocence and maintain their status with a recitation of the hardships they have endured in achieving their current status.[410] For example, consider the oblivious executive who remarked during a discussion of privilege, "I may be a White male, but I was the first in my family to go to college, which I had to finance myself because my family had little money. I can remember many dinners when the only thing on my plate was bread and bologna. Yet I was able to pull myself up by my bootstraps to become CEO."

Given the frequent invisibility of privilege, the resistance to accepting one's own privilege, and the challenges of changing the biases, cultural norms, and social, political, and economic systems that support privilege, it is predictable that for a leader to act to eliminate privileges from which she herself benefits is extremely difficult. Though privilege receives considerable attention in public forums, scant research-based evidence is available to provide guidance for addressing it. Simple logic suggests three steps: awareness and acknowledgment of one's privileges, empathy with grace, and taking action to equalize privileges.

Awareness and Acknowledgment

Often called "checking your privilege," awareness and acknowledgment of the privileges an individual enjoys is neither easy nor straightforward given the resistance a person must overcome. Two starting points are the systemic bias process through which privilege forms (see "Competency 5: Advancing Toward Equity") and Peggy McIntosh's essay, "White Privilege: Unpacking the Invisible Knapsack." Her essay is an excellent tool for gaining awareness of privilege. A useful way to move from awareness to acknowledgment is for leaders to read McIntosh's essay and write their own list of the privileges they enjoy due to their social group membership.

Empathy with Grace

Once privilege is acknowledged, it is vital to reflect on and experience the effects of privilege on those with fewer privileges. What privileges does a man enjoy in this organization that a woman doesn't? What advantages does that privilege confer? What privileges does a White woman enjoy that a Black or Brown woman doesn't? Empathy with grace comes from genuinely exploring one's privilege with openness, generosity, and compassion and responding to one's unearned privileges with appreciation and grace toward those with lesser privileges.

Taking Action to Equalize Privilege

People who are comfortable in their privileges are unlikely to renounce them. Indeed, they are more likely to resist actions that reduce their privileges. The superior approach is to act to increase the privileges of the least privileged.

In organizations, privilege manifests in a multitude of ways. Two of the most significant are being hired and receiving the support necessary for advancement. Although what you know and what you've done are critical in hiring, of equal or greater importance is who you know—greater importance because a candidate may never get to show what they know and what they've done without the right introduction. Being privileged often means having privileged family members and acquaintances who are likely to know people well placed in hiring organizations. Having little privilege means being relegated to responding to advertisements that appear on internet search engines. Expanding privilege to those with little privilege might mean offering bonuses to employees who recommend those from particular social groups for positions for which they are hired or requiring leaders to expand their personal networks into institutions that have significant numbers of qualified, lesser-privileged candidates, or sourcing candidates from institutions with significant numbers of qualified, lesser-privileged candidates, such as historically black colleges and universities.

Once inside an organization, a lesser-privileged employee is likely to come up against homophily, the "birds of a feather flock together" principle mentioned several times above. Homophily means that an employee whose characteristics most closely mirror senior managers is more likely to be deemed a "fit," be informally mentored and sponsored, receive higher performance evaluations, and have better access to key developmental opportunities.

For equality of privilege to persevere over the length of time necessary for legacy to evolve, senior leaders should consider all the ways in which privilege is manifested in the organization and then assiduously and rigorously work to expand privilege to those with less privilege.

FUTILITY

Futility is the limiting belief that there is little one person can do to right the injustice and exclusion experienced by underrepresented employees. It is the rare leader who can make lasting change through a series of grand, sweeping strokes. The truth of sustainable change is that it happens through many small actions taken time and time again by leaders throughout the organization. As Robert F. Kennedy expressed at Cape Town, "Each time a man stands up for an ideal, or acts to improve the lot of others, or strikes out against injustice, he sends forth a tiny ripple of hope, and crossing each other from a million different centers of energy and daring, those ripples build a current which can sweep down the mightiest walls of oppression and resistance"[411]—and bend the arc of the world's institutions toward justice.

Acknowledgments

THE IDEA FOR *LEADING DIVERSITY for Competitive Advantage* began in 2012 while serving as research director for the Conference Board's Research Working Group on Improving Employment Outcomes for People with Disabilities and as principal author of its monograph, *Leveling the Playing Field: Attracting, Engaging and Advancing People with Disabilities.* As my colleague Ivelys Figueroa and I surveyed the research literature on employing people with disabilities, we discovered little evidence-based knowledge to guide practice. As I later expanded that search to include all underrepresented people, I found a dearth of evidence-based practice to guide organizational diversity, equity, and inclusion. Thus began a nearly ten-year journey of research, practice, and writing to forge an evidence-based practice of diversity.

I faltered many times on that journey: What does a White guy really know about diversity? What would scholars think about my attempt to link diversity practice to scientific evidence? How could I forgo earning any income while I devoted myself full-time to research and writing? How could I keep telling my friends and family that I am working on a book that never seems to be finished? How could I sustain this journey with no certainty that the book would ever be published?

That I have made it to the finish is testament that researching and writing a book, as raising a child, takes a community. Though that community is too vast to individually thank everyone, I want to acknowledge and thank those who were so pivotal in completing this journey:

Most of all, my wife, Marlene Linkow, who saw into my heart that day on Oxford Street and never wavered, not for a second, in her belief in and support for this venture;

My three sons, Alex, Zack, and Nick, writers all, who have provided invaluable input, advice, and steadfast enthusiasm and support for this project;

Andrew Hahn, former assistant dean and professor emeritus at the Heller School for Social Policy and Management at Brandeis University, who, in the face of discrimination, taught me deep lessons about taking the high road and has been a paragon of loyalty and social commitment;

Walter Pressey, whose encouragement and support established me on the path that led inexorably to diversity leadership and strategy;

William W. Lynch, chairman of the Educational Psychology Department at Indiana University, whose faith in me guided a perplexed young man to self-confidence, endowing me with the agency that enabled this book;

Ken Barrett, Ted Childs, Jr., Deb Dagit, Veronica Villalobos, Melinda Wolfe, and Sharon Wong, who gave so generously and graciously of their knowledge and insights as chief diversity officers at the US Navy, IBM, Merck, the US Office of Personnel Management, Goldman Sachs, and Goddard Space Flight Center, respectively;

Rebekah Steele, who has so authentically, inclusively, and effectively expanded the boundaries of diversity practice, and whose feedback, encouragement, and referrals motivated me and sustained me through periods of self-doubt;

The W. K. Kellogg Foundation and Larraine Matusak and Robben Wright Fleming, who invited me to become a Kellogg

Fellow and supported my three-year odyssey to elaborate strategic thinking, providing the opportunity to study and interview a host of gifted strategic thinkers—including Vernon Jordan, Joan Ganz Cooney, Walter Wriston, and Faye Wattleton—and research, practice, and teach strategy;

Susanne Bruyère and Mary Wright, who invited me to join the Research Working Group on Improving Employment Outcomes for People with Disabilities at the Conference Board, unleashing my curiosity about evidence-based diversity practice and revitalizing my commitment to equity, and Rebecca Ray, who shines a bright light on the future of human capital;

The executives and their teams who partnered with me to pioneer and develop the diversity and strategy practices that are featured in this book, including John Van Scoter and Larry Sherrell at Texas Instruments/DLP, Kevin Kelly and David Denison at Fidelity Canada and Fidelity Investments Institutional Services, John Russell and Debbie Lewis at Loomis Sayles, Darry Callahan at Warren Petroleum/Chevron, Victoria Hubbell at CIBC, Kerry Tompson, Heather DeBlois, and Florence Chapman at Sobeys, Mike Markovits at GE Capital, Mike Ullman and Jim Wiggett of LVMH/DFS House, Kathi Hanley and Wayne Lowe of Toyota/TMMK, and Kai Sotorp at UBS Global Asset Management;

Ivelys Figueroa, whose deft research assistance informs the evidence base so critical to this work;

The reference librarians at Wellesley Free Library who assiduously tracked down even the most obscure references I requested;

Emmy Award–winning writer Gary Stuart Kaplan, who contributed much productive feedback to this endeavor;

And authors Keith Yocum and David Hughes and publisher Simon Holt of Elsevier, who guided me through the arcana of book publishing.

References

1   Michael Norton and Samuel Sommers, "Whites See Racism as a Zero-Sum Game That They Are Now Losing," *Perspectives on Psychological Science* 6, No. 215 (2011).

2   "Reverse Discrimination Complaints Rare, Labor Study Reports," *The New York Times*. March 30, 1995.

3   Scott Page, *The Difference: How the Power of Diversity Creates Better Groups, Firms, Schools, and Societies* (Princeton, NJ: Princeton University Press, 2007).

4   Wiley Online Library, "Sex Differences in Cognition," in *Encyclopedia of Cognitive Science* (John Wiley and Sons, 2014); and Kingsley Browne, "Sex Differences in Cognitive Abilities," in *Rethinking Sexual Equality* (New Brunswick, NJ: Rutgers University Press, 2002).

5   Viorica Marian and Anthony Shook, "The Cognitive Benefits of Being Bilingual," *Cerebrum*, September-October 2012, 5.

6   Faye Belgrave and Kevin Allison, *African American Psychology: From Africa to America* (Thousand Oaks, CA: Sage, 2014), 273-78.

7   Office of Federal Contract Compliance Programs, "Small Contractor Affirmative Action Program (AAP) Job Group Availability Determinations," US Department of Labor, retrieved Dec. 10, 2015, http://www.dol.gov/ofccp/scaap.htm.

8   US Equal Employment Opportunity Commission, *EEO-1 Job Classification Guide 2010*, retrieved Dec. 10, 2015, http://www.eeoc.gov/employers/eeo1survey/jobclassguide.cfm.

9   Maria Veronica Santelices and Mark Wilson, "The Case of Freedle, the SAT, and the Standardization Approach to Differential Item Functioning," *Harvard Educational Review* (Spring 2010).

10   ABC News, "Is the 'N-Word Going Mainstream?" retrieved Nov. 17, 2015, http://abcnews.go.com/2020/story?id=132632&page=1.

11   The complete lyrics, retrieved on January 6, 2022, are available at https://www.google.com/search?q=lyrics+to+sucka+nigga&oq=lyrics+to+sucka+nigga&aqs=chrome..69i57.8147j0j15&sourceid=chrome&ie=UTF-8.

12   Southern Poverty Law Center, "Straight Talk About the H-Word," Teaching Tolerance Project, retrieved Nov. 17, 2015, http://www.tolerance.org/magazine/number-40-fall-2011/feature/straight-talk-about-n-word.

13   Marina Bolotnikova, "Above All Else, Do Not Lie," *Harvard Magazine* (May 23, 2018), retrieved on May 25, 2018, from https://www.harvardmagazine.com/2018/05/commencement-class-day-chimamanda-adichie.

14   Theodore Roosevelt, *Citizenship in the Republic*, delivered at the University of Paris (April 23, 1910).

15   Michael Boren, "LGBT? LGBTQ? LGBTQIA? Hey Philly, what's the ideal acronym? *The Philadelphia Inquirer* (September 25, 2017), retrieved on July 30, 2022 from https://www.inquirer.com/life/inq/lgbt-lgbtq-lgbtqia-hey-philly-whats-ideal-acronym-20170925.html&outputType=app-web-view.

16   William Safire, "Language: Woman vs. Female," *The New York Times*, The Opinion Pages (March 18, 2007) retrieved Dec. 20, 2016, http://www.nytimes.com/2007/03/18/opinion/18iht-edsafire.4943390.html.

17   BLS Reports, *Labor Force Characteristics by Race and Ethnicity, Table 3. Employment Status of the Civilian Non-Institutional Population by Sex, Age, Race, and Hispanic or Latino Ethnicity, 2019*, US Department of Labor, Bureau of Labor Statistics, retrieved on November 8, 2021, https://www.bls.gov/opub/reports/race-and-ethnicity/2019/home.htm and *Labor Force Characteristics by Race and Ethnicity, Table 3. Employment Status of the Civilian Non-Institutional Population by Sex, Age, Race, and Hispanic or Latino Ethnicity,* 2009, Bureau of Labor Statistics, US Department of Labor, retrieved November 8, 2021, https://www.bls.gov/opub/reports/race-and-ethnicity/archive/race_ethnicity_2009.pdf

18   US Bureau of Census, *Educational Attainment in the U.S. 2010, Table 1: Educational Attainment of the Population 18 and Over, by Age, Sex, Race, and Hispanic Origin: 2010,* retrieved on November 8, 2021, from https://www.census.gov/data/tables/2010/demo/ educational-attainment/cps-detailed-tables.html; and US Bureau of Census, *Educational Attainment in the U.S. 2020, Table 1: Educational Attainment of the Population 18 and Over, by Age, Sex, Race, and Hispanic Origin: 2020,* retrieved on November 8, 2021, https:// www.census.gov/data/tables/2020/demo/educational-attainment/ cps-detailed-tables.html.

19   US Census Bureau, *Educational Attainment in the United States: 2018,* retrieved November 10, 2021, https://www.census. gov/data/tables/2018/demo/education-attainment/cps-detailed-tables.html; and the US Equal Employment Opportunity Commission, *2018 EEO-1 National Aggregate Report,* retrieved November 10 2021, from https://www.eeoc.gov/statistics/employment/jobpatterns/eeo1.

20   US Equal Employment Opportunity Commission, *2008 EEO-1 National Aggregate Report,* retrieved November 10, 2021, from https://www.eeoc.gov/eeo-1/2008-eeo-1-national-aggregate-report; and US Equal Employment Opportunity Commission, *2018 EEO-1 National Aggregate Report,* retrieved November 10, 2021, from https://www.eeoc.gov/statistics/employment/jobpatterns/eeo1.

21   Ibid

22   The Conference Board, *Mind the Gap: Factors Driving the Growing Racial Wage Gaps and Solutions to Close Them (2021),* retrieved January 1, 2022, from https://www.conference-board.org/ publications/growing-racial-wage-gaps.

23   Joseph Price and Justin Wolfers, *Racial Discrimination Among NBA Referees,* National Bureau of Economic Research, Working Paper (June 2007), retrieved July 12, 2016, from http://www.nber. org/papers/w13206.

24   Marianne Bertrand and Sendhil Mullainathan, "Are Emily and Greg More Employable Than Lakisha and Jamal? A Field Experiment on Labor Market Discrimination," *American Economic* Review, 94 No. 4 (September 2004): 991-1013.

25   Adrienne Colella and Arup Varma, "Disability-Job Fit Stereotypes and the Evaluation of Persons with Disabilities at Work," *Journal of Occupational Rehabilitation* (1999): 79-95 and Michelle Hebl, Jessica Foster, Laura Mannix, and John Dovidio, "Formal and Interpersonal Discrimination: A Field Study of Bias Toward Homosexual Applicants," *Personality and Social Psychology Bulletin*, 28 No. 6 (2002): 815-825.

26   Devah Pager, "The Mark of a Criminal Record," *American Journal of Sociology*, 108 No. 5 (March 2003): 937-75.

27   Claudia Goldin and Cecilia Rouse, "Orchestrating Impartiality: The Impact of 'Blind' Auditions on Female Musicians," *American Economic Review*, 90 No. 4 (September 2000): 715-741.

28   US Equal Employment Opportunity Commission, *Charge Statistics (Charges filed with the EEOC) FY 1997 Through FY 2021 (2022)*, retrieved on July 30, 2022, from https://www.eeoc.gov/statistics/charge-statistics-charges-filed-eeoc-fy-1997-through-fy-2021.

29   PEW Research Center, *A Survey of LGBT Americans* (June 13, 2013).

30   Sandy James, Jody Herman, Susan Rankin, Mara Keisling, Lisa Mottet, and Ma'ayan Anafi, *The Report of the 2015 US Transgender Survey,* Washington, DC: National Center for Transgender Equality (2016), 4.

31   "Non-Discrimination Laws," Movement Advancement Project, American Civil Liberties Union, retrieved June 7, 2016, from https://action.aclu.org/maps/non-discrimination-laws-state-state-information-map?iframe=1#.

32   Harris Interactive, *The ADA, Twenty Years Later*, Kessler Foundation and National Organization on Disability (July 2010), 56.

33   Lori Snyder, Jennifer Carmichael, Lauren Blackwell, Jeanette Cleveland, and George Thornton III, "Perceptions of Discrimination and Justice Among Employees with Disabilities," *Employee Responsibilities and Rights Journal*, No. 22, (2010), 8.

34   Bureau of Labor Statistics, *Persons with a Disability: Labor Force Characteristics* Summary, *Table 1. Employment Status of the Civilian Noninstitutional Population By Disability Status and Selected Characteristics, 2016 annual averages*, US Department of Labor, 2016, retrieved on January 5, 2018, from https://www.bls.gov/news.release/disabl.nr0.htm.

35   *Workplace Discrimination*, China Labour Bulletin, retrieved June 17, 2016 from http://www.clb.org.hk/content/workplace-discrimination#hukou; and *Guide to Discrimination Law in the PRC*, Mayer Brown JSM, retrieved on June 17, 2016 from http://www.clb.org.hk/content/workplace-discrimination#hukou.

36   *Discrimination at Work in Asia*, Factsheet, International Labour Organization (May 2007).

37   Matt Moir, "The Persecution of China's Muslim Uyghurs," *Religion and Politics* (August 9, 2016), retrieved February 13, 2017, from http://religionandpolitics.org/2016/08/09/the-persecution-of-chinas-muslim-uyghurs/.

38   Hugo Ñopo, Alberto Chong, and Andrea Moro, "What Do We Know about Discrimination in Latin America? Very Little!" in Hugo Ñopo, Alberto Chong, and Andrea Moro (eds.), *Discrimination in Latin America: An Economic Perspective*, Inter-American Development Bank and the World Bank (2010), 79-80.

39   *Women in Business and Management: Gaining Momentum*, International Labour Organization, United Nations (2015).

40   *Quick Take on Boards*, Catalyst Inc. Knowledge Center, (March 3, 2014).

41   *Pay Equity: A Key Driver of Gender Equality*, International Labour Organization, 2-3, retrieved June 7, 2016, from http://www.ilo.org/wcmsp5/groups/public/---dgreports/---gender/documents/briefingnote/wcms_410196.pdf. 2-3.

42   *Women at Work: Trends 2016*, International Labour Organization, 29.

43   United Nations, *Global Status Report on Disability and Development: Protoype 2015*, Department of Economic and Social Affairs (2015).

44   Justin McCarthy, "European Countries Among Top Places for Gay People to Live," Gallup (June 26, 2015), retrieved on June 24, 2016, from http://www.gallup.com/poll/183809/european-countries-among-top-places-gay-people-live.aspx?version=print.

45   *Figure 1: Tolerance in Africa*, Afrobarometer (2016): 3

46   *Report 2009*, Corporación Latinobarómetro, (2009): 52.

47   Charles Radcliffe, "The Real Cost of LGBT Discrimination," World Economic Forum (Jan. 5, 2016), retrieved on June 9, 2016 from https://www.weforum.org/agenda/2016/01/the-real-cost-of-lgbt-discrimination/

48   Lucas Paoli Itaborahy and Jingshu Zhu, *State-Sponsored Homophobia: A World Survey of Laws: Criminalisation, Protection and Recognition of Same-Sex Love*, 8th edition, International Lesbian Gay Bisexual Trans and Intersex Association (May 2013), retrieved on August 8, 2022, from https://www.almendron.com/tribuna/wp-content/uploads/2014/12/ilga-state-sponsored-homophobia-2013.pdf.

49   Jack Zenger and Joseph Folkman, "Are Women Better Leaders Than Men?" *Harvard Business Review*, March 15, 2012, retrieved on January 3, 2018, from https://hbr.org/2012/03/a-study-in-leadership-women-do.

50   Sonia Ospina and Erica Foldy, "A Critical Review of Race and Ethnicity in the Leadership Literature: Surfacing Context, Power, and Collective Dimensions of Leadership," *The Leadership Quarterly* 20 (2009): 876-896.

51   Peter Hom, Aimee Ellis, and Loriann Roberson, "Challenging Conventional Wisdom About Who Quits: Revelations from Corporate America," *Journal of Applied Psychology*, September 2008

52   Peter Linkow and Jan Civian, *Men and Work-Life Integration: A Global Study*, WFD Consulting and World-at-Work, May 2011, retrieved on November 15, 2017, from https://www.worldatwork.org/adimLink?id=51556.

53   Michael Norton and Samuel Sommers. "Whites See Racism as a Zero-Sum Game That They Are Now Losing." *Perspectives on Psychological Science,* 6, No. 3 (May 2011): 215–218, https://www.hbs.edu/ris/Publication%20Files/norton%20sommers%20whites%20see%20racism_ca92b4be-cab9-491d-8a87-cf1c6ff244ad.pdf.

54   Alice Eagly, "When Passionate Advocates Meet Research on Diversity, Does the Honest Broker Stand a Chance?" *Journal of Social Issues*, Vol. 72, 1 (2016), 199-222.

55   Minority Business Development Agency, *Fact Sheet: All Minority-Owned Firms* (2017) and *Fact Sheet: All Minority-Owned Firms* (2007), retrieved on November 11, 2021, from https://www.mbda.gov/page/us-business-fact-sheets.

56   American Express, *The 2019 State of Women-Owned Businesses Report: Summary of Key Trends*, 2019, retrieved on November 10, 2021 from https://s1.q4cdn.com/692158879/files/doc_library/file/2019-state-of-women-owned-businesses-report.pdf.

57   American Express, 7.

58   Jeffrey Humphreys, *The Multicultural Economy* 2019, Selig Center for Economic Growth, Terry College of Business, University of Georgia (2019).

59   Ibid

60   Michelle Yin, Dahlia Shaewitz, Cynthia Overton, and Deeze-Mae Smith, *A Hidden Market: The Purchasing Power of Working-Age Adults with Disabilities, American Institutes for Research (April 17, 2018)*, retrieved on November 11, 2021, from https://www.air.org/resource/report/hidden-market-purchasing-power-working-age-adults-disabilities.

61   Peter Linkow, *Leveling the Playing Field: Attracting, Engaging, and Advancing People with Disabilities*, The Conference Board (2013).

62   Michael J. Silverstein, Kate Sayre, and John Butman, *Women Want More: How to Capture Your Share of the World's Largest, Fastest-Growing Market*, New York: HarperBusiness (2009).

63   US Bureau of Economic Analysis, *Real Disposable Personal Income [DSPIC96]*, Federal Reserve Bank of St. Louis: (January 24, 2018), retrieved on January 24, 2018, from https://fred.stlouisfed.org/series/DSPIC96.

64   Michael Silverstein and Kate Sayre, "The Female Economy," *Harvard Business Review* (September 2009).

65   Small Business and Entrepreneurship Council, *Going Global: Resources for Entrepreneurs and Small Businesses* (2018), retrieved on January 25, 2018, from http://sbecouncil.org/resources/going-global/.

66   International Monetary Fund, *World Economic Outlook: Real GDP Growth* (October 2017).

67   Statista, *Gross domestic product (GDP) of the United States from 1990 to 2016 (in billion current U.S. dollars)*, The Statistics Portal, retrieved on January 3, 2018, from https://www.statista.com/statistics/188105/annual-gdp-of-the-united-states-since-1990/.

68   Trade Partnership Worldwide, LLC, *The Impact of Trade on U.S. and State-Level Employment: 2016 Update*, prepared for the Business Roundtable, January 2016, retrieved on January 3, 2018, from http://businessroundtable.org/sites/default/files/reports/Trade%20and%20American%202016%20FINAL.pdf.

69   Rick Newman, "Why US Companies Aren't So American Anymore," *US News and World Report*, June 30, 2011, retrieved on January 3, 2018, from https://money.usnews.com/money/blogs/flow-chart/2011/06/30/why-us-companies-arent-so-american-anymore.

70   Gary N. Siperstein, Neil Romano, Amanda Mohler, and Robin Parker, "A national survey of consumer attitudes towards companies that hire people with disabilities," *Journal of Vocational Rehabilitation*, vol. 22 (2005): 4-5.

71   IBISWorld, *Elderly & Disabled Services in the US: Market Research Report*, (December 2011).

72   BCC Research, *Disabled and Elderly Assistive Technologies*, (July 2011).

73   Stephanie Downey, Lisa van der Werff, Kecia Thomas, and Victoria Plaut, "The Role of Diversity Practices and Inclusion in Promoting Trust and Employee Engagement," *Journal of Applied Social Psychology*, 45 (2015): 35-44; and Charles Rodgers, Amy Richman, Barbara Nobles Crawford, and Hal Morgan, "The Drivers of Employee Commitment: Tools for Creating a Competitive Workplace," WFD Consulting (1998): 1-20.

74   See, for example, James Harter, Frank Schmidt, and Theodore Hayes, "Business-Unit-Level Relationship Between Employee Satisfaction, Employee Engagement, and Business Outcomes: A Meta-Analysis," *Journal of Applied Psychology*, 87, No. 2 (2002): 268-279; S. Badal and James Harder, "Gender Diversity, Business-Unit Engagement, and Performance," *Journal of Leadership and Organizational Studies*, 4, No. 2 (2014): 354-365; Amy Richman, "Everyone Wants an Engaged Workforce: How Can You Create It," *Workspan* (January 2006): 36-39.; and Tejaswi Bhuvanaiah and R. P. Raya, "Employee Engagement: Key to Organizational Success," *SCMS Journal of Indian Management* (December 2014): 61-71.

75   Rodgers, Richman, Crawford, Morgan, 10-11.

76   Rodgers, Richman, Crawford, Morgan, 17.

77   Deborah Dougherty, "New Products in Old Organizations: The Myth of the Better Mousetrap in Search of the Beaten Path, " PhD dissertation, Sloan School of Management, MIT (1987); Sara Kiesler, *Interpersonal Processes in Groups and Organizations* , AHM Publishing: Arlington Hts., IL (1978); Jeffrey Pfeffer and Charles O'Reilly, "Hospital Demography and Turnover among Nurses," *Industrial Relations*, 36 (1987): 158-173; and Marvin Shaw, *Group Dynamics: The Psychology of Small Group Behavior*, New York: McGraw-Hill (1971).

78   Warren E. Watson, Kamalesh Kumar, and Larry K. Michaelsen, "Cultural diversity's impact on interaction process and performance: Comparing homogeneous and diverse task groups," *Academy of Management Journal*, 36, no. 3 (1993): 599.

79   Thomas Kochan, Katerina Bezrukova, Robin Ely, Susan Jackson, Aparna Joshi, Karen Jehn, Jonathan Leonard, David Levine, and David Thomas, "The Effects of Diversity on Business Performance: Report of the Diversity Research Network," *Human Resource Management,* 42, no. 1 (2003): 3-21 (chrs.rutgers.edu/pub_documents/38.pdf).

80   Scott Page, *The Difference: How the Power of Diversity Creates Better Groups, Firms, Schools, and Societies* (Princeton, NJ: Princeton University Press, 2007).

81   Page, *The Difference*; Margaret Foegen Karsten, *Management, Gender, and Race in the 21st Century* (Lanthan, MD: University Press of America, 2006); Orlando C. Richard, Tim Barnett, Sean Dwyer, and Ken Chadwick, "Cultural Diversity in Management, Firm Performance, and the Moderating Role of Entrepreneurial Orientation Dimensions," *Academy of Management Journal*, 47, no. 2, 2004, pp. 255–266 (misweb.cbi.msstate.edu/~COBI/faculty/users/tbarnett/AMJ2004.pdf); and K. M. Thomas, *Diversity Dynamics in the Workplace* (Belmont, CA: Thomson Wadsworth, 2005).

82   Günter K. Stahl, Martha L. Maznevski, Andreas Voigt, and Karsten Jonsen, "Unraveling the effects of cultural diversity in teams: A meta-analysis of research on multicultural groups," *Journal of International Business Studies*, 41 (2009): 690–709.

83   Cone Communications, *Brands and Social Action: What Do You Stand Up For?* (2017): 2.

84   Ibid, 6.

85   Cone Communications, *2017 Cone Communications CSR Study* (2017): 15.

86   John Peloza, "The Challenge of Measuring Financial Impacts From Investments in Corporate Social Performance," *Journal of Management*, 35, No. 6 (2009): 1518-1541.

87   D. B. Turban and D.W. Greening, "Corporate Social Performance and Organizational Attractiveness to Prospective Employees," *Academy of Management Journal* 40, No. 3 (June 1997): 666.

88   Herman Aguinis and Ante Glavas, "What We Know and Don't Know About Corporate Social Responsibility," *Journal of Management*, 38, No. 4 (July 2012): 940-947.

89   Duncan Kennedy, "A Pluralist Case for Affirmative Action in Legal Academia." In *Critical Race Theory: The Key Writings That Formed a Movement*, 1st edition, edited by Kimberle Crenshaw (New York: New York Press, 1995), 164.

90   Peter Linkow, "Is Your Culture Aligned with Diversity?" *Profiles in Diversity Journal* (July/August 2005): 2.

91   Henry Mintzberg, Bruce Ahlstrand, and Joseph Lampel, *Strategy Safari: A Guided Tour Through the Wilds of Strategic Management*, (New York: The Free Press, 1998).

92   James Brian Quinn, *Strategies for Change: Logical Incrementalism*, (Homewood, IL: Richard D. Irwin, 1980), 15.

93   Kelly Acton et al., "Trends in Diabetes Prevalence Among American Indian and Alaska Native Children, Adolescents, and Young Adults," *American Journal of Public Health*, 92, No. 9 (September 2002): 1485-6.

94   Kenneth Andrews, *The Concept of Corporate Strategy*. Revised Edition. (Homewood, IL: Richard D. Irwin, 1980), 18.

95   Peter Drucker, *Managing for Results* (Oxford: Butterworth Heinemann, 1964): 10.

96   Paul Schoemaker, "When and How to Use Scenario Planning: A Heuristic Approach with Illustration," *Journal of* Forecasting, 10 (1991); Peter Schwartz, *The Art of the Long View: Planning for the Future in an Uncertain* World, New York: Doubleday (1996); and Kees van der Heijden, *Scenarios: The Art of Strategic Conversation*, Chichester, England: John Wiley & Sons (1996).

97   Ibid, 9.

98   Suzanne Heywood, Ruben Hillar, and David Turnbull, "How Do I Manage the Complexity in My Organization?" McKinsey & Co. (2007): 4.

99   Peter Linkow, "What Gifted Strategic Thinkers Do," *Training & Development*, 53, No. 7 (July 1999).

100   National Archives and Records Administration, "Executive Order 13583--Establishing a Coordinated Government-Wide Initiative to Promote Diversity and Inclusion in the Federal Workforce," *Federal Register*, 76, No. 163 (August 23, 2011).

101   United States Office of Personnel Management, *Guidance for Agency-Specific Diversity and Inclusion Plans* (November 2011).

102   Robert Merton, "The Unanticipated Consequences of Purposive Social Action," *American Sociological Review*, 1, No. 6 (December 1936): 894-904.

103   Robert Schafer and John Tait, *A Guide for Understanding Attitudes and Attitude Change*, North Central Regional Extension Publication 138 (Aug. 1986): 3.

104   Susan Fiske, "What We Know Now about Bias and Intergroup Conflict, the Problem of the Century," *Current Directions in Psychological Science*, 11, No. 4 (August 2002): 124.

105   Patrick Devine, Patrick Forscher, Anthony Austin, William Cox, "Long-Term Reduction in Implicit Race Bias: A Prejudice Habit-Breaking Intervention," *Journal of Experimental Social Psychology*, 48, No. 6 (Nov. 2012): 1270-71.

106   Thomas Pettigrew and Linda Tropp, "A Meta-Analytic Test of Intergroup Contact Theory," *Journal of Personality and Social Psychology*, 90, No. 5 (2006): 751-783.

107   Ibid, 1270.

108   W. Edwards Deming, *Out of the Crisis*, 2nd ed. (Cambridge, MA: The MIT Press, 2000): 315.

109   California State Personnel Board, Summary of the Uniform Guidelines on Employee Selection Procedures, Test Validation and Construction Unit: 3, retrieved on May 1, 2020, from https://home.ubalt.edu/tmitch/645/articles/summary_of%20_uniform_guidelines-1.pdf.

110   Max Bazerman and Dolly Chugh, "Decisions Without Blinders," Harvard Business Review (January 2006).

111   Anthony Greenwald and Thomas Pettigrew, "With Malice Toward None and Charity for Some," *American Psychologist*, 69, No. 7 (2014): 669-684.

112   Thomas Pettigrew and Roel Meertens, "Subtle and Blatant Prejudice in Western Europe," *European Journal of Social Psychology*, 25, No. 1 (1995): 57-75; and Roel Meertens and Thomas Pettigrew, "Is Subtle Prejudice Really Prejudice?," *Public Opinion Quarterly*, 61, No. 1 (1997): 54-71.

113   Donn Byrne, "Interpersonal attraction and attitude similarity," *The Journal of Abnormal and Social Psychology*, 62, No. 3 (1961): 713-715.

114   Quoted in Po Bronson and Ashley Merryman, "Even Babies Discriminate: A Nurtureshock Excerpt," *Newsweek, March 24, 2015*, retrieved on June 4, 2022, from https://www.newsweek.com/even-babies-discriminate-nurtureshock-excerpt-79233.

115   Herminia Ibarra and Prashant Deshpande, "Networks and Identities: Reciprocal Influences on Career Processes and Outcomes," INSEAD (2004): 1-34.

116   Ibid, 3.

117   Minority Corporate Counsel Association, *The McDonalds Story*, retrieved on Oct. 21, 2016, from http://www.mcca.com/index.cfm?fuseaction=Feature.showFeature&featureID=112.

118   Herminia Ibarra, "Race, Opportunity, and Diversity of Social Circles in Managerial Networks," *The Academy of Management Journal*, 38, No. 3 (1995): 673-703.

119   Ibid, 680.

120   For an introduction to organizational network analysis, see Rob Cross's organizational network analysis website at http://www.robcross.org/network_ona.htm and his book with co-author Andrew Parker, *The Hidden Power of Social Networks: Understanding How Work Really Gets Done in Organizations* (Boston: Harvard Business Review Press, 2004).

121   "The Stereotype Threat to Workplace Diversity: Dr. Claude Steele Mesmerizes Audience," DiversityInc., retrieved Aug. 2, 2016, from http://www.diversityinc.com/diversity-events/the-stereotype-threat-dr-claude-steele-mesmerizes-audience-video/.

122   Bettina Casad and William Bryant, "Addressing Stereotype Threat is Critical to Diversity and Inclusion in Organizational Psychology," *Frontiers of Psychology*, 7, No. 8, National Center for Biotechnology Information (Jan. 2016), 2-5, retrieved July 29, 2017, from http://www.ncbi.nlm.nih.gov/pmc/articles/PMC4718987/pdf/fpsyg-07-00008.pdf; and Caryn Block, Sandy Koch, Benjamin Liberman, Tarani Merriweather, and Loriann Roberson, "Contending With Stereotype Threat at Work: A Model of Long-Term Responses," *The Counseling Psychologist*, 39, No. 4 (2011), 581.

123   Loriann Roberson and Carol Kulik, "Stereotype Threat at Work," Academcy of Management Perspectives, 21, No. 2 (May 2007), 36.

124   Casad and Bryant, 8.

125   Laura Kray and Aiwa Shirako, "Stereotype Threat in Organizations: An Examination of Its Scope, Triggers, and Possible Interventions," in M. Inzlicht and T. Schmader (eds.), *Stereotype Threat: Theory, Process, and Application* (NY: Oxford Press, 2011), 182.

126   ReducingStereotypeThreat.org, "What can be done to reduce stereotype threat?," retrieved Aug. 2, 2016, from http://www.reducingstereotypethreat.org/reduce.html.

127   From Gordon Allport's *The Nature of Prejudice* (1954) to Henri Tajfel's social identity theory the idea of division into in-groups and out-groups with in-group favoritism instead of hostility is well established.

128   Erika Harrell, Lynn Langton, Marcus Berzofsky, Lance Couzens, and Hope Smiley-McDonald, *Household Poverty and Nonfatal Violent Victimization, 2008-2012*, Special Report, US Department of Justice (November 2014): 1.

129   The National Minority Supplier Development Council, *Economic Impact Report: The Effects of NMSDC Certified Minority Business Enterprises on the U.S. Economy* (2014): 5-7, retrieved on September 23, 2016, from http://www.nmsdc.org/wp-content/uploads/Economic_Impact_Report_FINAL.pdf.

130   *Final Interagency Policy Statement Establishing Joint Standards for Assessing the Diversity Policies and Practices of Entities Regulated by the Agencies*, retrieved on May 16, 2020, from www.sec.gov/rules/policy/2015/34-75050.pdf (2015): 27-36.

131   Susan Fiske, 127.

132   Bob Altemeyer, "The Other 'Authoritarian Personality,'" in *Political Psychology: Key Readings*, ed., John Jost et al. (New York: Psychology Press, 2004): 85-106, retrieved March 6, 2017, from http://www.uky.edu/AS/PoliSci/Peffley/pdf/altemeyer%20The%20Other%20Authoritarian%20Personality.pdf.

133   Ibid, 85-6.

134   Ibid, 99.

135   Ibid, 90.

136   Ibid, 89.

137   Ibid, 86-88.

138   Claudia Goldin and Lawrence Katz, "The Most Egalitarian of All Professions: Pharmacy and the Evolution of a Family-Friendly Occupation," Working Paper No. 18410, National Bureau of Economic Research (2012), retrieved from https://www.nber.org/papers/w18410.

139   Kimberlé Crenshaw, "Why Intersectionality Can't Wait," *The Washington Post* (September 24, 2015), retrieved on Sept. 6, 2016, from https://www.washingtonpost.com/news/in-theory/wp/2015/09/24/why-intersectionality-cant-wait/?utm_term=.8a48c69d0d60.

140   Ibid.

141   Wiebren Jansen, Sabine Otten, Karen van der Zee, and Lise Jans, "Inclusion: Conceptualization and Measurement," *European Journal of Social Psychology* (2014), DOI: 10.1002/ejsp.2011.

142   Gregory Walton and Geoffrey Cohen, "A Question of Belonging: Race, Social Fit, and Achievement," *Journal of Personality and Social Psychology*, 92, no. 1 (2007): 82-96.

143   Jason McPherson, Tim Hancock, Steven Huang, and Jessica Huang, *2018 Diversity and Inclusion Report*, Culture Amp and Paradigm, https://blog.cultureamp.com/2018-diversity-inclusion-report.

144   Walton and Cohen, "A Question of Belonging," 82.

145   Wendell Cockshaw and Ian Shochet, "The Link Between Belongingness and Depressive Symptoms: An Exploration in the Workplace Interpersonal Context," *Australian Psychologist*, 45, no. 4 (December 2010): 283-289.

146   Gregory Walton, Christine Logel, Jennifer Peach, Steven Spencer, and Mark Zanna, "Two Brief Interventions to Mitigate a 'Chilly Climate' Transform Women's Experience, Relationships, and Achievement in Engineering," *Journal of Educational Psychology*, 107, no. 2 (2015): 469.

147   Maxwell Huppert, "Employees Share What Gives Them a Sense of Belonging at Work," *Inside the Mind of Today's Candidate*, LinkedIn (April 2017), https://business.linkedin.com/talent-solutions/blog/company-culture/2017/employees-share-what-gives-them-a-sense-of-belonging-at-work.

148   Jansen, et al., "Inclusion: Conceptualization and Measurement," 16.

149   Glenn Malone, David Pillow, and Augustine Osman, "General Belongingness Scale (GBS): *Personality and Individual Differences*, 52 No 3 (February 2012): 311-316.

150   Michael Kernis and Brian Goldman, "A Multicomponent Conceptualization of Authenticity: Theory and Research," *Advances in Experimental Social Psychology*, 38 (2006), 294-301, DOI: 10.1016/S0065-2601(06)38006-9.

151   Brené Brown, "The Power of Vulnerability," TEDxHouston, YouTube, https://www.ted.com/talks/brene_brown_on_vulnerability?language=en.

152   Ralph Van den Bosch and Toon Taris, "Authenticity at Work: Development and Validation of an Individual Authenticity Measure at Work," *Journal of Happiness Studies*, 15 (2014): 34, DOI 10.1007/s10902-013-94133, 34.

153   Kernis and Goldman, "A Multicomponent Conceptualization of Authenticity," 345-348.

154   Rob Goffee and Gareth Jones, "Managing Authenticity: The Paradox of Great Leadership," *Harvard Business Review* (December 2005): 4, https://hbr.org/2005/12/managing-authenticity-the-paradox-of-great-leadership.

155   Van den Bosch and Taris, "Authenticity at Work," 24.

156   Wilmar Schaufeli, Arnold Bakker, and Marisa Salanova, "The Measurement of Work Engagement with a Short Questionnaire," *Educational and Psychological Measurement*, 66, no. 4 (August 2006): 702.

157   Astrid Emmerich and Thomas Rigotti, "Reciprocal Relations Between Work-Related Authenticity and Intrinsic Motivation, Work Ability and Depressivity: A Two-Wave Study," *Frontiers in Psychology*, 8 (March 2017): 1.

158   Ibid, 2-3.

159   Ibid, 2.

160   Boris Ewenstein, "Ahead of the Curve: The Future of Performance Management," *McKinsey Quarterly* (May 2016): 1-11, https://www.mckinsey.com/business-functions/organization/our-insights/ahead-of-the-curve-the-future-of-performance-management; and Marcus Buckingham and Ashley Goodall, "Reinventing Performance Managment: How One Company is Rethinking Peer Feedback and the Annual Review, and Trying to Design a System to Fuel Improvement," *Harvard Business Review* (April 2015): 1-10, https://hbr.org/2015/04/reinventing-performance-management.

161   Gallup, *State of the American Workplace* (2013): 46.

162   Sohee Park and Sunyoung Park, "Employee Adaptive Performance and Its Antecedents: Review and Synthesis," *Human Resource Development Review*, 18, No. 3 (2019), 294-324; Elaine Pulakos, Sharon Arad, Michelle Donovan, and Kevin Plamondon, "Adaptability in the Workplace: Development of a Taxonomy of Adaptive Performance," *Journal of Applied Psychology*, 85, No. 4 (August 2000), 612-624; Karen van Dam, "Employee Adaptability to Change at Work: A Multidimensional, Resource-Based Framework," in *The Psychology of Organizational Change*, eds. Shaul Oreg, Alexandra Michel, and Rune Todnem By (Cambridge, England: Cambridge University Press, 2013), 123-142; and Karen van Dam, Tanja Bipp, and Joris van Ruysseveldt, "The Role of Employee Adaptability, Goal Striving and Proactivity for Sustainable Careers, in *Handbook of Research on Sustainable Careers*, eds. Ans De Vos and Beatrice van der Heijden (Cheltenham and Camberley, England: Edward Elgar Publishing, 2015), 190-204.

163   Justin Berg, Jane Dutton, and Amy Wrzesniewski, "Job Crafting and Meaningful Work," in *Purpose and Meaning in the Workplace*, eds. Bryan Dik, Zinta Byrne, and Michael Steger (Washington, DC: American Psychological Association, 2013), 81-104.

164   Paul Spector, "Perceived Control by Employees: A Meta-Analysis of Studies Concerning Autonomy and Participation at Work," *Human Relations*, 39, No. 11 (1986): 1005.

165   Jay Cone, "In Times of Change, Go Slow to Go Fast," retrieved Nov. 24, 2015, http://interactionassociates.com/insights/blog/times-change-go-slow-go-fast#.VlSFAG_smic.

166   Brugh Joy, *Joy's Way*, A Map for the Transformational Journey (New York: Tarcher/Putnam, 1979).

167   Frauke Meyer, Deidre Le Fevre, and Viviane Robinson, "How Leaders Communicate Their Vulnerability: Implications for Trust Building," *International Journal of Educational Management*, 31, No. 2 (2017): 221-235, https://doi.org/10.1108/IJEM-11-2015-0150.

168   Ibid, 222.

169   David Bartz and Dallas Bartz, "Confidence, Vulnerability, and Empathy: Friends to Managers," *International Journal of Business and Social Science*, 8, No. 10 (October 2017): 3.

170   Alan Lee, Sara Willis, and Amy Wei Tan, "Empowering Leadership: A Meta-analytic Examination of Incremental Contribution, Mediation, and Moderation," Journal of Organizational Behavior, 39, No. 3 (March 2018): 307.

171   Stein Amundsen and Øyvind Martinsen, "Empowering Leadership: Construct Clarification, Conceptualization, and Validation of a New Scale," Leadership Quarterly, 25, No. 3 (2014): 7. DOI: 10.1016/j.leaqua.2013.11.009.

172   Ibid, 8-13.

173   Michael Hui, Kevin Au, and Henry Fock, "Empowerment Across Cultures," 35, No. 1 (January 2004): 46-60.

174   Geert Hofstede, Culture's Consequences; Software of the Mind, 2nd edition (Thousand Oaks, CA: Sage, 2001)

175   Lee, Wills, and Wei Tian, "Empowering Leadership," 307.

176   Allan Lee, Dara Willis, and Amy Wei Tan, "When Empowering Employees Works, and When It Doesn't," Harvard Business Review, Reprint H046XV (March 2, 2018): 3.

177   Amundsen and Martinsen, "Empowering Leadership," 14; and Scott Seibert, Gang Wang, and Stephen Courtright, "Antecedents and Consequences of Psychological and Team Empowerment in Organizations: A Meta-Analytic Review," Journal of Applied Psychology, 96, No. 5 (2011): 981-1003.

178   Amundsen and Martinsen, "Empowering Leadership," 67-69.

179   Lee Konczak, Damian Stelly, and Michael Trusty, "Defining and Measuring Empowering Leader Behaviors: Development of an Upward Feedback Instrument," Educational and Psychological Measurement, 60, No. 2 (April 2000), 307-308.

180   Josh Arnold, Sharon Arad, Jonathon Rhoades, and Fritz Drasgow, "The Empowering Leadership Questionnaire: The Construction and Validation of a New Scale for Measuring Leader Behaviors," Journal of Organizational Behavior, 21 (2000), 268-269.

181   Monica Forret and Thomas Dougherty, "Networking Behaviors and Career Outcomes: Differences for Men and Women?" Journal of Organizational Behavior, 25, No. 3 (May 2004): 421.

182   Herminia Ibarra, "Personal Networks of Women and Minorities in Management: A Conceptual Framework," *Academy of Management Review,* 18, No. 1 (1993): 56.

183   Forret and Dougherty, "Networking Behaviors and Career Outcomes," 421.

184   Ibarra, "Personal Networks of Women and Minorities in Management," 61.

185   Catalyst, *Connections that Count: The Informal Networks of Women of Color in the United States* (2006): 10.

186   Ibarra, "Personal Networks of Women and Minorities in Management," 71.

187   Ibarra, "Personal Networks of Women and Minorities in Management," 61.

188   Jeffrey Hall, "How Many Hours Does It Take to Make a Friend?," *Journal of Social and Personal Relationships* (2018): 1-19, DOI: 10.1177/0265407518761225.

189   Monica Forret and Thomas Dougherty, "Correlates of Networking Behavior for Managerial and Professional Employees," *Group & Organization Management,* 26, No. 3 (September 2001): 305.

190   Ibid, 306-307.

191   Hans-Georg Wolff and Daniel Spurk, "Developing and Validating a Short Networking Behavior Scale (SNBS) from Wolff and Moser's (2006) Measure," *Journal of Career Assessment, 28, No. 2 (2020): 302.*

192   John Doris, *Lack of Character: Personality and Moral Behavior* (New York: Cambridge University Press, 2002): 5.

193   Christine Porath, "Half of Employees Don't Feel Respected by Their Bosses," *Harvard Business Review,* (November 19, 2014): 2, https://hbr.org/2014/11/half-of-employees-dont-feel-respected-by-their-bosses.

194   Ibid, 2.

195   Ibid, 3.

196   Christine Porath and Christine Pearson, "The Price of Incivil-

ity: Lack of Respect Hurts Morale—and the Bottom Line," *Harvard Business Review* (January-February 2013): 2.

197   Dana Kabat-Farr and Lilia Cortina, "Chapter 7: Selective Incivility: Gender, Race, and the Discriminatory Workplace," in *Gender and the Dysfunctional Workplace*, ed. Suzy Fox and Terri Lituchy (Northampton, MA: Edward Elgar, 2012), 113-114.

198   Porath and Pearson, "The Price of Incivility: Lack of Respect Hurts Morale—and the Bottom Line," 3.

199   Christine Pearson, Lynne Andersson, and Christine Porath, "Assessing and Attacking Workplace Incivility," *Organizational Dynamics*, 29, No. 2 (2000): 128.

200   Kristie Rogers and Blake Ashforth, "Respect in Organizations: Feeling Valued as 'We' and 'Me,'" *Journal of Management*, 43, No. 5 (May 2017): 1581.

201   Ibid, 1587-88.

202   Ibid, 1591.

203   David Garvin, "How Google Sold Its Engineers on Management," *Harvard Business Review* (December 2013): 6.

204   Andrea Ellinger, Alexander Ellinger, and Scott Keller, "Supervisory Coaching Behavior, Employee Satisfaction, in Warehouse Employee Performance: A Dyadic Perspective in the Distribution Industry," *Human Resource Development Quarterly*, 14, No. 4 (winter 2003): 435-457; Andrea Ellinger, Alexander Ellinger, Daniel Bachrach, Yu-Lin Wang, and ABE Baş. "Organizational Investments in Social Capital, Managerial Coaching, and Employee Work-related Performance," *Management Learning*, 42, No. 1 (2010):257-270; Marcia Hagen, "Managerial Coaching: A Review of the Literature," *Performance Improvement Quarterly*, 24, No. 4 (2012): 17-39; and Grace McCarthy and Julia Milner, "Managerial Coaching: Challenges, Opportunities and Training," *Journal of Management Development*, 32, No. 7 (2013): 768-779.

205   Ann Gilley, Jerry Gilley, and Elies Koulder, "Characteristics of Managerial Coaching," *Performance Improvement Quarterly*, 23, No. 1 (2010): 55.

206   Hagen, "Managerial Coaching," 23.

207   Gilley, Gilley, Koudler, "Characteristics of Managerial Coaching," 62.

208   Globoforce, "Employee Experience as a Business Driver," SHRM/Globoforce, Recognition Survey (2016): 18.

209   Manuel London and James Smither, "Feedback Orientation, Feedback Culture, and the Longitudinal Performance Management Process," *Human Resource Management Review*, 12, No. 1 (Spring 2002): 81-100.

210   Jane Brody Gregory and Paul Levy, "Employee Feedback Orientation: Implications for Effective Coaching Relationships," *Coaching: An International Journal of Theory, Research and Practice* (2012): 3.

211   London and Smither, "Feedback Orientation," 86.

212   London and Smither, "Feedback Orientation," 81.

213   Jane Brody Gregory and Paul Levy, "It's Not Me, It's You: A Multilevel Examination of Variables That Impact Employee Coaching Relationships," *Consulting Psychology Journal: Research and Practice*, 63, No. 2 (2011): 67-88.

214   Ibid, 1.

215   Anthony Grant and Sean O'Connor, "The Differential Effects of Solution-focused and Problem-focused Coaching Questions: A Pilot Study with Implications for Practice," *Industrial and Commercial Training*, 42 (2010): 102–111.

216   Brody and Levy, "It's Not Me, It's You," 88.

217   David Noer, *Coaching Behaviors Inventory: Participant Workbook* (Greensboro, NC: Noer Consulting, 2019).

218   Beth Linderbaum and Paul Levy, "The Development and Validation of the Feedback Orientation Scale (FOS)," *Journal of Management*, 36, No. 6 (November 2010): 1401.

219   Guy Berger, "Will This Year's College Grads Job-Hop More Than Previous Grads?" LinkedIn (April 12, 2016), https://blog.linkedin.com/2016/04/12/will-this-year_s-college-grads-job-hop-more-than-previous-grads.

220   Amy Adkins, "What Millennials Want From Work and Life," Gallup Workplace (May 10, 2016), https://www.gallup.com/workplace/236477/millennials-work-life.aspx.

221   "National Study From Bridge Shows Outdated Knowledge Can Mean College-Educated Employees Need Workplace Learning," Bridge (March 29, 2016), https://www.getbridge.com/news/press-releases/national-study-bridge-shows-outdated-knowledge-can-mean-college-educated.

222   "Seventy Percent of Employees Unhappy with Career Opportunities," CEB (November 16, 2015), retrieved from https://www.prnewswire.com/news-releases/seventy-percent-of-employees-unhappy-with-career-opportunities-300178571.html.

223   Jeffrey Greenhaus, Saroj Parasuraman, and Wayne Wormley, "Effects of Race on Organizational Experiences, Job Performance Evaluations, and Career Outcomes," *Academy of Management Journal*, 33, No. 1 (March 1990): 65.

224   Ibid, 65.

225   Monica Higgins and Kathy Kram, "Reconceptualizing Mentoring at Work: A Developmental Network Perspective," *The Academy of Management Review*, 26, No. 2 (April 2001), pp. 264-288

226   Ibid, 268.

227   Ibid, 264.

228   Monica Forret and Thomas Dougherty, "Networking Behaviors and Career Outcomes: Differences for Men and Women?" *Journal of Organizational Behavior*, 25 (2004), 430-433.

229   Boston University Medical Center, *Building Your Developmental Network*, retrieved from https://www.bumc.bu.edu/facdev-medicine/files/2009/12/Developmental_Network-AssessmentKramandHiggins.pdf.

230   Claire McCarty Kilian, Dawn Hukai, and Elizabeth McCarty, "Building Diversity in the Pipeline to Corporate Leadership," *Journal of Management Development*, 24, No. 2 (2005), 160-61.

231   Maria Kramer, Scott Seibert, Sandy Wayne, Robert Liden, and Jesus Bravo, "Antecedents and Consequences of Organizational Support for Development: The Critical Role of Career Opportunities," *Journal of Applied Psychology*, 96, No. 3 (2011), 486.

232 See, for example, Claire McCarty Kilian, Dawn Hukai, and Elizabeth McCarty, "Building Diversity in the Pipeline to Corporate Leadership," *Journal of Management Development*, 24, No. 2 (2005), 155-168; and Katherine Giscombe and Mary Mattis, "Leveling the Playing Field for Women of Color in Corporate Management: Is the Business Case Enough?" *Journal of Business Ethics*, 37 (2002), 103-119.

233 Belle Rose Ragins, "Relational Mentoring: A Positive Approach to Mentoring at Work," in K. Cameron and G. Spreitzer, eds., *The Oxford Handbook of Positive Organizational Scholarship* (New York: Oxford University Press, 2012), 520.

234 Ibid, 520.

235 Cynthia Emrich, Mark Livingston, and David Pruner, *Creating a Culture of Mentorship*, Heidrick and Struggles (2017), retrieved on August 4, 2022, from https://www.researchgate.net/publication/323106316_Creating_a_Culture_of_Mentorship.

236 Lisa Baranik, Elizabeth Roling, and Lillian Eby, "Why Does Mentoring Work? The Role of Perceived Organizational Support," *Journal of Vocational Behavior*, 76, No. 3 (2010): 366.

237 Lillian Eby, Marcus Butts Jaime Durley, and Belle Rose Ragins, "Are Bad Experiences Stronger Than Good Ones in a Mentoring Relationship? Evidence from the Protégé and Mentor Perspective," *Journal of Vocational Behavior*, 77 (2010), 82.

238 Nancy Carter and Christine Silva, "Mentoring: Necessary But Insufficient for Advancement," Catalyst (2010), 3.

239 Heather Foust-Cummings, Sarah Dinolfo, and Jennifer Kohler, "Sponsoring Women to Success," Catalyst (2011), 3-5.

240 Ragins, "Relational Mentoring," 250.

241 Foust-Cummings, Dinolfo, and Kohler, "Sponsoring Women to Success," 7-8.

242 Ragins, "Relational Mentoring," 524.

243 Charles Greer and Meghna Virick, "Diverse Succession Planning: Lessons From Industry Leaders," *Human Resource Management*, 47, No. 2 (Summer 2008), 358.

244 Kevin Groves, "Integrating Leadership Development and Succession Planning Practices," *Journal of Management Development*, 26, No.3 (2007), 248.

245   See, for example, Seval Gündemir, Astrid Homan, Carsten de Dreu, and Mark van Vugt, "Think Leader, Think White? Capturing and Weakening an Implicit White Leadership Bias," PLOS, (2014), retrieved from https://www.ncbi.nlm.nih.gov/pmc/articles/PMC3885528/; Pew Research Center, *Men or Women: Who's the Better Leader* (2008); and Jack Zenger and Joseph Folkman, "Research: Women Score Higher Than Men in Most Leadership Skills," *Harvard Business Review* (June 25, 2019).

246   Alice Eagly, Steven Karau, and Mona Makhijani, "Gender and Leadership Style: A Meta-Analysis," *Psychological Bulletin*, 117 (1990), 137.

247   Alice Eagly and Jean Lau Chin, "Diversity and Leadership in a Changing World," *American Psychologist*, 65, No. (April 2010), 781.

248   Ibid, 783.

249   Alice Eagly and Steven Karau, "Role Congruity Theory of Prejudice Toward Female Leaders," *Psychological Review*, 109, No 3 (2002): 576.

250   Arpi Festekjian, Susanna Tram, Carolyn Murray, Thomas Sy, and Ho Huynh, "I See Me the Way You See Me: The Influence of Race on Interpersonal and Intrapersonal Leadership Perceptions," *Journal of Leadership & Organizational Studies*, 21, No. 1 (2013), 114.

251   Festekjian, Tram, Murray, Sy, and Huynh, "I See Me the Way You See Me," 105.

252   Ingmar Björkman, Mats Ehrnrooth, Kristiina Mäkelä, Adam Smale, and Jennie Sumelius, "Talent or Not? Reactions to Talent Identification," *Human Resource Management*, 52, No. 2 (April 2013), 195-214.

253   See, for example, Training Industry, *The State of the Leadership Training Market* (2019); and Laci Loew and Karen O'Leonard, *Leadership Development Factbook 2012: Benchmarks and Trends in U.S. Leadership Development*, Bersin by Deloitte (July 2012).

254   Pierre Gurdjian, Thomas Halbeisen, and Kev in Lane, "Why Leadership-Development Programs Fail," *McKinsey Quarterly* (January 2014), 2-3.

255   Training Industry, *The Leadership Training Market* (March 2019), 1-2.

256   Morgan McCall, "Recasting Leadership Development," *Industrial and Organizational Psychology*, No. 3 (2010), 4.

257   Ibid, 4.

258   Margaret Hopkins, Deborah O'Neil, Angela Passarelli, and Diana Bilimoria, "Women's Leadership Development Strategic Practices for Women and Organizations," *Counseling Psychology Journal: Practice and Research*, 60, No. 4 (2008), 358.

259   Ibid, 358.

260   Ryan Smith and Golnaz Tabibnia, "Why Radical Transparency Is Good Business," *Harvard Business Review* (October 11, 2012). Retrieved on August 4, 2022, from https://hbr.org/2012/10/why-radical-transparency-is-good-business.

261   Todd Zenger, "The Case Against Pay Transparency," *Harvard Business Review* (September 30, 2016), retrieved from https://hbr.org/2016/09/the-case-against-pay-transparency.

262   Zoë Cullen and Ricardo Perez-Truglia, "How Much Does Your Boss Make? The Effects of Salary Comparisons," National Bureau of Economic Research Working Paper No. 24841 (August 2018): 1, retrieved from https://www.nber.org/papers/w24841.

263   Kim Elsesser, "Pay Transparency Is the Solution to the Pay Gap: Here's One Company's Success Story," *Forbes* (September 5, 2018), retrieved from https://www.forbes.com/sites/kimelsesser/2018/09/05/pay-transparency-is-the-solution-to-the-pay-gap-heres-one-companys-success-story/#129cc4305010.

264   US Equal Employment Opportunity Commission, *Harassment*, retrieved from https://www.eeoc.gov/laws/types/harassment.cfm.

265   Johnson & Johnson, *Position on Providing a Safe and Harassment Free Workplace*, retrieved July 10, 2022,, from https://www.jnj.com/about-jnj/policies-and-positions/our-position-on-providing-a-safe-and-harassment-free-workplace.

266   Sandra Burud and Marie Tumolo, *Leveraging the New Human Capital: Adaptive Strategies, Results Achieved, and Stories of Transformation* (Boston: Nicholas Brealey Publishing, 2004).

267   Brie Weller Reynolds, "More Professionals Struggling with Work-Life Balance, Flexjobs Survey Finds" (February 5, 2018), retrieved from https://www.flexjobs.com/blog/post/professionals-struggling-with-work-life-balance-flexjobs-survey/.

268   Kim Parker, Julianna Menasce Horowitz, and Rachel Minkin, "COVID-19 Pandemic Continues to Reshape Work in America," Pew Research Center (February 2022): 4, retrieved on May 22, 2022, from https://www.pewresearch.org/social-trends/2022/02/16/covid-19-pandemic-continues-to-reshape-work-in-america/.

269   Andrew Chamberlain, "What Matters More to Your Workforce Than Money," *Harvard Business Review* (January 17, 2017), retrieved from https://hbr.org/2017/01/what-matters-more-to-your-workforce-than-money.

270   James Bond and Ellen Galinsky, "What Difference Do Job Characteristics Make to Low Income Employees," Families and Work Institute (November 2012), retrieved from http://www.familiesand-work.org/site/research/reports/low-income_employees.pdf.

271   Edgar Schein, *Organizational Culture and Leadership* (San Francisco: Jossey-Bass, 2010).

272   Flannery Stevens, Victoria Plaut, and Jeffrey Sanchez-Burks, "Unlocking the Benefits of Diversity: All-Inclusive Multiculturalism and Positive Organizational Change," *The Journal of Applied Behavioral Science*, 44, No. 1 (March 2008): 121.

273   Ibid, 121.

274   Victoria Plaut, Kecia Thomas, Kyneshawau Hurd, and Celina Romero, "Do Color Blindness and Multiculturalism Remedy or Foster Discrimination and Racism?, *Career Directions in Psychological Science*, 27, No. 3 (2018): 203.

275   Adapted from the Program on Intergroup Relations, University of Michigan; the Dialogue Center, Lehigh University; and the American Bar Association.

276   Clive Fletcher and Caroline Bailey, "Assessing Self-Awareness: Some Issues and Methods," *Journal of Managerial Psychology*, 18, No. 5 (2003): 396.

277   Ibid, 396.

278   Angelo DeNisi and Avraham Kluger, "Feedback Effectiveness: Can 360-degree Appraisals Be Improved?" *Academy of Management Executive*, 14, No. 1 (2000): 130.

279   Ibid, 132.

280   Ibid, 132.

281   Paul Mabe and Stephen West, "Validity of Self-Evaluation of Ability: A Review and Meta-Analysis," *Journal of Applied Psychology*, 67, No. 3 (1982): 293-4.

282   David Dunning, Chip Heath, and Jerry Suls, "Flawed Self-Assessment: Implications for Health, Education, and the Workplace," *Psychological Science in the Public Interest*, 5, No. 3 (2004): 71-73.

283   Bianca Bernstein and Conrad Lecomte, "Supervisory-type Feedback Effects: Feedback Discrepancy Level, Trainee Psychological Differentiation, and Immediate Responses," *Journal of Counseling Psychology*, 26 (1979): 301.

284   Jonathon Brown, "Accuracy and Bias in Self-knowledge'" in C. R. Snyder and D. R. Forsyth (Eds.), *Pergamon general psychology series, Vol. 162. Handbook of social and clinical psychology: The health perspective* (Elmsford, NY: Pergamon Press, 1991): 158.

285   Marissa Lombardi, "Assessing Intercultural Competence: A Review," *NCSSSMST Journal (Fall 2010): 15-17.*

286   James Jones and Santiba Campbell, "Cultural Psychology of African Americans," *Online Readings in Psychology and Culture*, 3, No. 1 (2011): 6.

287   Touré, *Who's Afraid of Post-Blackness?: What It Means to be Black Now* (New York: Free Press 2011): 20.

288   See Geert Hofstede and Gert Jan Hofstede, *Cultures and Organizations: Software of the Mind* (New York: McGraw-Hill, 2005); Fons Trompenaars and Charles Hayden-Turner, *Riding the Waves of Culture: Understanding Diversity in Global Business*, Second Edition (New York: McGraw-Hill, 1998); and Shalom Schwartz, "Universals in the Content and Structure of Values: Theoretical Advances and Empirical Tests in 20 Countries," *Advances in Experimental Social Psychology*, 25 (1992).

289   Hofstede and Hofstede, *Cultures and Organizations*, 46.

290   Ibid, 59.

291   Ibid, 76.

292   Ibid, 76.

293   Ibid, 104.

294   Ibid, 120.

295   Ibid, 120.

296   Ibid, 167.

297   Ibid, 189.

298   Ibid, 210.

299   Ibid, 225.

300   Ibid, 225.

301   Robert House, Paul Hanges, Mansour Javidan, Peter Dorfman, and Vipin Gupta, eds., *Culture, Leadership, and Organizations: The GLOBE Study of 62 Societies* (Thousand Oaks, CA: Sage, 2004), 5.

302   Ibid, 3.

303   House, Hanges, Javidan, and Goodwin, *Culture, Leadership, and Organizations*, 676-678.

304   Leslie Ashburn-Nardo, Kathryn Morris, Stephanie Goodwin, "The Confronting Prejudiced Response Model (CPR): Applying CPR in Organizations," *Academy of Management Learning & Education*, 7, No. 3 (2008), 333.

305   Lauri Hyers, "Resisting Prejudice Every Day: Exploring Women's Assertive Responses to Anti-Black Racism, Anti-Semitism, Heterosexism, and Sexism," *Sex Roles*, 56, No.1 (February 2007), 7.

306   Alexander Czopp, Margo Monteith, and Aimee Mark, Standing Up for a Change: Reducing Bias Through Interpersonal Confron-tation," *Journal of Personality and Social Psychology*, 90, No. 5 (2006): 785.

307   Alexander Czopp and Margo Monteith, "Confronting Prejudice (Literally):Reactions to Confrontations of Racial and Gender Bias," *Personality and Social Psychology Bulletin*, 29 (2003): 532–544.

308   Hyers, "Resisting Prejudice Every Day," 7.

309   Lauri Hyers, "Alternatives to Silence in Face-to-Face Encounters with Everyday Heterosexism: Activism on the Interpersonal Front," *Journal of Homosexuality*, 57, No. 4 (2010): 545.

310   Czopp, Montieth, and Mark, "Standing Up for Change," 786.

311   Jacqueline Nelson and Kevin Dunn, "Bystander Anti-Racism: A Review of the Literature," *Analysis of Social Issues and Public Policy*, 11, No. 1 (2011): 265.

312   Ibid, 272.

313   S. Plous, "Responding to Overt Displays of Prejudice: A Role-Playing Exercise, *Teaching of Psychology*, 27, No. 3 (2000): 2.

314   Nelson and Dunn, "Bystander Anti-Racism,"279.

315   Nelson and Dunn, "Bystander Anti-Racism," 270-272.

316   John Ruskin, *The Works of John Ruskin Volume 5: Modern Painters III*, eds. Edward Cook and Alexander Wedderburn (New York: Cambridge University Press, 2010), 331.

317   Labor Force Statistics from the Current Population Survey, Table A-13: Employment Status of the Civilian Noninstitutional Population by Age, Sex, and Race

318   Ibid, Table A-13.

319   Digest of Educational Statistics, *Tables 322.20, 323.20, and 324.20*, National Center for Educational Statistics (2018).

320   Michael Porter, *Competitive Strategy: Techniques for Analyzing Industries and Competitors* (New York: The Free Press, 1980); and Michael Porter, *Competitive Advantage* (New York: The Free Press, 1985).

321   Adapted from Michael Porter, *Competitive Advantage: Crerating and Sustaining Superior Performance* (New York: The Free Press, 1985): 12.

322   Chief Marketer, "P&G Launches My Black is Beautiful Campaign" (August 10, 2007), retrieved from https://www.chiefmarketer.com/pg-launches-my-black-is-beautiful-campaign/.

323   David Thomas, "Diversity as Strategy," *Harvard Business Review* (September 2004), 2.

324   Ibid, 2.

325   Government Services Administration, IT Accessibility Laws and Policies, GSA Government-wide IT Accessibility Program, retrieved on September 13, 2019, from https://www.section508.gov/manage/laws-and-policies.

326   Bureau of Labor Statistics, "Table 11. Employed persons by detailed occupation, sex, race, and Hispanic or Latino ethnicity," Labor Force Statistics from the Current Population Survey (2018).

327   National Center for Education Statistics, "Table 318.30: Bachelor's, master's, and doctor's degrees conferred by postsecondary institutions, by sex of student and discipline division: 2016-17," *Digest of Education Statistics* (2018).

328   Labor Force Statistics from the Current Population Survey, *Table 11. Employed Persons by Detailed Occupations, Sex, Race, and Hispanic or Latino Ethnicity*, Bureau of Labor Statistics (2018), retrieved from https://www.bls.gov/cps/cpsaat11.htm.

329   See, for example, Scott Seibert and Maria Kramer, "The Five-Factor Model of Personality and Career Success," *Journal of Vocational Behavior*, 58, No. 1 (February 2001), 1-21, retrieved from https://www.sciencedirect.com/science/article/abs/pii/S0001879100917573; and Timothy Judge, Chad Higgins, Carl Thoresen, and Murray Barrick, "The Big Five Personality Traits, General; Mental Ability, and Career Success Across Life Span," *Personnel Psychology*, 52, No.3 (Autumn 1999), 621-652, retrieved from https://onlinelibrary.wiley.com/doi/abs/10.1111/j.1744-6570.1999.tb00174.x.

330   Ian Bates, Sherly Meilianti, Christopher John, and Lina Bader, "Pharmacy Workforce Intelligence: Global Trends Report," International Pharmaceutical Federation (2018), 17.

331   American Association of Colleges of Pharmacy, *Academic Pharmacy's Vital Statistics* (2019), retrieved from https://www.aacp.org/article/academic-pharmacys-vital-statistics.

332   American Institutes for Research, *The AIR Index: The Pay Gap for Workers with Disabilities* (2015), retrieved from https://www.air.org/resource/air-index-pay-gap-workers-disabilities; Eileen Patten, *Racial, Gender Wage Gaps Persist in U.S. Despite Some Progress*, Pew Research Center (2016), retrieved from https://www.pewresearch.org/fact-tank/2016/07/01/racial-gender-wage-gaps-persist-in-u-s-despite-some-progress/; and Crosby Burns, *The Gay and Transgender Wage Gap*, Center for American Progress (2012), retrieved from https://www.americanprogress.org/issues/lgbt/news/2012/04/16/11494/the-gay-and-transgender-wage-gap/.

333   Maeve Duggan, "Gaming and Gamers," Pew Research Center (December 2015), retrieved from https://www.pewinternet.org/2015/12/15/gaming-and-gamers/.

334   Kelsey Gee, "In Unilever's Radical Hiring, Resumes Are Out, Algorithms Are In," Fox Business (2017), retrieved on August 11, 2022, from https://www.foxbusiness.com/features/in-unilevers-radical-hiring-experiment-resumes-are-out-algorithms-are-in.

335   Ibid.

336   Bart Turczynski, "Hiring & Recruiting Statistics: Job Search, Interview, Resume Stats 2019," Zety (2019), retrieved from https://zety.com/blog/hr-statistics#job-interview-statistics.

337   Aaron Smith, "Searching for Work in the Digital Era," Pew Research Center (November 2015), retrieved from https://www.pewresearch.org/wp-content/uploads/sites/9/2015/11/PI_2015-11-19-Internet-and-Job-Seeking_FINAL.pdf.

338   Ibid.

339   Pew Research Center, *Internet/Broadband Fact Sheet* (June 2019), retrieved from https://www.pewinternet.org/fact-sheet/internet-broadband/.

340   National Center for Education Statistics, "Table 318.30: Bachelor's, Master's, and Doctor's Degrees Conferred by Postsecondary Institutions, By Sex of Student and Discipline Division: 2015-16," *Digest of Education Statistics: 2016 Tables and Figures* (2017).

341   Bart Turczynski, *Hiring and Recruiting Statistics*; and Jacquelyn Smith, "7 Things You Probably Didn't Know About Your Job Search," *Forbes* (April 2013), retrieved from https://www.forbes.com/sites/jacquelynsmith/2013/04/17/7-things-you-probably-didnt-know-about-your-job-search/#139c2bc13811.

342   Will Evans, "You Have Six Seconds to Make an Impression: How Recruiters See Your Resume," Ladders (March 2012), retrieved from https://www.theladders.com/career-advice/you-only-get-6-seconds-of-fame-make-it-count.

343   See, for example, Nikki Graf, Anna Brown, and Eileen Patten, "The Narrowing, But Persistent, Gender Gap in Pay," Pew Research (March 22, 2019), retrieved from https://www.pewresearch.org/fact-tank/2019/03/22/gender-pay-gap-facts/; and PayScale, *The State of the Gender Pay Gap 2019: Women of Color Face Multiple Barriers to Advancement in the Workplace* (2019), retrieved from https://www.payscale.com/data/gender-pay-gap.

344   Andreas Liebbrandt and John List, "Do Women Avoid Salary Negotiations? Evidence from a Large Scale Natural Field Experiment," *Management Science*, 61, No. 9 (October 2012), 1, retrieved from https://www.researchgate.net/publication/256038947_Do_Women_Avoid_Salary_Negotiations_Evidence_from_a_Large_Scale_Natural_Field_Experiment.

345   Morela Hernandez, Derek Avery, Sabrina Volpone, and Cheryl Kaiser, "Bargaining While Black: The Role of Race in Salary Negotiations," *Journal of Applied Psychology*, 104, No. 4 (2019), 581.

346   Liebbrandt and List, 3.

347   Adam Smith, *The Wealth of Nations*, 3rd ed. (London: William Strahan 1784).

348   Stephen Humphrey, Jennifer Nahrgang, and Frederick Morgeson, "Integrating Motivational, Social, and Contextual Work Design Features: A Meta-Analytic Summary and Theoretical Extension of the Work Design Literature," *Journal of Applied Psychology*, 92, No. 5 (2007), 1332-1356.

349   Humphrey, Nahrgang, and Morgeson, "Integrating Motivational, Social, and Contextual Work Design Features," 1333-1345.

350   Edward Deci and Richard Ryan, "The Empirical Exploration of Intrinsic Motivational Processes," in Leonard Berkowitz (ed.) *Advances in Experimental Social Psychology*, 13 (New York: Academic Press (1980): 39-80.

351   Edward Deci, *Intrinsic Motivation* (New York: Plenum, 1975).

352 Society for Human Resource Management and Globoforce, "Using Recognition and Other Workplace Efforts to Engage Employees," SHRM Survey Findings (2018): 12.

353 Lauren Manheim, Sarah Moore, Leon Grunberg, and Edward Greenberg, "Pre- and Post-Termination Organizational Commitment and the Effects of Leaving," Institute of Behavioral Science, Research Program on Political and Economic Change, Working Paper PEC2003-0004 (November 2003): 8

354 Manheim, Moore, Grunberg, and Greenberg, "Pre- and Post-Termination Organizational Commitment and the Effects of Leaving," 1-32 and Connie Wanberg, Larry Bunce, and Mark Gavin, "Perceived Fairness of Layoffs Among Individuals Who Have Been Laid Off: A Longitudinal Study," *Personnel Psychology*, 52 (1999): 78-79.

355 Carol Kulik, Belinda Rae, Shruti Sardeshmukh, Sanjeewa Perera, "Can We Still Be Friends? The Role of Exit Conversations in Facilitating Post-Exit Relationships," *Human Resource Management*, 54, No. 6 (November-December 2015): 893-894.

356 Allan Lind, Jerald Greenberg, Kimberly Scott, and Thomas Welchans, "The Winding Road from Employee to Complainant: Situational; and Psychological Determinants of Wrongful-Termination Claims," *Administrative Science Quarterly*, 45, No. 3 (September 2000): 580-581.

357 See, for example, Richard Feinberg and Nina Jeppeson, "Validity of Exit Interviews in Retailing," *Journal of Retailing and Consumer Services*, 7, No. 3 (July 2000): 123-127; Joel Lefkowitz and Myron Katz, "Validity of Exit Interviews," *Personnel Psychology*, 22, No. 4 (1969): 445-455; and David Williams, Candice Harris, and John Parker, "I Love You—Goodbye: Exit Interviews and Turnover in the New Zealand Hotel Industry," *New Zealand Journal of Employment Relations*, 33, No. 3 (2008): 70-90.

358 Malcolm Patterson, Michael West, Viv Shackleton, Jeremy Dawson, Rebecca Lawthorn, Sally Mattis, David Robinson, and Alison Wallace, "Validating the Organizational Climate Measure: Links to Managerial Practices, Productivity and Innovation," *Journal of Organizational Behavior*, 26, No. 4 (June 2002): 405-407.

359 Hay Group, *Organizational Climate Survey*, Korn Ferry.

360   Michàl Mor Barak, David Chernin, and Sherry Berkman, "Organizational and Personal Dimensions in Diversity Climate: Ethnic and Gender Differences in Employee Perceptions," *Journal of Applied Behavioral Science*, 34, No. 1 (March 1998): 93.

361   Amy Richman, "Everyone Wants an Engaged Workforce: How Can You Create It," Workspan (January 2006): 38.

362   Retrieved on March 5, 2020, from https://nlwilmarsc-belly.savviihq.com/downloads/.

363   Corporate Leadership Council, *Attracting and Retaining Critical Talent Segments: Building a Competitive Employment Value Proposition*, Corporate Executive Board (2006): 7.

364   Ibid, 7.

365   Ibid, 8.

366   Christopher Collins and Jian Han, "Exploring Applicant Pool Quantity and Quality," *Personnel Psychology*, 57 (2004): 44.

367   Gartner, *Strengthen Your Employee Value Proposition*, retrieved on February 19, 2020, from https://www.gartner.com/en/human-resources/insights/employee-engagement-performance/employee-value-proposition.

368   Universum, *Employer Branding NOW* (2019): 22.

369   Karl-Johan Hasselström, *The Power of Differentiation*, Universum (September 20, 2018): 37.

370   Bailey Reiners, "Employee Value Proposition: How 25 Companies Define Their EVP," built in (April 6, 2022), retrieved August 5, 2022, from https://builtin.com/employer-branding/employee-value-proposition-examples.

371   Universum, *Employer Branding NOW* (2019): 17.

372   Corporate Leadership Council, *Attracting and Retaining Critical Talent Segments* (2006): 11.

373   Corporate Leadership Council, *Attracting and Retaining Critical Talent Segments* (2006): 16.

374 Tejaswi Bhuvanaiah and R. P. Raya, "Employee Engagement: Key to Organizational Success," *SCMS Journal of Indian Management* (October-December 2014): 63-65.

375 John Gibbons, *Employee Engagement: A Review of Current Research and Its Implications, The Conference Board (2006): Appendix A.*

376 Corporate Leadership Council, *Driving Performance and Retention Through Employee Engagement: A Quantitative Analysis of Effective Engagement Strategies*, Corporate Executive Board (2004): 7.

377 Aon Hewitt, *Global Employee Engagement* (2013), retrieved on March 13, 2020, from https://www.prnewswire.com/news-releases/aon-hewitt-analysis-finds-managing-and-improving-employee-engagement-is-key-to-achieving-revenue-growth-and-profitability-goals-209494171.html.

378 Steve Bates, "Getting Engaged," *HR Magazine*, (February 1, 2004): 5-6. Retrieved on March 11, 2020 from https://www.shrm.org/hr-today/news/hr-magazine/pages/0204covstory.aspx.

379 Towers Perrin, *Understanding What Drives Employee Engagement*, US Report (2003): 19-21.

380 James Harter, Frank Schmidt, and Theodore Hayes, "Business-Unit-Level Relationship Between Employee Satisfaction, Employee Engagement, and Business Outcomes: A Meta-Analysis," *Journal of Applied Psychology*, 87, No. 2 (2002): 273.

381 Towers Perrin/International Survey Research, *Engaged Employees Drive the Bottom Line* (2003): 2.

382 Corporate Leadership Council, *Driving Performance and Retention Through Employee Engagement*, 16.

383 Hewitt Research Brief, *Employee Engagement at Double-Digit Growth Companies* (2004).

384 IBM Kenexa, *The Impact of Employee Engagement.*

385   See, for example, Aon Hewitt, *2012 Trends in Employee Engagement* (2012); Kimberly Fitch and Sangeeta Agrawal, *Female Bosses Are More Engaging Than Male Bosses*, Gallup (May 7, 2015), retrieved on March 16, 2020 from https://news.gallup.com/businessjournal/183026/female-bosses-engaging-male-bosses.aspx; Sumaira Gulzar and Rafiq Teli, "Gender and Work Engagement: A Study of Academic Staff in Higher Education," *Arabian Journal of Business and Management Review*, 8, No. 2 (2018); Quantum Workplace, *2017 Employee Engagement* Trends (2017); Alice Reissová, Jana Šimsová, and Kateřina Hášová, "Gender Differences in Employee Engagement," *Littera Scripta*, 10, No. 2 (2017); and Sunita Shukla, Bhavana Adhikari, and Vikas Singh, "Employee Engagement–Role of Demographic Variables and Personality Factors," Amity Global HRM Review, No. 5 (2015).

386   Quantum Workplace, *2017 Employee Engagement Trends* (2017): 48, retrieved on March 16, 2020, from https://www.quantumworkplace.com/2017-employee-engagement-trends-report.

387   Ibid: 30, 32, 38, 42

388   Myung Jin and Jaehee Park, "Sexual Minority and Employee Engagement: Implications for Job Satisfaction," *Journal of Public and Nonprofit Affairs*, 2, No. 1 (2016): 3.

389   Valentini Kalagyrou, "Gaining a Competitive Advantage with Disability Inclusion Initiatives," *Journal of Human Resources in Hospitality and Tourism*, 13, No. 2 (2014): 124.

390   US Bureau of Labor Statistics, *Labor Force Characteristics By Race and Ethnicity, Table 1: Employment Status of the Noninstitutional Population 16 Years and Older By Gender and Race, 2020 Annual Averages (2020)*, retrieved on February 9, 2022, from https://www.bls.gov/opub/reports/race-and-ethnicity/2020/home.htm.

391   International Labour Organization, *Statistics on the Working-Age Population and Labour Force (2022)*, retrieved on February 9, 2022, from https://ilostat.ilo.org/topics/population-and-labour-force/.

392   Charles Rodgers, Amy Richman, Barbara Nobles Crawford, and Hal Morgan, *The Drivers of Employee Commitment: Tools for Creating a Competitive Workplace*, WFD Consulting (1998): 10-17.

393   Society for Human Resource Management, *SHRM Survey Findings: Diversity and Inclusion*, 2014 retrieved April 17, 2018, from https://www.shrm.org/hr-today/trends-and-forecasting/research-and-surveys/pages/diversity-inclusion.aspx.

394   Louise Fitzgerald, Fritz Drasgow, Charles Hulin, Michele Gelfand, and Vicki Magley, "Antecedents and Consequences of Sexual Harassment in Organizations: A Test of an Integrated Model," *Journal of Applied Psychology*, 82, No. 4 (1997): 586.

395   American Psychological Association, *APA Dictionary of Psychology* (2022), retrieved on August 7, 2022, from https://dictionary.apa.org/mental-model.

396   Jeffrey Pfeffer, "Changing Mental Models: HR's Most Important Task," *Human Resources Management*, 44 No. 2 (Summer 2005): 123-128.

397   Asma Khalid, "Warren Apologizes To Cherokee Nation for DNA Test," National Public Radio (February 1, 2019), retrieved on August 7, 2022, from https://www.npr.org/2019/02/01/690806434/warren-apologizes-to-cherokee-nation-for-dna-test.

398   See Ray Birdthisell, *Kinesics and Context: Essays on Body Motion Communications* (Philadelphia: University of Pennsylvania Press, 1970); and Albert Mehrabian and Susan Ferris, "Inference of Attitudes from Nonverbal Communication in Two Channels," *Journal of Consulting Psychology*, 31, No. 3 (1967): 248-252.

399   Mehrabian and Ferris, "Inference of Attitudes from Nonverbal Communication in Two Channels."

400   Allan Pease and Barbara Pease, *The Definitive Book of Body Language: The Hidden Meaning Behind People's Gestures and Expressions* (New York: Bantam, 2006): 5.

401   See, for example, Richard Beckhard and Wendy Pritchard, *Changing the Essence: The Art of Creating and Leading Fundamental Change in Organizations* (San Francisco: Jossey-Bass, 1992); Rosabeth Moss Kanter, *The Change Masters: Innovation and Entrepreneurship in the American Corporation* (New York: Simon & Schuster, 1983); John Kotter, *Leading Change* (Boston: Harvard Business School Press, 1996); George Litwin, John Bray, and Kathleen Lusk Brooke, *Mobilizing the Organization: Bringing Strategy to Life* (Hemel Hempstead, UK: Prentice Hall, 1996); and Harrison Owen, *Spirit: Transformation and Development in Organizations* (Potomac, MD: Abbott Publishing, 1987.

402   Peter Eavis, "Why Not Treat Diversity Like a Profit?" *New York Times* (July 15, 2020): B1-3.

403   David Thomas, "Diversity as Strategy," *Harvard Business Review* (September 2004): 2.

404   Ibid, 2.

405   IBM, *2019 Benefits and HR Programs: Employee Benefit Summary* (2019).

406   Bryan Kim, "Acculturation and enculturation," in *Handbook of Asian American Psychology*, eds. F. Leong, A. Inman, A. Ebeco, L. Lang, L. Kinoshita, and M. Fu (Thousand Oaks, CA: Sage Publications, 2007): 141-158.

407   Thomas Watson, Jr., *A Business and Its Beliefs*, IBM (1962), retrieved on August 8, 2022, from https://www.ibm.com/ibm/history/ibm100/us/en/icons/bizbeliefs/#:~:text=%E2%80%9CI%20firmly%20believe%20that%20any,faithful%20adherence%20to%20those%20beliefs.

408   Sara Jordan-Bloch, VMWare Women's Leadership Innovation Lab, Stanford University, retrieved on August 8, 2022, from https://womensleadership.stanford.edu/people/sara-jordan-bloch.

409   Theodore Roosevelt. "Citizenship in a Republic." 1910. Delivered at the University of Paris, April 23, 1910. Retrieved on August 8, 2022, from https://www.thepublicdiscourse.com/2022/04/81972/.

410   Taylor Phillips and Brian Lowery, "Herd Invisibility: The Psychology of Racial Privilege," *Current Directions in Psychological Science*, 27, No. 3 (2018), 156.

411   Robert Kennedy. "Day of Affirmation." National Union of South African Students, University of Cape Town, delivered June 6, 1966, retrieved on August 8, 2022, from https://www.jfklibrary.org/ learn/about-jfk/the-kennedy-family/robert-f-kennedy/robert-f-kennedy-speeches/day-of-affirmation-address-university-of-capetown-capetown-south-africa-june-6-1966.

Index

Page numbers in italic indicate figures or tables.

A

H

I

T

V

W

CPSIA information can be obtained
at www.ICGtesting.com
Printed in the USA
BVHW032246090123
655974BV00017B/117